TANTRIC ART AND MEDITATION

The Vajra Mandala

TANTRIC ART AND MEDITATION

The Tendai Tradition

Michael Saso

Tendai Educational Foundation · Honolulu

ISBN 0-8248-1363-4

Camera-ready copy was prepared by the author

The paper used in this publication meets the minimum requirements
of American National Standard for Information
Sciences/-permanence of Paper for Printed Library Materials
ANSI Z39.48-1984

Distributed by
University of Hawaii Press
2840 Kolowalu Street
Honolulu, Hawaii 96822

TABLE OF CONTENTS

ACKNOWLEDGEMENTS

The author would like to thank the Rev. Ikuta
Koken, who patiently allowed me to learn about
the meditations, mantra, and mudra of Tantric
Buddhism for two-and-a-half years of daily lessons,
translations, and ritual practice at Bishamondo
Temple, Yamashina, Kyoto. I am also deeply indebted
to the Rev. Yamada Ettai, the Ozasu titular head
of Enryaku-ji, Mt. Hiei, Kyoto, whose willing
approval made this study possible. Finally, the
generosity of the Rev. Ara Ryokan, director of
the Tendai Institute of Honolulu, made the publication of this book a reality.
I must also acknowledge the patience of my two
daughters Theresa and Maria who accompanied me
to Kyoto, and the interest of my mother Beatrice
Saso, and so many others for whom the exploration
of inter-religious dialogue is a meaningful
experience.

FOREWORD

Japanese Tantric Buddhism has produced two Major schools, the *Taimitsu* Tendai Buddhism, founded by Saicho (Dengyodaishi), and *Tomitsu* Shingon Buddhism, founded by Kukai (Kobodaishi). Shingon was the earliest standard of Tantric practice, brought from China in 807 CE. The Goma Fire Rite was practiced when Saicho opened the first temples on Mt. Hiei. Tendai developed its own quite distinct Tantric practice when Ennin and other monks returned from China after 847 CE. Shikan style Zen meditation, Pure Land and Tantrism were taught by the monks of Mt. Hiei.

Ozasu, Rev. Yamada Ettai

Tantric Buddhism is called an "esoteric" practice because it is learned and transmitted orally, from master to disciple. Since Tantric ritual depended on a direct, oral tradition, the teachings became divided into many ritual schools. From the early Ishin and Danna schools came the Homan, Anoo, and Sanmai schools of Mt. Hiei today. Tendai holds that enlightenment comes from within the self, the so-called Hongaku shiso. During Japan's religious reformation (400 years before Europe), Jodo, Shinshu, Zen, and Nichiren broke away from Tendai and rejected Tantric Buddhism. Tantric art and meditation still have a profound influence on Buddhism today.

To prepare this book Michael Saso went to one of the most renowned Homan masters of Mt. Hiei, the Rev. Ikuta Koken. With the permission of the chief Abbot of Mt. Hiei, the Rev. Yamada Ettai, he studied the oral tradition for ten years. These pages, sponsored by The Tendai Institute, present a summary of that study for inter-religious understanding.

The Rev. Ara Ryokan, Tendai Institute, Hawaii

INTRODUCTION

My interest in Tantric Buddhist meditation began in 1967, when I was first introduced to a *Cheng-i* Orthodox Taoist master named Chuang Teng-yun, in Hsinchu city, north Taiwan. Master Chuang practiced a form of vajra or thunder meditation that was filled with siddham sanskrit mantra and tantric mudra (hand symbols) very much like those used by Tibetan monks. The Taoists of north Taiwan who used these ritual meditations did not know the meaning of the sanskrit words, but used them for their resonant power; each of the mantra, when sounded, summoned a spiritual image or vision, to be used in the tantric form of meditation.

In 1972 while residing in Hokkaido, I was taken to a Goma Fire Rite for a *yakubarai* exorcism on the occasion of my 42nd birthday. The Goma Fire Rite was performed by a monk named Suzuki of the Tantric Shingon Buddhist sect of Japan. I was fascinated not only by the beauty and perfection of Rev. Suzuki's ritual, but by the astonishing realization that many of the mudra hand gestures and mantric words used during the Goma were similar to those used by Taoist master Chuang of Hsinchu. After the rite was over I approached the Rev. Suzuki, and asked to see the ritual manual he had used, which contained illustrations of the mudra and Chinese phonetic characters giving the pronunciation of the siddham sanskrit words. The mudra and Chinese phonetic mantra were analogous to those in my Taoist manual, brought with me from Hsinchu, Taiwan.

It was not until 1974, on coming to the University of Hawaii to teach in the Department of Religion, that I was able to pursue the comparative research of Buddhist and Taoist meditation further. Honolulu, Hawaii, perhaps like no other place in the world, provides an environment where many forms of Asian cultural and religious practice are found together in one place. Here on the celebration of the first year of Tendai Tantric Buddhism coming to Hawaii from Hieizan, northeast of Kyoto, in Japan, I met the Rev. Ara Ryokan, and saw the Chief Abbot of Mt. Hiei and head of Tendai Buddhism, Ozasu Yamada Ettai perform the Goma. The Tendai version of the Goma Fire Rite was different from the Shingon version I had seen in Hokkaido in two important ways. Tendai Buddhism makes a clear distinction between popular *Kengyo*, devotional Buddhism for the people, and Tantric *Mikkyo* Buddhist practice for the monk. The laity may choose to meditate on the Goma (*Nai Goma*, i.e., interiorize the Goma) in the Tantric manner, or pray for blessings in the popular interpretation of the Goma. Either way, i.e., whether seeking "union" or "favors," the meditator is in the presence of the sacred, the transcendent, or the other shore.

The second great difference, a more profound distinction for the reader to understand, is the difference in the Buddhist Yogacara and Madhyamika schools of practice. Shingon Buddhism, following the Yogacara tradition, emphasizes oneness between the phenomenal and the pure, idealized Buddha world. The visions of the two mandalas are to be kept in the mind. All else is burned away, as the meditator unites him or herself with the transcendent aspects of the Buddha. Tendai Buddhism on the other hand adopts the Madhyamika attitude to reality. The meditator in this time honored form of Buddhist practice does not judge the world to be real or illusory, but suspends all judgment of reality and inner mind vision as well. Thus the Tendai meditation teaches the meditator to burn away the vision itself, so that nothing is left in the heart or mind bent on union. The Tendai way can be compared to the "Dark Night" of the western mystic tradition, the *Cloud of Unknowing*, and the words of Paul "The eye cannot see, the ear hear, or the mind conceive the vision of God (the Transcendent)."

The reader may test these ideas by following the meditations in the following pages. In the Lotus World meditation, the meditator unites him or her self with the figure of Vairocana Buddha doing Zen meditation, emptying the center of the body, voiding mind and heart of all image. In the Vajra meditation the reader is led in a counter-clockwise motion from the ninth bottom right square upward through the eighth, seventh, sixth square, and so on, into the center of the Vajra-thunder world for union with Buddha Vairocana performing Vipasyana meditation. In this step, everything received from the Buddha is given away, for the sake of all sentient beings. Nothing is kept for the meditator. Finally in the Goma rite, (which appears first in the text, but is performed last in the rite of initiation), the meditator burns away all images of the transcendent, as father, mother, savior, cosmic, and folk religion. No image is left, no desires, not even ashes remain from the burning interior fires of the Goma. Only then can one be truly united with the transcendent "other shore."

The ritual meditations described and interpreted in these pages derives from the Japanese Tendai Buddhist tradition, a Tantric form of Mahayana Buddhism dating from the Heian Period, Kyoto, Japan. The founder of Tendai Buddhism, Saicho, also known as Dengyo Daishi, went to China in 803 A.D., and studied T'ien-t'ai Buddhism and the writings of Chih-i at Mt. T'ien-t'ai, located in the Chekiang Province of southeast China, and Tantric Buddhism at Lung-hsing temple in Yueh-chou for almost a year. Another great Japanese monk named Kukai also traveled to China in that year, and went to the T'ang Chinese capital Ch'ang-an city of west China where he too studied tantric Buddhism, returning to Japan after three years in 807 A.D. Saicho however returned to Japan in 804 A.D. and founded Tendai Buddhism atop Mt. Hiei, to the north of Kyoto city. Kukai founded Shingon Buddhism on Mt. Koya, far to the southwest of Kyoto after his return to Japan. The Tantric Buddhism brought back by these two famous monks to Japan is no longer practiced in China.

Both men brought back the Lotus, Vajra, and Goma meditation rites to early ninth century Japan. Even though Tantric ritual had been in use before these two great monks journeyed to China, the Goma Fire especially became one of the most popular forms of ritual after their return to Japan until today. Japanese men in their forty-second year, and women in their thirty-third year, are advised to attend the Goma for Yakubarai exorcism and blessing as the midlife crisis approaches. So efficacious is the rite thought to be, that all forms of blessing, health, enlightenment, perfection, and even the suppression of one's enemies are thought to be derived from its devout performance. As taught by the meditating tantric masters of Hieizan in Kyoto, the Goma is a vehicle for burning away all impediments to enlightenment, and union with the transcendent Buddha bright-as-the-sun, Vairocana.

The Goma fire rite was first performed in Vedic India, perhaps even before the Aryan invasions of the Indus valley in 1500 B.C. A two volume masterpiece on the fire rite, published by Fritz Stahl with contributions by some of the world's foremost authorities on the Goma was published in 1983 under the title *AGNI: The Vedic Ritual of the Fire Altar*, (Asian Humanities Press, Berkeley). The rite was used as an offering and enticement to the god of fire, Agni, who was thought to send fire down to earth on the back of a large bird for man's benefit. Archaeological remains and modern versions of the rite show that in its most primitive form, the Agni Hottra (Goma) was offered on a huge stone or terra-cotta altar shaped like a bird. Grains, liquids, and the mythical soma plant were offered to Agni and the other deities who came down from the Indo-european heavens to be wined and dined.

The rite was offered to win divine favors for the people, and as a means of divine union for the priests performing the ritual. Perhaps in the ritualized humor of India's primitive wisdom, the gods of the superior light skinned Brahmin caste were thought to be burned away in the minds of the dark-skinned native Dasyus. Almost from the beginning, the Goma could be offered simultaneously for both reasons. The common lay folk sought nature's good things, while the priestly caste or those seeking perfection offered the fire rite to burn away all impediments to union with the transcendent.

When the Buddha preached his new religion between 560 and 483 B.C., the rites of the Brahmin caste and its belief system, with notions of reincarnation for the privileged, were cast aside. The new doctrines of Buddhism taught that salvation or enlightenment could be won by selfless compassion. Sorrow and suffering were caused by selfish desire. Burning away selfish gain by acts of compassion (the Mahayana interpretation of Buddha's doctrines) did away with the need for Brahmin religion and all its rites. The Goma was certainly not a part of the Buddha's original doctrines. With other Brahminic parapher-nalia, it was left aside by those who espoused Buddhist doctrines.

But after a thousand years of growth and spread, when Buddhism became indeed a religion for export, flourishing more on foreign soil than in its native environs, a Tantric form of practice that is, a holistic ascetic that sought enlightenment through the use of mind, mouth, and body became popular in India and China. In this new form of Buddhist practice, the teachings of the Buddha were portrayed by bodily hand dance (mudra), devo-tional chant (mantra) and geometric or cosmic centered meditation, (mandala). This tantric form of Buddhism traveled across Tibet into China in the sixth and seventh cen-turies A.D., where it was influenced by and mutually molded Taoism in the Central Kingdom.

The Womb or Lotus world mandala (Garbha Datu) was not a part of the ancient Vedic religion, but was invented as a later Buddhist form of Tantric ritual meditation. The Lotus-Womb world is found in artistic representations throughout the kingdoms of north India, Ladakh, Nepal, Mongolia, and Tibet. It is easily identified by the four gates, squares, or rectangles leading to a circular lotus in the center of the mandala. The figure of Vairocana, the Buddha as sunlight with hands folded in the dhyana meditation mudra, makes the Lotus-womb world easy to identify. It is described in Tantric Buddhist texts of the T'ang period, and was most probably brought to China in the 7th-8th century C.E. It's spiritual goal in these pages is to unite the meditator with the vision of Vairocana, Buddha bright as the sun in the posture of samatha (Zen) meditation.

The Vajra mandala, sometimes translated "Diamond" or "Adamantine" mandala, actually refers to the thunder-lightning weapon symbolic of awakening and enlightenment by the rays issuing from the body of Vairocana. The nine sectored Vajra world as preserved in Japan today is found in Chinese and Japanese Buddhist iconography. Indian origins supposedly favored a six sectioned version. The nine sections of the Vajra mandala are analogous to the Taoist Lo-shu magic square, a nine-segmented chart that is model for the Chinese temple, walled city, and the ancient Taoist sacred dance called "The Steps of Yu" (禹 步). The two mandala became part of a systematic four-fold ritual meditation, necessary to the initiation and ordination of a tantric Buddhist priest. Whether this system was found in China and brought back to Japan, or developed by the holy monks who brought Tantric Buddhism to China between 803-845 CE, is warmly debated by modern scholars. It's purpose is to unite the meditator with Vairocana Buddha in the posture of Vipasyana or "empty center" meditation.

Some scholars believe that forms of Tantric Buddhism first reached Japan by 752 A.D., when the Chinese monk Ganjin came to the Nara court and received a warm hero's welcome. The monks Kukai and Saicho went to China fifty years later to study a form of Tantric Buddhist practice imported to China in the late 7th and early 8th centuries of T'ang dynasty China. These practices proved both pleasing and meaningful to the Japanese of the Heian period. Tendai Buddhism was especially influential in spreading a more devotional *bhakti* form of the Goma, while the Shingon sect of Kukai practiced the more powerful *siddhi* exorcistic form of the fire rite. The Shingon Goma and its founder Kukai have been widely studied and appreciated abroad, while the quiet devotional monks of Mt. Hiei, the Tendai sect, kept their esoteric Goma fire rite on the aloof heights of the sacred mountain.

The Tantric rituals brought back to Japan by Kukai (Kobodaishi) had a much more profound effect on Heian period Japan than did those of Saicho. The monks of Mt. Hiei felt inferior to the monks trained by Kukai on Mt. Koya. At first Kukai shared his secrets with Saicho's followers, but as Shingon political power grew, the Tendai monks no longer shared the secrets brought back to Japan by Kukai. The monk Ennin, third master of Mt. Hiei, traveled to China in 835 and spent ten years studying Tantric Buddhist ritual on Mt. Wutai and in Ch'ang-an City, until the Huang Chao rebellion in 845-847 and the persecution of Buddhism in China forced him to return to Kyoto. The Goma and other tantric rites brought back by Ennin emphasized the Susiddhi and the Heart Sutras, and therefore were spiritually quite different from the religious methods of Kukai based on the Risshyo-Naya Sutra. The Tendai Goma used today reflects these differences, born in the spiritual milieu of Heian period Japan.

Even though the Tendai and Shingon Goma rites seem to be the same in structure, the Tendai rites are in fact different in content and goals. Tendai tends to lay more importance on devotion, symbolized by the Lotus symbol, while Shingon derives power from the emphasis on the Vajra thunder bolt symbol. This symbolic difference can be seen in the order in which the rituals are performed. Tendai performs the Lotus meditation before the Vajra mandala rite, while Shingon places Vajra before Lotus.

The manner in which the legs are folded in the half lotus position at the beginning of the Tendai Goma also illustrates this difference. The left leg, which stands for Vajra, is placed over the right leg, which stands for Lotus, in the Tendai fire rite. Thus the left foot which stands for power is burned away, while the right foot, devotion, is preserved and protected from the fire. The Shingon monks usually place the right leg over the left when performing their version of the Goma. These and other subtle differences, as well as the content and style of the eidetic (moving) visualizations make the two forms of Goma quite different in style and in spirit.

Tendai Buddhism practiced on Mt. Hiei had a deep and profound influence on later Japanese Buddhism. All of the reformation sects, (Japan experienced a religious reformation 400 years prior to Europe, during the 12-13th century Kamakura period) represented break-aways from the parent Tendai organization. Dogen who later founded Japanese Zen Buddhism, Nichiren, Honen who founded Pure Land, and Shinran who founded the popular Jodo Shinshu were all trained on Mt. Hiei, and learned there how to perform the Goma. All rejected this complicated rite as something to be left aside in the religious reformation. Yet the Goma continues until today to be popular in Japan as a means of exorcism, prayer for blessing, and a form of disciplined devotion.

The Goma rite presented here is representative of the Tendai tradition, as it is practiced today and taught on Mt. Hiei, Kyoto. The translation is sometimes literal, and sometimes interpretative, according to the oral instructions of the Mt. Hiei teachers. The mudra hand symbols, and mantra chants, as well as the visualizations and meditations which accompany the translation, are taken from manuals used on Mt. Hiei. The author-translator was required to live as a monk and perform the Goma a total of thirty-six times before being granted permission to translate the text. The teachings of the Goma are ordinarily given by the Ajari-masters only after the postulant has received the *tokudo* rite of initiation and undergone the sixty day *shugyo* trial with a Hieizan master.

Only after learning the *Ju-hachi Do* Eighteen Path meditation, (the introductory rite which always precedes the Goma), and practicing the lotus World and Vajra World meditations, will the Ajari master teach the pupil how to perform the Goma. Following the sixty day *shugyo* period of intense trial and instruction, the novice is given a *kancho* ordination and licensed to perform ritual when called upon to do so for the people, or for his or her own devotional practice. Some monks choose to continue on for a hundred day trial, and others follow the thousand day "return to the mountain peak" trial, during which time thirty kilometers are run daily for three months over a seven year period, and the monk does not eat or drink for nine whole days.

The translator underwent the sixty day training in 1980 with the Ajari master Ikuta Koken, abbot of Ryu-o Ji on Mt. Hiei, and head of the Bishamondo temple, Yamashina, Kyoto. The training and preparation continued until 1985, when the Lotus-womb Mandala (Taizo-kai) and Vajra mandala (Kongo-kai) meditations were learned, and the translation work begun. With a grant from the Japan Foundation in support of the project, a translation of the Taizo-kai Lotus-womb World meditation, and the Kongo-kai Thunder World meditation, was completed, with notes explaining the siddham sanskrit seed words and meditations passed on orally by the Ajari masters. The following pages represent a summary of the translations (published separately, under the title *Fire, Lotus, Vajra: the meditations of Tendai Tantric Buddhism*, Delhi: Scholar's Press, 1990), in order to give an understanding of the tantric meditation process, and a glimpse of the beautiful art that accompanies its practice in a popular, usable form.

The meditative rites described below are based upon the following works, used by the monk-instructors of Mt. Hiei: 1) the *Kokuyaku Seikyo Daikei*, four volumes, Tokyo: Kokusho Kankokai; 2) the four volume ritual manuals of the Honman sect, entitled *Juhachi-Do, Taizo-kai, Kongo-kai*, and *Goma Ku Shiki*, woodblock photo-offprint, Mt. Hiei; and 3) the *Shido Gyoki Shiso*, Anou sect, Mt. Hiei, Kyoto. A fourth set of instructions published by the Sanmai sect of Mt. Hiei were also referred to, but not used in the present presentation. These special volumes are printed and sold to the monks who come to Mt. Hiei to study and practice Tantric paths to Buddhist enlightenment.

A special word must be added here on the meaning of the term tantric, or "esoteric" Buddhism. All of the details of the four rituals, the Eighteen Path Mandala, the Lotus World, the Vajra World, and the Goma Fire Rite summarized here are taken from my larger volume on Tantric meditation published in India. There are no secrets, no "esoteric" teachings that cannot be bought and studied separately from the Ajari masters. Just as one cannot study nuclear physics without a competent instructor, or learn to drive a car without instructions, so too the Tantric rites require a person trained in ritual to be performed properly. The making of tofu (bean curd cakes), driving a car, learning to sew a dress or suit, are skills that must be learned from a teacher. This volume, therefore, is an introduction to a practice that must be experienced and visualized to be mastered.

It must not be thought that the Tantric rites are so secret that noone but a chosen few may learn them. One may approach the monks of Mt. Hieizan, pay a fee, and learn to perform the rites much as enrolling in any other sort of school. Tantric Buddhism therefore does not mean *secret* so much as *physical*, that is, the rites must be learned by physically doing them. This is because Tantric Buddhism by definition is the use of body (mudra or hand-dance), mantra (chant), and mandala (patterned meditation) to reach enlightenment. The prayer of *kenosis* or emptying mind of images and heart of desires is the goal of the holistic, total body tantric meditations.

In this sense, Tantric Buddhism is not secret or privileged information. It is no more secret or privileged than a university course on the New Testament in the hermeneutic tradition, or a night school course on wine tasting that must be paid for and attended for credit. The word *mikkyo* in Japanese, which bears the connotation of a "secret" teaching, does not so much mean privileged as it does orally transmitted instructions. The hand gestures (mudra), mantric chants (mantra), and eidetic visions (mandala) must be seen and practiced in order to be understood. In presenting these materials in class lectures, I sometimes use a videotape (*The Goma Fire Rite*, Univ. of Hawaii, Relig. Dept.)

in order to further enhance the experience of the Goma. But nothing can substitute for a trip to the sacred mountain, where the Goma can be seen as it is performed by the Ajari master.

In finding a teacher, the novice may choose from a variety of holy monks and masters. The Honman sect, Anou sect, and Sanmai sect are presently the most popular on Mt. Hiei, Kyoto. The Goma ritual below follows the instructions of the Rev. Ikuta Koken, who is an Ajari master in the devotional (bhakti) oriented Honman sect. The differences between this and the more simplified Anou and the Shingon influenced Sanmai sects are minimal. All three oral sources ces were used as references in presenting the Lotus, Vajra, and Goma rituals.

The Goma rite is divided into three major sections, namely: 1) before the fire; 2) during the fire; and 3) after the fire. The stages are easily recognized, since a fire is lit in the circular furnace-receptacle placed in the middle of the Goma altar at the beginning of stage two. The fire is no longer stoked and begins to go out at the beginning of stage three. The spectator may easily follow the rite by using this manual in conjunction with the performance, or simply watch the drama unfold visually.

The first stage consists of a lengthy purification and litany, followed by the Eighteen Path (eighteen stage) mandala meditation called *Ju-hachi Do*. This entire first section always precedes all major tantric rituals, including the Vajra World and Lotus World meditations, as we will see below. Scholars do not agree about the origins of the Eighteen Path mandala. Some say it comes from India, while others believe it was invented by Kukai after his return to Japan. Since elements of the rite are found in both Buddhist and Taoist rituals in China, a position between the two extremes seems to be appropriate. The Juhachi-do contains elements from India, China, and Japan.

The following structural outline will help the reader understand the order of Tendai Tantric ritual. The Ju-hachi Do meditation consists of a series of powerful eidetic visions in which the monk creates around him or herself pillars and walls of flames, inside of which are mentally constructed a sacred area where the meditations take place. Once constructed, the monk envisions a great ocean within the sacred area, in the center of which is a mountain. Atop the mountain is a pavilion, holding a sacred lotus throne. From the center of the lotus springs the seed word *Ah*. The word changes first into a lute, then a sword, and finally becomes the terrifying vision of Acala, surrounded in flames. Acala's stern face is a warning that the meditator must be pure and filled with feelings of compassion in order to proceed further. On the understanding of this vision of Acala rests the efficacy of the four subsequent meditations. The Lotus-womb world and the Vajra world meditations are performed within the structure of the Eighteen Path Mandala.

The definition of Tantric meditation as "eidetic vision" is understood through the vision of Acala as taught in the Eighteen Path mandala. The word *eidetic*, from the Greek word eidos, means a vision or image that is alive and moving. No two times is the vision ever the same. Part two of the Goma, the fire rite itself, uses powerful eidetic imagery to portray the various aspects of the Buddha as purifying, as father, mother, savior, cosmic, and folk centered, all are "burned away" in the Goma, a preparation for true union with the empty *sunya* void of T'ien-t'ai meditative practice.

The Goma fire ritual itself is begun by constructing a mandala of wood. The first three sticks, laid in the form of a triangle over the mouth of the furnace symbolize the three worlds, Buddha, Lotus, and Vajra mandala. Eight sticks laid four-by-four in a square represent the visible world and the eight directions. The final three sticks laid in a triangle atop the fire stand for my own body -- head, chest, and belly, or the intellect, will, and intuition. All of these images are to be burned away in the fires of the goma. The process of burning can be compared to the three stages of the spiritual life described in the writings of the western mystics. The writings of western mystics describe these stages in terms of purification, illumination, and union. Between the second illuminative stage and final union occurs a form of kenotic emptying, a "dark night" of the senses and intellect. During this period the intellect and will are emptied or darkened. The process within the Goma of burning away images and desires, symbolized by the offerings and the sticks of wood, is analogous to the apophatic or emptying process of the mystic experience. Thus the Goma is truly a form of mystic kenosis, i.e., a prayer of total self-emptying.

The Tendai Goma fire rite is composed of six meditations, or eidetic "moving" visualizations which are burned away in the flames. As each image is envisioned, the four offerings to the right side of the altar, representing bad deeds, and the six offerings in the center of the altar representing good deeds, are thrown into the flames. Both good and bad deeds are a hindrance to true awakening. The twelve inch long sticks of wood, representing the twelve nidhanas, or causes of recycling desires, are added to the flames. Thus the Goma burns away will and intellect, leaving nothing behind, not even ashes, in the mental imagery of the meditating monk. The images are as follows:

1. Agni, the image of Buddha as fire (see p. 22).
2. Butsugen Bomu, i.e., Buddha Locana (see p. 23).
3. Usnisa/The white-robed Tara (Kannon) (p. 24).
4. Acala and Vairocana together (p. 26).
5. The Buddha, Lotus, and Vajra worlds (p. 27).
6. Acala surrounded by the twelve deities of ancient
   Vedic India (p. 30).

When the six sets of offerings have been completed, and the visions burned away in the flames, a seventh meditation called "entering samadhi" is performed. The practitioner sees her/his heart, the heart of all sentient being, and Vairocana, as one. Once emptied of all selfish hindrances, mental images, and desires, the life of the devotee can be given to acts of true compassion for others. Compassion is the test of true union with the non-dual, transcendent. If the meditator does not spend the rest of his or her life caring for the good of others, the text warns, the Goma, Lotus, and Vajra meditations were in vain.

In the Tendai version of the meditations, the Lotus-womb mandala is first performed by the meditator, in order to totally purify the inner self, and fill the body with the image of Acala and Vairocana. Once that Vairocana has been "locked" in the heart, the meditator then performs the Vajra meditation, in which all of the benefits of the Lotus world are given away. One steps into the Lotus world in a clockwise motion, and gives away the merits and visions of the Vajra world in a counter-clockwise motion. Once that the interior has been emptied of Lotus and Vajra, then all of the visions are burned away by the fires of Agni in the Goma. Since the Goma is frequently seen throughout Japan, while Lotus and Vajra are preserved for the top of the sacred mountain, we present the Goma first in these pages, and save the beautiful pictures and visions of the two hidden mandala for the later sections of the presentation.

The art work found in this volume was prepared for publication by the wonders of Hewlett-Packard scanjet, an IBM/AT motherboard with add-ons from many sources, WS2000+ word processor, and the beautiful 10 pt. Times-Roman font of HP Laserjet. The wood block prints were provided by Bishamondo temple, Yamashina, Kyoto, courtesy of the Rev. Ikuta Koken. The kindness and generosity of the Rev. Ara Ryokan made the research and publication possible. The photos of the various mandala are from 16th century paintings preserved in the archives of the Bishamondo temple, one of the few collections of Tendai art preserved from the ravaging fires of Odo Nobunaga in 1571. The Rev. Haba Jion of Tokyo, The Rev. Keishin Taki, director of the Tendai central offices in Sakamoto, lake Biwa, the Rev. Monzeki Umeyama, and many others helped the publication of this volume, for which I am very grateful.

The original text of the Goma was written in siddham sanskrit seed words and Chinese, with Japanese katagana written beside the sanskrit in order to facilitate pronunciation. In each case, the meaning of the Sanskrit or the Chinese is indicated by the accompanying Japanese notes and explanation. We have chosen not to give the Sanskrit pronunciation or diacritical marks in this interpretation. The practitioner must learn to pronounce the words in the Japanese manner when performing the Goma under the directions of a master on Mt. Hiei. The complete version of the text, published by Scholar's Press, Delhi, provides all of the mantra used in the Kongo-kai, the Taizo-kai, and the Goma ritual meditations (see above). The Japan Foundation Grant which has provided for the preparation of this volume also includes the forthcoming translations of the above three works. For further study of the two mandalas, see the definitive work of Adrian Snodgrass, *The Matrix and Diamond World Mandalas in Shingon Buddhism*, New Delhi: Aditya Prakashan, 1988, Two Volumes, with illustrations. The pioneer work of Ryujun Tajima, *Les Deux Grands Mandalas et la Doctrine de l'Esoterisme Shingon*, Tokyo/Paris: 1959, and Taiko Yamasaki's *Shingon: Japanese Esoteric Buddhism*, Boston: Shambala, 1988, sensitively translated by Cynthia and Richard Peterson, are also quite helpful.

I am very grateful to the many people who helped prepare this volume. The Sanskrit seed words and English romanization can be found in the larger volume published by Prof. Lokesh Chandra, the Culture Press, Delhi, India. An earlier version of the text was edited and typed for printing by Donna Bair. The oral instructions and patience of Rev. Ikuta Koken made the translation a possibility, along with the gentle kindness of the Ozasu Yamada Ettai, head of Tendai Buddhism, who encouraged the completion of this project. Whatever errors and inaccuracies are found, are solely the translator's fault. The Goma, Lotus, and Vajra meditations presented in this volume will, it is hoped, prove helpful for interfaith and cultural understanding.

I. THE MEDITATION ON FIRE
Section 1. Purification

I. *Initial Purification*.

The following are performed before entering the altar room. Using ordinary tap water, cleanse the hands and the mouth. Put on clean clothing, including white underwear (symbolizing purity), grey monk's clothes, and the yellow robe worn over the left shoulder called *kesa*. Holding the kesa (yellow robe) in the left hand. With the right hand form the Wind-Fist Mudra, i.e., fold the thumb into the palm and bend the four fingers down over it. Move the hand toward the kesa three times, imagining that purifying water is sprinkled on it. Recite each time "Om, be cleansed, svaha!" Then tie the kesa over the left shoulder, symbolically covering the left hand, which in India is considered to be impure, and chant: "Om! don the pure Vajra robe, Hum!"

II. *Perform the goshimbo mudra to purify the body*:

A. Purify the Three Sources of karmic activity, mind, mouth, and body. To do this, form the *Gassho* Joined-Hands Mudra, as follows: place the hands before the chest with the palms pressed together and recite:

> Om! May the self arising,
> All dharmas, and my nature be purified! Kham!

B. *Butsu-bu Samaya*: Purify the Buddha World mudra. Form the Buddha world mudra: place the hands before the chest with the palms facing each other, the fingers pointed upward. Allow the bases of the palms, the tips of the thumbs and the little, ring, and forefingers to touch. Keep the tips of the middle fingers slightly apart, thereby forming the shape of a partially-opened lotus. Recite :

> Om! Tathagata, be cleansed, Svaha!

C. *Rengei-bu Samaya*: Purify the Lotus World mudra. Form the Rengei (Lotus) mudra: Keeping the bases of the palms and the tips of the thumbs and little fingers together, open out the middle and forefingers to represent a fully-opened lotus and recite:

> Hail! Lotus World, be cleansed, Svaha!

D. *Kongo-bu Samaya*: Purify the Vajra World mudra. Form the Vajra Mudra: With backs of palms together, little fingers and thumbs intertwined, recite:

> Om! Vajra World, be cleansed, Svaha!

E. *Hi-ko go-shin*: Armor protects the body. Form the Armor Mudra: With palms facing each other, little and ring fingers intertwined, middle fingers extended and touching at tips, forefingers extended and slightly bent, thumbs parallel and touching, press the "five places" (belly, heart, mouth, left shoulder, right shoulder, head) and recite:

> Om! Vajra fire, protect me, Svaha!

III. *Enter the Hall while holding the Beads and the Vajra*.

A. Preparing to Enter the Hall: at the entry way form the Three-Pronged Vajra Mudra: Press the tip of the little finger into the palm with the tip of the thumb, extending the ring, middle, and forefingers. Make a counter-clockwise circular motion three times, then a clockwise circular motion three times, each time reciting

> Om kiri kiri vajra, Hum! Phat!

1

Picture within one's heart a moon one inch in diameter. In the center of the moon visualize a lotus. In the center of the lotus place the Sanskrit letter *Ah* (𑀅). Expand the lotus and place it between you and the altar.

B. Purification by Water: At the entry way, dip a twig (if available) or three fingers into the holy water on the right and touch them to the body three times, reciting each time:

Om amirite Hum Phat!

(Om! Sweet dew of immortality, Hum! Cleanse me!)

C. Enter the Hall. Snap the fingers of the right hand three times, reciting "Hum, Hum, Hum." Step over the smoking elephant-shaped incense burner, right foot first, seeing all of the Buddhas of the Dharma world welcome my entrance. The incense and the light coming from the Buddha's wisdom eye cleanses all my impurities.

Om! Light piercing eyes, purify me, Um! Phat!

D. Proceed to the Front of the Buddha Altar. Enter the room, picturing one's self to tread across the petals of the large lotus placed there by the imagination. Recite:

I have come from infinite past worlds, eternally passing through this world of life and death. So many good and evil deeds have I committed, they are without number. As I stand before Acala I empty my heart. Just as the Buddhas of the past have repented, I too now repent and seek to avail myself of their power. I do so in order to purify and save all sentient beings. By this great vow may their impurities, as well as my own, be cleansed.

E. *Jo Sango*: Repeat the mantra for purifying the Three Karmic actions, as in II.A above. With palms pressed together, recite:

Om! May the self arising, my nature, and all the

Dharmas be purified, Kham!

F. Bow to Acala, (Fudo Myo-o), seen standing by the altar. Place palms together, then kneel with palms facing upward and touch the "five places" (forehead, two palms, two knees) to the floor. While doing so, recite:

I take refuge in and honor *honzon* worthy, the holy

one, the supremely holy, supremely compassionate,

Lord Acala. By his power we achieve enlightenment.

G. Sit at the Goma altar in Half-Lotus Position. Climb onto the cushion directly in front of the Goma altar. Sit cross-legged with the left leg (symbolizing the vajra) over the right (symbolizing the lotus). Straighten the clothes. Take the lids off the incense burner and the water containers.

IV. *Use powdered Incense, to purify oneself.*

To purify the self, take a pinch of incense from the box of powdered incense at the left of the altar, and rub it between the hands. Take another pinch and touch it to the lips, and then rub some on the chest. Recite "*So ken to gi*." See all five places (belly, heart, two shoulders, and mind) as empowered and purified by the power of Acala, when reciting the mantra.

2

V. *Burn Grain Incense.*

      A. Using the forefinger, the middle finger, and the thumb, take a pinch of grain incense from the box to the left of the altar, and place it in the middle incense bowl on the altar. Do this three times. Recite inwardly:

> May the fragrance of this incense purify and fill the
>
> Dharma world in ten directions, by Tathagata's power.

      B. Next place a pinch of the grain incense in the hand-held incense burner, and repeat the silent prayer, as above.

VI. *Perform the Goshimbo* as in step II. A-E, above.

A. Purify the three sources of karmic action, mind, mouth, and body. B. Purify the Buddha World (mind). C. Purify the Lotus World (heart). D. Purify the Vajra World (belly). E. Don Acala's Armor to protect the body.

VII. *Purify the incense and water.*

Hold the prayer beads in the left hand, and the vajra in the right hand; run the beads through the fingers forty-seven times outwards and fifty-four times towards the self, while chanting "Om kiri kiri basara um hatta." (Om, Vajra light purify! Hum! Phat!). See the vajra light purify the entire cosmos.

VIII. *Water Purification.*

      A. Purify the *Aka* Water with red and white light. There are two water bowls and two wooden water-sticks to the left of the altar-furnace. Take the stick to the left with the right hand and dip it into the water bowl on the left. Visualize two colored flames in the water: red (representing *Ram*, the male aspects of the Buddha) and white (representing *Bam*, the female aspects of the Buddha). With a circular motion mix the two colors, three times counter-clockwise and three times clockwise, reciting "Ram Bam" each time. See the colors blend into a bright pink purifying light.

      B. Purify the entire cosmos with water.

1. Purify the Self: dip the same water-stick into the water and touch it to the forehead three times, reciting each time *Om amirite um hatta*.

2. Purify the San-Tan (Three Worlds): move the stick horizontally before you from left to right, reciting *Om amirite um hatta*, once to purify heaven, slightly lower to purify the earth, and lower still to purify the underworld.

3. Purify the Offerings: pass the stick three times left to right over the offerings, each time reciting "Om amirite um hatta."

4. Purify the Goma Hall, while reciting "Om amirite um hatta" only once. Tap the stick on the rim of the water bowl nine times to purify the eight directions and the center.

IX. *Envision the Offerings purified with vajra lightning.*

Make a fist with your left hand and place it on the hip. With the right hand pick up the vajra and circle it in the air, three times counter-clockwise and three times clockwise, reciting "Om! Kili-kili Vajra Lightning, Hum! Phat!"

X. *Purify by Clapping the Vajra Thunder Hands.*

Clap the hands three times, reciting "Om! Vajra Clap, Hum! Phat !" (Lit., that which follows vajra lightning, thunder clap).

XI. *Purify by Snapping the Fingers.*

To drive away all evil, snap the fingers of the right hand three times, moving from above the left to the right knee while reciting "Om! Kili Kili Evil be gone, Hum! Phat!"

XII. *Expel Impurity with the triple prong vajra.*

Make a Triple-Pronged Vajra Mudra with both hands by placing thumb over the tip of the little finger and extending the fore, middle, and ring fingers outward. Place the right hand on the hip and move the left hand in a circular motion in front of the chest, three times counter-clockwise and three times clockwise, reciting "Om! Kili kili Vajra, Hum! Phat!"

XIII. *Purify again with Water.*

    A. Pick up the right side water-stick with the left hand and dip it into the purifying water. Dab the water onto the right palm beneath the ring finger. Put down the water-stick. Press the thumb of the right hand to the base of the ring finger and fold the four fingers over the thumb. Do the same for the left hand, folding the fingers down over the thumb.

    B. Cleanse the Buddha world: Keeping the hands in the above mudras, place the left hand on the hip and hold the right hand before the head. Perform a knocking motion toward the head, and recite "Om! Enlightened Benevolent Ones, Jyah!" three times.

    C. Cleanse the Lotus world: Keeping the left hand on the hip, hold the right hand before the chest and again with a the knocking motion recite three times "Om! Spotless Ones, Jyah!"

    D. Cleanse the Vajra World: Keep the left hand on the hip; hold the right hand before the belly and with a knocking motion toward self recite three times "Om! Vajra grip, Jyah!"

XIV. *Purify the cosmos with Vajra Light.*

    A. Purify the external Buddha World. Rub the palms together, spreading the water from the right hand to the left. Place the thumb of each hand over the fingernail of the little finger, extending the three other fingers, like a vajra trident. Holding the right hand upward with the elbow bent and the palm facing forward, touch the three extended fingers of the left hand to the right elbow. Circle the air three times clockwise with the right hand, reciting: "Om! Vajra light purify the deva-spirit world with thy power, Hum! Phat!"

    B. Purify the external Lotus World. Using the same hand positions, circle the right hand clockwise three times, reciting "Om! Brightest light, illumine the great (Lotus) blessing, Svaha!"

    C. Purify the external Vajra World. Using the same hand positions, circle the right hand clockwise three times, reciting "Om! Vajra light, protect us, Svaha!"

XV. *Purify the cosmos with the Vajra Deed Bodhisattva Mudra.*

Form the Vajra Deeds Bodhisattva Mudra: press down the little finger of each hand with the thumb. Cross the wrists, right over left. Perform a circling motion three times counterclockwise, reciting "Om! Vajra Kharma, ken!"

XVI. *Kongo Wheel Mudra.*

Perform the Kongo Wheel Empowering Mudra: Place the palms together, intertwining the ring and little fingers. Place the middle fingers over the index fingers, with the thumbs together and recite:

4

In the name of the Three Worlds, Nam! And all the
Tathagata who dwell therein, Nam! May the spotless,
Purest great wheel, the eternal, unmoved vajra, purify
the   three causes (mind, mouth, body) and effects
(words, desires, deeds) of evil; by the power of thy
triple wisdom victorious, Tram! Svaha!

XVII. *Kigan: Prayers of Petition.*

A. Take up the incense thurible, the five-pronged vajra, and the beads in the left
hand. With the right hand hold the instrument to strike the bell.

1. Strike the bell and recite the following prayer:

In order that the dharma may forever be honored,
benefiting both man and heaven, protecting the
children of the Buddha, burning away all sin,
giving birth to good, bringing about true
enlightenment for the benefit of the entire Dharma
world equally, we invoke the following.

2. Envision Vairocana Buddha and recite:

Hail Great Vairocana Buddha! Strike the gong.

3. Envision the Acala and recite:

Hail Great Honzon Worthy Acala! (gong)

XVIII. *Invoking the Spirit World.*

Recite the following prayer to the spirits: "Let us begin by honoring Brahma, Indra, Prthivi,
the earth spirits, and all the spirits of the three worlds--heaven, earth, and underworld.
May they protect all the children of the Buddha, including myself, blessed by the protective
star-sign under which I was born. May all the cities of the kingdom be at peace. May all
the great spirit forces protect our sacred mount Hiei, bring peace, and protect tantric Buddhism. With the great Spirit of the Red Mountain (a Shinto shrine on Mt. Hiei) may they
exorcise the demon kings, the underworld officials, the masses suffering in hell, the great
ocean dragon spirits, the yaksa and asura demons. To the utmost may those who inhabit
the empty Dharma World, those who follow the two teachings (the true way and the ex-
pedient way), the heavenly spirits, and the earthly forces, may they all take joy in the
Dharma and be filled with subtle light, greatly respecting the Sangha. May all spirits cross
over to the shore of wisdom, i.e., *prajna-paramita* enlightenment.

Recite the phrase *Hanya shingyo*, ring the gong, and again say: "By the virtue of
the Prajna Paramita Sutra...gone, gone, gone to the other shore. Arrived at the other
shore. Enlightened. So be it. The Great Heart Sutra!" (ring gong.)

XIX. *Name and summons all the Spirits.*

With beads, vajra, and incense burner in the left hand, and the mallet for striking the gong
in the right hand, recite:

For the sake of the great founders of Tantric Buddhism,
Nagarjuna, Pu-k'ung, Hui-kuo, the three national heroes,
(Kobodaishi, Denkyodaishi, Ennin, or Jikakudaishi) that
Their vows may be full and complete,

5

In the name of Vairocana,   (gong)

And the holy one, Acala.   (gong)

XX. *Prayers of Petition.*

The meditator takes the mallet for striking the gong in the right hand, and the incense thurible in the left, and recites the following petitions, striking the gong each time a Buddha or Boddhisattva is invoked:

For the emperor of China, may he live 10,000 years.

Hail, Great Vairocana Buddha.   (gong)

Hail, Honzon worthy Acala.   (gong)

For the Emperor of Japan, may his desires be fulfilled.

Hail Great Vairocana Buddha.   (gong)

Hail Honzon Worthy Acala.   (gong)

For the Great Palace Tree (i.e., the Shogun) peaceful rule!

Hail Great Vairocana Buddha.   (gong)

Hail Honzon Worthy Acala.   (gong)

For the four seas, fair winds, bumper crops, and peace for the people!

Hail Great Vairocana Buddha.   (gong)

Hail Honzon Worthy Acala.   (gong)

May all the mountains be at peace, free from disaster, and filled with joy. May the disciples of popular and tantric Buddhism be filled with learning and progress, bringing to fulfillment the path of the Buddha.

Hail Great Vairocana Buddha.   (gong)

Hail Honzon Worthy Acala.   (gong)

May I, servant of the Buddha, have all the impurities and hindrances of my karmic deeds burned away and my good and compassionate desires fulfilled, and my interior at peace; may all sentient being [through thy power] be filled with joy, one with the Dharma, and equally filled with blessing.

Hail Great Vairocana Buddha.   (gong)

Hail Honzon Worthy Holy Acala.   (gong)

Hail Buddha Locana Boddhisattva.   (gong)

Hail Ekaksara-Usnisa-Chakra.   (gong)

Hail Avalokitesvara Boddhisattva.   (gong)

Hail Kundali Light King.   (gong)

That all sentient beings choose the Dharma path.

Hail Great Vairocana Buddha.   (gong)

Hail Honzon Worthy Holy Acala.   (gong)

Hail Vajrasattva Worthy.   (gong)

Hail Ekaksara-Usnisa-Chakra.   (gong)

Hail Manjusri Boddhisattva.   (gong)

Hail Sarva Tri-Ratna (Three Treasures) (gong)

XXI. *Offering the gifts for all sentient beings.*

Continue to hold beads, vajra, and incense burner in the left hand and the mallet to strike gong in right hand. See all of the leaves, flowers, and other items as universal offerings. Chant the following three times: "May these liturgies respectfully be offered that all might eternally be one with the three treasures--the Buddha, the Dharma, and the Sangha." Recite the following verses:

> May all those here present, each worthy, kneel in
> obeisance, respectfully take up fragrant flowers, and
> according to Dharma-custom present them as offerings.
> May these clouds of incense and flowers spread everywhere in
> the ten directions as offerings, nourishing all the Buddhas,
> Buddha avatars, and Bodhisattvas. May the innumerable voices
> of those receiving these clouds of incense and flowers be
> heard by all. May these clouds of incense and flowers be
> as a great pavilion of light, spreading out to the cosmos
> without limits. We present boundless, limitless offerings to
> the Buddha, offered respectfully on behalf of all beings.

Put down the incense burner.

XXII. *Chant in Honor of the Lotus World.*

    A. Form the Vajra Mudra. Hold the beads and the single pronged vajra between the palms with the fingers slightly intertwined. Uplift the heart and in the imagination see the following Buddhas one by one. Picture the self bowing to the ground at each name.

1. Envision Vairocana above the center of the mandala. Recite:
> Hail Purest Dharma Body Vairocana Buddha.

2. Envision Ratnadhvaja in the East. Recite:
> In the Eastern Quarter Ratnadhvaja Buddha.

3. Envision Samkusumita-Raja in the South. Recite:
> Hail in the southern quarter Samkusumita Buddha.

4. Envision Amitabha in the West. Recite:
> Hail in the western quarter, Buddha of Eternal Life.

5. Envision Divyadundubhi Megha Nirghosa in the North. Recite:
> Hail in the northern quarter, drum of heaven, thunder sounding Buddha.

6. Envision Samantabhadra (Fugen) in the Southeast. Recite:
> Hail in the southwest, Samantabhadra Boddhisattva.

7. Envision Manjusri in the Southwest. Recite:
> Hail in the southwest, Manjusri Boddhisattva.

8. Envision Avalokitesvara (Kannon) in the Northwest. Recite:
> Hail in the northwest, Avalokitesvara Boddhisattva.

9. Envision Maitreya in the Northeast. Recite:
> Hail in the northeast, Maitreya Boddhisattva.

10. Envision Buddha Locana (Butsugen Bu Mo) below center. Recite:
> Hail Buddha Locana Boddhisattva.

B. Continue performing the Kongo Mudra and recite the following three times:

> We offer our respects to the Great Mandala Lord,
> the Holy Source of Light, the Great Enlightened One [Acala].

C. Continue performing the Vajra Mudra and recite the following:

> We offer our respects to the four great Light Kings
> (Trailokyavijaya, Kundali, Yamantaka, and Vajrayaksa), the
> enlightened ones, the great enlightened ones. We offer our
> respects to the greater and lesser Isvara, the stars of the
> twelve stems, of the twenty-eight constellations, and of all
> the phenomenal heavens. We offer our respects to the Three
> World Mandala (the Buddha, Lotus, and Vajra Worlds).

XXIII. *Sudden Awakening.*

A. Form the awakening mudra by linking the little fingers and pointing the forefingers outwards, allowing them to touch at the tips. Awaken all the Buddhas and bodhisattvas just envisioned before you by reciting "Om! Vajra awaken! Hum!"

B. Form the Vajra Joined-Hands Mudra: Interlace the tips of the four fingers and cross the thumbs. Invoke the Three Worlds, and purify the altar again by reciting "Hail, Three worlds, all the tathagata therein, Nam! Spotless, most pure, by the great cakra wheel, always unchanging, ceaselessly purify the three causes and effects of evil, by thy triple wisdom fulfilling this purifying act, victory thine! Tram! Svaha!"

XXIV. *Announcing the Petitions.*

With the left hand, pick up the five-pronged vajra, beads, and incense burner. With the right hand pick up the gong mallet and strike the gong once. Recite the following:

> With upright hearts we make our vows: We only beg Vairocana, Acala, and all
> their entourage -- the bright Acala with eight youths, the twelve great heavens, the
> triple and five-tiered worlds, all the worthies and myriad saints, the entire void
> dharma world, and all manifestations of the triple treasure --may each one read
> these vows with us, each pronouncing the vows of compassion. May each come
> down to be here in this sacred place, to practice together the three tantra (of
> mind, mouth, and body). May the lost souls all benefit from these vows as we
> firmly commit ourselves to the (task) before us. May you (Acala) protect these
> children of the Buddha, including myself. May you wipe out all guilt of sin and
> give birth to deeds of good. May you grant us eternal blessing and health. Despite
> whatever oppression might occur, whatever misfortunes, whatever calamities, may
> you protect the weary who find the way hard and the weak who otherwise would
> not persevere. Let them all be fulfilled. May our homes be at peace and may all
> humanity be filled with joy, extending even to the whole world, benefiting all.

XXV. *Five Great Vows of the Bodhisattva.*

Continue to hold the incense burner, beads, and vajra in the left hand. Recite the following:

> All sentient beings I vow to save.
> All wisdoms and blessings I vow to practice.
> All Dharma paths I vow to follow.

All Tathagata I vow to serve.

The highest enlightenment I vow to fulfill.

Help me, child of the Buddha, to accomplish these vows.

Section 2. *Ju-Hachi Do*
The Eighteen Path Mandala Meditation

The first five steps constitute the Goshimbo, as in II.a-e, above:

I. *Purify the Three Sources of Karma, mind, mouth, and body*. With palms pressed together recite:

> Om! May Self-arising, all Dharmas, and my nature be purified, Kham!

II. *Purify the Buddha World*: With hands formed as a partially-opened lotus, or hands open as a bowl, recite:

> Om! Tathagata be cleansed, Svaha!

III. *Purify the Lotus World*: With hands formed as a fully-opened lotus, recite:

> Om! Lotus be purified, Svaha!

IV. Purify the Vajra World: With backs of palms together, little fingers and thumbs inter-twined, recite:

> Om! Vajra be purified, Svaha!

V. *Armor Protects the Body*: With palms facing each other, little and ring fingers inter-twined, middle fingers extended and touching at tips, forefingers extended and slightly bent, thumbs parallel and touching, press the "five places" (belly, heart, mouth, left shoulder, right shoulder, and head) and recite:

> Om! Vajra flames, protect me, Svaha!

See protective flames envelope the body and void the mind.

VI. *Envision the Great Pillar of Earth*.

Form a mudra by interlocking the ring and middle fingers with the little and forefingers pointing outward and touching at the tips; let the thumbs point toward the body and also touch at the tips. Make a circular motion three times clockwise above the head, reciting:

> Om! Kili kili, Vajra, Great Vajra, firmly
>
> cover me with thy net, Hum! Phat!

See the mudra become a great vajra pillar, flowing out from the hands, spiraling upward to the extent desired. It becomes like a great beacon of fire. Vajra lightning surrounds and protects the meditator as the net of vajra flames fills the meditation area.

VII. *Envision a Vajra Wall of thunder and lightning flames*.

Open out the thumbs and turn the hands until the palms face inward. In a horizontal plane in front of the meditator, move the hands in a circular motion, clockwise. Recite three times:

> Om! Firm, so firm, Vajra wall surround me, Hum! Phat!

As the mantra is recited, the mudra becomes a great vajra weapon, from which flows a measureless vajra flame, encircling the entire altar. The fire-lightning hardens into a wall.

VIII. *Dojo kan*: Visualization of the *Ah* Sacred Seed Word.

9

A.   Form the Contemplation Mudra by placing the hands in the lap, palms upward, with the right hand over the left and the thumb tips touching. Directly in front visualize a great net spread over the vajra wall. Inside this net is a great ocean. In the center of the ocean is a precious mountain. On top of the mountain is an altar. In the center of the altar is a great eight-petalled lotus, on top of which there is a lion throne. On the throne is a seven-storied precious tower, surrounded by pillars bedecked with heavenly embroidered curtains, decorated with jewels and clouds of gems and bells. There are tapestries and banners on the walls. Everywhere can be heard the tinkling sound of chimes. It is grand and awe-inspiring.

On all sides, clouds of incense arise. Petals of flowers fall like gentle rain. Beautiful music can be heard. Precious viands of heavenly drink and food are laid out. A bright red Mani pearl sheds light all around. In the midst of the pavilion there is a great mandala, at the heart of which is the seed word *Ah* [곅]. The seed word becomes a stone piba (lute). Above the stone lute is the seed word *Kam* [곅]. The *Kam* becomes a great sword. The great sword turns into Acala. His color is bluish black. His face is round and full. In his right hand he grasps the sword of wisdom and in his left hand he holds a coiled rope. He is wrapped in measureless, swirling flames which give birth to samadhi. Though his countenance is extremely angry, infinite compassion flows from his heart.

B.   Offering Food to Acala. Form the mudra by placing the palms together and folding down the middle fingers. The thumbs should be parallel. The tips of the forefingers, ring fingers, and little fingers should be touching. Raise and lower the touching forefingers seven times, reciting each time:

Om Vajra, born of the void, Koh!

Envision the boundless food offerings in the pavilion being offered to Acala. Form the Vajra Fist Mudra: Make a fist with each hand by placing the thumb under the tips of the other four fingers. Place the fists on the hips and recite:

Om! Vajra hand, Hum!

C. With the right hand pick up the single-pronged vajra. Circle it in the smoke from the incense burner three times in front of the heart, thinking of it as a sun and reciting *Hum! Hum! Hum!* Raise it to the chest three times, while reciting the mantra. Pick up the vajra bell with the left hand. Place the right fist on the waist and recite *Om Vajra!* Ring the bell while reciting *Ken da um.* (Ring the bell nine times in the morning, seven times in the evening). Put down the bell. Touch the belly, heart, shoulders and forehead with right hand in Vajra Fist mudra.

IX. *Sending out three Chariots.*

With the palms held upward, intertwine the four fingers. Pass the thumbs outwards across the tops of the fingertips and back under the fingertips three times, reciting *Om toro toro um* each time. The mantra represents the sound of the chariot wheels which are sent forth to welcome the Buddha World, the Lotus World, and the Vajra World, respectively.

X. *Inviting the Chariots to enter.*

With the palms upward, intertwine the four fingers, and pass the thumbs towards the chest over the tops of the fingertips and back away under the fingertips three times. Picture each of the three mandala worlds directly in front of the self, waiting to come in. Recite the following mantra three times:

> In the name of all Tathagata of the Three Worlds, Nam!
> Om! blazing Vajra flames, Holy Acala,
> All Boddhisattva, come, Svaha!

XI. *Invite the Worthies inside the body of the meditator.*

    A. Leaving the fingertips intertwined, turn the hands over so that the fingertips are now pointing downward. Bring the bases of the palms together with the thumbs parallel to each other. Move the thumbs inward three times, reciting each time:

> Om! Benevolent Buddha world, enter, Kyah!

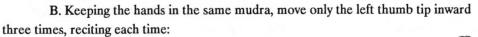

Envision the mandala of the Buddha World to enter the head.

    B. Keeping the hands in the same mudra, move only the left thumb tip inward three times, reciting each time:

> Om! Pure Lotus world, enter, Kyah!

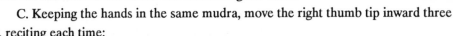

Envision the mandala of the Lotus World entering the chest.

    C. Keeping the hands in the same mudra, move the right thumb tip inward three times, reciting each time:

> Om! Vajra fire Holy Acala Great awakened, enter, Svaha!

Envision the mandala of the Vajra World entering the belly.

XII. *Expel any evil that may have entered the body at this time.*

    A. Form the Three-Pronged Vajra Mudra with each hand: i.e., extend the forefinger, middle finger, and ring finger. With the tip of the thumb press down the little finger. Maintaining this mudra, place the right hand on the waist, and raise the left hand over the head and move it in a circle, three times counter-clockwise, then three times clockwise. Recite each time:

> Om kili kili Vajra, Hum! Phat!

Envision a net covering self, keeping out all evil thoughts.

    B. Using the same mudra, place the left hand on the waist. Raise the right hand, palm facing outward, and bend the fingertips three times to purify the three karmic actions, by the power of the Buddha, Lotus, and Vajra worthies. Recite each time:

> Om! Made one, fulfill thy purifying vows in us, Svaha!

XIII. *The Vajra Net.*

Form the Vajra Net mudra: place the hands together, intertwine the middle fingers and fold them downward. The forefingers and little fingers extend and touch at the tips. The thumbs are parallel, tips touching the middle joint of the third finger. Maintaining this mudra, raise the hands above the head and move them circularly, clockwise, reciting each time:

> Om! Vajra net, protect us on all sides, Hum! Phat!

Envision a Kongo net spreading over oneself and the altar, supported by the vajra wall and pillar.

XIV. *Pavilion of Fire Mandala.*

Build an imaginative fire which encloses the entire sacred area. Form a mudra by holding the hands in front, palms up, with the right hand resting lightly on the left palm. Envision a fierce fire spiraling out beyond the Vajra wall and filling the entire room. Recite:

> Om! One with Agni-fire, Hum! Phat!

XV. *Offer the Five Real Items to the left of the altar.*

A. *Aka*: Pure Water. Pick up the bowl containing the water using the forefinger, middle finger, and thumb. Circle it in the smoke of the incense clockwise three times, then place it in the palm of the left hand. With the right hand form the Three-Pronged Vajra Mudra: the middle, fore, and ring fingers extend and the thumb presses down the little finger. Using this mudra, to the right of the bowl of water make a circular motion counterclockwise, blessing the water by saying *Om kiri kiri Vajra Hum! Phat*! Now hold the bowl between your palms with the four fingers extending upward and the thumbs touching.

Hold it at the level of the head and recite *Namaku samanda bodanam...* Hold it at the level of the heart and recite *Gya gya-na...* Hold it at the level of the belly and recite *Sama sama sowaka*. (In the name of all Buddhas, with the void made one! So be it, Svaha!) Recite inwardly "By the means of this purified water I wash away all the defilements of my body, never to turn away from my vows as a Bodhisattva. By this act I demonstrate my sincerity to fulfill these vows."

B. *Incense*. Pick up the bowl containing the incense using the forefinger, middle finger, and thumb. Circle it in the smoke of the incense clockwise three times, then place it in the palm of the left hand, as above. Now hold the bowl between the palms with the four fingers extending upward and the thumbs touching. Hold it at the level of the head, as above, and recite *Namaku samanda bodanam*. Hold it at the level of the heart and recite *Gya gya na...* Hold it at the level of the belly and recite *Sama sama sowaka*.

C. *Leaves*. Pick up the bowl containing the leaves, using the forefinger, middle finger, and thumb, as above. Circle it in the smoke of the incense clockwise three times, then place it in the palm of the left hand. Now hold the bowl between the palms with the four fingers extending upward and the thumbs touching. Repeat the triple offering, as above. Hold it at the level of the head and recite *Namaku samanda bodanam*. Hold it at the level of the heart and recite *Gya gya na...* Hold it at the level of the belly and recite *Sama sama sowaka*.

D. *Rice*. Pick up the bowl containing the rice using the forefinger, middle finger, and thumb. Circle it in the smoke of the incense clockwise three times, then place it in the palm of the left hand. Now hold the bowl between your palms with the four fingers extending upward and the thumbs touching. Hold it at the level of the head and recite *Namaku samanda bodanam*. Hold it at the level of the heart and recite *Gya gya na...* Hold it at the level of the belly and recite *Sama sama sowaka*.

E. *Fire*. Form the Fire Mudra with the right hand: press down the nail of the forefinger with the thumb. Press the ring and little fingers into the palm. Crook the middle finger. With the fingertips of the left hand touch the base of the right wrist, as if holding up a torch. Hold this Fire Mudra at the level of the head and recite *Namaku samanda bodanam*. Hold it at the level of the heart and recite *Gya gya na...* Hold it at the level of the belly and recite *Sama sama sowaka*.

XVI. *Offer the Five Items again as Universal Symbols*. Instead of real, concrete items, a hand symbol or mudra is used to represent the offering of the five sense and consciousness, the six parameters, (paramitas) whereby the Boddhisattva attains Buddhahood: charity, precepts, perseverance, energy, meditation, and wisdom.

A. *Aka*: Pure Water Cleanses the Heart. The offering of symbolic water is lengthy, and includes the following meditations:

1. Form the Empty Palms Mudra: with palms upward and side by side, the outside edges of the little fingers and the palms touching, bend the fingertips toward oneself, with the thumbtip beneath the forefinger. Place the mudra at the level of the head, heart, and belly, reciting each time *Om kyamara sowaka*. (Om! Open, Lotus. Svaha!) See a lotus blooming in the heart.

2. Form the Eight-Petalled Lotus Mudra by placing the base of the palms together, extending the ring, middle, and forefingers, and allowing the tips of the little fingers and thumbs to touch. Hold this mudra at the level of the head, and envision oneself as offering a lotus to the Buddha World. Again recite *Om kyamara sowaka*. Hold this mudra at the level of the heart and offer a lotus to the Lotus World. Recite *Om kyamara sowaka*. Hold the mudra at the level of the belly and offer a lotus to the Vajra World. Recite *Om kyamara sowaka*.

3. Universal Offering to the entire Buddha World. Form the vajra mudra by intertwining the four fingertips and crossing the right thumb over your left. Silently think the following:

 Welcome to all of the worthies who come here. Due to the original vow of (Amida) Buddha may you come down to this sacred area, take your preordained seats, and receive these symbolic offerings.

4. Many-tiered Great Mandala World. Form a mudra by intertwining the little and ring fingers of both hands. Allow the tips of the middle fingers to touch. The forefingers and thumbs are open. Move the mudra in a circle three times clockwise, and three times counterclockwise, seeing a great golden moon surrounding the self. Then touch the five places, i.e., the belly, heart, shoulders, throat, and head, while reciting: "Sealed by the Great Original Vow! Svaha!" Envision the power of the third light King Kundali protecting oneself from all forms of Siddhi powers and other impure spiritual forces.

Now repeat the Five Offerings in the form of symbolic mudra.

B. Symbolic offering of Powdered Incense. Place the right hand before oneself with the palm facing outward. With the left hand hold the right wrist. Visualize powdered incense being rubbed on the bodies of all the Worthies of the Buddha, Lotus, and Vajra worlds. Recite "In the name of all Buddhas may this incense purify all sentient beings. Svaha!"

C. *Keman*: Symbolic offering of Leaves and Flowers. Form the Keman flower mudra: place the palms upward with the little, ring, and middle fingers intertwined. Allow the forefingers to touch at the tips and the thumbs to rest by the sides of the forefingers. Visualize the hands as flowers being laid in front of the all the Buddhas. Recite "In the name of all Buddhas, may Great Compassion be born in all sentient beings, Svaha!"

D. Symbolic offering of burning incense. Form the Burning-Incense Mudra: Place the palms upward with the backs of the fingertips of the little, ring, and middle fingers touching. The forefingers are extended and the thumbs rest beside them. Visualize incense smoke surrounding all the Buddhas of the three worlds and recite: "In the name of all Buddhas may this incense fill and purify the entire Dharma world. Svaha!"

E. Symbolic offering of a Bowl of Rice. Form the Bowl of Rice Mudra by cupping the palms together with the little fingers flush and the other fingertips touching. The thumbs are flush with the palms. Visualize rice in your palms being offered to all the Buddhas of the three worlds and recite "In the name of all Buddhas, Arara Kyara, make this offering into a wondrous feast. Svaha!"

F. A symbolic offering of Light. With the right hand form the Fire Mudra as in XV.E above. Visualize the middle finger as a flame extending outward to flood the Buddha, Lotus, and Vajra worlds with light. Recite "In the name of all Buddhas may the brilliant Tathagata light fill the great void. Svaha!"

XVII. *General Offering of the gifts to the entire cosmos.*

A. Form the Clasped-Hands Vajra Mudra: Place the palms together with the tips of the four fingers intertwined and the right thumb crossed over the left. Recite the following: "Today, I hereby offer to all the Buddhas these gifts. May they together purify the dust of the real world and the image-world. May the real world and the image-world be washed in the Dharma sea. In reality, all of these wonderful offerings are the Dharma World, the sea which washes away all impurities."

Visualize the four Dharma bodies: the Phenomenal, Noumenal, the Noumenal-Phenomenal, and the Body Non-Hindered by Phenomena or Noumena. Picture the Buddha, Lotus, and Vajra worlds as being continuously nourished by these offerings.

B. The Empowering Mudra and Mantra. Form the clasped hands Kongo Mudra: Place the palms together with the tips of the four fingers intertwined and the right thumb crossed over the left. Recite "In the name of all Buddhas, Ken! (Wisdom of the Void). May we be born in the great void! Svaha!"

XVIII. *Entering Samadhi.*

A. In Praise of Acala. Using the same mudra as above, recite "In the name of all Buddhas and Boddhisattva! By the power of thy ordination (Acala) may compassion blossom in all sentient beings everywhere. Svaha!"

B. In Praise of the Four Types of Wisdom. Using the same mudra, recite "Om! Vajrasattva help us receive the vajra jewel, highest attainable vajra dharma, vajra song, vajra deeds. Svaha!" See Acala as having these four types of wisdom: Perfect Mirror Wisdom, All Things Equal Wisdom, Wondrous Perception, and Wisdom which Enlightens All Beings.

14

C. Enter Samadhi (A Symbolic Vision of Acala). Form the Samadhi Mudra: Place the hands on the lap with palms upward. Rest the left hand in the palm of the right and allow the thumbs to touch at the tips. See the heart as a great, round moon, above which is the word *Kam* (猭). The *Kam* becomes a sword. The moon and the sword fill the entire Dharma World, so that there exists only one great moon and one great sword. The sword becomes Acala. Bring the figure of Acala inside you, and allow his merits to become part of you. See that internally, Acala is filled with kindness and compassion, even though externally he manifests anger and fury. Envision that one's own body and the body of Acala are now one.

Section 3. Introduction to the Goma

I. *The Konpon-In and the Honzon-In mudra which are used in this step must be given by a master to his or her disciple.* The mantra to be recited is "In the name of all Vajras, Nam! O Great Fiery-Angry One! Destroyer of Evil! Hum! Trah! Tah! Kam! Mam!"

II. *Protecting Mudra.* Buddha Locana is here asked to protect the practitioner. Intertwine the little, ring, and middle fingers at the tips. Bend the forefingers and allow their tips to rest on the tips of your thumbs, which are parallel and flush. Raise and lower the tips of your forefingers, keeping them touching each other. Recite "Om Buddha Roshana! Svaha!"

III. *Summon Agni, The Vedic Spirit of Fire.*
Place the right hand in front of oneself, palm outward, with the thumb folded into the palm. Hold the right wrist with the left hand. Bend and straighten the forefinger of the right hand three times to summon Agni. Envision Agni coming as in the form of Vairocana (Buddha as sunlight). Recite "Om! Agni! Svaha."

IV. *Mudra used during the fire ritual.*
There are six different mudra that can be used at this point in the ritual, according to the number of segments that the monk or nun plan to use during the fire rite. The mudra and mantra shown here are used for a six step Goma of blessing and devotion (Kei Ai). The rite can have anywhere from three (a short service), to five (the standard Shingon service) or six mudra (Tendai practice) as described below. The first mudra declares the purpose for which the fire rite is offered.

Place the palms together and intertwine the ring fingers. Extend the little and middle fingers and allow them to touch at the tips. Extend the forefingers and allow them to remain open. The thumbs are placed parallel and flush. Recite "Om! Purify all obstacles to union in us, Oh Vajra! Svaha!"

V. *Mudra for Grasping the Beads.* Using both hands, grasp the beads between the thumb and ring finger of each hand. Move the beads through the fingers three times reciting each time "Om! made one with Vajra by these sacred (secret) words, Hum!"
Place the beads between the palms leaving the tassels hanging free. The meditator prays silently at this point, for his/her own private intentions. Recite: "Om! Great light shining from thy crown (O Vairocana). Svaha!

VI. *Invocation of the Visions To Be Seen During the Goma.*

A. Four Invocations to the Buddha as sunlight, Vairocana (Dainichi Nyorai). Pick up the single-pronged vajra with the left hand. Place it between the thumb and palm. Hold the beads between the thumb and ring finger of each hand to perform the following incantations:

1. Run the beads through the ring fingers and thumbs ten times, each time reciting "Om bira um ken."

2. Run the beads through once, reciting "Om! Buddha Locana, Svaha!"

3. Run the beads through twice, reciting "Borom borom."

4. Run the beads through ten times, reciting "Namaku samanda basara nam senda makaroshana sowataya um tarata kam man."(For a translation, see #3.I above).

B. Mantra for the Goma which Blesses the community. Continuing to hold the single-pronged vajra between the thumb and palm of the left hand, run the beads through once, reciting "Om saruba haba dakana basara sowaka."(Pg. 1. Mantra #D).

C. Mantra for Agni, the Spirit of Fire. Running the beads through once, reciting "Om agyana ei sowaka." (Hail Agni! Svaha!) Visualize Acala with a red body, yellow hair, three eyes, and four arms. (N.b. Agni is here identified with Acala).

D. Mandala of the Northern Constellations (the Big Dipper and the Twelve Earthly Stems). Run the beads through once, reciting "Om gyara kei shu jibariya hara hatta juchi ramaya sowaka." Visualize Buddha Locana (Lord Ram) surrounded by the sun, moon, thunder, wind, and seven stars of the dipper.

E. The Twenty-Eight Constellations. Visualize the white-robed Tara (Kannon or Avalokitesvara with forty-two arms) while reciting "Om dakisha tara-niri sodani ei sowaka."

F. The Three Buddha Worlds Together. Visualize the three worlds, i.e., the Buddha, Lotus, and Vajra mandala, and recite "Om asaha Svaha!"

G. Mantra of All the Heavens Together. Visualize the twelve spirits of the Vedic religion surrounding Acala. Recite "Om rokya rokya kyaraya sowaka."

The preparations are now complete, and the Goma is about to begin. The meditator uses the same process outlined above when beginning the Goma, the Lotus Mandala, and the Vajra Mandala meditations. In the following pages we will present 1) the meditations of the Goma Fire Rite; 2) the meditations of the Lotus Mandala, and 3) the meditations of the Vajra Mandala, assuming that the above steps have been performed first. At the end of the three meditations, the above "Eighteen Path Mandala" ritual is reversed. The eighteen steps are therefore an approach and an exit from the sacred area of mental visualization. In the closing stages of the three tantric rites, the meditator may also insert a reading of the Four Noble Truths, the Eightfold Path, the Twelve Nidanas (Twelve Causes of non-enlightenment), and the Heart Sutra, as devotion and time permit.

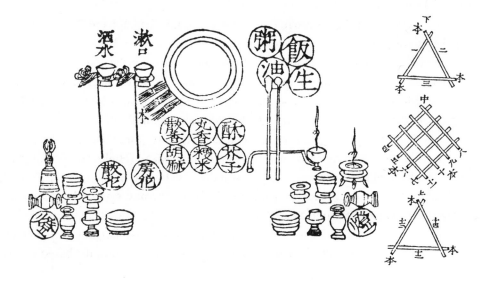

17

Section 4. The Goma Fire Meditation
Part One: The Vision of Acala

I. *Entering the Goma Rite*.

Place the palms together before the chest with the single-pronged vajra and the beads be-
tween them. Offer a silent prayer according to your own intentions in performing the
Goma (for example, the Goma can be used for *Kei-ai*, devotion). Recite three times
"Namaku samanda basara nam senda makaroshana sowataya um tarata kam man."
(Mantra #I, "In the name of all Vajras, Nam! O Great Fiery Angry One! Destroyer of Evil!
Hum! Trah! Tah! Kam! Mam!")

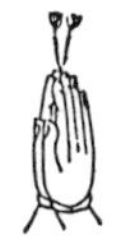

II. *Special Mudra of Acala*.

The mudra used in this step must be transmitted from master to disciple.

III. *Arrange the Goma Altar for the Fire Ritual*.

   A. Remove all *Ju-Hachi Do* articles to the two sides of the altar.

   B. Place the four offerings representing the bad deeds to be burnt away -- red
beans, white beans, rice, and oil -- to the right of the fire.

   C. Place the six offerings representing good deeds -- powdered incense, sesame
seeds, grain barley, sesame seeds, and poppy seeds -- directly in front of the fire altar, as
shown in the diagram. Follow the arrangement shown in the illustration.

   D. To the left of the fire place the *So Ko* water for refreshing the guests. To its
left place the *So Ko* ladle. To the left of the *So Ko* ladle place the *Sha Sui* water, for
purification. To the left of the *Sha Sui* water place the *Sha Sui* ladle.

   E. Place the bowl of joined leaves and the bowl of separate leaves diagonally to the
left of the water. These leaves are used to summon and send away the Buddhas and spirits.

   F. Place the twelve inch pine sticks, representing the Twelve Nidanas and all our
desires, on the table to the left of the practitioner.

   G. Place the fan (for fanning the flames), and the small broom (for sweeping the
altar) on the table to the right of the practitioner.

IV. *The First Vision*. The Agni Fire Altar.

   A. Wrap the beads around the left wrist. Using the left hand, count out fourteen
sticks into the right hand. Then place the sticks into the left hand, and purify them with the
Vajra mudra and mantra, as follows: with the right hand form the Vajra Mudra: extend the
ring, middle, and forefingers outward. Press the tip of the little finger down with the
thumb. Move the hand in a circular motion, three times counter-clockwise then three
times clockwise, reciting each time "Om kili kili Vajra Hum! Phat!"

   B. One by one, dip the top and bottom of each stick into the oil and lay it on the
stove of the altar, reciting each time "Om agyana ei sowaka." (Hail Agni! Svaha!) The first
three sticks form an equilateral triangle, with the base toward the meditator. Form the left
side of the triangle first, then the right, then the base. The next four sticks are placed
diagonally and parallel, running southwest to northeast (the altar is considered to be
North). The next four sticks are also placed diagonally and parallel, this time running
southeast to northwest. The final three sticks form a triangle. Form the base first, then the

left side. Before placing the last stick on the right, after it has been dipped, flip it over so that the tail (marked in black) is pointed away from you. Place it on the triangle in that manner.

C. Light the fire. Take either a stick that has been fire-blackened before the ritual or a knotted stick with pitch and dip it in the oil bowl to the right of the altar. Hold the tip in the candle flame until it lights. Holding it in your left hand, form the Vajra Mudra with the right hand and make a circular motion, three times counter-clockwise and three times clockwise, reciting each time "Om kili kili Vajra Hum! Phat!" Thrust the burning stick into the center of the altar stove in order to light the Goma fire.

D. Purify the fire with Water: pick up the Shasui water ladle which has been placed to the left of the Soko water ladle. Dip the Shasui water ladle into the Shasui water (water for purification). See the characters for *Ram* [𑖨] and *Bam* [𑖤] in the water. Flick a drop of water onto the fire and recite three times "Om amirite Hum! Phat!"

E. Fan the fire: pick up the fan with the right hand and rest the right hand in the palm of the left. Open the fan and fan the flames three times, reciting each time "Om boji bara um." Put the fan down.

F. Offer a sprig of leaves: throw a sprig of leaves into the fire. Visualize a four-petalled lotus opening in the middle of the flames. Recite three times "Om agyana ei geki sowaka." Visualize the Yellow Haired Acala form of Agni to come into an open lotus in the middle of the flames.

G. *Kongo Gassho* (Vajra joined hands): form the Kongo Gassho Mudra by placing the palms together with the fingertips slightly intertwined. See in the middle of the flames a great lotus. Above it is the seed word *Ram* [𑖨], which becomes the great fire light worthy, Agni. His body is red and his hair is yellow. He has three eyes and four arms. Fire and light radiate from his body.

H. Invitation. Continuing to perform the *Kongo Gassho* mudra, think to oneself:

> Respectfully bowing my head, I here today invite the great, highest, and worthy Ka-Ten (Agni), the great immortal from the central heaven. By this mantra we respectfully beg you alone to come down here and partake of this offering.

I. Summoning Mudra. Place the right hand before the chest palm outward with the thumb folded into the palm. With the left hand grasp the right wrist, while leaving the fingers of the left hand extended. Bend the index finger of the right hand down three times to summon Agni (seen as a form of Vairocana). Recite: "Om Agni! Welcome! Svaha!"

J. Four-Character Binding Mudra. While performing the mudra and mantra, see Agni bound and locked in the flames.

1. With wrists crossed, lock the little fingers together, keeping the backs of the palms toward oneself. Recite "Jya."

2. Keeping the little fingers locked together, bring the backs of the palms together and recite "Um."

3. Maintaining the above hand position, interlock the forefingers and recite "Bam."

4. Maintaining the above hand position bend the ring and middle finger of each hand down over the thumb. Maintaining this position place the hands in front of the chest with the interlocked forefingers aimed at the fire. Recite "Ko." This binds Agni in the fire.

K. A refreshing Drink. Dip the *So Ko* water ladle into the *So Ko* water and flick a drop of water into the fire three times, reciting each time "Om! Desires fulfilled! Vajra! Void!"

L. *Nai Goma*: the Interior Fire Meditation. All the karmic deeds of all sentient beings are to be purified, burned away by this fire. The Interior Goma creates the Bodhi enlightened heart. The external fire is a symbol for burning away all interior thoughts, both good and bad, all troubles and desires, so that nothing, not even ashes, are left in the unconscious mind.

Hold the beads, vajra, and large oil ladle in the left hand. Pick up the small oil ladle in the right hand. Cross the heads of the ladles in front of the forehead, left over right, forming a triangle with the body as the base. Meditate as follows:

When visualizing the Interior Goma, those performing it must realize that all things arise and are born from the effects of karmic i.e., willed deeds, on the mind. To purify the impediments arising from words and deeds, i.e., to attain liberation from them, we must be able to burn away the causes of our deeds by the so-called Bodhi [enlightened] heart-mind. This is the goal of the Interior Goma. If we examine the fire of the visible world, we see that it burns things and turns them into ashes. But this flame [of the Interior Goma] is not the same. It is a violent purging wisdom within the self which burns away all positive as well as negative images. It is a sudden devouring flame which leaves no ashes remaining as residue in the voided heart-mind.

The three places, body, fire, and altar, become one. I.e., the great altar, a sacred area, becomes the Goma fire. The Goma becomes my body; my body becomes Ka-Ten (Agni, Acala); Agni becomes Vairocana. Body, mouth, and mind are fused together in a fiery meditation of interior alchemy. The three, fire, Agni, and I are equal; there is no differentiation. The three bodies, made one, are visualized to expand and fill the entire Dharma (mind) World. They neither arise nor are they annihilated, when separated from words and the images which bear words. The meditator is born in the realm of no birth, where there is nothing which is not diffused by purifying light from Vairocana.

Meditating at the gateway of *Ah* [꙰], the gateway to outer reality and inner imagination, the Goma fire prevents all the seeds of desires from arising. Entering into the violent cutting wisdom of Vairocana's light, the meditator sees him/herself suddenly becoming a great burning flame, in the center of which is the image of Acala holding a sword and a coiled rope. The swirling flames devour karmic deeds and mental images. The mind, like a wooden vessel laden with avidya, ignorance, never again can return to a state of attachment to words, images, or desires. Nothing remains, no residue is left from these meditative flames.

The meditator next envisions the human heart, purged by the flames of the Bodhi light, washed in a great compassionate water. He/she sees the water of compassion pouring into the body, flowing through it like sweet, white dew. It washes away the evils of the ten directions, cleanses the hearts of all sentient beings, washes away all worries, all troubles. In the meditative vision the waters fall like dew on the petals of a newly budding Bodhi flower. One by one the petals manifest five seed words:

Ah
Bam
Ram
Kam
Ken

The meditator now sees these five seed words become a five-storied stupa. The stupa becomes the body of Vairocana (Dainichi Nyorai, Great Sun Tathagata). The body of Vairocana is the Dharmakaya (The Dharma Body). This is the secretly-transmitted internal Goma, a meditation that can be performed privately as well as publicly during the Goma ritual.

M. Burning the Four Offerings that represent our bad deeds. (Note: Though each item is offered three times, the offering is actually put into the fire only once. Then the offering bowl is hit twice to symbolize the three separate offerings being made.)

1. Take the small ladle in the right hand, the large ladle in your left. Dip the small ladle into the oil and scoop three spoonfuls into the large ladle. Put down the small ladle. Using both hands empty the contents of the large ladle into the fire. Recite "Om Agni! Svaha!" Repeat the procedure three times.

2. Next, holding the small ladle with both hands, pour oil onto the fire three times, reciting each time "Om Agni! Svaha!"

3. Using the seed ladle, throw three spoonfuls of red beans onto the fire, reciting each time "Om Agni! Svaha!"

4. Again using the seed ladle, throw three spoonfuls of white beans onto the fire, reciting each time "Om Agni! Svaha!"

5. Again using the seed ladle, throw three spoonfuls of rice onto the fire, reciting each time "Om Agni! Svaha!"

N. Separate Leaves. Throw three separate leaves over the fire, reciting "Om Agni! Svaha!"

O. Pick up three sticks, dipping each of them, one by one, into the soma (honey and oil mixed), and toss them into the fire. Recite each time "Om Agni! Svaha!"

P. Burn the six sets of offerings in the center of the altar that represent our good deeds. Hold the single-pronged vajra between the thumb, ring, and middle fingers of the right hand. Pinch up the offerings from the small brass bowls while making a resounding sound of the brass vajra against the rim of the bowl.

1. Toss seven pinches of poppy seeds into the fire, reciting each time "Om Agni! Svaha!"

2. Toss seven pinches of barley seeds into the fire, reciting each time "Om Agni! Svaha!"

3. Toss fourteen pinches of sesame seeds (goma) into the fire, reciting each time "Om Agni! Svaha!"

4. Toss three pinches of grain incense into the fire, reciting each time "Om agyana ei sowaka."

5. Toss three pinches of powdered incense into the fire, reciting each time "Om Agni! Svaha!"

6. Take the small ladle in the right hand, the large ladle in the left. Dip the small ladle into the oil and scoop three spoonfuls into the large ladle. Put down the small ladle. Using both hands empty the contents of the large ladle into the fire. Recite "Om Agni! Svaha!" Perform the offering three times.

Q. Prayers of Petition. Meditate silently on the following:

May these offerings of respect to the Agni protect and preserve all the children of the Buddha. May our vows of compassion always be fulfilled.

R. Dip the bamboo stick into the So Ko water and flick a drop of water into the fire three times, reciting each time "Om Desires fulfilled, Vajra! Void!"

S. Leaf-Sprig Offering dispels the vision. Throw a sprig of leaves over the fire, allowing it to land to the left of the stove. Recite "Om Agni! Be gone, be gone! Svaha!"

T. Words of Farewell. With palms pressed together in the gassho mudra, quietly chant: "Our sole wish is that Agni returns to his proper throne."

U. Mudra of farewell. Place the right hand before the chest palm outward, with the thumb folded into the palm. With the left hand grasp the right wrist, with the fingers of the left hand extended. Bend the ring finger of the right hand down three times to send Agni away. Recite: "Om Agni! Begone Begone! Svaha!"

Part Two. *Yo Dan*: The Vision of Buddha Locana.
Burning Away the Fatherly Aspects of the Buddha

The second vision of the goma follows the same format as the rubrics in Part One, except for the following:

I. Add three sticks of wood to the fire, instead of fourteen.

II. When throwing the sprig of leaves into the fire, see the image of Buddha Locana sitting in the middle of a lotus in the center of the fire where the leaves landed. Around him see the seven stars of the Big Dipper and the twelve stem-constellations (Precious Vase, Fish, Green Sheep, Cow, Male, Crab, Lion, Lady, Good Fortune, Tree Grub, Bow, Dragon Head).

III. Recite the mantra "Om! Lord Ram who enlightens nature from within, Svaha!" ("Om gyara kei jibariya hara hatta ji shu chi ramaya ei geki sowaka.") (The sanskrit seed words bears the connotation of welcoming Lord Ram, slayer of Lanka who kidnaped Lady Sita. Ram, or Lord of Light purifies and empties the interior for union in this Bakhti tradition).

IV. Contemplation of the Buddha Locana vision. Envision in the middle of the fire a lotus throne, on top of which is the seed word *Ken* [𑀓]. The word becomes Buddha Locana (Butsugen Bu Mo), the fatherly aspects of Vairocana Buddha. Around Buddha Locana see the five elements as five planets: Saturn is in the center and represents the earth element. Jupiter is to the East and represents wood. Mars is to the South and represents fire. Venus is to the West and represents metal. Mercury is in the North and represents water. To the East of Jupiter is the Sun, representing yang. To the West of Venus is the Moon, representing yin. Outside the circle of the planets there is a circle comprised of the twelve stem-constellations. In the area between the two circles are the seven stars of the Big Dipper.

The second stage of the Goma rite is performed in exactly the same manner as the first, as listed from paragraphs A. through R. above. The following change is observed in the second stage through the sixth stage, for sending off the vision:

U. Sending-Off Mudra. From the second to the sixth stage of the Goma, the sending off mudra is as follows: cross the wrists right over left. Link the little fingers. Allow the forefinger of each hand to touch the thumb. Flick the index finger off the thumb three times, reciting each time "Om! Lord Ram who enlightens nature from within, begone! Begone! Svaha!"

Part Three of the Goma Fire Rite is performed exactly the same as the first and second stages, except for the following changes:

I. The Third Stage of the meditation envisions the Great Moon Orb One Word Gold Wheel Usnisa Buddha. In the oral tradition, the vision is changed into the thousand armed Kannon (Avalokitesvara) surrounded by the Twenty-Eight Constellations, i.e., the motherly aspects of Buddha Vairocana.

II. When throwing a sprig of leaves into the fire, visualize a great golden wheel where the leaves land. The golden wheel is changed into a great golden moon, in the center of which is a lotus throne surrounded by twenty-eight lotus blossoms, representing the stars of the twenty-eight constellations.

III. Recite the mantra "Om dakisha tara nijiri sodani ei sowaka!" for each of the offerings and invocations. (The mantra has a double meaning: "Om! Constellations that devour evil by thy chant," the textbook meaning, is supplanted by "Om! White-robed Tara whose voice purifies, Svaha!" in the oral Ajari tradition).

IV. The Meditation. See in the center of the fire a great lotus pavilion, in the center of which is the seed word *Borom* [家]. The word *borom* becomes a great gold moon, in the center of which is a lotus, and Usnisa Gold Moon Buddha (Ichi-Ji Kin Rin Butcho). In the lotus is also the white-robed Tara (Kannon), who is surrounded by the spirits of the twenty-eight constellations.

Offer all of the seeds, grains, oils, wood, and leaves as in the first and second stages, substituting mantra of the Usnisa Buddha and White-robed Tara at each invocation.

Part Four. *Honzon Dan*: Union with Acala and Vairocana

I. Build a Vairocana Altar in the center of the flames. Wrap the beads around the left wrist. Using the left hand, count out fourteen sticks into the right hand, and follow the directions for building the fire to Agni in Part One. The first three sticks, representing the Buddha, Lotus, and Vajra worlds, are laid on the fire in the form of a triangle. Next place eight sticks on the fire, which symbolize the entire visible cosmos. Last, lay on three sticks in a triangle pattern, that stand for the head, heart, and belly of man. The fire thus represents the macro and microcosm, filled with the triple mandala.

Follow the order of the first three stages, except for the following changes:
1. Recite the mantra to Acala-Vairocana, as follows: "Namaku samanda basara nam senda makaroshana sowataya um tarata kam man." (In the name of all Vajras, Nam! O Great Fiery-Angry One! Destroyer of Evil! Hum! Trah! Tah! Kam! Mam!). Use this mantra for all of the offerings and invocations.
2. Throw two sprigs of leaves in the fire. Envision a lotus in the center of each sprig. In the center of the first lotus see the seed word *Ah* [罗]. The seed word *Ah* becomes Vairocana (Dainichi Nyorai). In the second lotus see the seed word *Kam* [汉]. The seed word *Kam* becomes Acala (Fudo Myo-o). Always envision Acala together with Vairocana during the fourth stage of the meditation.
3. Perform the meditation with the two ladles held in a triangle over the head, as in stage one. The words of the meditation are the same as in stage one, except for the following:
Envision the five-wheel seed words:

Ah
Bam
Ram
Kam
Ken

See these five seed words become a five-storied stupa. This stupa becomes the body of Dainichi Nyorai, the Dharma Body. Vairocana's wisdom fire flows from above, from the enlightened land down to the Avici Hell of eternal suffering, the place from which all illusions, karmic deeds, and sorrows arise, into the world of illusions filled with evil and calamities. Throw all of this world of illusion into the raging fires. It will not be reborn. There will be no ashes, no remnants. Relying on the power of this vision, we can leave behind the impediments of this world. Due to the merits of these offerings, peace and stillness will fill us, filled with the desire to fulfill the vow of compassion.
4. When burning the sacrificial items, each of the offerings are doubled, one set each for Acala and Vairocana.
5. When throwing the six offerings of good deeds into the fire, tap the various brass dishes 100 times (or an approximation thereof), while reciting the Acala mantra "Namaku samanda basara nam senda makaroshana sowataya um tarata kam man."

6. Mix the contents of the three bowls -- poppy, barley, and sesame seeds -- together in one of the bowls, and toss it into the fire, reciting the Acala mantra. Then take thirty-six sticks, dip both ends into the oil, and throw them into the fire, reciting the mantra.

7. Purify oneself of all faults by the fiery light of Vairocana. Press the palms together. Fold down the ring fingers. Open out the forefingers. The thumbs are parallel and flush. Recite seven times "Om saruba haba dakana basara ya sowaka." (Om! All faults are burned away by the vajra-wisdom fire. Svaha!). Then envision Vairocana in the fire. See the heart of Vairocana to be like a lotus. The lotus becomes a wheel of light. The wheel of light becomes the entire Dharma World. Think quietly to oneself:

> All the Buddhas are nourished by these sacrifices equally.

> All barriers are burned away. Endless joy fills my heart.

Send off Acala and Vairocana as in the second stage of the goma, with the linked finger "seeing off" mudra.

Part Five. Burn Away All Worthies of the Three Mandalas, i.e., the Buddha, Lotus, and Vajra worlds

I. Adding Wood. Dip both ends of four sticks into the soma oil in the center of the altar and place them on the fire, parallel, running southwest to northeast. Dip both ends of another four sticks into the oil and place them on the fire, parallel, running southeast to northwest. Dip both ends of one stick of wood into the oil and place it on the center of the fire, running east to west. The first three sticks are accompanied by reciting the mantra "Om! Ah! (Buddha World) Svaha!" See the Buddha world placed directly over the fire. The second three sticks placed on the fire are accompanied by the mantra "Om! Sa! (Lotus World) Svaha." Envision the Lotus World directly over the fire. The third three sticks placed on the fire are empowered by the mantra "Om! Va! Svaha!" Envision the Vajra World directly over the fire.

II. The Fifth Stage of the Goma Fire rite follows the same order as the first four stages, with the following exceptions:

1. When summoning the Three Worlds, throw three single leaves into the fire together, reciting "Om! Ah, Sa, Va, welcome! Svaha!" Envision the three worlds burning in the fire. See all the worthies of the three worlds in the middle of a lotus blossom beneath the three worlds.

2. During the meditation see in the midst of the flames the three seed words *Ah* [𑀅], *Sa* [𑀲], and *Va* [𑀯]. These three seed words become the three mandala, the Buddha, Lotus, and Vajra worlds. Use the mantra "Om! Ah, Sa, Va, Svaha!" for all of the offerings and invocations of the fifth stage.

3. After burning the six items that represent all good deeds, place the hands before oneself, palms up, curving the fingers up slightly to form a single cup. See in one's cupped hands all the merits accrued from doing this Goma. Offer up these blessings so that all sentient beings may be enlightened. Recite "Om! In the name of all Buddhas, may all sentient beings be enlightened, Svaha!" Then say to oneself inwardly:

> Now we have passed through the entire Dharma World. All
> deeds and impediments have been burnt away; all beings may
> pass over to the shore of enlightenment.

Think to oneself that all the remnants of good as well as evil deeds, all visions of Buddha are burnt away in the Goma fires.

4. All of the remaining seeds are now put together in a single bowl. One of the keman leaves are ripped into small pieces, and laid on the top of the bowl. These mixed seeds are used as the food offerings to the spirits envisioned in the sixth, i.e., the last section of the Goma.

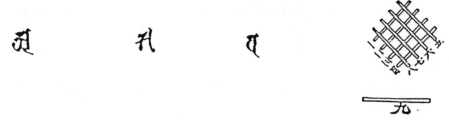

27

Part Six. Burn Away the Spirits of the Entire Cosmos

In the sixth stage of the Goma an imaginary vision of the spirits of the Vedic religion, Chinese and Japanese folk religion, and all other religious traditions are burned away. The reason for burning away all man made notions of the absolute at this point of the Goma is to confirm the fact that in all mystic or kenotic (emptying) religious traditions, "the eye cannot see, the ear cannot hear, nor can the mind conceive" the experience of union with what is transcendent, "on the other shore."

When adding wood to the fire in the sixth stage, throw only three sticks into the fire. Do not dip them in oil. Recite "Om! fiery, brightly burning dark skinned one (Acala)! Svaha!" Use this mantra for all of the offerings and invocations, except as follows:

1. When inviting the vision into the fire, throw a handful of separate leaves into the flames, reciting "Om! fiery, burning Dark One, welcome! Svaha!"

2. Meditation. Form the Vajra Clasped-Hands Mudra: Place the palms together with the tips of the fingers intertwined, the thumbs crossed right over left. Envision in the center of the fire the seed word *Kam* [呪]. See the seed word Kam become the four-armed Acala, surrounded by the twelves spirits of the heavens in all ten directions around Acala. Maintaining the Mudra, recite the following:

> I respectfully bow my head and invite the four-armed Acala
> Worthy and all the heavenly spirits in the ten directions,
> begging them to come down here, to be present and to receive
> these Goma offerings.

3. Empowering the Mixed Offerings. Prepare the bowl of mixed offerings by the following mudra and mantra. Touch the middle finger of the right hand to the thumb. Rub the middle finger on the tip of the thumb, then snap three times, reciting "Om! In the name of all Tathagatas, let us contemplate, Om! By these offerings may we attain birth, peace, on the other shore, Svaha!"

4. Turn the right hand so that it is now palm upward. See in the hand the seed word *Vam* [鑁]. See the seed word *Vam* slip from the hand into the fire and become a huge twelve-petalled lotus. There is one petal for each of the twelve heavenly spirits. Recite "In the name of all Buddhas! Vam!" Then, grasping the seed ladle, offer one scoop of the seeds to each of the worthies, as the mantra is recited:

a. *Acala.* "In the name of all Vajras, Nam! Trah! Destroyer of evil, Great Angry, Fiery Resplendent One, Hum! Trah! Kam! Mam!" Visualize Acala in the center of the flames.

b. *Indra.* "Om Indaraya Svaha!" Visualize Indra on the east side of the flames.

c. *Agni.* "Om Agni! Svaha!" Visualize Agni to the southeast side of the flames.

d. *Enma* (Yama: King of Hell). "Om Enma! Svaha!" Visualize Enma on the south side of the flames.

e. *Raksasa.* (Rasetsuten). "Om Raksasa! Svaha!" Visualize Rasetsuten on the southwest side of the flames.

f. *Varuna* (Suiten: Water Spirit). "Om Barodaya! Svaha!" Visualize Suiten on the west side of the flames.

g. *Vayu* (Futten: Wind Spirit). "Om Bayabei! Svaha!" Visualize FutTen on the northwest side of the fire.

h. *Vaisravana* (Tamonten, Bishamon). "Om Beishira manaya! Svaha!" Visualize Bishamonten on the north side of the fire.

i. *Isvara* (Jizaiten: Spirit Free from Delusion). "Om Ijyanayei! Svaha!" See Jizaiten to the northeast of the fire.

j. *Brahma* (Bonten). "Om Lord Brahma! Svaha." Visualize Bonten directly above the center of the fire.

k. *Prthivi* (Jiten: Earth Goddess) "Om Privithi! Svaha!" Visualize Jiten directly below the center of the flames.

l. *Surya* (Nitten: Spirit of the Sun). "Om Surya! Svaha!" Visualize Nitten to the northwest of the flames.

m. *Chandra Devi* (Gatten: Lady Ruler of the Moon). "Om Chandra! Svaha!" Visualize Gatten to the southwest of the fire.

n. Sources of Light (Sun, Moon, and the Big Dipper, the second stage of the Goma fire rite). "Om! Lord Ram who enlightens nature from within, Svaha!" Visualize the sources of light directly above the head of Acala (Fudo Myo-o).

o. The Twenty-Eight Constellations. "Om! White Robed Tara! Svaha!" Visualize the twenty-eight constellations surrounding the center of the fire altar.

p. All the Heavens. "Om! Brightly shining, Dark One! Svaha!" Visualize the Buddha, Lotus, and Vajra worlds inside the fire.

q. All the Spirits. "Om! Brightly shining, Dark One! Svaha!" See the flames enveloping Acala to leap forth and burn away the entire vision.

5. Put down the seed ladle and pick up the bowl with the seed mixture. Recite "Om! Be purified! Hum! Phat!" Throw the remaining seeds into the fire.

6. Dip both ends of seven sticks in the soma oil. Throw them into the fire, reciting "Om! Brightly shining, Dark One! Svaha!"

7. Pick up the single-pronged vajra with the left hand. Hold the beads between the thumbs and middle fingers of both hands. Pull the beads through your fingers once, representing one hundred times. Recite "Om! Brightly shining Dark One! Svaha!"

8. Using both hands, scoop three spoonfuls of oil into the fire, reciting "Om! Brightly shining Dark One! Svaha!" Stack up the Goma offering bowls and place them, along with the ladles, to the side of the altar.

9. Offering up the Buddha's teachings (Dharma). Form the Kongo Clasped-Hands Mudra: Place the palms together with the tips of the fingers intertwined, the thumbs crossed right over left. Recall the Four Noble Truths: All of life is conditioned by suffering; suffering is caused by desire; annihilate desires; choose the (eightfold) path of compassion.

Continuing to perform the Kongo Clasped-Hands Mudra, recall the the Twelve Nidanas, i.e., the obstacles to enlightenment: i. Ignorance (avidya); ii. Actions produced by ignorance (samskara); iii. First consciousness in the womb (vijna); iv. The mental function of naming (nama-rupa); v. Six judgments: five senses plus the mind (sadayatana); vi. Touch (sparsa); vii. Sense Perception (vedana); viii. Desire (trsna); ix. Attachment (upadana); x. Clinging to existence (bhava); xi. Birth (jati); xii. Old Age, Death (jaramaran).

Continuing to hold the Kongo Clasped-Hands Mudra, recall the *Roppara Mitsu* Six Perfections: i. Giving (dana); ii. Precepts (sila); iii. Perseverance (ksanti); iv. Assiduity (virya); v. Zen Meditation (dhyana); vi. Hannya: Wisdom (prajna).

10. The sixth section of the Goma fire rite ends with the monk sending off the visions, sweeping off the front of the altar with a small broom, and replacing the offerings and implements used during the Eighteen Path meditation.

Part 7. Concluding Meditation of Union

The meditator performs the final meditation while assuming the "contemplation" or Zen meditation mudra, right palm placed over the left. Envision a great moon disk filling the microcosm (the meditator's body). In the center of the disk is the seed word *Kam* [釤], symbol of self united to Vairocana. While contemplating the vision, realize inwardly:

> The reason why the Dharma is not understood is because I have never realized that my heart and the Buddha heart are one and the same. My heart and that of all sentient beings are one. The Buddha world, my heart, and all sentient beings are now united as one. We are not different. My body is Vairocana. Vairocana is I.

(The oral tradition here says that tears of gratitude pour forth from the heart of the meditator upon realizing this truth).

The other shore of enlightenment, the shore of wisdom (Prajna Paramita, the wisdom parameter) is only reached because the light emanating from Vairocana, symbolized by the fires of the Goma, have burned away all obstacles in me. It is not by my merits, but by the light of Vairocana-Amida-Acala (all three are now seen as one) that enlightenment is attained in the Tendai Tantric tradition.

It is crucial that any merit or good received from the ritual be given away for all sentient beings. The person offering the Goma must give away not only all of the gifts, but any spiritual attainment that might have accrued to him or herself during the meditation. The following prayer is recited:

> I now give away all of these gifts, one-by-one, all of the dust and ashes of the real and phenomenal, which comprise the whole ocean of Dharma world; Dharma world is indeed identical with these offerings. I offer all four Dharma bodies, (phenomenal, noumenal, noumenal and phenomenal body as one, noumenal body without hindrance). The three worlds (past, present, future) are always nourished by these gifts...

The Goma Fire Rite ends by reversing the order of the Juhachi-do meditation, as seen in the first part of the meditation, i.e,, before the fire was lit. The officiant once again offers of the five visible items (on the left side of the altar), and the six symbolic mudra, as before. He/she sends back the visions by the chariot mudra, rings the bell, and performs the *Goshimbo* five purificatory mudra, to end the rite. As the meditator bows deeply to Acala and leaves the sacred area, the closing words of the Goma, Lotus, and Vajra meditations warn that the ritual was in vain if henceforth the life of the meditator is not filled with compassion and helping love towards others.

II. THE LOTUS WOMB MEDITATION
Introduction

The Lotus Mandala meditation uses Tantric prayer, i.e., mind, mouth, and body, (mandala patterned visualization, mantric chant, and mudra hand dance) for the purpose of achieving Buddhist awakening. The goal of the meditation is to "put on" or assume by total body prayer the aspects of a Buddha or enlightened person. Since there is nothing that I can do as a person limited in space and time to merit this awakening by my own deeds or power (jiriki), it is necessary to achieve the "crossing over" or attainment of the absolute with the help of one who has already crossed over to the other shore, that is, by the power of another (tariki). This "other" is seen to be the central figure of the Lotus Mandala, Vairocana, the Buddha of infinite light and compassion.

Vairocana, the Buddha of Infinite Light and Compassion, (pronounced Vairochana in sanskrit, *Dai-nichi Nyorai* in Japanese) is assisted in this task of awakening the meditator by the Great Light King Acala, (Achala, *Fudo Myo-o*). During the course of the mandala liturgy, the meditator is made to see a series of startlingly realistic visualizations (called "eidetic" or moving visions) identifying with Buddha as in a mirror. In a manner analogous to the powerful Spiritual Exercises of Ignatius of Loyola, or the words of Paul calling the early christians to "put on Christ," the Buddhist monks and nuns who perform these liturgies put on the body, heart, and mind of Vairocana-Acala.

It is important to repeat, in the Tendai version of this rite, that the "putting on" of the aspects of Vairocana, who is the equivalent of Acala, Amida, and any other aspect of a Tathagata or enlightened being,(we must not be attached to the name or the vision) is not done through any merit or power of my own. The light and saving grace of the absolute non-conditioned state is always shining on me, like the sun in the heavens. I am told to simply open my mind, heart, and body to the vision, like a lotus opening to the light of the sun. The seed of enlightenment, envisioned as the sanskrit seed-word *Ah* is aready planted there, waiting to be watered and awakened. In this sense, the Greek letters Alpha-Omega and the sanskrit *Ah* and *Om* are similar, i.e. symbols of the infinite origin and infinite return to origin. The Lotus meditation is an opening, a watering and flowering of the seed word *Ah*, waiting in my heart to blossom and bear fruit, the result of awakening to union.

The Lotus World meditation, as in the case of the Goma and the Vajra rites, is structured by the Eighteen Path Mandala, which acts as an introduction and an exit from the sacred area in which the meditation takes place. The following structure quides the meditator through a clockwise process into the center of the Lotus World, where union is achieved with a vision of Vairocana meditating in the Zen-lotus position.

I. Purification. (As in the Eighteen Path Mandala).
    1. Entrance rite.
    2. Summoning and petitions.
    3. The first offerings.
    4. Chant of the Lotus mandala.
    5. The Nine Songs of praise.

6. Vows of the Boddhisattva.

7. *Goshimbo*, a series of six mudra-mantra to purify the meditator.

II. Building the Lotus Altar.

1. Awaken and summon the spirits of the Lotus Mandala.

2. First eidetic vision: generate the Lotus Stupa.

3. Putting on the 32 aspects of the Tathagata's body.

III. Contemplate the Lotus mandala.

1. The great ocean meditation.

2. Lotus flower and vajra hand meditations.

3. Lotus King and Lotus Center meditation.

4. Self, Tathagata, and Dharma are one.

5. Give away merit to all sentient beings.

6. The mandala wheel and its colors.

7. Contemplate each Buddha of the Mandala.

IV. Invite the Buddhas inside the Mandala.

1. Point to the Mandala entrance.

2. The meditator becomes Acala.

3. Don the armor, clasp the sword of Acala.

4. Ring the bell, invite the Buddhas to enter.

5. With binding mudra, bolt the gates, purify with sword.

6. Welcome the Buddhas with water and flowers.

7. Offer prayers and vows to the Buddhas.

V. Put on the body and merits of Vairocana.

1. Protect the body with vajra armor.

2. Cast out all evil thoughts and spirits.

3. Purify the four directions and three worlds.

4. Again lock and guard the four gates of the Mandala.

VI. The six offerings.

1. Offer the six gifts (water, incense, flowers, burning
   incense, rice, and light), the concrete aspects of reality.

2. Offer the six gifts as symbols, i.e., the phenomenal aspects of reality.

VII. The Samadhi Meditation.

1. Envision the Lotus Mandala, as AH seed word generated.

2. Mudra and mantra of Vairocana.

3. Enter Samadhi meditation (vipassana).

4. Chant with beads and mudra.

5. Envision self as Buddha Locana.

VIII. Offerings of Thanks, exit through Eighteen Path mandala.

(Reverse the process of stage one, above).

The goal of the Lotus Mandala Meditation is union with Vairocana in the center of the microcosm, signified by identification with the various images of the Lotus World. The goal of the Vajra Mandala meditation, which immediately follows the Lotus ritual, is to give away all of the benefits of the Lotus and Vajra worlds, in a true emptying or kenosis experience of the meditator's mind and heart. The images of both mandala are but *upaya*, convenient skillful means for achieving the third of the four noble truths, the annihilation of desires, and the thoughts that lead to them. In the philosophy of emptiness that Tendai Buddhism, and the world's great mystic traditions follow, emptiness (kenosis, the dark night of intellect and senses) is the basic condition for "achieving the other shore." The meditations of Tantric Buddhism are therefore a method for kenotic union.

The Lotus-womb Mandala

34

Part 1. Purification

The first stage of the Lotus meditation is the same as the Eighteen Path mandala rite found in Part One, section two, above. The following changes are oberved:

    A. The chant in honor of the Lotus World sings the praises and envisions the center of the mandala as follows:

1. Vairocana, in the center, the Dharma Body manifestation.
2. Ratnadhvaja, *Tohobodofu* in the east, or top of center.
3. Samkusumita, *Kakaihufu* in the south, left of center.
4. Amitabha Buddha, *Buryoshufu* in the west, below center.
5. Divyadundubhi, *Hotsuho Tenko Rai-infu*, north, right of center.
6. Samantabhadra Boddhisattva, southeast of center.
7. Manjusri Boddhisattva, southwest of center.
8. Avalokitesvara Boddhisattva, northwest of center.
9. Maitreya, *Miroku* Boddhisattva, northeast of center.

    Below the center of the Lotus World mandala envision the Five Light Kings, as seen in the illustration, from right to left:

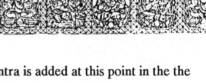

10. Acalanatha, (Fudo Myo-o).
11. Trailokyavijaya, (Gozanze).
12. Kundalin (Gundari), or Vajra Kundalin.
13. Enma, King of Hell (Enma).
14. Vajra Yaksho (Yakisha).

    B. Visualize the *Ah* seed word. A special mantra is added at this point in the the Lotus World, while the monk or nun forms the clasped hands mudra with empty center:

> In the name of all Buddhas
> *Ah*𑖀 is one with me
> The Three (Dharma, Lotus, Vajra) one with me,
> One thou art with me, Svaha! So be it!

The mantra is repeated five times, and the mudra is pressed to the five places, (belly, heart, shoulders, throat, and dissolved over the head). Body, mouth, and mind (*shin-ku-i*) are called "samaya," i.e., same or one with the Buddha, Lotus, and Vajra worlds. The oral teaching here intervenes to show the following correspondences in the greater cosmic order:

Head	yi	(mind)	Buddha	Dharma body	mandala
Mouth	ku	(heart)	Lotus	Reward body	mantra
Body	shin	(belly)	Vajra	Response body	mudra

    In a more profound sense, as learned in the Eighteen Path meditation, my heart, the tathagata, and all sentient beings must be seen as united (samaya) or symbolically one. Samaya has a four fold sense here, that is, equally possessing the Buddha nature (the ability to be enlightened), I share in the original vow of Amida to save all sentient beings, prevent all obstacles from arising, and bring about complete and sudden enlightenment in self and others. The identity of self with the compassionate vow of the Tathagata (Amida, Vairocana, or any image of Buddha) is but an *upaya* a convenient and skillful means to awaken one's mind, heart, and body from the sleep of ignorance. From this awakening it becomes possible to dwell in a state of deep meditation, realizing that life and death are equal, beginning and end are a single process, a single *Ah* seed word buried deep in my heart, the center of the Lotus.

The *Ah* seed word is therefore the basis for the Lotus world meditation, the first letter of the Siddham (Tantric) alphabet. The disciple is told by the Ajari master to throw him or herself into the womb of the *Ah* lotus world, at this point, and realize for the first time that enlightenment takes place within my own heart. The bodhi-awakened heart mind is born from the *Ah* seed in the depths of the Lotus world. The *Ah* seed word is the basis for all subsequent awakening, realized for the first time in the recitation of the above "entering Buddha samaya" mantra. The ten fingers of the empty center mudra, held straight up, symbolize the oneness of Buddha (right hand) and I (left). The middle fingers are now slightly opened, symbolizing that the *Ah* seed word within me has now been awakened, opened to a light that does not lead to the arising of wordly thoughts, a light not gained by merit, that permeates the entire cosmos.

C. The second mudra of the Lotus World meditation is symbolic of the reward body, born from the *Ah* seed word. The *Ah* seed word turns the Dharma body into the compassionate Lotus-reward body, in the meditator's heart. The mudra is formed by touching the extended index fingers together, with third, fourth, and fifth fingers pressed down over the thumbs. The mantra invokes the seed word *Kam* to effect the transformation.

Hail, All Buddhas!
Dharma world
Self-risen (innate disposition)
Within me! Kam!

See a fire springing from the fingertips, that fills and purifies the entire world, burning away all mental images, all worries and all impediments arising from my deeds (N.b. karma means deeds, not destiny or fate). The fire is a bright red in color. From the midst of the flames arises a black Acala whose sword and flames cut away all impediments. A wind then arises which fans the flames, turning them into a Lotus, symbol of the Buddha's "Reward" body being born. The meditator is now told to see that his or her body is one with the very fibre, the warp and woof of the cosmos. "My body is the dharma world, and from it is born the Lotus, symbol of love and compassion."

D. Third, the meditator performs the "Revolving the Dharma wheel" mudra and mantra meditation. The fingers are interlaced, left palm facing outward and right palm inward, with thumbs bent back and touching (see the illustration). The eight fingers intertwined represent the eight aspects of the Buddha's life, (descent from the Tusita heavens, conceived, born, renounce the world, defeat temptations, enlightenment, revolve the dharma wheel by teaching, and entry to nirvana). The mudra and mantra meditation "Revolve the Dharma Wheel," by forming the mudra and revolving it three times to the right, then touching the five places, the belly, heart, throat, shoulders, and forehead. By so doing the Response body of Vairocana, with folded palms in the "middle way" meditation of Samatha concentration, is made one with my body, symbolized by the two thumbs touching.

Hail all ye Vajra-Buddhas!

Vajra and my body one, Kam!

The eight fingers are also interpreted to mean the eight fold path of enlighenment, now realized in the putting on of the Vajra or Response-body. The Lotus wheel thus gives birth to the Vajra world, making the Eighteen Path Mandala (Dharma body), the Lotus Mandala, and the Vajra world meditation a single process. The visualizations of the Vajra World are found in Part Three of the study, below, brought to fullest realization in the central Vajra Assembly hall meditation. The Buddha's *eightfold path*, or the eight aspects of the enlightened Buddha are interpreted to be (1) the recognition of causal dependence, (2-6) hear, see, smell, taste, speak, and think no evil, (7) Samatha (Zen) concentration and (8) Vipasyana centering and emptying meditation, respectively. My body is now one with the Three Bodies of Buddha, and the Lotus Meditation may now begin.

E. Part One of the Lotus Meditation ends with three mudra and mantra meditations, which provide a transition from the Eighteen Path mandala into the powerful visions of the Womb world. These consist in 1) Donning the armor of Vajra compassion, 2) Using the seed word *Ram* to purify and enlighten the mandala, 3) Purifying and invoking the earth spirits to protect the altar area, making it into a pure land for performing the meditations.

1. The first mudra-mantra meditation is called "Donning the Vajra Armor." The empty hand Lotus mudra is first formed, (clasped hands, empty center), and the index fingers are drawn down so that they touch the first joint of the third "fire" finger. The mantra is then recited, and the mudra is touched to the five places (belly, heart, throat, shoulders, head):

In the name of all Vajras,

Om! Vajra Armor, Hum!

Next, the vajra-thunder mudra is formed, by pressing the four fingers down over the thumbs. The index fingers are now extended, and the meditator sees the seed words *Om* and *Don* at the tip of each finger. A dark blue thread of light issues from each finger, and vajra armor is tied onto the twelve places of the body in eidetic vision by repeating the words *Om-Don* and touching the finger tips, as if tying cords and armor around the body. The twelve places are: the waist, (back to front), the left knee and right knee, belly, hips, breastplate, left and right shoulders, throat, left and right head, and helmet. The manner of tying the cords, order of tying, and pronunciation of the seed words differs for each of the three sects, and each Ajari master. The meditator sees him or herself become Vajrasattva, a dark bodied armored figure holding a five pronged vajra and a bell. The external visage of Vajrasattva is angry, but his heart is filled with compassion.

2. The second transition mudra is called "Contemplation of the seed word RAM." The seed word *Ram* is symbol of Buddha Locana, a Buddhist adaptation of Lord Ram and the spirit of Bakhti devotion in the newly popular Hindu religion of India, out of which Tantric Buddhism developed in the Fifth and Sixth century, before its coming to T'ang dynasty China. (See the Buddha Locana meditation on pg. 23, the second Fire meditation). The seed word *Ram* is located in the center of the forehead of the meditator, and corresponds to the fire triangle directly above the center of the Lotus World, as well as the central ornament in the crown of Vairocana and Buddha Locana (see illustration, pg. 34).

The Oral hermeneutic tells the meditator to see the center of his or her forehead filled with a bright white light, as if a shining pearl were inserted there. The pearl turns into the seed word *Ram*, and the light emanating from its center purifies my body and the entire Dharma world. The fire mudra is formed, by pressing the fingers over the thumbs, then extending the index fingers and touching them at the tips, while reciting the mantra:

> In the name of all Buddhas, Ram!

The pearl in the center of the forehead now becomes bright as the morning sun. From the bright white center red flames emanate, surrounding the triangle above the center of the Lotus Mandala, and filling the altar and sacred area in front of the meditator. The seed word RAM generates the fire triangle of the lotus and vajra stupa, and the fires of love or bakhti that fill the meditator's heart.

The last mudra and mantra of Part One of the Lotus meditation invoke all the Tathagatas, by their power and merit alone, to protect and purify the meditator as he or she enters the Womb World. The clasped hands with hollow center mudra, basic sign of the Lotus meditation is formed, and then the fourth or "water" fingers are opened slightly. As the mantra is recited, the mudra is moved in a circle three times to the left, and three to the right, and then pointed upward to heaven, and downward to the earth. Finally, the mudra touches the five places and is dissolved over the head.

> In the name of all thou Tathagata
> All terror and fear be gone!
> All of these gateways let us enter,
> By thy help, Kham! Ken!
> Protect us with thy great strength,
> By all thy Tathagata merit,
> Hum! Hum! Trat! Trat!
> Oh Thou incomparable ones Svaha!

Part 2. Become Tathagata Buddha

The second stage of the Lotus meditation has three parts, I) purification, II) interiorizing the Lotus stupa, and III) by the power of Vairocana (tariki   ) the putting on of the thirty-two aspects of a Tathagata. As part two of the dramatic rite begins, the meditator calls on the primordial spirits of mother earth for protection from the evil temptress Mara, as the Buddha did under the Bo tree long ago. Just as Buddha called on the earth to witness his purity of intention, by pressing his hand to the ground, so too the meditating monk or nun here places the right hand on the ground while reciting the mantra.

I. *Purification*

A. Purification of earth. The *kesa* saffron colored robe, draped over the left shoulder of the monk or nun, (leaving the right shoulder bare, as in Indian sadhu-monastic custom), is used to cover a portion of the ground in front of the right knee of the meditator. Taking the five pronged vajra in the left hand and pressing it against the heart, the right hand is placed on top of the robe spread out in front of the right knee. The right hand is touched to the earth with the fingers stretching toward the left knee. The earth is pressed eight times, one for each line of the mantra.

> Oh Thou lady Devi, come here before me,
> Tell all the Buddhas, to help me cross over,
> And practice wisdom's superior ways,
> Thus able to pass to the other shore.
> May Mara's legions be destroyed and broken,
> And I saved by Shakyamuni's merits;
> Evil's victory thus fully suppressed,
> By drawing this sacred Mandala, Kham!

The right hand pressed to the ground eight times represents the wisdom of the five Buddhas of the Lotus center, and the three bodies (dharma, reward, and response body) of the Buddha. Just as Buddha called on the earth to witness his own resolute rejection of the temptress Mara's vision, so too the meditator is warned to cast aside all selfishness, impurity, and anger in order to continue on in the meditation.

B. Build a protective wall. Grasping the five pronged vajra between the two hands, with the fingers folded down over the knuckles, the meditator now sees the earth to be a firm and strong ally. Strengthened by the thunderbolt held in the clenched hands, the three seed words *Om!* *Bu!* and *Ken!* are recited, creating a triple wall of earth's friendly spirits to surround the outermost edges of the mandala, and keep out all impurities.

C. Purification with water. The meditator now picks up the *sanjo* bamboo ladle, dips it in the *shasui* pure water (as in the Juhachi-do recitation) and purifies the Lotus altar. The altar is sprinkled three times, to purify the Dharma, Lotus, and Vajra worlds, then the eight directions, beginning with the northeast "Gate of Demon," while the mantra of purification is recited:

> In the name of all Buddhas
> One with the absolute
> One with the void

Everywhere penetrating
Original nature purified
Dharma world washed clean. Svaha!

D. Purification with Incense. Now taking the hand held incense burner in both hands, the meditator recites the following verse:

Oh all ye Buddhas, take pity on us sentient beings
We only beg that you keep in mind our needs,
Here and now I address each strong and holy one,
Firmly bring Privithi (Mother Earth) too under your care.
May all Tathagatas, and children of the Buddha,
Never forget their vows of compassion, be by our side!
I invoke the siddhi-strength of mother earth here,
to confirm in us thy protecting power.

E. Invitation of the spirits to enter. The incense burner is laid down on the altar, and the two hands are formed in the shape of an open bowl, as in the illustration. The invitation of Privithi is now chanted:

Hail Privithi, Come! Svaha!

The meditator sees Mother Earth Privithi enter the sacred area, and be purified by the flames and sword of Acala. All of the Tathagatas then affirm their vows to protect earth and all sentient beings. The mudra of firm earth is formed while reciting the mantra:

In the name of all Buddhas,
May all Tathagata blessings dwell in us.
May stainless spotless Acala
Purify our original nature, Svaha!

Visualize that the fire seed words *Ram* and *Ah*, from which the Lotus world and the state of compassionate enlightenment spring, are implanted in the womb of mother earth, visualized as the altar in front of the meditator. The seed word *Ram* is seen as a flame that burns away the seed word *Ah*, all Siddhi powers, and all visions of the Buddha until a state of kenotic emptiness remains. Thus the ultimate goal of the Lotus and Vajra meditations, in the Tendai tradition, is a state of emptiness (sunya, k'ung 空 or hsu 虛) realized by compassion and love in everyday living.

II. *Interiorize the Lotus Stupa.*

In step two, the meditator "puts on" or interiorizes the Lotus Mandala. The monk or nun envisions a square earth cakra, base of the five layered stupa, as generated by the seed word *Ah*, springing from an open lotus. The seed word *Ram* is directly above the *Ah* character, burning it away, and with it all worries, pride, desires, and reason, source of intellect and thought. All logic, philosophy, and spiritual attainment must be given away, in a true "dark night" of the spirit and senses. The entire Lotus world, envisioned in the next stage of the meditation, is also meant to be burned away. I.e., earth, water, fire, wind, and space are seen as a process of meditatively emptying the Dharma world. The ashes left from *Ram* fire are washed away by water, dissipated by wind, and finally left void and empty, so that nothing is left. Only when empty can true awakening *hongaku* 本覺 be realized, and this only by the power of Acala-Vairocana.

40

A. In the first step of the vision process, the meditator's body becomes the Lotus stupa. I.e., earth is below belly, water above navel, fire in heart, wind in throat, space in the head of the meditator. The seed word *Ah* is envisioned to be in the heart, and the seed word *Ram* is directly above the crown of the head. The flames emanating from the seed word *Ram* are seen to descend and burn completely my mind, emptying all worries and thoughts therefrom. The flames descend and burn the heart and entire body, so that only the seed word AH remains, from which no thoughts and no images arise. The seed word is then brought down and placed at the base of the spine, below the belly. The flames now produce the image of Vairocana deep inside, which arises and fills my entire body.

The Lotus world arises from the body purified by the *Ram* and *Ah* meditation above. The flames produce five seed words, *Ah Vi Ram Hum Ken*, the basic dharani or mantra of the Lotus world, (Abira-um-ken), then change into five Ah syllables (A, Aa, Am, Ah, Ak), and finally into the five cakra syllables of the Vajra, *Ah, Hrih, Trah, Hum, Vam*, as follows:

i. The five seed words of the Lotus and Vajra worlds:

A	Bi	Ra	Um	Ken	(lotus)
Ah	Hrih	Trah	Hum	Vam	(vajra)

ii. The elements and their symbols:

earth	water	fire	wind	space	(element)
square	circle	triangle	moon	peak	(stupa)

iii. The colors or aura envisioned in the symbols:

yellow	white	red	black	rainbow	(lotus)
green	yellow	red	white	rainbow	(vajra)

iv. The corresponding place in the meditator's body:

below navel	above navel	heart	mouth-nostrils	crown	(body)

v. The corresponding mudra or hand symbol:

fifth	fourth	third	index	thumb	(mudra)

B. The meditator is now ready to become the body of Vairocana by putting on or imagining the above symbols to be a part of his or her own body. The mudra and mantra for becoming the five wheel cakra are as follows:

1. Form the fire mudra, and see the seed word *Ah* to be in the heart, and the seed word *Ram* to be above the crown of the head. Touch the mudra to the head three times, and see red flames burst forth from the *Ram* character, and burn away all images from my mind, and empty my body. Then press the mudra to the belly, and see the *Ah* seed word descend and rest below the navel. Recite the mantra three times:

In the name of all Buddhas, Ram!

2. Form the five pronged vajra mudra, and press it to the belly, seeing the seed word *Ah* dwelling there. It is a bright gold in color, and changes into a square, the cakra or symbol of earth within me, the color yellow.

In the name of all Buddhas, Ah! nata buddhanam Ah!

41

3. Form the eight petal Lotus Blossom mudra, and hold it above the navel, seeing there the seed word *Vam*. Its color is white. It changes into a circular cakra, symbol of the element water, and it emits a bright white light.

> In the name of all Buddhas, Vam!

4. Form the fire mudra (as in No. 1 above) and hold it above the heart, seeing there the seed word Ram. Its color is a fiery red, and it changes into a triangle, symbol of the element fire within me. It emanates a bright red light.

> In the name of all Buddhas, Ram!

5. Form the wind mudra, and hold it in front of the face. See the seed word *Kam* between nose and mouth, a dark blue-black in color. It changes and becomes a quarter moon, symbol of the element wind inside me. Its color is an effulgent blue-black.

> In the name of all Buddhas, Kam!

6. Form the space mudra, and hold it above the crown of the head. Envision there the seed word *Ken*, color of the rainbow, which changes into the space cakra, the shape of the leaf of a Bo tree. The color of space includes all colors.

> In the name of all Buddhas, Ken!

The stupa formed inside my body now changes into the shape of Vajrasattva, seated with a bell in the left hand and a five pronged vajra in the right, pressed against the heart. The meditator now sees the Lotus mandala produce first a blossoming flower with eight petals, surrounding Vairocana in the center. The Lotus is the blossom out of which springs the fruit or harvest of the Vajra World mandala. Thus all of the images of the Lotus and Vajra world are contained in the *Ah* seed word that springs from the earth of the Womb matrix mandala.

C. The meditator next sees the dharma waters of the second circle sprinkling on the lowest square earth cakra, causing the lotus to blossom, and the vajra world to spring forth as fruit from the lotus' center. The vision is interpreted to mean that the Lotus Mandala gestates the Vajra mandala. The triangle above the Lotus mandala center is symbol of this relationship, in that it represents burning away the three impediments (desires, worries, sorrow) and gives birth to the three bodies (dharma, reward, response) of the Buddha, and the four *paramitas* or "crossings" symbolized by the four Boddhisattva that occupy the four interstices of the Lotus center. The four Boddhisattva stand in the following relationship to Vairocana:

Ah	Vam	Ram	Kam	Ken
Vairocana	Fugen	Manjusri	Kannon	Maitreya
Awaken	practice	awaken	awaken	upaya skill
heart	yoga	mind	intuition	for others
Earth	Water	Fire	Wind	Space

D. The meditator now must contemplate the entire Lotus world, and relate each segment of the mandala to his or her own body. Just as the center of the lotus turns into a stupa that fills my interior, so, too the entire Lotus word must be imprinted on my exterior body. To do this, it is necessary to pause and look at the Lotus mandala for a moment, and then relate the twelve major figures pictured there to twelve places in my own body.

1. By looking at the Lotus Mandala, the meditator can easily distinguish the central figures of the twelve halls that surround the center. Directly beneath the eight petaled Lotus Center are the five great light kings, with the figures of Fudo Myoo (Acala), Gozanze (Trailokyavijaya), Gundari, Enma, and Vajrayaksa. Directly beneath these terrifying visions are the prominent figures of the thousand armed Kannon (Avalokitesvara) and the 108 armed Vajra King, to the left (north) and right (south) of the base. Kannon represents the entire left side of the lotus world, while Vajra King rules the entire right side, i.e., the Vajra world. Directly above the Lotus center is the three sided Wisdom symbol (a blazing triangle), the figure of the historical Buddha, and Manjusri, in ascending order. To the left and right of Manjusri are Maitreya and Buddha Locana.

```
                Manjusri
                Buddha
     Buddha Locana  Maitreya
            Triangle
     All          All
     of the  Lotus  of the
     Lotus  Center  Vajra
     World          World
        The Five Light Kings
     1000 arm      108 Arm
     Kannon        Kongo Zo-o
          Sunyata-Space
          Susiddhi-devotion
```
Twelve halls of the Lotus Mandala

2. The twelve halls in the Lotus world mandala are points of focus for the above meditation. These twelve images are now to be imprinted on the body of the meditating monk or nun, with a seed word in place of each figure, thus "empowering" or imparting to the devotee the devotional aspects of the image. The order of imprinting is as follows:

Place	seed word	Image
1. left ear	Am	Maitreya (Miroku Bosatsu)
2. right ear	Ahm	Buddha Locana (Butsugen Bomu)
3. crown	Ken	Buddha (Vairocana)
4. forehead	Ahk	Triangle, P'ien-chih Yin
5. rt. shld	Tsan	The Lotus World
6. lt. shld	Su	The Vajra World
7. throat	Kam	Lotus center, nine worthies
8. heart	Kah	Paramita Boddhisattva
9. over navel	Ram	Trailokyavijaya (Gozanze)
10. bl. navel	Rah	Acala (Fudo Myoo)
11. rt. leg	Vam	1000 armed Avalokitesvara
12. lt. leg	Vah	108 armed Kongo Zo-o

43

The meditation is performed while holding the Karma mudra, as in the illustration, (clasped hands, thumbs and little fingers raised and touching, third "fire" fingers pressed inwards and down), and pressing it to each of the twelve places in turn. Recite the mantric seed word proper to each place, and visualize the respective seed word to be imprinted there on one's body. The seed word then changes and becomes the image of the Buddha or Boddhisattva, so that the Lotus Mandala is imprinted on the body of the meditator.

3. The twelve visions represent the twelve causes of rebirth, i.e., the twelve nidanas washed pure by the light of the Lotus and turned into twelve causes of enlightenment. (Refer to pages 29-30 for the twelve causes). The number twelve also symbolizes the twelve earthly stems, signs of cycling change in nature. Thus the twelve months of the Chinese lunar year, and the twelve times five or sixty year cycle, are transformed from symbols of change to causes of enlightenment in the Tantric meditative system. This is accomplished by making each of the twelve symbols of change into a seed word of enlightenment, in the Lotus mandala meditation.

4. In a manner analogous to the Kepher symbol of the Kabbalah system, the meditator now ascends one step higher to the crown over the head, and envisions the "King of a Hundred Lights" i.e., the image of Vairocana in the seed word *Am* to fill the entire Dharma world with a bright white light. The hands are formed in the intertwined vajra mudra (see illustration) and held over the head as if wearing a crown. The seed word *Am* is envisioned over the head, a bright red in color, emanating a piercing white light with hundreds of rays that fill the entire cosmos. The mudra is moved back and forth three times while reciting the mantra, then dissolved over the head as if undoing the top knot of hair over Vairocana's head.

In the name of all Buddhas Ah!

The *Ken* seed word at the crown of the head in the above twelve seed word meditation and the *Am* character of Maitreya and Buddha Locana are seen to emanate from one higher source, i.e., Vairocana, the Buddha of light emanating from within the body of the meditator. The *Kah* character above the heart, the *Ram* character above the belly, and the AH character that generates the lotus from the earth below are in fact a part of a single process of purification and refinement. This process continues in the following mudra and mantra meditations, and culminates in the final internalization of the *Trikaya* Three Bodies of the Buddha below. The *Am* character of the crown cakra represents the Dharma body, the *Kam* character of the heart is the Reward body, and the *Ram* above the belly is the Response body of Vairocana. The meditator forms the "Non-arising heart-mind" mudra and presses it to the heart while reciting:

Hail all Buddhas, Ah!

He or she then forms the fire mudra for burning away all impurities at the belly and recites the mantra:

Hail all Buddhas, Ram!

next, using the same fire mudra, he or she presses the index fingers to each eye and recites the mudra, while seeing the eyes purified by a bright red light:

Hail, all Buddhas, Ram!

44

E. The white and red flames that swirl through the body of the meditator now burn away all vestiges of reason, so that knowledge based on sense or intellect does not arise. Bodhi enlightenment follows from the state of non-arising thought, that is, the light of *Ah* and *Ram*, surging from the two index fingers, create a wisdom light in the heart which gives birth to a Lotus, the source of *sunya* (k'ung 空) void non-arising wisdom. The wisdom light has now purified the entire body, head, heart, belly, and eyes, (*Am, Ah, Ram, Rahm*). The fifth and last phase of this stage of the meditation follows, in which the five Buddhas of the central Lotus flower are interiorized as seed words.

The five mantra of completion are chanted, while the basic vajra mudra is re-formed. For the first time the meditator sees the images of the five Buddhas as five wheels, inserted inside his or her own body. The *kuden* oral teachings of an Ajari master are required here to complete the meditation. The seed words are repeated three times, once for each of the triple bodies of the Buddha:

Dharma body:	Ah	Vam	Ram	Kam	Ken
Reward body:	Ah	Vi	Ra	Um	Ken
Response body:	Ah	Ra	Ha	Sya	Na

F. The above process of tantric meditation had two goals, as follows: 1) purification and 2) eidetic visualization of the Lotus world imprinted inside the meditator's body. Before going to the last goal 3) of the second meditation, i.e., the putting on of the thirty-two aspects of a Tathagata, the meditator pauses to "give away" or externalize the five cakra of the Lotus world, so that they fill and enlighten the entire cosmos. The rite is called "Contemplation for externalizing the five cakra wheels," and begins with a vision of the seed word *Ram*M, the bright red flames from which purify the external world from all impediments to enlightenment. The ordinary things of the world now become adamantine instruments of the Vajra World. The Lotus cakra are envisioned in reverse order, beginning with the crown and ending with the square earth *Ah* cakra at the base.

> In the name of all Buddhas, Ram! (World is a vajra tool).
> In the name of all Buddhas, Kem! (Basic nature is pure).
> In the name of all Buddhas, Kam! (Blue wind fills world).
> In the name of all Buddhas, Ram! (Red fire purifies all).
> In the name of all Buddhas, Vam! (White water cleanses).
> In the name of all Buddhas, Ah! (Yellow earth gestates).

III. *Put on the Thirty-two Aspects of Tathagata Buddha.*

The third goal of the second part of the Lotus meditation is to "put on" of the thirty-two aspects of a Tathagata Buddha. The Tathagata of the Lotus World meditation is here interpreted to be Vairocana, but the meditator is told not to be attached to any form of the Buddha. The thirty-two aspects include the vision of all four Buddhas and the four Bodhisattvas of the center, as well as the other major figures of the mandala. Tathagata is therefore a generic term for the potency within the self for enlightenment. Buddhist images and statues are not idols for worship, but symbols of what the meditator should be, if truly enlightened.

The first three aspects of a tathagata are the *Trikaya*, the three Dharma, Reward, and Response bodies of the preceding meditations. The fourth through the twenty-eighth meditations put on the dress, body, and thoughts of all Buddhas. The the twenty- ninth through thirty-second meditations assume the identity of the four great Bodhisattva, Fugen, Kannon, Manjusri, and Miroku, (Samantabhadra, Avalokitesvara, Manjusri, Maitreya). Part Two of the Lotus World meditation ends with two highly esoteric visions of the female aspects of enlightenment. The process of interiorizing the Tathagata is as follows:

1. The Dharma Body. Form the Lotus Bud mudra. There is no distinction between self and Buddha. The Three (Dharma, Lotus, Vajra) are made one, equal in origin, Svaha!

2. The Reward Body. The fire mudra is formed, and the "Dharma world gives birth" mantra recited, uniting self to Lotus:

> Hail all Buddhas, The Dharma World gives birth,
> Self-arising, one with my nature, Ham!

3. The Response Body. The mudra for revolving the Dharma wheel is formed, and the mantra recited, uniting self with the Vajra:

> Hail all Vajras, Vajra and my body united, Kam!

4. The Sword of Wisdom cuts away knowledge. The wisdom sword mudra is formed, and the mantra recited:

> Hail all Buddhas, Oh great sword of pure spotless Dharma,
> All things self-arising from Dharma nature are revealed by
> cutting self from knowing. The act of total faith in
> Tathagata, frees from passion, Hum!

5. The Dharma Conch. By blowing the Dharma conch, the Tathagata awakens all sentient beings to the realization of nirvhana. The Dharma conch mudra is formed (thumbs tucked under index fingers, wind, water, and earth fingers extended), and the mantra sung:

> Hail all Buddhas, Ahm!

6. The Boddhisattva Vows to bless all beings. The hands are formed in the eight petaled open lotus mudra; the AH mantra for bringing the blessing of the Reward body to all creatures sung:

> Hail all Buddhas, Ah!

7. The Great Wisdom of the Vajra. The blessing of Vajra wisdom is invoked for self and all creatures. The five pronged vajra mudra is formed, and the mantra sung:

> Hail all Vajras, Om!

8. The Tathagata Crown. The Usnisa crown of Amida, seen as a trousseau of hair rising above the head, is symbolized by mudra and mantra:

> Hail all Buddhas, Hum! Hum!

9. The Tathagata Forehead. The vajra fist, thumbs tucked under the four fingers, folded down over the palms, is formed with both hands. The left hand is pressed to the waist, and the right knuckles are placed against the forehead.

> Hail all Buddhas!

> In void, vast endless space,
> Pure, spotless Dharma manifest, Svaha!

46

10. Tathagata Brow. Using the same mudra, the knuckles are pressed against the brow. The meditator sees that the mind of non arising purifies the causes of arising in others.

> Hail all Buddhas,
>
> Ah! Ham! Jah!

11. The Buddha's Begging Bowl. The meditator takes the two ends of the kesa robe and holds them between the left and right palms, folded in the Zen samadhi mudra. The robe represents the armor of the monk, who has chosen the holy path of Buddhist perfection. The hands represent the bowl with which the monk or nun begs for food, a sign of separation from the "Three possessions," i.e., death, birth, and attachments. Abstinence from dead things, celibacy (abstinence from birth and arising thoughts) and giving   away all possessions, real and spiritual, are symbolized by the Buddha bowl mudra. As the mantra is recited, all gifts and offerings are seen as vehicles of enlightenment, when given away.

> Hail all Buddhas, Vah!

12. Freedom from Fear. The left hand now holds both ends of the monk's *kesa* shoulder robe and the right hand is held up, palm outward, symbolizing the freeing of all sentient beings from fear and anxiety.

> Hail all Buddhas!
>
> Always, everywhere victory, victory,
>
> Fear overcome, Svaha!

13. Fulfillment of the Buddha's Vow to make self and vajra one. The left hand continues to hold the kesa, and the right hand now is lowered and points outward, in the gesture of Amida giving saving enlightenment to all sentient beings. The light issuing from the Vajra world floods over the meditator, who recites:

> Hail all Buddhas, Vows fulfilled,
>
> Vajra and I made one, Svaha!

14. The Compassionate Eyes of Buddha. The fire and water fingers of the right hand are extended, and the thumb holds down the bent wind and space fingers (see illustration). The left hand, forming the vajra mudra, is pressed to the left waist. The mudra is touched to the left and right eyes, so that the fire (third) finger touches the right eye, and the water (fourth) finger touches the left eye. The mantra is recited twice:

> Hail all Buddhas, for thy
>
> Great, pure, most auspicious endowment,
>
> The compassion filled Tathagata eyes, Svaha!

The meditator pauses here to meditate, as follows: "By purifying these eyes of flesh, may I put on the eyes of the Buddha, to see the deepest mysteries of the Tathagata world. The fleshly eyes see all the allurements of the world. But the the dharma realized eye (right-lotus) sees the hearts of all sentient beings, and the wisdom eye (left-vajra) sees the roots, the origin of non-arising. By both eyes we can see the difference in the real 實 and the 假法 phenomenal.

15. The Tathagata Cord. The hands are formed in the Amida mudra, while the meditator considers: "Those who do bad things bring evil on themselves, while those who do good bless all those around them." While reciting the mantra, the cord of the Buddha, gold in

color, is seen to stretch out and rescue all those caught in emotional attchments and the sickness born from them. The touch of the cord brings about a total act of faith and trust in Tathagata Buddha (Amida).

> In the name of all Buddhas,
>
> Hey, hey, great cord, long, boldly
>
> Heal all illness in the sentient world,
>
> Manifesting total trust in Tathagata, Svaha!

16. The Buddha's Heart. From a folded fist, fingers and thumbs tucked in, extend the fire fingers to touch straight up. Realize that wisdom's sign is a compassionate heart, filled with a great and overwhelming awakening to do good and help others. Recite the mantra while pressing the mudra to the heart:

> Hail all Buddhas,
>
> Born of Wisdom, compassion's fragrance, Svaha!

17. Buddha's Belly. With the same folded fist as above, extend the fourth or water fingers, and press the mudra to the belly, while recalling that wisdom and immortality *amrte* are born from the water (belly) cakra. The sweet dew of the Lotus world's VAM water extinguishes the fires of the burning intellect, and brings life to Lotus and Vajra.

> Hail all Buddhas,
>
> Give birth to immortality (amrte) Svaha!

18. Buddha's Waist. Extend the water finger of the right hand only, and see one's body put on Tathagata's wisdom body, and the golden color of a Buddha.

> Hail all Buddhas,
>
> Tathagata's body be born, Svaha!

19. The Buddha Storehouse (Belly). Extend the fire and earth fingers, with thumbs pressed against the folded index fingers and press the mudra to the belly. See the body enveloped in the purifying rays of the sun, emanating from the mudra at the belly. Light fills the entire body, washing away all defilements and memories of past grudges or worries. A bright mani pearl is seen to be contained within the storehouse cakra of the lower abdomen, filled with compassionate wisdom. The pearl now turns into a light wheel radiating outward, filling the entire cosmos.

> Hail all Buddhas!
>
> The Tathagata body is born! Svaha!

20. Universal Light, Buddha's Halo. Fire fingers rounded and touching, index (wind) fingers opened and extended, the thumbs are bent inward so that the image of a light held in the hands is created. The mudra is circled to the right three times, and the meditator envisions light to diffuse everywhere in the cosmos:

> Hail all Buddhas,
>
> Light blazing round thy head,
>
> Tathagata halo, arc arising, Svaha!

When the body is pure, an aura of light surrounds it, emanating from a mani pearl in the earth cakra below the belly. The light ascends and turns into the halo or arc of wisdom that is around the head of Buddha. This subtle light of wisdom touches the spiritual as well as the physical order. The thumbs pressed inwards hide the Dharma body, the pearl-like source of *sunya* emptying that arises from the seed word *Ah* and fills the Lotus world with awakening wisdom.

21. The Tathagata Armor. Form the armor of fire mudra, and touch it to the five places, while visualizing the self putting on the bright Vajra armor. The armor gives the power to suppress evil and carry out the work of a Buddha.

> Hail all Buddhas!
> Oh light of the Vajra,
> Shine brightly, Hum!

22. Tathagata's Tongue. Form the upright clasped hands mudra, and tuck the thumbs inward, while visualizing one's tongue to become the tongue of Buddha. The mantra empowers the meditator to teach as a Buddha and preach the Vajra Dharma.

> Hail all Buddhas!
> Oh tongue of the Buddha,
> Source of true Dharma, Svaha!

23. Buddha's Speech. Thumbs extended, index and water fingers folded, fire and earth extended, touch the lips with the mudra, and see the eight superior qualities of the Buddha's voice instilled in my own speech. The eight virtues are: 1) pleasant, 2) easy to understand, 3) harmonious, 4) soft spoken, 5) no error, 6) no lies, 7) dignified, 8) deep and far reaching in wisdom.

> Hail all Buddhas, Tathagata's words,
> Filled with all wisdom, and beauty, Svaha!

24. Buddha's Teeth. Index fingers pressed down over the thumbs, fire, wind, and earth fingers touching, press the mudra to the teeth and see one's mouth and sense of taste to be Buddha's. Now we can taste the best of all tastes, and in moving be the source of Dharma teaching.

> Hail all Buddhas!
> With Tathagata's teeth, best of all tastes,
> Attain birth in the Tathagata's world, Svaha!

25. Buddha's Discourse. Spread the index fingers outwards, touch the mouth with the mudra, and see how the fears of all creatures are dispelled by the Buddha's harmonious discourse. By preaching the correct Dharma, no obstacles from within, or incorrect interpretations from outside, can harm the self or others.

> Hail all Buddhas!
> Thy inconceivably wonderful words,
> Whose effect is felt everywhere, Purifying sounds, Svaha!

26. Buddha's Ten Powers. Thumbs and space (little) fingers tucked inward, wind, fire, and water extended, hold the mudra in front of the chest and pray for the ten powers, as follows: 1) know right and wrong, 2) know past, present, and future, 3) know all worlds and levels of existence, 4) know what others think and desire, 5) know our basic capacities,

6) know the results of all kinds of practice, 7) know all forms of meditation, 8) know the changes of all sentient beings, 9) know birth and death, and 10) know how to destroy all evil passions. Recite the mantra, and at the recitation of the three seed words *Hum, Sam, Jam*, see that the ten powers are realized in the real, phenomenal, and void realms:

> Hail all Buddhas!
>
> The ten powers, May I have each one!
>
> Hum! Sam! Jam! Svaha!

27. The Buddha's Thoughts. With fire, water, and earth fingers upright and touching, bring index (wind) fingers straight down over the thumbs, and press the mudra to the forehead. Meditate on how all sentient beings are meant to attain the benefits of rebirth into the empty dharma world, a void absolute free from all limitations. Recite the mantra, as follows:

> Hail all Buddhas!
>
> From Tathagata's thoughts,
>
> All benefits arise.
>
> By oneness with the void absolute,
>
> Identity of opposites, we are not two, Svaha!

28. Awaken to the Equality of all things with Dharma. Form the mudra by folding thumbs and water fingers down, with the remaining fingers upright. See my nature, all things, and the Dharma as equal by nature. Recite the mantra, as follows:

> Hail all Buddhas!
>
> All Dharmas everywhere realized,
>
> Tathagata attained, Svaha!

29-31, Put on the Three Signs of a Boddhisattva. The wisdom of the Boddhisattva Fugen, compassion of Kannon, and care for all sentient beings of Manjusri are assumed by repeating the mudra and mantra three times. Hold the fire, water, and earth fingers upright, and bring the index (wind) fingers down to touch the first joint of the middle finger. Hold the mudra in front of the chest, and recite the mantra three times:

> Hail all Buddhas!
>
> Dharma everywhere present,
>
> Frees from passion.
>
> Everywhere manifest,
>
> Great thou art, wonderful, Svaha!

32. The Boddhisattva of Mercy, Maitreya. Using the same mudra as above, the meditator now puts on the last aspect of a Tathagata, the merciful compassion of Maitreya. Ponder how all Tathagata, the Dharma and Lotus worlds arise from the seed word AH of the mandala. The fruit of the seed word is a great, universal compassion. The compassion of the Tathagata is like a rain falling from heaven that purifies and brings life to all beings.

> Hail all Buddhas!
>
> Invincible Victor,
>
> The hearts of all sentient beings
>
> Do thou touch and fill, Svaha!

Part Two of the Lotus meditation now ends with two special invocations to the female aspects of the great light kings of the Lotus world, the *Vidyarajni*. These lady Buddhas are seen to dwell in a state of samadhi meditation, nourished by a sweet dew that is offered to all sentient beings, good and bad alike, for salvation. The Lady Light Queens are eight in number: 1)Tara, 2) Svetyarka, 3) Pandaravasini, 4) Vilokani, 5) Ekajata, 6) Gauri, 7) Yasamati, and 8) Bhrkuti. The index fingers are pressed against the first joint of the fire fingers and the mantra sung to invoke these eight figues of the Lotus world to dissolve all obstacles to the enlightenment of sentient beings of the three worlds, past, present, and future.

> Hear us as follows, may all those who are
> One with the void, and not one with the void,
> All equally everywhere accept the Tathagata vows
> And be one with thee, best, auspicious void, Svaha!

Lastly the Eight Lady Light spirits are invoked to keep all sentient beings from harm. The right palm is laid over the left, and the mudra is circled right and then left three times. The thirty-two aspects of the tathagata are placed inside the palms, and given away by the meditator to all sentient beings. The marks of the Tathagata bless the whole world, alleviate suffering mankind, heal illness, and lead all sentient beings to the other shore. In giving away all benefits of the meditation, the monk and nun are reminded that the only benefit to self is attained by benefitting others.

> Hail all Tathagatas And all Tathagata paths. That the mind be always void,
> Be aware only of the unmoveable absolute, Svaha!

51

Part 3. Meditate on the Lotus Mandala

The third stage of the Lotus ritual consists in a lengthy contemplation of the Lotus World Mandala. After envisioning the twelve hallways of the mandala, the meditator sees him/herself bathed in the saving and illuminating light of Vairocana. The series of eidetic visualizations contain some of the most powerful imagery in the Tantric meditative tradition. The meditation is divided into ten steps. The details of the ritual are kept to a minimum, and the visible artistic effects emphasized.

I. *The Great Ocean.*
Envision in front of the self the seed word *Viṭ*, on top of the earth cakra. It now changes into a great ocean. It is filled with the waters of the Eight Virtues (pure, cool, good-tasting, soft, moistening, comforting, thirst-quenching, and nourishing). It rests on the earth cakra, and is contained within a five-pronged jewel vajra, as its shores.

II. *The Lotus Flower.*
See a lotus flower to be planted in the center of the great ocean. The stem of the lotus is a vajra, and the eight petals of the lotus are seen to open amid the five prongs of the vajra. The vajra and lotus planted in my belly.

III. *The Flower Pavilion.*
Envision a ten spoked karma wheel beneath the lotus blossom, between the vajra and the lotus. The ten spoked wheel, plus vajra and lotus, represent the twelve seed words of the Lotus mandala, imprinted in my body in Part Two of the Lotus Meditation. These twelve seed words are now related to the five cakra within the body, as follows:

Hail all Buddhas

Eternally gone beyond

The incomplete Dharma world,

Am, Ken, Am, Ah, (Space cakra, Vairocana)

Sam, Sah, (Earth cakra, Maitreya and Amida)

Ham, Hah, (Wind cakra, Tengu, Divyadundubhi)

Ram, Rah, (Fire cakra, Hofu, Samkusumita Raja)

Vam, Vah, (Water cakra, Kaiho, Ratnadhvaja)

Svaha! So be it!

Ram, Rah, (Body, mudra, Dharma body)

Hra, Hah, (Mouth, mantra, Reward body)

Ram, Rah, (Mind, mandala, Response body)

Svaha! So be it!

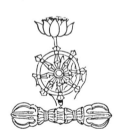

Now see a five pronged vajra, representing the five central buddhas of the stupa, and a three pronged vajra, for the Three Tantric sources of prayer, i.e., mind, mouth, and body, atop the lotus.

IV. The Vairocana is King of the Marvelous Lotus Throne.
Envision in front of the meditator an eight petaled white lotus, in the center of which is the seed word *Ah*. The Lotus is austere and perfect in its beauty, containing within itself all precious things, the storehouse of the self-arising lotus world. The *Ah* character now turns into the figure of Vairocana, King of the Lotus World. See that if one goes "down" or out-

ward from the *Ah* character, all sentient beings evolve. Going "up" or inwards, Boddhi awakening is realized. But enlightenment is not something attained, like a jewel or accomplishment for the self. Only by Vairocana's aid is this awakening to be attained, and only by giving away through acts of compassion and "emptying" all virtues and accomplishments can Vairocana be seen.

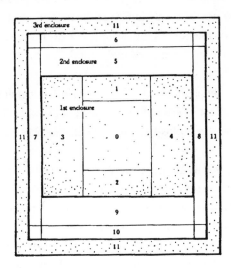

0. The Lotus-Womb Mandala Center
1. Hall of Wisdom-fire
2. Hall of the Light Kings
3. Hall of Compassion (Avalokitesvara)
4. Hall of Vajra-Lightning
5. Hall of Sakyamuni Buddha
6. Hall of Manjusri Boddhisattva
7. Hall of Earth Storehouse (Ksittigarbha)
8. Hall of Samantabhadra
9. Hall of Kenosis-emptying
10. Hall of Susiddhi devotion
11. Outer Hall, Guardians and Folk Spirits

V. *Contemplate the Mandala*.

The above four steps are now summarized in the Mandala or Tao-ch'ang contemplation. The meditator assumes the Samadhi mudra by holding the right hand over the left in the lap, thumbs touching. There are forty-one lines to the meditation, summarized as follows:

1. See on top of the earth cakra the ocean of water perfumed by the eight virtues. From the middle of the ocean arises a five pronged vajra, stem of the marvelous white eight petaled lotus. Between vajra and lotus is a ten spoked karma wheel, platform of the Lotus. See the lotus fully open, revealing the golden pestil center, which contains the seeds of the Flower Storehouse world. In the center of the golden pestil is the seed word AH.

2. Light issues from the *Ah* seed word and spreads out in the four directions, filling the entire Dharma world.

3. There are four gates leading outward from center, that is, one gate in each direction, leading to east, south, north, and west (the gates at the outer rim of the Lotus Mandala, see illustration). These four gates are symbols of the fourfold path of the Madhyamika school of emptiness, i.e., the four tetralema that lead to the "middle way" of no judgment: i) the gate of affirming judgment; ii) the gate of empty or non-affirming; iii) the path of neither affirming or denying; and iv) the path of simultaneous holding and emptying. The four paths now multiply into four-times-four, or sixteen external lotus petals, seen as pathways or connectors to the other shore of transcendent experience. Eight petals are for popular Buddhist chant, and eight petals are for tantric Buddhist meditation, the vajra-lotus path.

4. Recollect that the eight petals of the lotus in fact generate the three and five pronged vajra world, as effect or fruit of meditation. The oral tradition here interposes a lengthy explanation of the three-plus-five interrelated stages of the Tendai tantric process as follows:

a. The three pronged vajra is a samaya-symbol of consecrating or "crowning" the meditator in the triple path of tantric meditation. I.e., the mind is purified by the emptying fires of meditation, a white pathway of light issuing from the first prong of the vajra. The heart is filled with red fires of bakhti devotion, seen as a bright red fiery path issuing from the second prong of the vajra. The whole body is filled with a bright golden-yellow light, seen as a path combining the rules of a monk and the samatha-vipasyana wisdom meditation of the belly, issuing from the third prong of the vajra:

i) Dharma-mind, emptying purification, white light.
ii) Lotus-heart, compassion, devotion, red light.
iii) Vajra-belly, wisdom, bodily intuition, gold light.

b. The five pronged vajra is a symbol (samaya) of the colors and iconography of the central figures of the Vajra world mandala i.e., the five Dharma-bodies to be "put on" by the meditator in the last stage of the tantric meditation process. The Lotus and Vajra meditations must therefore be seen as part of a single meditative process, from Lotus to Vajra to absolute emptiness.

i) Vairocana: Dharma world & original self are one, center, sun.
ii) Aksobhya: Wisdom to see things as they are, east, mirror.
iii) Ratnasambhava: Wisdom to see all things equal, south, fire.
iv) Amida: Wisdom to see all things with compassion, west, lotus.
v) Amoghasiddhi: Wisdom to help others cross over, north, Buddha.

5. Envision a half-open lotus directly above the ten pronged karma wheel, underneath the open lotus. This vision represents compassion manifest in concrete, physical giving. Thus, the offering of water, powder incense, flowers, burning incense, rice, and light are symbols the six paramitas (crossings) from the shore of suffering to the shore of union with the absolute, by acts of compassionate giving.

6. Now envision the open lotus, atop the half open lotus of giving. Contemplate the eight petals of the lotus in the center of the mandala. Each petal has an image of the Buddha or Boddhisattva imprinted on it, as in the illustration. Realize that the Lotus blossom was able to open and manifest itself because of the concrete practices taught in the third,

fourth, and fifth stages above. The practices are conditions, not causes of awakening, i.e., the light of Vairocana issuing from the Lotus center, not my deeds, is the cause of the Lotus flowering. Giving compassion empties and purifies the selfish desires that are obstacles to realizing presence of the Lotus within.

7. See how Vairocana is seated on the golden pestil throne in the center of the Lotus mandala. The light flowing from the lotus fills me with Vairocana's wisdom.

8. Envision the eight petals around the center of the Lotus. The images of the four Buddhas and four Boddhisattvas are symbols of Vairocana's vow to enlighten and save all sentient beings. The effervescent light that constantly flows from the center of the lotus is mediated by the eight figures, each of which manifests the Buddha nature in a different way. The Lotus world in fact manifests the Buddha nature that must be found within me. I.e., the four Buddhas and four Boddhisattvas of the Lotus represent the ways that I must manifest the Buddha nature.

9. The Lotus Flower with Vairocana in the center is therefore the cause of enlightenment, and the seeds of the lotus, numerous as the sands of the sea, are the effect of Vairocana's power to enlighten, planted in my body to grow and blossom.

10-12. The seeds that blossom bear fruit within me, symbolized by the mudra, mantra, and eidetic vision of the nine central figures of the mandala. Thus, I must first see the eight petals surrounding the central circle of the Lotus. At first, the circles are empty, but are seen to glow with a bright light. Next the meditator sees the seed words glowing in each petal. Lastly, the seed words turn into the living vision of the nine Buddhas. The true vision of the Buddha nature is the empty circle, as cause, while the fruit or effect of the meditation is the image of the Buddha printed on my heart.

13-15. From the center of the Lotus issues twelve rays of light, that spread and fill the entire lotus mandala, and are imprinted on my body as twelve seed words (see above, #3, flower pavilion). Four of the rays of light issue directly from Vairocana in the center. Two rays issue from each of the four surrounding Buddhas, i.e., the seed words *Sam* and *Sa* issue from Amida in the west, and are imprinted on my two shoulders. The seed words *Ham* and *Hah* issue from Amoghasiddhi in the north, and are printed on my heart. RAM and *Rah* issue from Ratnaketsu in the east, and are printed above the belly. *Vam* and *Vah* issue from Samkusa in the south, and are printed on my knees. Thus the images in the Lotus world that correspond to these twelve positions (see Part Two, above, the meditation on the twelve branches), are fruits of the compassion of the five central Buddhas. Note also that the number twelve symbolizes the twelve nidhanas, now changed from causes of recycling to gateways or paths to enlightenment. The light issuing from the Lotus center is therefore cause, and enlightenment the fruit or effect of tantric meditation.

16-18. Now see the entire Womb world-lotus mandala to be filled with a myriad lotus blossoms, each connected to the center by a ray of light emanating from the center. The meditator is free at this point to envision the mandala as he or she wills. The eidetic or moving aspects of the vision are important, and the Ajari now instructs the novice to contemplate the central figure of the Lotus throne, i.e., Vairocana, and see how all fears and obstacles are overcome by this awakening vision. The rays of light emanating from Vairocana fill the entire void space of the world and bring enlightenment to all sentient beings.

19-22. The palace around the central figure of Vairocana is now analyzed by the meditator. The walls are covered with pearls, symbols of the teachings and vows of Buddha fulfilled. Row upon row of pillars fill the central palace, connecting it to the outer halls of the mandala. The petals of the lotus are giant pillars moving outward to fill infinite space. The ceiling and draperies keep out all worldly thoughts and desires, and protect all sentient beings who seek enlightenment.

23-28. The body of Vairocana is adorned with jewels, and the crown has six ornaments, representing the six paramitas marks of wisdom: 1) charity, 2) precepts, 3) perseverance, 4) strength, 5) Zen meditation, 6) prajna wisdom. The flowing robes represent leaving the world of desire. The clouds of incense and flowers that fill the air around the Buddha represent the spirit of giving, kind words, kind conduct, and working together. The flowers and petals pour from the sky like rain, adorning the earth with compassion and blessing.

29-30. The sounds of beautiful chant and music fill the Lotus world so that all who hear it are filled with loving compassion. Those who hear the music of the Lotus spontaneously break out in song themselves, that purifies the sense of hearing and fills the boundless void with joy.

31-34. The meditator is now filled with a wondrous peace, which like the pure Aka water in the ritual vases, washes away worries and fills the mind and judgment with wisdom. Just as the flowers of the Lotus world open in timely sequence, morning to night, opening and bearing fruit, so by the light of the Lotus center all sentient beings are illuminated everywhere and at all times, by the merit and grace of Vairocana.

35-38. All of the earth is now seen to be wrapped in Samadhi meditation. Just as Lady Wisdom (Lotus or Womb world is here seen to be a lady) chooses concentration (Zen) as the interior goal of meditation, so the goal of the male Vajra world is outgoing Vipasyana intuition. The process of crossing to the other shore is seen to have two stages, i.e., interior enlightenment of the Lotus World, and external awakening to the need of all sentient beings through the Vajra meditations.

39-41. The Lotus world is now called an *upaya* skillful means to help all sentient beings attain interior enlightenment. By chanting, singing, and dancing the wonders of the Dharma-womb world, all one's own visions of the Lotus, the saving light of Vairocana and the worthies are given away for the sake of all other sentient beings. The Lotus world therefore is meant to be a popular aesthetic-art experience for universal enlightenment, as well as a vehicle of tantric meditation.

VI. *The Three Signs of Strength.*

The Text of the Lotus meditation now turns to the Eighteen Path Mandala (Page 3o, above) for a simple poetic offering of my self, joined to the strength of the Tathagata Vairocana and the entire Dharma world, as a universal puja for all sentient beings (vajra palms mudra):

I hereby give all my strength
Through the power of the Tathagata,
And the merits of the entire Dharma world,
To be a universal *puja* offering.

VII. *The vision of Universal Nourishing.*

The mudra of the offering for Universal Nourishing is formed (see illustration), and while reciting the mantra, the monk or nun sees self become Akasagharba (Kokuzobosatsu):

Om! Born in the Void Space Vajra, Koh!

The meditator is now told to give away the vision of the Great Ocean and the Lotus World, the Dharma world, and merit gained from Vairocana, as an offering for all sentient beings. Now he or she has indeed become a "Void storehouse," ready to perform the Samadhi meditation of concentration on emptiness. The symbols of the three powers given away are interpreted to be the incense, flowers, sacred music and dance, (mantra and mudra) which now fill the entire world with their awakening fragrance. See that all the joys, glory, and adornments of the world pass away and turn to ashes, while only the experience of the void remains.

VIII. *The Great Cakra Altar.*

The meditator now forms the vajra binding mudra, and sees the entire Lotus mandala to be brought into the self as if by drinking from a cup. The mudra is pointed inwards to the altar, outward to the Buddha, upward to the sky, and downward to the heart. Finally, it is touched to the crown, forehead, and lips, as if printed on the cosmos, and then sipped into the body. The mandala is bound to the self while reciting the mantra:

Om! Vajra cakra, Hum!

IX. *The Paths to the Center.*

The meditator sees that there are three paths to the empty center of the mandala, represented by the five, three, and single pronged vajra. The five pronged vajra represents the five cakra of the Lotus center. The three pronged vajra represents the three paths of tantric Buddhism, mudra, mantra, and mandala. The single point vajra represents the mind empty of all thoughts, ready for samadhi meditation and union.

A. *The Five Central Cakra.* The meditation on the five central cakras is called "The path to the multicolored world." The five pronged vajra mudra is formed, and the meditator envisions the five central cakra, as follows:

1. The mudra is pressed to the heart, and the seed word *Ra* is seen to be planted there, emanating a white color, for Vairocana. The mantra is recited three times, and the mudra is revolved in a circle three times to the right, starting from the northeast.

Hail all Buddhas, Ra!

The recitation opens a white pathway to the mandala's center.

2. Again pressing the mudra to the heart, the seed word *Ram* is envisioned, emitting a bright red light. The *Ram* seed word and the red light stand for the Buddha of the Eastern quarter, Ratnaketsu. The mantra is recited, and the mudra revolved three times, opening a red pathway to the east of center.

3. The yellow road to the south is opened by envisioning the seed word *Kyah*, and the Buddha Samkusumitara, while revolving the mudra and reciting the mantra.

4. The blue road to the west is opened by envisioning the seed word *Ma*, and the Buddha of Immeasurable Life (Amida). The mantra is recited and the mudra revolved three times.

5. The black road to the north of center is opened by envisioning the seed word *Ka* and the Buddha of the northern sector Dundhubi (Tengu Raion). The mantra is recited and the mudra revolved three times.

i) The meditator sees that all five paths, each with its own color, leads to the center of the mandala, where the meditation of union with Vairocana takes place. The meditation is repeated, using the same seed words:

In the name of all Buddhas, Ra, Ram, Kyah, Ma, Ka!

ii) A second set of five paths is then constructed mentally that lead to the five external halls surrounding the center, i.e., 1) the hall of wisdom above the lotus flower; 2) the hall of the light kings below center; 3) The halls of Kannon-Ksittigharba to the left; 4) the halls of Vajra-purification to the right; and 5) the hall of the Void Storehouse Boddhisattva below the Hall of the Light Kings, where the figures of the 1,000 armed Kannon and the 108 armed Vajrasattva are so prominent.

B. *The Three Intermediate Paths to the Center.* Next the three pronged vajra is invoked, and three pathways, red, yellow, and white in color, are constructed to the three sections that stand between the outer walls and center. The same mudra is used, and the mantra recited:

In the name of all Buddhas, Ra, Ram, Kyah

A red pathway is constructed to the Hall of Buddha, a Yellow path to the Hall of Manjusri, and a white path to the Susiddhi hall of wondrous self-emptying compassion.

C. *The Outer Wall, a Third Path to Center.* The seed word *Ra* is envisioned, emitting a bright white light that fills the outermost hall of the Lotus Mandala. The mudra is formed and mantra recited three times:

In the name of all Buddhas, Ra!

The meditator sees that in fact there is only one path to the center, a single bright white light that burns away all visions, and completes the kenotic process in the fires of the internal Goma, that leave no ashes. (See the Goma Fire Rite, Page 26).

X. *Contemplation of the Lotus Mandala.*

The meditator now forms the Samatha-Zen mudra, right palm over left in the lap, thumbs touching. In front of him/her is seen the image of Vairocana on his throne, superimposed on a full white moon, and a lotus blossom. Each worthy of the mandala is seen to be seated on a similar throne, inside a great round moon. The meditator recites the mantra "In the name of all Buddhas, Ah!" The mantra generates the image of the seed word *Ah*, emitting a bright gold color. The *Ah* seed word is placed in the middle of an open lotus flower, within the bright moon orb. From this point, the *Ah* character is seen to change into the lotus stupa, a square, circle, triangle, half moon, and crown, as in the illustration:

Ken

Kam

Ram

Vam

Ah

The stupa changes into the figure of Vairocana, sitting in the Zen samadhi posture of meditation. A gold light emanates from Vairocana's body, and illumines each figure of the Lotus mandala. The manifestation is called the "Transcendent, form purifying Dharma body" of Vairocana, which now emanates a crackling and sparkling light that fills the entire cosmos, past, present and future. The meditation ends with the realization of Vairocana's (i.e., Amida's) vow to save all sentient beings, and how this vow is represented by the light that penetrates to my own innermost depths, revealing all of my own true features. My body is made pure by this light, so as to "become Acala" in the next, fourth stage of the Lotus Mandala meditation.

The fourth section of the Lotus meditation is divided into sixteen mudra and mantra recitations. The climax of the meditation is the "putting on" of the aspects of Acala, *Fudo Myo-o* The meditator must follow the instructions of the Ajari master in every precise detail, envisioning in him or herself all of the aspects, paraphernalia, of the great light king Acala. The meditation may be performed interiorly as well as liturgically, in which case, if no incense burner or altar implements are at hand, the details of the meditation can be totally imagined in the mind of the meditator.

I. *Prepare the Way.*

The meditator picks up the incense burner between both hands, and holding it in front of the chest, moves it to the right in a circle three times, while seeing in the imagination a pathway to be opened and purified for all of the Buddhas of the pure void Dharma world to have access and entrance to the Lotus world. The mantra is recited thrice:

> I take refuge in the marvelous (susiddhi) powers of the
> Vajra to make a brilliant, thundering light path, to
> protect, blazing, binding, beating, Hum! Phat!

II. *Become Acala.*

Both hands are formed into the anger mudra, bent index and little fingers raised, fire and water fingers bent down over the folded thumbs (see illustration). The mudra is first held to each knee, then the knuckles joined and held to the heart. By reciting the mantra, the meditator sees him or her self become Acala, able to cut away all worldly ties and prevent any thoughts from arising in the heart-mind.

> In the name of all Vajras, Kam!
> Hail! One with Vajra, Kam!

III. *One with Acala's Flames.*

The third mudra and mantra cause the flames of Acala to surround one's own body, thus making me able to purify the mandala and the altar of meditation. Form the fire mudra, and press it to the chest, while reciting:

> In the name of all Vajras, Ram!
> Hail! One with Vajra flames, Ram!

IV. *Acala's sword and scabbard.*

The fourth eidetic vision represents the high point of the Tantric contemplative tradition, in which the meditator learns the saving compassion mantra of Acala, and the sword-and-scabbard mudra of the Pole Star, shared with the Taoist, Shinto, Shugendo, Yamabushi, and other esoteric movements in Asia. The thumb of left and right hand is pressed down over the fourth and fifth fingers, with the index and third (fire) fingers extended, like a sword. The right hand represents the sword of wisdom that cuts away all thoughts and desires, both good and bad. The left hand represents the scabbard, i.e., the mind and heart of the meditator, made void and empty so as to be filled with samadhi-wisdom. The manner of performing the meditation, reciting the mantra, and moving the mudra belongs to the oral tradition, and must be learned from an Ajari master. The mantra, the same used in the fourth stage of the Goma Fire rite, is as follows:

In the name of all Vajras, Great Fiery-angry one, destroyer
of evil! Hum! Trat! Kam! Mam!

The meditation is performed while reciting the mantra and moving the two mudra in the following six stages:

1. Place the scabbard (left hand) on the left knee, and place the sword (right hand) over it, inserting the sword (index and fire fingers) into the scabbard:

2. Envision the hair and braid of Acala on my head. Take the sword from the scabbard, and, imagining the hair of Acala to be piled on my head, slowly bring the scabbard down past the cheek, seeing the braid of Acala hanging down to my left shoulder. Re-insert the sword into the scabbard, and lay both hands on the left knee.

3. Envision my face and body to be Acala. Remove the sword from the scabbard, and hold the scabbard (left hand) against the right nipple, palm facing outward. Now lift the sword (right hand) slowly past the right chin and cheek, and let it rest over the left eye. See how Acala's left eye is half closed. Now envision my face and body to become Acala's.

4. Touch the five places of the body with the tip of the sword, that is, the forehead, right and left shoulder, right and left knee. Recite the mantra for each place touched, and see the armor of Acala placed on one's own body.

5. Bring the sword and scabbard together, and move both hands to the right once in a circle. Insert the sword into the scabbard, and lay both on the knee, without reciting the mantra. Then touch sword and scabbard to the heart, forehead and crown of the head. Bow prostrate to the ground three times, and dissolve the mudra over the head.

6. Join the hands in the prayer mudra, and see my body now totally identified with Acala. Recite the mantra once, seeing all negative thoughts about others, and all judgmental reasoning burned away by Acala's flames.

V. *The Vajra Hand.*

Form the two fists in the vajra mudra, and press them to left and right waist, saying "Hail Vajra fist, Hum!" Then pick up the five pronged vajra in the right hand, and revolve it to the right three times, while saying "Hum! Hum! Hum!"

VI. *The Vajra Bell Invites All.*

Pick up the bell in the left hand, and ring it nine times, as in the Eighteen Path Mandala, saying *Ken-da-um* as the bell rings. Envision the tones of the bell to fill the entire lotus world, inviting each worthy to be present for a banquet.

VII. *Invite the Worthies with Acala's Hook.*

In place of the chariot mudra of the Eighteen Path and Goma rites, form the closed fist wind mudra, right index finger extended, symbol of Acala's hook. Recite, "Hail all Ye Buddhas, all Ye indestructible Tathagata, come by this hook to fulfill all Boddhi deeds, Svaha!" The Boddhi deeds are, 1) care for all sentient beings, 2) alleviate all fear, 3) perform meditation 4) see self and all others as equal.

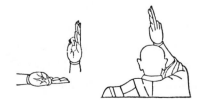

VIII. *Acala's Cord.*

Form the special mudra that binds self to Vairocana, and recite the mantra: "Hail all Buddhas! By this great rope of Acala and thy great magnanimity, may all illness and harm be prevented in the world of sentient beings, by showing total faith in Tathagata Svaha!" See self now bound to all of the worthies in the Lotus world, with the same relationship as they to Vairocana.

IX. *Acala's Lock.*

Form the lock mudra with both fists joined, and recite the mantra: "In the name of all Vajras, Hum! Binding, breaking, Oh Thou born of Vajra, nothing can destroy Thee, Svaha!" See the union of self to Acala and Vairocana to be eternal, nothing can ever tear it away.

X. *Acala's Bell.*

Form the special bell mudra, and now ring the bell symbolically, while reciting the mantra: "Om! Vajra bell, Ken-da-a". Move the hand as if ringing a bell, and see all of the worthies invited by Acala to a banquet within the Lotus world. Note that the four binding mudra and mantra just recited belong to the *Jah! Um! Vam! Koh!* genre of binding mudra used in the Goma fire rite to bind the vision of the spirit in the flames, and here to bind the vision to the self. The hook draws in Acala's image. The rope keeps out external images and binds self to Buddha's mind. The lock preserves the image of Acala within, and the bell welcomes all Buddhas to the banquet.

XI. *Purify the Lotus World Again.*

As the gates of the Lotus world are opened, and the multitude of worthies and outermost layer of spirits enter, the sword mudra of Step Four above is repeated, to purify any impure spirit or thought that may have crept in during the meditation. Repeat the Great Compassion mantra, while performing the mudra:

    1. sword and scabbard circle once, then rest on the left knee.

    2. scabbard is placed over left breast, sword raised to right forehead, facing outward. Move it to the right in a circle, three times, forbidding any evil demon or impure thought to invade the sacred area during the time that the Buddhas are entering.

    3. Move the sword upward and then bring it down, seeing a net cover the sacred area, protecting it from any evil.

    4. Touch the five places, then re-insert the sword in the scabbard, on the left knee.

    5. leave the sword in the scabbard, and touch both together to the heart and head.

    6. Touch the crown of the head, front and back, and bow deeply, dissolving the mudra over the head.

XII. *Manifest Samaya* (Sameness or Oneness with the Lotus).

Hold the folded hands over the top of the head, and recite the samaya mantra, making self, Buddha world, and Lotus mandala one and the same. "In the name of all Buddhas, may they who are not the same, the three together be one and the same, Svaha!"

XIII. *The Offering of Pure Aka Water.*

Pick up the Aka water bowl in the right hand, and purify it by holding it over the incense burner. Then respectfully place it in the left hand, and form the right hand into the sword mudra as above. Recite the Great Compassion Mantra twenty-one times while performing this process (3 x 7). Revolve the sword to the left, then to the right three times each. Then hold the water bowl between the two hands, formed into the eight petaled lotus mudra. Chant the poem written below, then hold the bowl of water at the head, heart, and belly, while chanting the mantra:

> May our bodies, by this pure water
> Be washed clean of all stains,
> Thus not neglecting (Buddha's) original vows,
> Proven within us, all duties fulfilled.
> Hail all Buddhas, One and same with the void, Svaha!

The third finger and thumb of the right hand are dipped into the water, and sprinkled three times to dharma, (head), lotus (heart) and vajra (belly level and altar). The Aka is then put down.

XIV. The hands are shaped into the chrysanthemum mudra, and the mantra is repeated, offering the symbolic or phenomenal-dharma aspects of the pure Aka water three times, to Buddha, Lotus, and Vajra worlds.

> Hail all Buddhas, One with the Void, Svaha!

XV. The hands are formed into the Lotus mudra, and the meditator sees flowers offered to all the worthies of the Lotus world, as each of the worthies is seated on his or her Lotus throne:

> Hail all Buddhas, Ah!

XVI. The fourth stage of the Lotus meditation ends with a brief prayer to all the assembly of worthies in the Lotus Mandala. The hands are formed in the vajra mudra, and the poem recited:

> Welcome all thou worthies,
> From vows of compassion come,
> Down here to this sacred place,
> Please, now, take thy thrones,
> And accept from us these offerings.

Part 5. The Concluding Meditations of the Lotus-womb World

I. *Put on Vajrasattva's Armor.*

The fifth stage of the Lotus Meditation begins with the re-affirmation of the purifying power of the sword mudra. The meditator repeats the mantra of compassion, and moves the sword mudra three times to the left and right in a circle, right hand sword inserted into the left hand scabbard. He or she then forms the five pronged vajra mudra, and touches the five places, belly, heart, throat, shoulders, and head. The word *Ken* appears over the head shedding a gold light, while the seed word *Vah* appears in the heart, emitting a bright white light.

A. The meditator changes the vision of Acala into the appearance of Vajrasattva, while reciting the mantra:

> In the name of all Vajras, Hum!
> Hail all Vajras, Hum!

The meditator is reminded at this point that the Dharma can only be understood when separated from words. The gold and white lights emanating from the Vajra vision empty the mind and heart of all concepts, images, and desires arising from the vision of the Lotus world. The three pronged vajra mudra is circled right three times, then touch the five places. The mantra assists the meditator don the armor of Vajrasattva.

> Hail all Vajras, fierce great wrath, Hum!

B. The mudra and mantra of the Lotus Meditation Part One, Sec. 7.4, "Donning the Vajra Armor" is repeated. A blue cord emanating from the finger tips, now ties the armor of Vajrasattva to the twelve places of the body:

> Om! Vajra Armor, Hum!

As the armor is tied to each of the twelve places (See Page 6, above) the words Om! Ton! are repeated. When completed, the right hand points to the ground, recalling how after the Buddha's enlightenment and attainment of spiritual insight, the evil temptress Mara appeared from the earth in sensuous vision. The evil to be expelled now is the pride that the vision of heavenly things can cause. If the vision of the Lotus world, or the heavenly worthies makes us lose compassion, then all of the meditations of Lotus and Vajra worlds are wasted. As the mantra is recited, a bright gold net covers the Lotus world, protecting it from all thoughts of pride and spiritual superiority. Demons are empowered by the mind's visions of self-perfection. The mantra is called "The Medicine of the Immortal of the Western Heavens," i.e., the vision of Amida's light flooding from the western heavens, not my own power, brings enlightenment.

> Hail all Buddhas! Oh Thou of great strength
> Who has attained the ten powers, show forth
> Thy Great compassion, Svaha!

C. The vision of Bhrkuti is now seen, an avatar or type of angry Avalokitesvara, with a violent countenance and four arms, each with a different mudra (beads, vows fulfilled, lotus, vase). The Ajari master explains at this point that the vision of Amida,

Avalokitesvara (Kannon) and Buddha Locana are different aspects of a Buddha. The meditator must not be attached to any image, but see each part of the mandala as related to the whole.

D. The vision of the total Lotus world is now before the meditator, who has realized the presence of the mandala within his or her body. But the awakening to the Lotus must not be ephemeral, a brief encounter with a world of iconographic splendor. The interior palace of transcendent, void presence, (the word *Le Llupuri* palace is used to symbolize the void lotus) must now be cleansed of all images and seed words. The special vajra purifying mudra is formed, and the mantra of cleansing recited:

> In the name of all Buddhas,
>
> Oh Le Luppuri palace,
>
> Be cleansed, no image, Svaha!

The Lotus World has now become a void and pure palace, with no image and no seeds of thought remaining.

II. *Locking the Gates to the Lotus Mandala*

A. The meditator sees the four great guardians, the *Shitenno* 四天王 at the four gateways to the mandala, who hasten to close the doors so that the state of void sunya in the Lotus world never be lost. The final meditation takes place in two stages: 1) The four great kings at the four gates are seen to repeat the words of cleansing purification. 2) Then Acala locks the gates, so that no thought and no desire may arise therein. The mudra of locking is repeated four times, sealing the heart of the lotus. The Lotus World has become a source of eternal enlightenment.

1. Envision the Guardian of the East, Jikokuten (Dhrtarastra), "No Fear." Form the mudra, and revolve it to the right and left, three times each, then touch the five places, and recite the mudra:

> Hail all Buddhas, Va!
>
> Le Luppuri Palace,
>
> Clean, pure, Svaha!

Visualize the self standing in the center of the Lotus, and look out the East gate of the mandala. There see the seed word*Va* above an open lotus flower. The word changes into the great protector quardian Jikokuten, who destroys all fear. His body is gold and his robes are bright white. He has an angry expression, and carries a staff in the right hand.

2. Envision the Guardian of the North, Tamonten (Vaisravana). Also called Bishamonten, he destroys all evil. Form the mudra, and revolve it to the right and left three times, then touch the five places and say:

> Hail all Buddhas, Vah!
>
> Le Luppuri palace,
>
> Clean, pure, Svaha!

Envision an open lotus in the middle of the north gate, atop which is the seed word *Vah*. The word changes into Tamonten, (Vaisravana) or Bishamon, Protector from all evil. His body and clothes are a bright white. He holds a sword in his right hand and a stupa in his left.

65

3. Envision the Guardian of the West, Komokuten (Virupaksa) who stops sorrow. Form the mudra, and move it the left and right three times, then touch the five places while reciting:

> Hail all Buddhas Sah!
> Le Luppuri palace
> Clean, pure, Svaha!

See an open lotus flower in the center of the west gate, over which is the seed word *Sah*. It changes into the great protector from suffering Komokuten (Virupaksa). His body is the color of pink, like a flower free of all sorrow. His clothes are crimson, and in his right hand he holds a vajra spear.

4. Envision the Guardian of the South, Zojoten (Virudhaka) who prevents all harshness and anger. Form the mudra and revolve it to the left and right three times, then touch the five places and say:

> Hail all Buddhas, Kam! Ken!
> Le Luppuri palace,
> Clean, pure, Svaha!

See an open lotus in the middle of the south gate, over which are the two seed words *Kam* and *Ken*. The words turn into the Great Protector form all harshness and anger, Zojoten (Virudhaka) whose face resembles the image of Bhrkuti, seen above. His body is dark in color, and his clothes are a deep black. He wears a flanged helmet. His left fist is pressed to the waist, and in his right hand he holds a tancha sword.

     B. The gates of the Lotus world are now locked and bolted, showing the immense difference between the spirit of the Womb-Lotus, and the male Vajra. The Lotus is female, a womb from which enlightenment is gestated, and therefore a place to be carefully sealed off and protected from all impurities and worldly evil. The meditation of the Lotus world is performed first in the Tendai tradition, because the meditator must be first filled with the selfless wisdom of compassion, as proof of true enlightenment. Only after wisdom and compassion are fixed deeply in my own heart can I step forth and do the deeds of a Buddha in the exterior world. The Vajra world meditation is then performed, in which the blessings received from the Lotus are given away to all sentient beings. The philosophy of Sunya emptying is thus practically realized in the two tantric meditations.

1.The four gates are first locked with the special mudra of protection, formed by inserting the index finger of the right hand into the closed left fist, then bolted by inserting the index finger of the left hand into the closed right fist. The meditator sees him or herself again changed into the countenance of Acala, to perform the mudra and mantra of locking. The sequence is repeated four times, once for each of the four gates, to the east, north, west, and south of the mandala. The point of the meditation is to realize that the Lotus world is preserved interiorly by keeping the vajra vow of compassion exteriorly, i.e., the vow of Amida-Vairocana to alleviate the suffering and save all sentient beings. The countenance of Acala is seen to radiate bright red and white flames, as the mantra is recited:

> Hail all Vajras!
> Oh Thou who cannot bear to see suffering,
> Great fierce one (Acala), devour,

Fulfill all the Tathagata vows,
for all of us, let it be done, Svaha!

The right index finger is inserted into the left fist, and turned to the right, locking the gate.

2. The gates are next bolted, with the following mantra:

Hey! Now for the other side!
Great violent fierce one, devour, digest, hurry,
Why so slow! Fulfill the original vow, remember, Svaha!

The left index finger is inserted into right fist, and turned to the left, bolting the gate.

III. *The Concluding Rites*.

The sixth, seventh, and eighth stages of the Lotus meditation are a reversal of the Eighteen Path mandala, as in Chapter One, pages 9-14, and page 31 above.

A. The six visible gifts, representing concrete deeds of compassion, and the six symbolic mudra representing the six paramitas of wisdom are offered, the meditation on the Dharma, Reward, and Response body of Vairocana, are repeated.

B.The meditation on the Lotus stupa, Chapter Two part 7 is also repeated, and the structure of the entire Lotus Mandala slowly and thoroughly contemplated. The samadhi posture of Zen meditation is assumed, right palm over left, thumbs touching. The meditator and Vairocana have the same posture, are in fact the same person. As the closing lines of the Eighteen Path Mandala are recited, the meditator is reminded to "go forth and do deeds of compassion," if the Lotus meditation was truly meaningful.

III. THE VAJRA THUNDER MEDITATION
Part 1. Purification

I. The Vajra Mandala meditation begins with the purification and Eighteen Path mandala meditations as in Chapters I and II above, except for the following changes:

A. Use the mantra of Trailokyavijaya, i.e., Nisumbha (Jpn.: Gozanze) to bless the water and offerings:

> Om Nisumbha vajra, Hum!

B. Bless the offerings with the three pronged vajra in the right hand, left fist to the waist:

> Om Nisumbha Vajra Hum!

C. Visualize the Buddhas of the Vajra Mandala, instead of the Lotus and Goma worlds:

> Kham! Vajra World Mandala!

Lift the head and look at the hanging mandala scroll; or envision the mandala in the imagination, in the sky directly above the meditator. Visualize each Buddha, from the center, through the right to the left sides, in clockwise fashion moving outward.

D. Awaken the Buddhas of the Vajra World. Form the Vajra awakening mudra, i.e., little fingers intertwined, index fingers extended and touching, thumbs tucked under the third and fourth fingers, bent in a fist. Recite the mudra three times, seeing each of the Buddhas of the Vajra world awaken and begin to move and talk (eidetic or moving vision):

> Hail, Vajra world, awake! Hum!

E. Pay obeisance to the four Buddhas of the Vajra center. Bow to each of the four Buddhas that surround Vairocana Buddha, in the center of the Vajra, beginning with the bottom or east side, and moving counter clockwise to the north or right side.

1. *The Buddha of the East*, Aksobhya (Ashuku). Imagine that in my heart there is the seed word *Hum*, emanating a bright yellow color. See it change and become a five pronged wisdom vajra. Then see my own body change into the five wisdom vajra, so that each particle of dust in my body is permeated with Vajrasattva, (i.e., *Ashuku*, (Aksobhya). Then visualize offering my body entirely to Aksobhya, and all of the Buddhas of the astern sector, while reciting the mantra:

> Hail, All Tathagatas! In your service
> Take my body as an offering.
> All Tathagata Vajra protect me, Hum!

2. *The Buddha of the South*, Ratna Sambhava (Hosho). Imagine that the seed word *Trah* is directly above my forehead, a deep blue-black color. See it change and become a Vajra jewel. Then see that my body too changes so that each particle of dust within me is permeated by Vajra-ratna, the Vajra Jewel; that is, I have put on the aspects of Vajrasattva, Ratna Sambhava Buddha. Then envision the offering of my body completely to Ratna Sambhava and all of the Buddhas of the southern sector, while reciting the mantra:

> Hail all Tathagatas, puja ordained, we offer ourselves.
> All ye Tathagatas, Consecrate us! Trah!

3. *The Buddha of the West*, Amida of Immeasurable Life. Visualize that in the mouth there is the seed word *Hrih*. It is red in color, and it changes into an eight-petaled Lotus Blossom. See my body also change into an eight-petaled lotus, so that each particle of dust within me is permeated with the the Vajra Dharma of Amida. Then chant the mantra, seeing my body and all of my abilities completely offered to Amida and the Buddhas of the western sector:

> Hail all tathagatas! For an on-going puja,
> Take me as an offering.
> Oh all ye Tathagatas, Oh Vajra Dharma,
> Mam. Hrih! Revolve me! Hrih!

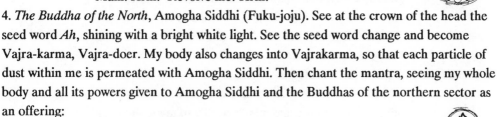

4. *The Buddha of the North*, Amogha Siddhi (Fuku-joju). See at the crown of the head the seed word *Ah*, shining with a bright white light. See the seed word change and become Vajra-karma, Vajra-doer. My body also changes into Vajrakarma, so that each particle of dust within me is permeated with Amogha Siddhi. Then chant the mantra, seeing my whole body and all its powers given to Amogha Siddhi and the Buddhas of the northern sector as an offering:

> Hail all Tathagatas!
> For puja deeds, take me as an offering.
> Oh all Tathagatas, into Vajra Karma,
> Convert my deeds. Ah!

F. Perform the Grand Mudra of the Vajra Holder. First, kneel on the right knee, form the vajra clasped hands mudra, then separate the palms, and hold them over the head, as if putting a vajra crown on the top of the head. Recite the phrase *Om Vajra Vih* ("Hail, Vajra victor!"), then hold the palms outward, parallel to each other, and move them to the height of the chest. First, move the right hand in a circle three times, then move the left hand in a circle three times, as if dancing. While performing the mudra, visualize self becoming Vairocana Tathagata. Recite the mantra three times, as follows:

> Hail all Tathagatas, with body, mouth, mind.
> Vajra ritual, let us do it! Hail, Vajra Victor!

When finished, tuck the right knee back into the half lotus position, and join the two hands in the vajra-anjali mudra. Meditate on the self made one with Vairocana, and breathe in the the light issuing from Vairocana's headpiece, circulating it through the body, as breath. Experience joy in this first visual union with Vajra wisdom. Then continue with the Eighteen Path mandala, substituting Trailokyavijaya for the name of Acala in the text.

G. *Chant in Honor of the Vajra World Buddhas.*

> All hail Oh thou eternal resident of the Three Worlds, pure,
> Wondrous Dharmakaya, Vajra World Great Compassionate Vairocana!
> All hail Oh Vajra-strength self-arisen body, Aksobhya Buddha!
> All hail Oh blessed, finely adorned body, Ratna Sambhava Buddha!
> All Hail Oh wisdom body, received to help others, Amida Buddha!
> All Hail Oh bringer of change, transformed body Sakyamuni Buddha!
> Hail thou four Paramita Boddhisattva worthies!
> Hail thou sixteen Boddhisattva worthies!
> Hail thou eight Puja Boddhisattva worthies!

Hail thou four helpers of wisdom Boddhisattva worthies!

Hail Oh all thou Buddhas and Boddhisattvas of the Vajra World!

H. *The five repentances.*

Form the Vajra-anjali mudra, and see oneself bowing down to the feet of the five central Buddhas, grasping their knees in sorrow and repentance.

1. First, recite the verses of obeisance and respect:

> I take refuge in all the Buddhas of the Ten directions,
> Most victorious wondrous Dharma enlightened multitude.
> By thy doing, body, mouth, and mind are purified;
> Profoundly moved, I clasp my hands and bow in respect.
> I take refuge and bow my head in obeisance to the great
> compassionate, Vairocana Buddha!

2. Next, recite the prayer of repentance:

> Oh all of ye in the midst of beginningless revolving,
> From body, mouth and mind's deeds, so many sins born!
> Let us join with Buddha and Boddhisattva's repentance,
> Let us now be like them, our sorrow one with theirs,
> Take refuge and bow our heads in obeisance to
> The Great, Compassionate Vairocana Buddha!

3. Last, Hymn of Joy in following the Buddha:

> Now let us again respond with joy from heart's depths.
> A joy gained from all the blessing of wisdom attained!
> All Buddhas and Boddhisattvas are now fulfilling vows,
> Of bearing in us the blessing of the three Vajra deeds.
> To cause awakening, hear their words, sentient ones!
> They are the root of good attained; follow their joy!
> Take refuge and bow in respect to the Great,
> Compassionate, Vairocana Buddha!

4. Invite the Buddhas to be present:

> Again let us envision each Buddhas seated in the Mandala.
> I personally invite each one to spin the Dharma wheel,
> Each and every light of the world to sit in the mandala.
> Awaken eyes, open the gates, shine on the three realms!
> I here, today, bend my knees and first do thou invite,
> To spin the highest, wondrous wheel of the Law.
> All of ye Tathagata, masters of the Three Worlds,
> Approach together, do not hold back, O enlightened ones.
> I invite you all today to be eternally present,
> Never forget thy compassionate vows to save the world.
> Take refuge and bow in respect to the Great Compassionate
> Vairocana Buddha.

5. Pronounce the Vajra vows:

> Come oh ye blessing of repentance and joy,
> Let us never lose the Bodhi enlightened heart-mind.
> May each Buddha and Boddhisattva, wondrous multitude all,
> Always be our best of friends, never cast us aside.
> Help us leave the eight hardships, born with no distress.
> May our destiny be to dwell in wisdom, body thus adorned,
> Parted from life's allurements, taste compassion's wisdom
> At last fulfilling the ability to pass to the other shore
> Of abundant joy, richly nourished, born in Buddha's race.
> May the holy ones be constant, warm, fulfilling family,
> Bringing to us the *four unhindered ways of speaking* (know
> the dharmas, understand their meaning, able to speak in
> any language, and joy for those who listen to us teach),
> And the *Ten Self-possessed Freedoms* (acts, heart & mind,
> appearances, deeds, birth, attachments, desires, spiritu-
> al power, Dharma, wisdom), the *Six Transcendental facul-*
> *ties*, (to go anywhere, see anywhere, hear from great dist-
> ances, know others thoughts, past lives, destroy passion),
> and bring to fulfillment our ability for *Zen* meditation.
> Just as Vajra Banner and Samantabhadra have done, we too
> Vow that all merit (of the Tathagata) be given to all,
> By homage and praise to Great Compassionate Vairocana!

I. The meditator now takes the beads, single-pronged vajra, and hand held incense burner in the left hand, strikes the chime with the right hand, then with implements grasped in both hands chants the vows of the Vajra Mandala World:

> With upright heart I make these vows,
> Promising solely to Vairocana,
> And the whole Vajra world mandala,
> The nine assemblies of the cakra altar,
> The four Buddhas of the four passageways,
> The eight offerings, the four assistants,
> The sixteen Great Boddhisattva,
> The Teacher who orders the body transformed,
> Gozanze (Trailokyavijaya) Master,
> Four Great, Eight great, All the Great Angry Ones
> The worthies of the Eighteen Assemblies,
> All the holy ones of the outer Vajra wall,
> They who protect the Dharma, heavenly horde,
> May they all repeat their original vows,
> Come down here, now, to this sacred area
> And partake of these Puja offerings.
> Protect us, children of Buddha, may all the good

Vowed in our hearts, be fulfilled, completed,
Fill the entire Dharma world, equally helping all!

J. Continuing to hold incense, beads, and vajra, pronounce the Five Great Vows of the Boddhisattva (as in Chapter I, pages 8-9).

K. *Contemplation on the Four Immeasurable Minds.*

1. The immeasurable mind of kindness. Envision one's mind to be filled with the immeasurable pure and gentle kindness of Samantabhadra *(Fugen)*. See that the six realms of rebirth (deva, human, animal, preta, asura, demon) and the four kinds of arising birth (womb, egg, moisture-born, and avatar or transformed body) all sentient beings have within themselves the original nature of a Tathagata, a potential realized by oneness with the Boddhisattva *Fugen* and *Maitreya*.

O Great Maitreya, pervade me!

2. The immeasurable mind of compassion. Envision all sentient beings to be filled with loving compassion. Even though the six realms of rebirth and the four kinds of arising birth, all sentient beings are immersed and sinking in the sea of life and death, still each one has within the depths of its own being the nature of Akasagharba, the Vajra Storehouse *Kokuzo Bosatsu*. Then recite the mantra, begging that all sentient beings achieve union with Akasagharba.

Oh Great compassion, pervade!

3. The immeasurable mind of Joy. Next one must see the mind purified and cleansed, by reason of which the six realms of rebirth and the four kinds of arising birth, all sentient beings, are purified and cleansed. This is because in the depths of their being they have the potency to be a true dharma storehouse. Thereupon recite the mantra, praying that all sentient beings may experience union with Avalokitesvara, Kanjizai Bosatsu.

O wondrous joy, pervade!

4. The immeasurable mind of equanimity. See, with a mind of equanimity, that all sentient beings, the six paths and the four arising births, are separate from "me" and "mine", and that in the depths of their being they are in fact one with the marvelous Dharma storehouse. Now chant the mantra, praying that each and every sentient being realize oneness with the void, empty storehouse Vajra-sattva Boddhisattva.

O great relinquishing, pervade!

This concludes Part One of the Vajra Mandala meditation.

Samantabhadra   Akasagharba   Avalokitesvara   Vajrasattva

Part 2. Enter the Vajra Mandala

In the second stage of the Vajra Mandala liturgy, the meditator uses mental visualization, mantric chant, and mudra hand dance to progress through the ninth, eight, and seventh halls of the Vajra world. These are 9) the Hall of Trailokyavijaya's *samaya* symbols, 8) the Hall of Identification with Trailokyavijaya, (*Gozanze*), and 7) the *Naya* (Jpn: Rishyu) Hall of mental purification. The liturgy begins with a six step visualization in which the meditator assumes in eidetic vision the aspects of Vajrasattva, the disciple of Vairocana Buddha.

I. *Vajra Eyes Meditation.*

See the seed word *Ma* over the right eye, which changes and becomes a moon. Then see the seed word *Ta* over the left eye which also changes and becomes the sun. Form the left and right hands into a fist with the thumbs tucked under the fingers. Press the left fist to the left eye, and right fist to right eye. See a five pronged vajra light shoot forth from each eye into outer space. Leap onto the light, and ride it into outer space, and see all of the Buddhas and Boddhisattvas, the multitudes of the Vajra world, to be filled with joy and happiness. Return the fists to the waist, and holding them there. See this meditation as a purifying dharma, that offers the self as a concrete purified offering, freed from all stain and dirt, cut off from worldly ties. See the self offering garlands of flowers and incense to all of the Buddhas, while reciting the mantra:

> Hail, Oh Vajra Eyes, Ma-Ta!

II. *The Vajra-anjali mudra.*

Join the hands joined with fingers upright and intertwined. This is the basic mudra for the vajra meditations. The left hand represents Zen or Samatha concentration, and the right hand represents Vipasyana or emptying wisdom. The ten fingers are symbols of the ten crossings (paramitas, or connectors to the Buddha-Vajra world): 1) the altar, 2) the precepts, 3) forbearance, 4) striving, 5) Zen meditation, 6) understanding, 7) *upaya* skillful means, 8) vows, 9) strength, and 10) wisdom. The mudra symbolizes that I am only able to have these virtues by realizing that I am united with the Buddha nature, not by any striving on my own. A gold light emanates from the mudra, covering my body and protecting it, like a statue of the Buddha covered in gold, from worldly desires and attachments. Recite the mantra:

> Hail, Oh Vajra palms!

III. *Vajra Bonds.*

Pull the fingers down over the fists, seeing all bonds to the desires, glories, and praise of the world thereby cut off, and self bound instead to oneness with the vajra world.

> Hail, Vajra Bonds!

IV. *Open the heart.*

Next, lift the fingers so that they extend upwards at a 45 degree angle. Hold this mudra first to the right nipple, and see the seed word *Trah* there. Then move the mudra to the left nipple, and see the seed word *Ta* imprinted there. Then bring the mudra to the center of the chest, and pull the hands apart like a door opening. Recite the mantra three times:

> Hail Vajra Gates, Open!

See the heart, closed off by the former Lotus World meditation, now about to open. The three obstacles, mind, deeds, and suffering are obliterated, and the three sources of karmic deeds, body, mouth, and mind, are purified.

V. *Summon wisdom into the heart.*

Envision an open lotus in front of the heart with the seed word *Ah* on top of it. Using the above mudra, pull the fingers down over the fists, and tuck the thumbs inside the closed fist three times, seeing the seed word *Ah* and the lotus to be drawn inside me. The lotus and the seed word glow with a brilliant pink and gold light, which diffuses and fills my body with breath, as it enters inside me. Recite the mantra three times:

Hail Vajra, enter Ah!

VI. *Close the Gateway to the Heart.*

With the thumbs still tucked inside the fists, pull down the index fingers over the thumbs, locking them inside. See the entrance to the heart closed, so that wisdom will never again leak out, or depart from me. Recite the mantra three times:

Hail Vajra clenched fist! Vam!

VII. Enter the ninth hall of the Vajra Mandala, the Samaya Assembly of Gozanze and Fugen (Trailokyavijaya and Samantabhadra), who purify and enlighten the meditator as he/she enter the Vajra Mandala. The hall consists of a series of symbols (samaya) which purify the mind of words, logical reasoning, and attachment to ideas. Note that the motion of the Vajra Mandala meditation is counterclockwise, i.e., it proceeds from the bottom right hand corner upwards in a counter-clockwise direction to union with Vairocana in the center of the mandala.

A. The two figures of Gozanze (Trailokyavijaya) and Fugen (Samantabhadra) dwell in the ninth hall. See oneself become one with and united to the Boddhisattva Samantabhadra. See that Samantabhadra (Fugen) is in fact an aspect of Vajrasattva, the disciple of Vairocana. He holds a five-pronged vajra bell in his left hand, pressed to the waist, and a five-pronged vajra in his right hand, pressed to his heart, and sits inside a moon cakra. See him as if in a mirror in front of oneself, as a reflection of the self. Now recite the mantra three times, saying:

Hail symbol, I and Thou One!

B. The visual union of self with Vajrasattva brings to me the realization that the nature of the Tathagata and all sentient beings is the same; that is, I now am one with the Tathagata's vow to enlighten and save all sentient beings, to burn away the worries of all sentient beings, and awaken all sentient beings to enlightenment.

C. The Ninth Hall is an Assembly of Wondrous Joy. Press in the middle fingers so that they point downward beneath the folded palms. Press this mudra, like an arrow, to the heart, thereby destroying all intellectual images and willed desires. The arrow destroys both vehicles, Theravada and Mahayana, and by thus emptying the heart-mind of all words, images and desires, brings about great interior peace and joy. Recite the mantra three times saying:

Om! Hoh! One with great joy!

VIII. *Enter the Eighth Hall.*

Enter the Eighth Hall of Trailokyavijaya, and become Gozanze. Cross the right hand over the left, and attach the two little fingers by hooking them together. Imagine that the two index fingers are the protruding teeth of Gozanze (see illustration). Move the fingers by pulling them inward and outward, and envision the body of Fugen (Samantabhadra) to change and become the terrifying body of Gozanze (Trailokyavijaya).

A. See Gozanze dancing in front of me, with eight arms and four heads portraying laughter, anger, fear, and terror. Four teeth (two upper and lower) protrude from his mouth. His body is surrounded by roaring flames. The left leg is extended straight outward, and the right leg is bent, trampling over the sky. Move the mudra to the right nipple, left nipple, point to the earth, then touch the heart, shoulders, throat, and crown of the head, finally dissolving the mudra over the top of the head as the mudra ends:

> Hail Sumbha Nisumbha Hum!
> Away, Away, Hum!
> Depart all evil, Hum!
> Come save us, Hoh!
> Oh Honored Vajra, Hum! Purify!

B. While reciting the last line, revolve the mudra to the right three times, purifying heaven and earth; then to the left three times, to enlighten all sentient beings. Then touch the four places, i.e., heart, shoulders, throat, and forehead. Dissolve the mudra over the head.

C. The Lotus-stupa symbol. Form the Great Sword Stupa mudra, the third "fire" fingers bent at the top joint and touching, index fingers extended, right thumb over left, symbolizing the vajra stupa that arises out of a Lotus. Hold the mudra slightly above the forehead, and see my body become Avalokitesvara, (Kanjizai Bosattsu), who holds a lotus bud in the left hand and a Dharma wheel in the right (between the index and little fingers). Press the mudra to the belly, and recite the mantra three times, seeing that my original nature is purified by the power of the Vajra-stupa sword.

> Hail Vajra-stupa, We are one, I and Thou!

D. The Dharma Wheel. Keeping the hands joined, fold down the index and third fingers, and bring up the little fingers so that they cross in an upright position. Envision the mudra to be a Dharma wheel, which revolves and burns away all the Alaya seed-conscious mind, and all attachments to the Theravada and Mahayana vehicles. Move the mudra three times to the right in front of the heart, and see the Dharma wheel to be spun by Gozanze, while the light issuing from his vajra hand purifies me from all desires and instills in me the thirty-seven seeds (preparation for the thirty-seven Buddhas) of the Vajra world meditation.

> Hail, Takki (Gozanze) destroyer,
> Great desire-free Vajra, Thou who truly
> grasps the Vajra, Thah! (spin the wheel).

IX. *Enter the Hall of Transcendent Desire.*

Envision the Eighth Hall of the Naya (Lady Buddha) Assembly. The meditator now enters the Seventh Hall of the Vajra World, the Rishyu Assembly of Void Wisdom. First, gaze on the Naya World (Rishyu) Mandala, and realize that all sentient beings enter the Buddha world, and cross over to the other shore, not by any merits of their own, but solely by the great, purifying vajra light. By virtue of the vajra power alone are they able to attain to the wisdom mind, and leave behind worldly love and desire. The one great desire is therefore to be void of desire, to be one with *Aizen Myo-o*, the spirit of mystic love, ruler of the Naya Assembly. He/she is the Buddha who purifies the soul of desire.

A. Form the mudra by folding the fingers down over the closed fists, and tuck the right thumb over the left into the interior of the closed fist. Recite the mantra three times, while pressing the right thumb into the interior three times:

> Hail wondrous pleasure, Vajra,
> Hook! Enter! Bind! Joy!
> I and Thou, Thou and I, same!

B. The Great Joy of Entry into the Naya Hall. As the meditator enters the Naya Hall, i.e., the Rishyu Assembly, he/she sees that mind and heart must be emptied of all Dharma, thoughts, and desires. Envision all sentient beings, by the grace and power of Gozanze, to quickly prove the power of the Tathagata by realizing within themselves the Grand Enlightenment of compassion, i.e., self-emptying wisdom. The Great Desire for compassionate wisdom is realized by union with Vajrasattva-Aizen. Use the same mudra as above, but leave the right thumb within the closed fist, without moving. Recite the mantra once:

> Oh great joyful Vajra,
> Realized for all sentient beings,
> Hook! Enter! Bind! Joy in them!
> Wondrous Joy! I and Thou One!

C. Summon forth all the transgressions of all sentient beings. Envision that all sins, transgressions, and guilt for them are purified by the power of Aizen Vajrasattva. Form the mudra by extending the middle fire fingers straight upward, like a sword. Then bring the index fingers up to touch the first joint of the third fingers. All of the sins and transgressions are seen to be summoned by moving the index fingers up and down, as if summoning them to be impaled on the sword of Vajrasattva.

D. See a huge black cloud, as of all evil demons, my sins, and guilt for them, as well as the transgressions of all sentient beings, arising from the three sources of evil (mind, mouth, body) to be impaled on the Vajra sword. Recite the mantra, feeling great sorrow for sins but compassion for the transgressors:

> Hail, all guilt, be pulled here!
> Purify it, Oh Vajrasattva!
> By being one with it! Hum! Phat!

E. Crush the transgressions. Pull down the index fingers from the previous mudra, and press the fingers and thumbs inside the fist, leaving the third fire fingers extended as a sword. The fingers and thumbs inserted inside the fist represent all transgressions and guilt, which will be purified and destroyed from within the Naya (Rishyu) assembly. See the black cloud of guilt and sin to be pressed inside the closed fist, and annihilated by a white light emanating from the center of the Rishyu hall. Breath this white light inside my body, thus purifying it by the power of Vajrasattva and the Naya assembly. Recite the mantra, and upon reaching the final mantric seed words *Hum! Tra! Ta!*, snap the extended third fingers three times, seeing all guilt for transgressions dissolved:

> Oh Vajra hand, conquer, destroy,
> From all evil bonds and ties,
> From all evil conditions, release us!
> Make all sentient beings, all Tathagatas
> One with Vajra! Hum! Trah! Ta!

F. Purification of Karmic Impediments. Form the great wisdom sword mudra, by pressing the index fingers over the upright thumbs, and crossing the extended third, fourth, and fifth fingers. Recite the mantra, and see that all of the obstacles created by my actions is destroyed by the light of the Vajra.

> Hail vajra deeds washed clean
> by the all-encircling protector!
> One with the true Buddha, Hum!

Touch the mudra to the right ear, and visualize a great lotus, symbol of compassion, to fill the heart and cleanse it of all karmic remains, and obstacles to enlightenment.

G. Achieving Enlightenment. Leave the little fingers and thumbs extended and touching, while folding down the index, third, and fourth fingers over the knuckles. Touch the left side of the head, completing the second stage of the Vajra meditation with an *abhiseka* or consecration of the self by anointing with Vajra light. See a moon with a lotus inside pass into the body from the left side of the head, filled with the Lady Wisdom Vajra, a female Amida. This vision is called the moon Amida, or the Lady Amida. Recite the mantra:

> Hail, moon above, blessings given for all,
> Oh great lady Vajra, Hum!

H. Form the samadhi mudra. Precepts fulfilled, mind and heart emptied, meditate for a moment on the Rishyu-kai mandala. The meditator here pauses to gaze at the Naya Assembly, i.e., the Rishyu Kai, seeing each of the Vajra images therein to be joined in union to me, through mudra, mantra, and eidetic visualization. By the power of Aizen Vajrasattva in the center, and each of the aspects of the vajra depicted in the mandala, the four passions (desire, pleasure, love, ecstasy) are totally purified and the intellect emptied of all hindering thought. The seventeen images of the Rishyu-kai are as follows:

1. Center, Vajrasattva (Kongosatta) Pure Love.
2. East, Istvara (Yokukongo, or Ishokongo) will and intellect.
3. South, Kelikilavajra (Shokukongo) sensuous touch.
4. West, Ragavajra (Aikongo) sensual love.
5. North, manavajra (Mankongo) delight.
6. Southeast, Manojavajrini (Yokukongonyo) lady desire.
7. Southwest, Kelikilavajrini (Shokukongonyo) lady touch.

8. Northwest, Ragavajrini (Airakukongonyo) lady love.

9. Northeast, Manavajrini (Mankongonyo) lady delight.

10. Vajralasi (Kongoki Bosatsu) dance.

11. Vajramala (Kongoman Bosatsu) garland.

12. Vajragita (Kongoka Bosatsu) song.

13. Vajranrtya (Kongobu Bosatsu) dance.

14. Vajrankuca (Kongoku Bosatsu) enticement.

15. Vajrapaca (Kongosaku Bosatsu) ensnare.

16. Vajrasphota (Kongosa Bosatsu) lock.

17. Vajraveca (Kongorei Bosatsu) bell.

The meditator has now purified all thoughts, desires, sensuous attractions, and impulses for physical love. In the tradition of the mystics, the human impulses, mind, mouth, and body are filled only with love and attraction for the sacred. In the Tantric Buddhist sense, the empty, void, transcendent, other shore, symbolized by Vairocana in his/her many manifestations, is now the object of the meditator's entire attention, symbolized by the feminine aspects of the Naya world Buddhas.

Part 3. Enter the Void

In the third phase of the Vajra ritual, the meditator passes through the sixth and fifth halls of the mandala, that is, union with Vairocana and the four central Buddha images surrounding him, and comes to rest in the third hall of Puja offerings, and the second hall of pure, undefiled wisdom. The goal of the third part of the meditation is to receive an *abhiseka* ordination or consecration from Vairocana, and then empty the self totally by "giving away" the merits gained by the meditations, to enlighten all sentient beings. The process of enlightenment is clearly based on a compassion that gives away everything to totally empty the self.

I. *The Single Mudra Hall.*

The first of the meditation takes place in the Single Mudra Assembly, *Ichi-in kai*, at the top (west) of the mandala. The meditator assumes the mudra of Samadhi (Zen) meditation, fingers intertwined, palms up, thumbs touching, and the third "fire" fingers bent upward and touching the thumbs. The mudra is placed in the lap, and the vision of the stupa is seen to arise in the center of the palms. The five segments of the stupa symbolize the five signs of Buddhahood attained:

1) Square (base), awakened, earth.
2) Circle, purified, water.
3) Triangle, firmed, fire.
4) Quarter moon, pervading, wind.
5) Stupa crown, become one, space.

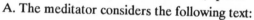

A. The meditator considers the following text:

Clearly see that all Dharma nature originates from within the mind. Worries piled upon worries, from the worldly cares and the desire to enter therein. All are a phantom, a flickering flame, like the Castle of Gandarva, or a burning wheel of fire, an echo from an empty valley. If in this Samadhi vision of self, you do not see into your own body and mind, then dwell a while in stillness and extinction, and in the end, you will know true wisdom! If indeed you can peer into the center of the void, see how all the Buddhas, numerous as sesame seeds, fill the limits of the great void realm! See one's body as proof of the ten Buddha paths; [Envision, work for, welcome, honor, call on, understand, rely on, offer to, respond to, pray to Buddha]. Dwell in the void between Dharma (mind) and reality. All of the Tathagatas of this empty realm, snap their fingers to awaken and enlighten us! Announce to all good disciples, give proof of what is awakened in you! A single path, of pure simplicity. Not even by Vajra Yoga practice, nor by all kinds of wisdom, can the above experience be attained. But do not be proud of this one experience; we must be filled with Samantabhadra's wisdom. Only then can we attain the highest true awakening, When body and mind are stilled, unmoved! From samadhi's depths we bow to the Buddhas. Hail, all ye Tathagata, Let us now bow at your feet!

B. The meditator now perceives him or herself to put on the five aspects of Vairocana, who is seated alone in the center of the One Mudra Hall:

79

1. *Penetration of the Bodhi enlightened heart-mind.*

    O practitioner, when you experience this startling awakening from Samadhi's
depths, pay universal homage (to the Vajra world) saying:

> My only wish is that all the Tathagatas
> Might manifest themselves here before me
> As I perform these Sadhana prayers and offerings.

All of the (Vajra world) responds with one voice:

> You must gaze into your own heart-mind!

And when you have heard these words,
Just as told, gaze into your own heart,
And gaze at length in a state of inner peace,
Repeatedly envision self prostrate at Buddha's feet.
Pray without ceasing to the Most Victorious Worthy,
Saying, "I do not see my own heart-mind,
For what characteristics indeed does it have?"
Then all of the Buddhas respond, saying:

> Ah, mind hard to measure, depths hard to plumb,
> Give thy heart instead these mantric seed words,
> And let it sing until it is filled with light.

Now see the heart as a full moon, and the seed word
Ah floating there, as it were, in a sea of mist.
Understand, at last, inner contemplation's source.
Hail, mind-heart piercing (Vajra), penetrate me!

2. *The Untainted Mind.*

The meditator reflects that the storehouse consciousness, by origin unstained, was pure and
clean, nothing false or evil therein. Now, if we realize the blessing of wisdom's presence in
the heart-mind kept like a pure round moon, and repeatedly perform the meditation of
emptying, what external things can ever harm us? Worry and troubles grow from words
planted within. Good and evil develop from what is held in the heart. The heart-mind
creates *Alaya* stored consciousness. Cultivate stillness, make it source of heart-mind, and
the six paramitas (charity, precepts, persevere, strength, Zen & Vipasyana) will flourish instead. Such a heart-mind will be great in its deeds. Reflect on the following:

> The storehouse consciousness, originally spotless, is pure and clean, no stain or
> falsity there. To dwell with true blessing and wisdom, is to see heart-mind as a
> pure, round moon. No substance, no distractions allowed there,
> Indeed, there is no moon there either. It is due to making blessing real for others,
> That my heart-mind is empty, like the pure full moon.

>> Skipping and dancing, the heart is filled with joy.
>> Repeatedly it sings to the heavenly worthies.
>> Now I have indeed seen my heart-mind.
>> It is pure and clean, like a full, round moon.
>> Leaving all worries, troubles, impurity,
>> Able to control all that mind holds and controls,

All the Buddhas respond to me, saying:

Your heart originally was like this, but when

It sojourned in the world's dust, it vanished.

The awakened heart-mind is a pure heart.

When you envision your heart as a pure full moon,

Then you will know the Buddha's enlightened mind.

Again We give you a heart-mind mantra;

Secretly recite it, while contemplating within.

Hail heart-mind enlightened! Arise from within me.

3. *Envision the Stupa.*

The meditator now puts on Vairocana's firm and strengthened Bodhi heart-mind. First, envision the stupa, as follows:

a. Vairocana Buddha, center section, as the seed word VAM:

b. Vajrasattva section, bottom or east sector, seed word HUM:

c. Ratna (Jewel) sector, south or left side, seed word TRAH:

d. Lotus or Amida sector, top or west side, seed word HRIH:

e. Amogha Action section, north or right side, seed word AH:

This vision is called a *samaya* or symbolic Vajra stupa, and it is kept in mind as the verse and mantra are recited:

Now that you can see the heart as a moon disk,

Round and full, glowing and radiating light,

All the Buddhas respond to the vision and say:

The Bodhi heart-mind, strengthen it!

Again let us teach you a heart-mind mantra;

See a circular Vajra stupa,

Like a moon-orb above the heart.

Inside the wheel revolves a seed word, Vam!

It becomes a Dharma wheel stupa.

Now once more intone the mantra: "Hail firm Vajra-lotus stupa!"

As the mantra is intoned, envision that the seed word *Vam* is implanted firmly in the center of the Vajra and Lotus stupa, making them one.

4. *Pervading fragrance.* My body becomes the stupa.

The fourth aspect of Vairocana is the all pervading fragrance of the Vajra-lotus, which spreads like a wind throughout the cosmos.

O thou meditator, now one with the moon orb,

Envision therein an eight petaled lotus.

Let it fill the entire Dharma world, everywhere,

So that there is only one great lotus blossom.

Now realize that your own body, with the Vajra

World's wisdom and Lotus World's reason, is one.

Form the lotus mudra with the left and right hands to symbolize a lotus blossom opening. Revolve the mudra three times to the right, and recite the mantra:

Hail! Spread everywhere, Vajra Stupa!

a. Visualize that the stupa and my body are one. See the lotus in the center of the moon inside my body turn into a stupa, that swells and fills the entire Dharma world.

b. See all of the Buddhas who fill the Lotus and Vajra worlds enter my my body. My body now glows with an effervescent light, the brilliance of which illumines the entire world and its myriad phenomena.

> Hail Vajra Stupa, my body! Vam!

c. Shrink the stupa. Envision the one great stupa that fills the entire world to become small again, the size of my body. See that all of the Buddhas of the void, empty space world also shrink with the stupa, and become part of my body. Recite the mantra :

> Hail vajra stupa, shrink!

5. The fifth aspect, *my body and Vairocana are one*.

Form the Great Sword mudra, the symbol of Vairocana. Then chant the following:

> I am the stupa body, resplendent on high, without limits.
> Again and again, all the Buddhas say it!
> I have become the Lotus body!
> Now is the time that all the Tathagatas
> Urge us on to the path of enlightenment.
> Envision my oun body to be the Honzon (Vairocana).
> Again, see myself, one with the stupa,
> Change and become the Great Vairocana!
> On my head is the five diadem crown,
> Dwelling within the symbolic mudra.
> Again we teach this mantric summons:
> Hail, All ye Tathagatas, See!
> I and Thou now are made one!

See the vajra-lotus stupa change and become Vairocana Buddha, head crowned with the five jeweled crown, body ornately adorned, hands held in the mudra of Vairocana (see illustration). The meditator should now envision the central hall of the Vajra Mandala, seeing how Vairocana extends the light issuing outward from this mudra to all the beings of the mandala, and the entire cosmos. (See explanation below Chap. 3, part 4).

II. *Embrace the Buddhas of the Four Mudra Hall.*

The meditator now enters the Hall of the Four Mudra Assembly, and puts on or assumes the characteristics of the four Buddhas who dwell there. The meditation is divided into two parts, this first in which the meditator embraces or "adheres to" the four Buddhas, and the second (II.B below) in which the meditator is consecrated by an *Abhiseka* crowning with flowers.

A. *Embrace Vairocana and the Four Buddhas.*

1. Embrace Vairocana. Continue to hold the Great Sword mudra of Part I.B.5 above, and while pressing this mudra to the heart, see that Vairocana is the source for the manifestation of all other Buddhas, so that by becoming Vairocana, I have fulfilled all the marks of a Buddha in myself. This fulfillment is possible by the light given by Vairocana to all sentient beings, and is due to no merits of my own. Due to the grace of Vairocana, I am able to see that the real and the phenomenal are both empty, not to be adhered to by judgment of any

sort, but simply perceived by the gaze of intuitive wisdom, i.e., *vipasyana* (jr-gwan, Jpn.: shikan 止観). See that the four Buddhas I am about to embrace emanate from Vairocana. Recite the Mantra, and press the mudra to the heart:

> Hail All Tathagatas, totally enlightened,
> Enduring Vajra, dwell here within me!

2. Embrace Vajrasattva, Buddha of the East. Vajrasattva, *Ashuku*, Buddha of the East or bottom circle of the mandala, an avatar of Acala the Unmoveable, is called forth and embraced by the seed word *Hum*. Recite the mantra:

> Hail, Vajrasattva, dwell within me! Hum!

3. Embrace Vajra Ratna, Buddha of the South. Next, embrace the Buddha of the right or south side of the Vajra Mandala, Ratna Sambhava, who is called forth the seed word *Trah*. Recite the mantra:

> Hail, Vajraratna, dwell within me, TRAH!

4. Embrace Amida, Buddha of the West. Next, embrace the Buddha of the top, or west side of the Vajra mandala, Amida, the Buddha of Immeasurable Life. Chant the mantra, Lotus Dharma made one with me:

> Hail, Vajradharma, dwell within me, Hrih!

5. Embrace Amoghasiddhi, Buddha of the North. Last, embrace the Buddha of the right or north side of the Vajra mandala, Amoghasiddhi. See Vajrakarma (i.e. Vajra deeds) inside me. Recite the mantra:

> Hail, Vajrakarma, dwell within me, Ah!

B. *The Abhiseka or consecration by crowning.*

The meditator now receives the *Abhiseka* or consecration of the self to the service of Vairocana Buddha by donning a crown.

1. Form the Vairocana sword mudra, and place this on the top center of the head, seeing self crowned and consecrated as Vairocana, and water sprinkled over the crown.

> Hail, all the Tathagata are ordained by Thee (Vairocana) Hum!

2. Form the Vajrasattva sword mudra, and touching this to the front of the head, see oneself consecrated by Vajrasattva:

> Hail Vajrasattva, ordain me, Hum!

3. Form the Vajra jewel mudra, and touch it to the right side of the head. See Vajraratna consecrate me with his crown:

> Hail, Vajraratna, ordain me, Trah!

4. Form the Dharma lotus mudra of Amida, and touch it to the back of the head. See Amida consecrate me with his crown:

> Hail, Vajra Lotus, ordain me, Hrih!

5. Form the Vajra deed mudra, and touch it to the left side of the head. See Amoghasiddhi consecrate me with his crown:

> Hail, Vajra Karma, ordain me, Ah!

III. *The Puja Offering Assembly Hall.*

The meditator now proceeds into the Hall of the Puja Offerings, to the left or south side of the Vajra mandala. Here he sees him or herself receive a flower lei from Vairocana and the four major Buddhas, while fastening the crowns on his head with mudra and mantra.

First, the individual mudra of each of the five Buddhas is formed, and while held to the heart, the mantra is recited once. Then while reciting the mantra two more times, form the thunder-vajra fist with both hands (thumb tucked into closed fist, index finger pressing thumb), and tie the crown to the front and back of the head by mime. Finally use the same thunder-vajra fist, and lay a lei garland of flowers around one's neck, as Vairocana receiving leis from the Buddhas of the four quadrants. Dissolve the mudra at the waist, when finished.

A. *The Flower Crowns.*

The Puja offerings are given by myself to Vairocana, and then by Vairocana to all the Buddhas of the Vajra world. Whatever I or any of the Vajra World worthies have received, must be given away for the sake of all sentient beings. I, too, must give my crown and flower wreath away, the equivalent of giving it to Vairocana. The same five mudra used in steps two and three above are formed during the recitation of the Puja offering mantra. The seed word VAM , identifying self with Vairocana, completes each of the mantra:

1. Receive a flower lay from Vairocana. "Om! Thou who ordains all Tathagata, crown me with thy flowers, Vam!"
2. "Hail, Vajrasattva, flower crown me, Vam!"
3. "Hail, Vajraratna, flower crown me, Vam!"
4. "Hail, Vajra Lotus, flower crown me, Vam!"
5. "Hail, Vajra Deeds, flower crown me, Vam!"

B. *Put on the Vajra Armor.*

In the following meditation the armor of Vajrasattva is tied to the nine places of the body by use of mudra and mantra. The meditator sees the armor attached to the body by a dark blue cord, tied to the forehead, right shoulder, left shoulder, heart, right side of chest, left side of chest, navel, right hip, and left hip respectively. The vajra armor assists me to bring saving compassion and happiness to all sentient beings by overcoming all forms of impurity, anger, resentment, envy, and selfishness. The preceding meditations of crowning and flower garlands were aimed at the interior, whereas the armor meditation strengthens us to do works of loving compassion in face of all opposition.

1. First form the Vajra armor mudra (palms upright and together, touch the index fingers to the first joint of the third fire fingers, with thumbs together and upright), and recite the mantra once. Then, while touching each of the nine places, recite the seed words *Om! Tom!* nine times. Use the extended index fingers to mime the tying of the cord, by turning them three times at each place. The word *Om* generates a blue cord, and the word *Tom* binds the armor with the cord.

In the name of all Vajras, Oh Vajra Armor, Hum! Om! Tom!

2. Vajra Clap. At this point the meditator has completely assumed the Vajra body, and claps in joy that the three vehicles (Theravada, Mahayana, and Tantrayana) all practice the Buddha's four noble truths and eightfold path equally. The Vajra assembly join the practitioner in clapping, as do the other monks who attend the Vajra liturgy. The Ajari masters in the solitudes of Mt. Hiei allow the practitioner to dance at this point, as an expression of joy while the other monks clap, and recite the mantra:

Hail, Vajra Clap, Hoh!

IV. *The Hall of Undefiled Wisdom.*

The meditator now enters the *Wei-hsi* Assembly of undefiled wisdom, the bottom left corner of the mandala assembly. Freed from passion and delusion, the meditator sees a great moon orb, which rests on an eight-petaled lotus. On the lotus throne is seated *Kongo Butcho* (Vajrasattva) in the full lotus position. In his left hand he holds the five pronged vajra bell pressed to his waist, and in his right hand a five pronged vajra pressed to his heart.

     A. Become Vajrasattva.

1. While contemplating this vision, see oneself in a state of symbolic oneness with Samantabhadra, that is, a person in whom meditation and practice are one. He or she recites the mantra, becoming one with undefiled wisdom:

        Om, Dwell in Vajra wisdom, Ah!

2. Take into one's hands the sword of undefiled wisdom:

        Hail, Vajrasattva, Ah!

3. The meditator now sees self become Vajrasattva:

        Hail, Vajrasattva, abundant joy, Ah!

     B. Perform the Four Binding Mudra.

The four binding mudra, *Jah, Hum, Bam, Koh,* are used to bind the eidetic (moving) vision to the meditator so that vision and viewer are one. In this case, the meditator is bound to Vajrasattva:

        Jah! Um! Bam! Koh! (Hook! Enter! Bound! Joy!)

     C. Prepare to Enter the Samaya Hall.

In this, the last meditation of Part Three, the meditator prepares to enter the lower, that is, the bottom center hall of the Vajra mandala, Part Four of the Vajra Mandala liturgy. First form the Wisdom Sword mudra of Samantabadhra, hands clasped in a fist with the third fingers straight up and touching. Recite the mantra, changing the vision of Vajrasattva into a symbolic image, as in the illustration:

        One with Symbol, Vam!

Then form the two vajra-thunder fists, thumbs tucked into the clenched fists, pressed down by the index fingers. Take the five pointed vajra in the right hand, and press it to the heart and the five pronged vajra bell in the left hand pressed to the hips, as in the picture of Vajrasattva. Then recite the mantra three times:

        I and symbol One! One with the great symbol!

Part 4. The Center of the Vajra

In the fourth part of the Vajra liturgy, the meditator enters the second Hall of Samaya symbols, at the bottom center of the Vajra mandala Here he/she envisions Mt. Sumeru, the center of the Buddhist cosmos. From there the meditator proceeds into the final, central hall of the Vajra world, to meditate on the grand vision of the Vajra assembly. Here Vairocana is seen in all his splendor. All of the other Buddhas and Boddhisattvas who serve him spread loving compassion and the light of saving wisdom to the entire cosmos. This fourth stage of the creative vision is the climax and high point of the Vajra mandala meditation.

I. *The Great Ocean.*

Form the Zen-Samatha mudra, open right palm over the open left palm, thumbs touching at the tips. Lay the mudra in the lap, and envision in front of the self a great ocean. The ocean is filled with fresh water made fragrant by the eight virtues (pure, cool, good tasting, soft, moistening, comforting, thirst quenching, and nourishing). In this ocean see the Vajra stupa arise, in reverse position, that is, with the space symbol on the floor of the ocean, arising through wind, water, earth, to Mt. Sumeru on top.

> A. *Envision the Vajra Stupa.*

1. See first the seed word *Ken* at the bottom of the ocean. The seed word becomes the space symbol, like the top of a stupa. Its color is that of the rainbow. Above the space cakra is the seed word *Kam*. It emanates a blue-black color, that shrinks and expands until it forms a quarter moon, symbol of the wind.

2. Next, above the wind cakra see the seed word *Vam* . It is white in color. Expanding and contracting it forms a great water cakra, circular in shape.

3. Above the water wheel now appears the seed word *Pra* . It is gold in color, and changes into a huge golden tortoise, symbol of the earth cakra. From it come forth resplendent, limitless rays of light that spread and diffuse everywhere.

4. On top of the turtle's back is the seed word *Su* , which turns into a wondrous, high mountain, adorned with the four treasures (gold, silver, gems, and crystal), which enthrone the Ruler of the Mountain (Vairocana).

5. See the seed word *Ken* on the mountain top. It changes and become seven gold peaks, surrounding Mt. Sumeru in orderly succession. The Great Ocean filled with the water of the Eight virtues surrounds the seven peaks. While contemplating this vision, separate the thumbs slightly, and move the fingers up and down, representing the waves of the ocean that move and sparkle in the light emanating from the mountains. Continue to hold the mudra at waist level, and recite the mantra:

> Hail, Pure Ocean, Hum!

> B. *Envision Mount Sumeru.*

Enclose the fingers and thumbs of both hands inside the clasped, closed fists, tucking the right thumb under the left. See this mudra to be the eight peaks of Mt. Sumeru (seven lesser peaks plus Mt. Sumeru, with Vairocana enthroned on seven lions). This image is now imprinted inside the heart of the meditator, while reciting the mantra:

> Om! Acala, Hum!

1. Contemplate the Sacred Mandala.

Now at the gateway of the central part of the Mandala, the meditator envisions the Vajra stupa that stands atop Mt. Sumeru. The hands are again formed in the Samadhi mudra, open palms with fingers intertwined on the lap, thumb-tips touching. See a wondrously high mountain, on the summit of which is a stupa made up of the five seed words, *Vam, Hum, Trah, Hrih, and AH*. See the stupa become a great palace, with four massive corners and four great gates at its base. See the ornate decorations that fill the interior of the palace.

2. Again, envision the exterior of the pavilion to be studded with all sorts of gems, bells, and precious ornaments, sparkling so brightly as to dim the splendor of the sun and moon.

3. Contemplate the Mandala Center, i.e., now envision the central hall of the Vajra Mandala. Within the great palace atop Mt. Sumeru is a great mandala, the center of the Vajra world. In the very center of the mandala is the seed word *Shin*𑀉, to the left and right of which are the seed words *Ah*𑀉 . The seed words change, and become a throne made of eight lions. Over the lions is a full moon, inside of which is a lotus throne. On the throne is the seed word *Vam*𑀉 , brilliant white in color. The word changes and becomes a stupa. The stupa then changes and becomes the Great Vairocana. His body is the color of the moon. On his head he wears the Five Buddha Jewel crown, and his body is clothed in the finest silk, adorned with splendid jewels. His hands form the "dwelling in wisdom" mudra, i.e., the upright index finger of the right hand is enclosed   between the thumb and index fingers of the left hand. Light emanates from the mudra.

4. A brilliant light also diffuses everywhere from the forehead of Vairocana. It spreads outward and fills the ten directions, i.e., the entire world without measure. Bright light flows everywhere from the body of Vairocana as well, from the chest, left and right shoulders, and back, in all four directions. A blue light shines from the front, gold from the right, red from the left, and rainbow colors from behind.

5. Embrace the Sacred Cakra of the Mandala Center.

Form the *Jah! Hum! Bam! Hoh*! mudra, embracing the entire cakra of the Mandala center. Then, while maintaining the last *Hoh* aspect of the mudra, lift the entwined fingers to the mouth and drink from the mudra, to symbolize the interiorization of the entire mandala center.

Hail, Vajra Cakra, Hum!

Jah! Hum! Bam! Hoh! (Hook, enter, bind, Joy!

6. Envision the entire central portion of the mandala, with each of the five central Buddhas seated on a special throne:

a. *Vam*, Vairocana, is seated on an eight lion throne.

b. *Hum*, Ashuku, is seated on a vajra throne.

c. *Trah*, Ratna, is seated on a horse-like throne.

d. *Hrih*, Amida, is seated on a pheasant throne.

e. *Am*, Amoghasiddhi, is seated on a latticed jewel throne.

> C. *Envision the Central Hall of the Vajra*.

See that the central Vajra hall is made up of three squares that enclose a circle, inside of which are five smaller circles. Four of these internal circles surround the central circle of Vairocana to the west (top), south (left), east (bottom), and north (right). To arrive at the central hall of the mandala, the meditator moved from square nine in the bottom right hand corner of the greater mandala, in a counter-clockwise direction, to square one in the center. Now the motion is reversed. The shining light from Vairocana, and the giving aspects of all the Buddha and Boddhisattva are sent outwards, in a clockwise direction. The figures in the central hall of the Vajra World are listed below (see illustration).

A. Vairocana, in the center of the assembly, is surrounded by the four paramita or connecting Buddhas:

a. Vajraparamita, who gives to Aksobhya [B] in the east;

b. Ratnaparamita, who gives to Ratnasambhava [C] in the south;

c. Dharmaparamita, who gives to Amida [D] in the west;

d. Karmaparamita, who gives to Amoghasiddhi [E] in the north.

B. Aksobhya, in the lower circle of the east gives light to the northeasterly direction through four Boddhisattva:

1. Vajrasattva, Boddhisattva of enlightenment, west;

2. Vajraraja, King of the Vajra Boddhisattva, north;

3. Vajraraga, Boddhisattva of love, south;

4. Vajrasadhu, Boddhisattva of joy, east.

C. Ratnasambhava, to the right or south of center gives light to the south and east through four Boddhisattva:

5. Vajraratna, Boddhisattva of precious gems, north;

6. Vajratejas, Boddhisattva of light, east;

7. Vajraketu, Boddhisattva of the banner, west;

8. Vajrahasu, Boddhisattva of the kind smile, south.

D. Amida (Lokecvaraja) of the top or west of center gives light to the southwest, through four Boddhisattva:

9. Vajradharma, Boddhisattva of the Law, east;

10. Vajratiksna, Boddhisattva of benefit for all,south;

11. Vajrahetu, Boddhisattva of causation, north;

12. Vajrabhasa, Boddhisattva of speech, west.

E. Amoghasiddhi, to the right or north of center, gives light to the north and west through four Boddhisattva:

13. Vajrakarma, Boddhisattva of deeds, south;

14. Vajraraksa, Boddhisattva who defends us, west;

15. Vajrayaksa, Boddhisattva teeth, east;

16. Vajrasamdhi, Boddhisattva fist, north.

F. The four corners of the inner circle of the mandala picture the lady Boddhisattva who bring puja-offerings to Vairocana:

a.2 Vajralasi, Boddhisattva of happiness, southeast;

b.2 Vajramala, Boddhisattva of adorned hair, southwest;

c.2 Vajragita, Boddhisattva of song, northwest;

d.2 Vajranrtya, Boddhisattva of dance, northeast.

G. The four corners of the inner square depict the four elements that surround and protect the *space* center of the circle. These are: I. Privithi, spirit of earth, seen as a female figure in the lower right corner; II. Agni, spirit of fire, in the lower left corner; III. Varuna the water spirit in the upper left corner, with nine dragon-like serpents in the coiffure; and IV. Vayu, spirit of wind, in the upper right corner.

H. The four corners of the second square depict the four Boddhisattva of external puja offerings to Vairocana:

a.3 Vajradhupa, Boddhisattva of burning incense, southeast;

b.3 Vajrapuspa, Boddhisattva of flower offerings, southwest;

b.3 Vajraloka, Boddhisattva of the Lamp, northwest;

b.4 Vajragandha, Boddhisattva of powder incense, southwest.

I. The second square also depicts the four Boddhisattva who assist Vairocana in the four directions, as follows:

a.4 Vajrankuca, Vajra Hook Boddhisattva, bottom, east;

b.4 Vajrapaca, Vajra Cord Boddhisattva, left, south;

c.4 Vajrasphota, Vajra Lock Boddhisattva, top, west;

d.4 Vajraveca, Vajra Bell Boddhisattva, right, north.

N.B. The Tendai version of this second square adds four images to each of the four sides of the hallway. The images are seen in clockwise order (right to left) from the lower northeast corner:

East quarter: Maitreya, Amogha Seer, Evil Destroyer, Stop Sorrow;

South: Incense Elephant, Vigor, Space Storehouse, Wisdom Banner;

West: Amida, Wisdom Protector, Light Net, Pure Moonlight Buddha;

North: Endless Wisdom, Manjusri, Vajra Storehouse, Samantabadhra.

J. In the spaces between these eight Boddhisattva of the second square are depicted the 1,000 Buddhas of the *Bhadrakalpa*, i.e., the Buddhas of past, present, and future who represent the innumerable transformations of Vairocana inside each one of us.

K. Finally, the third or outer square of the central assembly hall depicts the twenty spirits of the Vedic religion, whose images are shared with the folk religions of East Asia. The twenty figures, starting from the bottom right hand corner and proceeding clockwise (right to left), five to a side, are as follows:

1. Narayana, (Naraenden)

2. Kumara, (Kumaraten)

3. Vajrachinna, (Kongozaiten)

4. Brahman, (Bonten)

5. Indra, Cakra, (Taishakuten)

6. Aditya, (Nitten, Sun spirit)

7. Candra, (Gatten, Moon spirit)

8. Vajrabhaksana, (Kongojikiten)

9. Ketu, (Suiseiden)

10. Pingala, (Keiwakuten)

11. Raksasa, (Rasetsuten)

12. Vayu, (Futen, Wind spirit)

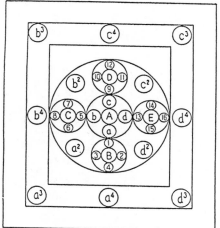

13. Vajravasin, (Kongoeten)

14. Agni, (Katen, Fire spirit)

15. Vaisravana, (Bishamonten)

16. Vajramukha, (Kongomenten)

17. Yama, (Enmaten)

18. Jaya, (Jobukuten)

19. Vinayaka, (Binayakaten)

20. Varuna, (Suiten, Water spirit)

    The four corners of the outer square depict the four great light kings, Acala (northeast), Yaksa (southeast), Kundalin (southwest), and Yamantaka (northwest). Vajra symbols surrounded with flames separate each of the figures in the outer square. The Buddhas and Boddhisattvas of the central assembly hall are each to be encountered in the next stages of the Vajra meditation.

Part 5. Give Away all Merit

The fifth section of the Vajra meditation is taken for the most part from the Eighteen Path mandala, as seen in Chapter I above. The following meditations and hymns are special to the Vajra ritual.

A. *Public Invitation to all the Assembly to Enter.*
See self as Vajrasattva formally inviting all of the worthies of the Assembly to enter the banquet hall. The entire assembly of the Central Hall is invited by a lengthy poem in siddham sanskrit meter called *Indra-vajra Upenda-vajra.* The meditator sees all of the Buddhas of the center Assembly, including the myriad Badhrakalpa Buddhas of the second square hall, float into the sacred area on clouds.

B. *The 108 Songs* for the Buddhas of the Vajra Center.
A song is sung for each of the worthies as they enter, consisting of eight phrases, four lines to a hymn.

C. *The meditator offers all of the gifts* emanating from Vairocana to the entire cosmos. The gifts are first collected by the offering is done by the four binding mudras:
1. See compassionate love grasped from within one's heart, and with joy offer it to others.
> Vajra Hook, Jah!
2. See the understanding of the Vajra world enter the mind of all others.
> Vajra bonds, Hum!
3. See that all of the benefits deriving from the Vajra Ritual meditation are not mine, but belong to Vairocana. They must be totally given away for the sake of all others. See also that I must break away from all selfish thoughts and deeds, to live as Vairocana.
> Vajra break the lock, Bam!
4. See that I am indeed one with Vairocana. Henceforth my life must be given entirely to Vairocana, in compassion and love for others.
> Vajra Joy, Hoh!

D. *Vajra Clapping.* The meditator now envisions him or herself offering a dance and clapping the hands in front of the assembly, as an expression of happiness and rejoicing. The hands are clapped and the mantra is recited three times:
> Om, Vajra clapping, Hoh, Hoh, Hoh!

E. *Offer pure Aka water to the assembly.* Pick up the bowl of pure *Aka* water, and offer it to the assembly to drink. The water here symbolizes the leveling or equalizing of one's own nature with the Vajra world, that is, all of the impurities and instabilities of phenomenal nature are washed clean and dissolved in the Aka water. The water is also symbolic of the sprinkling rite of ordination, *Kancho* that consecrated me totally to Vairocana.
> Water be purified, Hum! Phat!
1. The water is then offered first to Gozanze, then to all of the worthies. While holding the water in front of the three places, head, heart level, and belly, intone the Mantra:
> Hail, Nisumbha Vajra, Hum!
> May this water, originally pure at its source,
> Wash us all, make our bodies pure and stainless.

So that we never abandon the original vows,
Let this (water) be proof of duty fulfilled.
Hail, Vajra Water, Trah! Hum!

2. Next, put the water bowl back in its place, and form the mudra which symbolizes a universal water offering; fold the four fingers of both hands down over the thumbs, and repeat the mantra three times, seeing that all of my vows are fulfilled for eternity.

Hail Vajra Water, Trah! Hum!

F. *The Lotus Throne.*

Next, the meditator offers a beautiful, fully opened lotus to Gozanze (Nisumbha) and the entire multitude. See a fully opened pink lotus held in the hands. While forming the Open Lotus mudra, recite the mantra and offer the lotus:

Om, Open Lotus, Svaha!

G. *Ring the Vajra bell.*

1. The meditator now visualizes him or herself to be Samantabhadra, with a five pronged vajra in the right hand, and a five pronged vajra bell in the left. Fold the thumb of the both hands under the closed fist. Put left fist to waist, and touch the five places with the right fist, belly, heart, both shoulders, throat, and head, while reciting the mantra:

Om, Vajra Hand, Hum!

2. Next, bend the left hand downward from the wrist, fingers extended, imitating the ringing of a bell. Hold the right hand (vajra fist mudra) against the heart, and press the thumb of the left hand inward, ringing the bell three times while reciting:

Om, Vajra Bell, ring! HOH!

H. *Invite the Assembly to give offerings.*

Form the Vajra-anjali clasped hands mudra, and invite the assembly to attend the banquet. See that eight lady Boddhisattva respond to this summons, that is, the four internal puja Boddhisattva, and the four external puja Boddhisattva, (pages 21-23 above). The meditator here sees the eight lady Boddhisattva to awaken, and prepares for the next two visualizations:

1. The Puja-offerings of the Eight Boddhisattva.

a. Vajra Lassie Boddhisattva offers a smile.

b. Vajra Coiffure offers a splendid colored crown.

c. Vajra Songstress offers music.

d. Vajra Dancer fills the body with the Buddha's joy.

e. Incense Boddhisattva offers burning incense.

f. Flower Boddhisattva offers blossoms and fruit.

g. Lamp Boddhisattva offers light to the world.

h. The Ointment Boddhisattva offers powder incense.

I. *The Grand Offering of Food and Drink.*

The meditator envisions the Buddha of the West, Amida, to bring all sorts of flowers, incense, adornments, clothes, garlands, fronds, and branches to Vairocana and all sentient beings as offerings. The meditator sees that he or she too must offer these things to all sentient beings. The ritual follows the food offerings of the Eighteen Path mandala. The offerings conclude with the following prayer:

Today I offer this universal puja,
Each and every particle of dust,
All real (事) and phenomenal (理) things.
The real and phenomenal everywhere
are the entire Dharma ocean.
The Dharma ocean is in fact the total puja offering.
      The offering of self and others,
The four-fold Dharma body
(Self-born, received, transformed, one with Vairocana)
The Three Worlds (past, present, future)
Are equally an eternal offering.
Willing or unwilling, we are all bound together, one,
Self and others firmly residing
In the hidden storehouse of tantric treasure.

J. *The Hundred Word Mantra is sung to the Vajra.*

Hail Vajra Stupa, symbol of union, protect us!
Hail Vajra nature, be always present in me!
Let thy marvels be born in me,
Let thy love be present in me,
Fill me with thy nourishing presence,
Let all thy wondrous powers be granted to me,
Let all thy deeds, heartful blessings, be done by me,
Ha! Ha! Ha! Hoh!
Oh honored stupa, all Tathagata, never abandon me,
Lady Vajra born! To this great union awakened!

This ends part five of the Vajra meditation.

Part 6. Concluding the Vajra Meditation

I. The Sixth Stage: *Enter Samadhi*.

The sixth stage of the Vajra Mandala meditation, as in the Eighteen Path, Goma, and Lotus World rituals, consists in quiet contemplative experience of Samadhi meditation. The meditator assumes the position of Zen meditation, i.e., hands folded with palms up in the lap, thumbs touching. The heart-mind is envisioned as a huge full moon, in the center of which is a lotus. On top of the lotus is a seed word, the vision of which depends upon the specific meditation. Thus the Word *Ah* is used in the Eighteen Path and the Lotus Mandala, while the words *Ah* with *Kham* are used in the Goma. Here the word *Vam* is to be envisioned, which changes successively into Vairocana, the Vajra stupa, and then fills the entire Dharma world.

The ritual follows the order of the Samadhi meditation in the Eighteen Path Mandala, with the following changes.

A. *The meditation of Samadhi*.

1. See the seed word *Vam* atop a Lotus in a great moon disk. The seed word swells and becomes the vajra stupa, with the five seed words *Vam, Hum, Trah, Hrih, Ah*. This stupa swells and fills the entire Dharma world, and my body as well. It then changes into the form of Vairocana, with the five Buddha gems in the crown, body finely adorned, and the hands held in the vajra-wisdom mudra.

2. See that due to the power of Vairocana, through the seed words and vision before me, that words and speech must not be held onto (*Vam*), that the defilements of our deeds, good and bad, are washed away and purified (*Hum*), that the only treasure we have is the treasure of emptiness (*Trah*), and that emptying is possible only through compassion and giving (*Hrih*). Finally see that true bodhi enlightenment is due to the non-arising of deeds, attachments, and Dharma (*Ah*). Thus the work of Vairocana to enlighten all sentient beings by compassion is indeed my work.

B. *The Buddha Eye mantra*:

Chant the Mantra in Honor of Buddha Locana, as follows:

> In the name of all Buddhas, Ken!
>
> Void gift, most wonderful sign of union with the void,
>
> All unveiling strength, thine Eyes shine forth light,
>
> In Amoghavajra's name, Svaha!

This ends part six of the Vajra meditation.

II. *The Seventh Stage*.

The seventh and last stage of the Vajra mandala meditation is from the last stage of the Eighteen Path liturgy. The following additions are made to the concluding steps of the ritual, as described in Part One.

A. *Farewell to Each Hall of the Vajra Assembly*.

Hold the five pronged vajra, incense burner, and beads in the right hand, and strike the chime with the mallet in the right hand, while reciting a farewell to each part of the Vajra:

1. Farewell to the Three Worlds, Heavenly Multitude, may your joy in the Dharma ever increase! (strike the gong for each name).

2. Farewell to the Vajra World Mandala.

Form the Gozanze mudra, by crossing right hand over left, hooking the little fingers, and extending the index fingers like Gozanze's teeth. Recite the mantra and revolve the mudra to the left three times:

> Hail, Sumbha Nisumbha, Hum!
>
> Grrr! Grrr! (Out all evil) Hum!
>
> Kick out all evil, Hum!
>
> Forever and ever, Hoh!
>
> Honored Vajra, Hum! Farewell!

3. Dissolve the Vajra World mandala.

Form the Great Sword mudra, third fingers touching, bent at the top joint, index fingers extended, and recite the mantra to dissolve each of the nine assemblies:

> Om! Vajra! Muh!

4. See off the Assemblies.

Again form the Great Sword mudra. Hold a lotus bud, or a keman painted lotus leaf between the extended and tightly pressed third fingers. Kneel on the right knee to recite the mantra, and throw the petal into the air, feeling sorrow and regret at seeing off the assembly. Recite:

> May I hereby take all thy victorious merits,
>
> And give them away to all sentient beings,
>
> I only beg Thee, each holy one return to thy kingdom,
>
> Do not forget your original vow, to come back again!

5. Transfer the Merits to all sentient beings:

> Om! For the sake of all sentient beings,
>
> May these merits be transferred to all!
>
> Mandala dissolved, each return to their Buddha realm,
>
> Come again, Yea! O thou Stupa enlightened, farewell!

6. Farewell to each of the Five Central Buddhas.

Form the mudra for each of the five Buddhas, and recite the mantra of farewell, as follows:

   a.   Vairocana. The Great Sword mudra.

> Hail, Thou who enlightens all Tathagata,
>
> Dwell within me, Vajracitta!

   b.   East, Aksobhya:

> Hail, Vajrasattva, dwell within me, Hum!

   c.   South, Ratnasambhava:

> Hail Vajra Jewel, dwell within me, Trah!

   d.   West, Amida:

> Hail, Vajra Dharma, dwell within me, Hrih!

   e.   North, Amoghasiddhi:

> Hail, Vajra Deeds, dwell within me, Ah!

7. Homage to the *Abhiseka* crowning of the Five Buddhas.

Again form the mudra proper to each of the Five Buddhas, and touch it to the head while reciting the mantra:

a. Vairocana: who ordained all Tathagata in light, Hum!

b. Aksobhya: Hail, Vajrasattva who crowned me, Hum!

c. Ratnasambhava: Hail, Jewel who crowned me, Trah!

d. Amida: Hail, Vajra Dharma who crowned me, Hrih!

e. Amoghasiddhi: Hail, Vajra Doer, who crowned me, Ah!

8. Untie and take off the Armor.

Untie and remove the armor that was donned on page 84, above, using the Om-ton mudra and mantra:

> Oh Precious Vajra who ordained me,
>
> All ye mudra who strengthened and fulfilled me,
>
> (Thanks) for thy Wondrous Armour, Vam! Om! Don!

Repeat the last words OM-DON twelve times, while untying and removing the armor from the twelve places.

9. Vajra Clap to express thanks and joy.

> Hail Vajra Clap, Hoh!

10. Bow to the Four Buddhas, and Exit.

> Hail, all Tathagata offerings completed,
>
> Oh Vajrasattva take my consecrated body to serve thee!
>
> Oh Vajraratna take my consecrated body to serve thee!
>
> Oh Amida take my consecrated body to serve thee!
>
> Oh Amoghasiddhi take my consecrated body for thee!

11. Bow to each hall of the Vajra Assembly, and exit through the closing steps of the Eighteen Path mandala.

12. The meditator is again reminded that the Vajra Meditation was in vain if henceforth one's life is not filled with compassion and giving to others.

The Complete Handbook of
Video

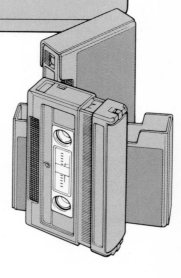

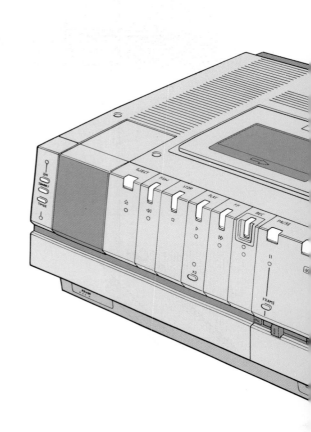

The Complete Handbook of
Video

**Everything you need to know
about video – from home
entertainment to everyday
office use**

David Owen / Mark Dunton

Penguin Books

Penguin Books Ltd., Harmondsworth,
Middlesex, England
Penguin Books, 625 Madison Avenue,
New York, New York 10022, U.S.A.
Penguin Books Australia Ltd., Ringwood,
Victoria, Australia
Penguin Books Canada Ltd., 2801 John Street,
Markham, Ontario, Canada L3R 1B4
Penguin Books (N.Z.) Ltd., 182–190 Wairau
Road, Auckland 10, New Zealand
First published 1982
Published simultaneously by Allen Lane
Copyright © Marshall Editions Ltd., 1982
Typeset by Servis Filmsetting Ltd.,
Manchester, U.K.
Reproduced by Gilchrist Bros. Ltd.,
Leeds, U.K.
Printed and bound in Belgium by Brepols S.A.

Edited and designed by
Marshall Editions Ltd
71 Eccleston Square
London SW1V 1PJ

Editor: Helen Varley
Assistant Editor: Helen Armstrong
Art Director: Paul Wilkinson
Artwork: Hayward & Martin
Retouching and Make-up: Roy Flooks
Picture Researchers: Helen Armstrong;
Mary Corcoran

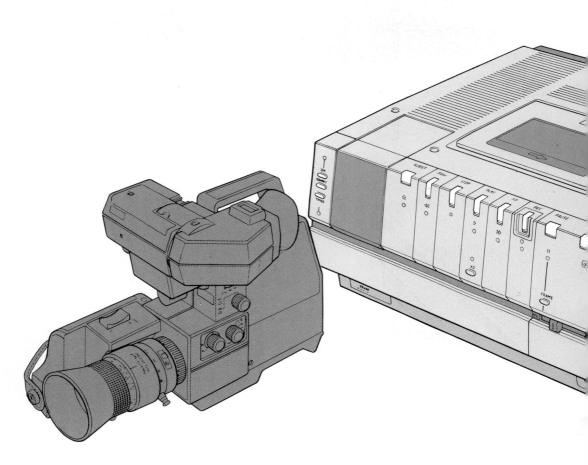

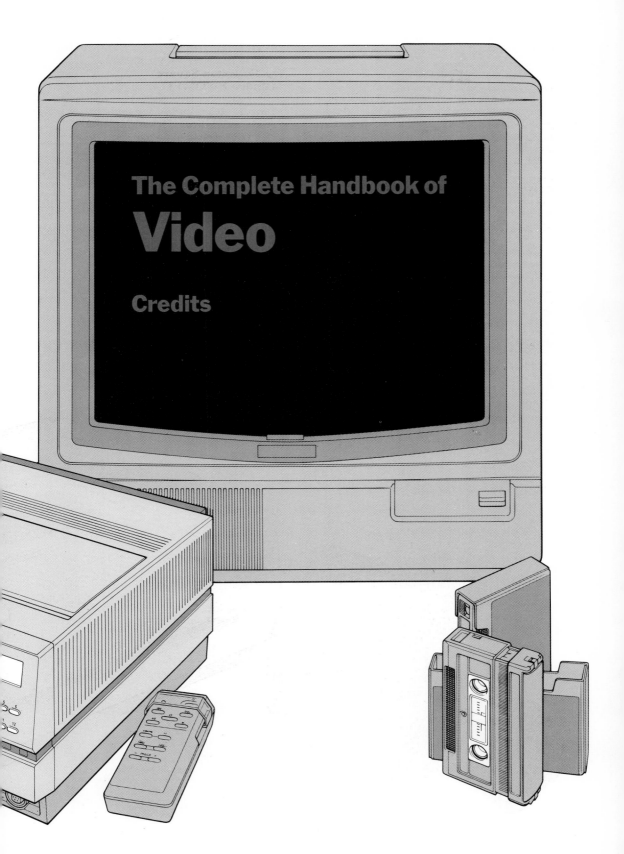

The Complete Handbook of
Video

Credits

continued overleaf —→

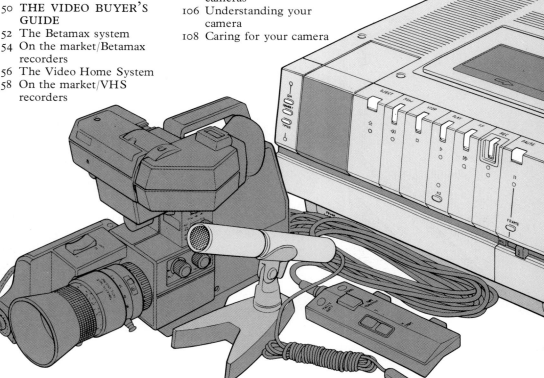

The Complete Handbook of
Video

Contents

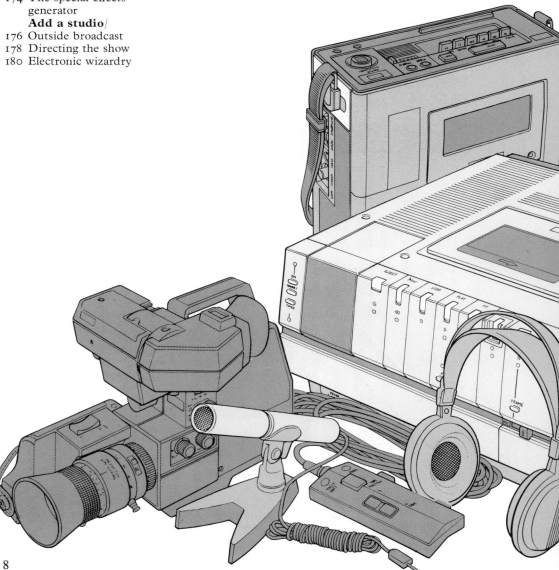

The Complete Handbook of
Video

Contents/2

9

The video user's guide

Video is a word which has become so familiar, and so fashionable, that it is all too easy to forget how recent is its impact on home entertainment. The idea of recording and playing back television pictures is as old as television: a primitive video disk was on sale in Selfridges of London in 1938.

Yet the first post-World War II experiments in recording television pictures and playing them back were not made with the domestic market in mind. The intention was to remove the stranglehold live television broadcasting imposed on the medium. Before video recording, sequences had to be shot on film, which was expensive, or they had to be transmitted live. Since broadcasting was closely tied to the evenings, this overloaded the studios and, moreover, any mistakes or hiccups in the production went out on the air immediately, giving the producer no chance to reshoot or edit them out afterwards. Repeats were impossible unless the production was shot all over again, or transferred to film.

Recording the signals which went out over the air on magnetic tape, just as in audio recording, seemed an obvious solution to the problem, but it proved amazingly difficult to achieve. To preserve a picture, vastly more complex information has to be recorded than with the highest-quality sound reproduction. Simply capturing the finer details of a picture meant a huge increase in the area of tape used to store the information. This meant, in turn, that the speed of the tape over the recording and playback heads had to be much higher than in audio recording.

After years of development, the American company Ampex produced the first working video recorders for broadcast use. These used four recording heads on a rotating drum, and two-inch (five-centimetre) wide magnetic tape. They were first shown to the public in April 1956 and used over the air at CBS's Hollywood studios seven months later.

Ever since then, more and more television has been recorded on tape, so that nowadays it is rare to see live broadcasts. The main exceptions are sports and other topical events, and even these are often recorded as they are transmitted, for later repeats or instant action replays.

Moving into the domestic market called for a much more portable system. Home recorders use narrower tape and a helical scan system. Although the first recorder using this system was patented in Germany in 1953, the prototypes were far too expensive and difficult to use. Friction between the tape and the heads meant that a tape could be used only once, and that every time it was used the machine had to be cleaned of tape particles.

Home video arrived in 1972, when the first cassette systems were produced: the original Philips VCR, still to be found in schools and colleges, and Sony's U-matic format, followed later by Sony's Betamax and the even more commercially successful VHS format, which used narrow half-inch (19 millimetre) tape. As the size of the tape became smaller, the cost of both recording and recorders fell quite dramatically and the stage was set for one of the biggest consumer booms of all time.

In most of Europe, sales of video equipment come second only to television sales, overtaking washing machines, radios, refrigerators, freezers and music centres. In 1980 a quarter of a million video cassette recorders (VCRs) were sold; this is rapidly rising to the million a year mark. The largest markets for video are in America and Japan where, by the end of the seventies, more than a million and a half recorders were sold each year.

Its versatility is one of the reasons for video's rapid success. Not only can a VCR be used for recording shows off air, and playing them back at any time, but ever more sophisticated timers, and the ability to record the picture broadcast on one channel while watching a different channel, make a video recorder a powerful aid to getting the best from television.

Video's other trump card is the ability to play back pre-recorded tapes from the fast-expanding choice on the market. Since most pre-recorded tapes cost considerably more to produce than the average audio album, they cost proportionately more to buy, but can be rented or borrowed.

So far and so fast has video come in the last decade that any predictions on future uses and markets are almost bound to be overtaken by reality. New developments, such as cable and satellite television, will add to the choice of material available for recording, and ever more sophisticated cameras, recorders and

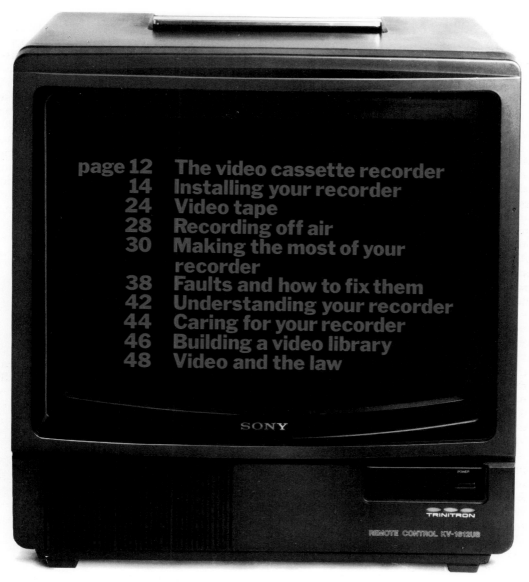

accessories will, in time, begin to rival the technical quality and flexibility of broadcast television.

Yet there is still a technical barrier between many television viewers and the video revolution. In Europe, technical know-how generally falls short of the level needed to operate video hardware with ease. Many a television addict, attracted by the storage capabilities of the VCR, finds it hard to choose from the glut of machines on the market. Those who solve the problem by renting may remain unaware that these expensive machines can do much more than memorize television for replay at a more convenient viewing time.

The next few pages attempt to overcome this technofear by bridging the technical gap. They analyze the basics of a video cassette recorder, and evaluate the trimmings. They explain where and how to install a video system, how it works and how to look after it. The most complex operations, such as tuning and timing, are analyzed.

By the time you reach the end you will know enough to read technical brochures with ease, and you may even begin to read the video press in order to keep up to date.

The video cassette recorder

The video cassette recorder (VCR) is the heart of a home video system. After the television set it is likely to be your first acquisition and it will certainly be more expensive. Whether you rent or buy, and whichever of the home video systems you eventually decide upon, all the machines you will consider having in your home have certain functions and facilities in common.

A VCR is designed to record sound and pictures in both black and white and colour on magnetic tape, and then to replay them when required. There are portable models, and home decks run from the electricity supply. These contain a tuner to enable the machine to record signals received from the antenna. The material recorded can then be played back on an ordinary domestic colour television set. You can also record one show using the VCR's tuner while you watch another station using the television's tuner.

All VCRs have a digital clock, and associated with it, a timer so that a show can be recorded when you are in bed or away from the house.

VCRs will play back tapes recorded on other machines as long as they are compatible. There are three different home video systems, or formats, currently available: VHS, Betamax and Video 2000. Each format will record only on tapes designed for it.

If your VCR and those of your friends are compatible, you can borrow and lend tapes you have recorded, or videograms (prerecorded tapes). These are expensive, but there are video libraries from which you can borrow cassettes of old and popular movies, educational or sports tapes, usually in VHS and Betamax, if not in all three formats. Prerecorded tapes have been available in VHS and Betamax for some time, and are now becoming available for the new and expanding Video 2000 format.

Some features, such as a footage counter which shows how much tape has been used, are standard on all VCRs. Others, such as fast picture search – the video equivalent of fast forward on an audio cassette recorder – have been available on the more expensive models, but are now appearing on budget machines. The more sophisticated facilities offered on the luxury models may seem confusing at first; they are hardly essential to the basic functioning. However, it is as well to be fully conversant with all these facilities

before you decide on a VCR because some of the apparently gimmicky extras may be just what you need.

For instance, if you always fall asleep during a movie, a warning buzzer to tell you when the the show is over might be a good idea. If you hate commercials, you need a remote control to fade them out. If you go away on business for weeks at a time, you need a sophisticated timer to keep up with your favourite television serials, but if you want a VCR to watch movies with your friends, and record television shows to watch later, a basic machine is all you require.

The Toshiba V-8600B, illustrated here, is a luxury Betamax model that offers a wide selection of the features currently available.

The 'Function' switch, 3, enables you to select manual or automatic (timer) use. When it is switched off, the signal from the antenna passes through to the TV set for normal viewing. When the 'Function' switch is set to 'On' the light above it illuminates.

When the 'Timer' switch, **4,** is pressed, the lamp below it illuminates and the VCR will begin recording at the time pre-set in the timer compartment, **2.** On this machine you can pre-set start and stop times.

On many machines, the power indicator light (above the 'Function' switch on this machine) will switch off when the 'Timer' switch is on.

All VCRs have a 24-hour clock, **5,** which can display pre-set recording times. This panel can display more information, including time left on the tape, or a warning that you have not yet loaded a cassette.

A recorded tape will never replay perfectly on any machine other than the one on which it was recorded. The 'Tracking' knob, **6,** will minimize interference if you play a borrowed cassette.

When the 'TV/VTR' switch, **7,** is set to the TV mode, you can watch one TV channel while recording another.

Into this panel you can connect a mike, **9;** an audio input, **10;** a camera, **11;** and a remote control, **12.**

Switch on your VCR by pressing the 'Mains' or 'Power' switch. This is usually located on the back panel, **1**, but may be in the position occupied by the 'Function' switch, **3**.

On this VCR, the 'Function' switch must also be pressed before the machine will record.

Only the most advanced home decks have an input socket for a video camera, so consider buying a portable deck (called a portapack) if you intend making home movies. A video camera, unlike a film camera, is not loaded with film. Instead, the picture is transmitted along a cable to the portapack and recorded on a video cassette.

Portapacks are battery powered, and more compact than home decks. The RCA SelectaVision 170, weighs 11 lb (about 5 kg). If you buy a tuner/timer unit it can be used to record broadcast TV

and to run from the home electricity supply. It has all the features of a good home deck, including a high-speed picture search, slow-motion playback and remote control.

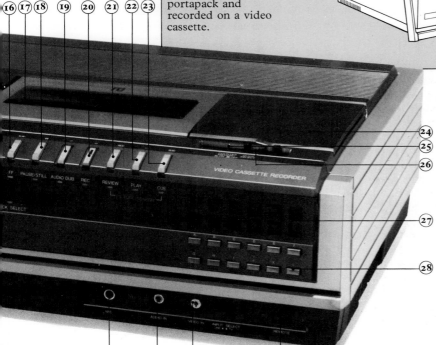

The **'Record' button, 20**, is usually operated together with the 'Play' button, **22**, to start recording. On this machine each controls a different function.

In the tuning compartment, 24, are controls for tuning each VCR channel to the locally available stations. Once the VCR is tuned in, the selector buttons, **28**, can be used to select a pre-tuned channel, and the appropriate indicator light, **27**, identifies it.

Most VCRs now have a picture search facility. This sophisticated machine has two: 'Cue', **23**, accelerates the tape forward and 'Review', **21**, reverses it, while retaining an image on the screen.

The 'Dew Indicator Lamp', 8, is a safety device not found on all machines. It warns that all functions have temporarily ceased because moisture has accumulated on the tape heads.

'Rewind', 14; 'Stop', 15; and 'Fast-Forward', 16; function as on an audio recorder. The tape disengages from the heads when 'Stop' is pressed.

The cassette-holder, 17, on a top-loading VCR rises when the 'Eject' button, **13**, is pressed. It may be spring-loaded or hydraulically operated, but has to be pressed down once the tape is in the holder.

Front-loading holders have a dust flap that folds away as the tape is pushed in, then closes over it.

'Pause', 18, stops the tape while keeping it in contact with the heads. This gives a still picture in playback, or temporarily interrupts a recording.

Press the 'Audio dub' button, 19, to record over a pre-recorded cassette using a mike. This automatically erases the previous recording.

The tape counter, 25, can be reset by a button, **26**, to 0000 at the beginning of a tape so that the starts and finishes of different shows can be noted.

13

Siting the recorder

If you are to get the best results from your VCR, it is worth while giving some consideration to its location in a room. Like all electronic devices, a VCR likes a dry, well-ventilated environment. Excessive heat or dust can damage its delicate circuits and precise moving parts.

Since information is recorded magnetically on video tape, stray magnetic fields can corrupt it. Recordings can suffer if the VCR or cassettes are placed too close to other machines with strong magnetic fields, such as audio recorders or stereo speakers. These have particularly virulent magnetic fields, which increase with the volume of sound. If possible, locate them at least two feet (60 centimetres) from television, tapes and VCR.

Remember that the VCR's magnetic field can affect other components of the video system. Never keep it on top of the television. It is wise to screen one component off from another by means of shelving. As a rule of thumb, leave one foot (30 centimetres) of space between them.

Placing and operating the VCR is largely a matter of common sense and convenience. A VCR is designed to work in a horizontal position, and make sure it is horizontal, because its tolerance for functioning when misaligned is relatively low. Keep the ventilation slots clear of surfaces that might inhibit air circulation through them, and above-all, position the VCR away from sources of heat such as radiators or convector heaters.

Do not stand your VCR on a surface which will transmit vibration from other domestic appliances – such as a suspended floor, for example. Cover the machine with a dust cover when it is switched off.

Damp is the VCR's worst enemy. Keep it in a warm room and do not subject it to extremes of temperature. If it is allowed to go cold and then moved to a warm room, moisture in the air will condense on the metal drum which carries the video heads, making the tape stick to it when it begins to spin. This can damage both tape and recorder. Most VCRs have a built-in protection against moisture condensing inside the casing. Some have internal heaters, but for these to work, the VCR must be kept connected to the electricity supply.

Never put anything on top of your VCR. You could block the ventilation grilles, and damage the casing.

TV sound quality can be improved by using hi-fi loudspeakers. Never remove the back of a TV receiver to gain access to the sound section. The easiest and safest way is to connect the VCR's audio output to a hi-fi system. For best reproduction of stereo material and mono television, the speakers should be placed at least 6 ft (1.8 m) apart, so that they and the listener form an equilateral triangle.

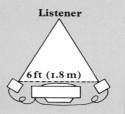

Most VCRs are top loaders. The cassette drawer opens for loading and unloading by rising about 2 in (5 cm) above the top panel. Allow for this when fitting a VCR into shelving.

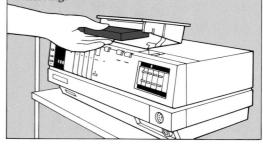

A video recorder should be near a TV receiver and antenna (aerial) input point. If you can, plug the VCR and the TV into different wall sockets to avoid the possibility of picking up an electrical hum. This can cause interference on the picture. If you want audio pick-up, the hi-fi system must also be nearby, but not on top, nor immediately adjacent to the VCR.

Postion the VCR away from doorways and other parts of the room where people walk, or reach across, and out of draughts, which may affect its performance.

Mobilize your video system with a purpose-built video cart, **1**, but beware of tripping over cables, **2**.

Trailing cables are dangerous and also untidy; keep them out of sight. Excess lengths can be wound into 12 to 15-in (30 to 40-cm) loops and secured with tape or a rubber band.

Site your video
system well away
from windows, **6**, and
fires, **3**. Direct heat
from a fire, or from
sunlight streaming
through a window,
can damage a VCR.
The rapidly changing
temperatures and
damp found near a
window will impair
the VCR's tracking
ability. If rain falls on
the VCR it can cause
a short-circuit.

Rack shelving, 4,
can be spaced to
accommodate video
system components of
unequal size, and
provides the screening
necessary to prevent
the magnetic field of,
say, a stereo speaker,
from affecting a
colour TV. Make sure
the VCR is not on top
of or touching the TV
– it should be at least
1 ft (30 cm) away.

The casing of a VCR
is pierced by
ventilation grilles
which permit free air
circulation. This is
essential because parts
of the workings heat
up with constant use.
To maintain an even
internal temperature
the grilles must be
kept clear, so make
sure there is at least a
half-inch (1.5 cm)
space around the
casing, **5**.

Never leave your
VCR on the floor.
Modern carpets, **7**,
made from artificial
fibres, can build up a
static charge which
may be transferred to
the VCR through its
ventilation grilles,
with disastrous
results. People
walking past can raise
dust which will
damage the video
heads.

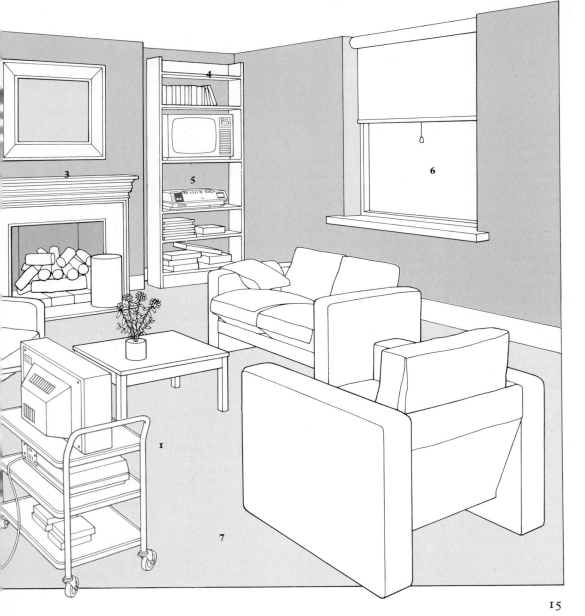

Furnishing with video

Video cabinets come in all shapes and sizes, from a simple rack to hold a VCR and a few tapes to a full console cabinet, holding the television set too. Philips make a complete home Video Centre. The custom-designed case holds a 26-inch (66-centimetre) colour television, a 6-inch (15-centimetre) black and white television monitor and a VCR.

When choosing a cabinet, consider what is to go inside. If it is to take the television set, either built-in behind doors or free-standing on top, the set's size and weight will determine the dimensions and construction. The standard size of $29\frac{1}{2}$ inches (75 centimetres) wide and $18\frac{3}{4}$ inches (45 centimetres) deep and $22\frac{1}{2}$ inches (57 centimetres) high allows for a 26-inch television, with VCR and cassette storage underneath.

Most cabinet designs allow for a reasonable distance between television tube, video motors and tape storage, to prevent the magnetic fields they set up from interacting to cause colour aberration on the tube, or partial erasure of a tape.

When making a cabinet for VCR only, the size depends on the dimensions of the particular model used. VHS and Betamax machines vary in width across the front panel from 17 inches (43 centimetres) for the smaller budget models up to nearly 20 inches (50 centimetres) for the top models. Older machines can be even larger and all Video 2000 models are over 20 inches (50 centimetres) wide. Portables, although smaller, will take up to $23\frac{1}{2}$ inches (60 centimetres) in width when side by side with a tuner. Depth will vary between 10 inches (25 centimetres) for some portables to a more normal 13 to $15\frac{3}{4}$ inches (33 to 40 centimetres) for home decks. Height also varies between 5 and 6 inches (13 and 15 centimetres) for most home decks, more for older machines, and as little as 4 inches (10 centimetres) for the newer portable machines.

Remember to leave enough hand-room at the sides to insert and remove the machine. There needs to be enough room at the back for all the leads to be plugged in without being bent too sharply, and it is important to leave enough air space for ventilation above and behind the recorder. Remember also to leave room for the mechanism to lift.

Alternatively the recorder can be placed on a sliding base, so that it pulls out sufficiently to allow access to the top loader.

Video furniture on the market ranges from shelves to add to a TV stand, to a full console cabinet with doors to match any décor, and high-tech designs with adjustable tubular aluminium supports, both free-standing or wall-mounted.

The simplest video stand is a platform, *left above*. The TV sits on top with the VCR underneath: far enough away to prevent interference.

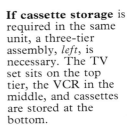

If cassette storage is required in the same unit, a three-tier assembly, *left*, is necessary. The TV set sits on the top tier, the VCR in the middle, and cassettes are stored at the bottom.

The TV video library case cabinet, *left*, is about 2 ft (60 cm) high, and will accommodate either a VCR and two tiers of cassettes, or a TV set, VCR and one tier of cassettes.

The Kee clamp can be used to build an interlocking pipe framework, in which shelves can be fixed. Different sizes of clamp are used to cope with different diameters of piping.

Rota-lock is another pipe-frame system. A chrome 'cage' holds the two pipes loosely together. A packing piece is bolted between them to make the joint rigid and safe for heavy loads.

Slotted angle, L-shaped steel sections, with a pattern of horizontal and vertical slot perforations, can easily be cut with a hacksaw, and bolted together to make a video rack.

T, X and L-shaped connectors can be screwed into the edges of flat wood panels to link them together in the form of a simple yet sturdy video storage cabinet.

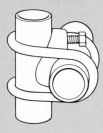
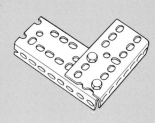
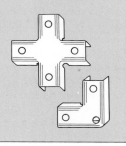

Video stands and carts, *below*, are the most versatile means of supporting video equipment. Carts run on castors and are, therefore, easily moved. The most

basic consists of a platform supported by a central column on a four-castor base, *below centre*. The platform is adjustable to take TV sets up to 39 in (100 cm) wide: the left

and right halves slide out to the required width.

The supporting column can be altered from 16 in (40 cm) to 39 in (100 cm).

Heavy-duty, two-

column designs, *below left*, should be used to support the larger TV sets, and the largest require a cart with the columns set wide apart, *below right*, for improved stability.

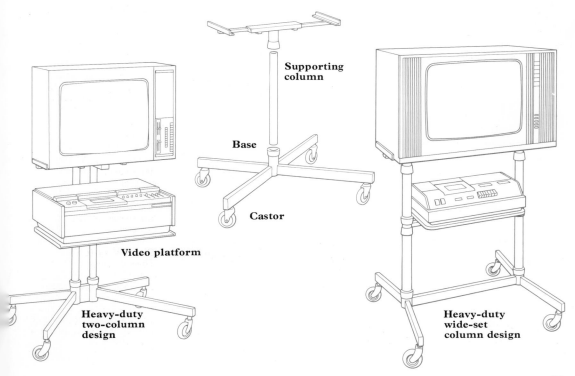

Supporting column

Base

Castor

Video platform

Heavy-duty two-column design

Heavy-duty wide-set column design

Connecting up

To connect your VCR to your television set you will need no fewer than four cables, and with each component you add to the system, the number multiplies. The AC lead powers the system; each of the other cables contributes to the flexibility, and the quality, of your video system. It is essential, therefore, that each cable is right for the job it has to do.

Why so many different kinds of cables? When the television signals which make up the picture and the accompanying soundtrack are broadcast, in order to make the journey from the transmitter to your receiving antenna, they have to be changed into very high-frequency waves.

These radio frequency (RF) signals cannot recreate the picture inside your television set in the form in which they arrive. They have to be changed back into low-frequency sound and video signals before being fed to the loudspeaker and picture tube. These same low-frequency signals are recorded on the video tape and reproduced when the recording is being played back.

This means that the input cable from the antenna must be coaxial cable (with one lead forming a central core, and the second forming a hollow tube around it) to carry the radio frequency signals from the antenna, and from the VCR, to the television set. Inside the VCR, the RF signal is converted into audio and video signals at a lower frequency for copying tape.

When the tape is played back, those signals must be converted once again into higher RF signals, so that they can be fed into the television set as if they were arriving directly from a transmitter.

This double conversion between VCR and television introduces a slight drop in quality. This is because most sets were designed simply to receive broadcast signals, and VCRs were designed to fit in with this. A television/monitor, however, can take the video and audio signals directly from the VCR and feed them into special sockets on the television set. This involves extra single-core cables used for low-frequency signals.

On semi-professional equipment, where sound quality is important, or where the sound signals have to be carried over long distances – in camera extension leads, for example – twin-core cables, which pick up less electrical interference from outside sources, are used.

To fit a coaxial connector, cut off $1\frac{1}{2}$ in (4 cm) of outer casing, fold back the metallic braiding **I**, and cut away about $\frac{1}{2}$ in (12.5 mm) of core insulation.

Fit the plug collar and the braid clamp, **2**, then fit the pin unit and solder the cable core to the pin. Cut off the surplus wire from the end of the pin and screw on the plug body, **3**.

- Outer casing
- Plug collar
- Metallic braid
- Braid clamp
- Core insulation
- Cable core
- Pin unit
- Pin
- Plug body

Power

Every VCR, home deck or portable, uses 12-volt (V) direct current (DC) electrical power. Portables have 12V batteries, but models with AC input have to work from the national system. This is usually alternating current (AC); few countries use DC.

AC alternates on a frequency of 50 or 60 Hertz (Hz) per second. This frequency determines the national frame rate: 50Hz systems have a rate of 25 frames per second; 60Hz systems have a rate of 30 frames per second.

Voltages differ nationally. In the USA and Europe the national standard is 110V; in the UK it is 220V. There are adaptors to enable American VCRs to be connected to British power supplies, but most VCRs have a multi-position switch, enabling them to function under either standard. Be careful not to operate it by mistake: if it is set to 110V and plugged into a 220V socket, all the fuses will blow.

While the VCR is recording it consumes only as much electicity as a domestic light bulb.

The 3-core power cable supplies AC electricity. In the USA, cable and plugs are bought sealed together; in Europe it is now standard for three-core cables to be colour-coded: brown is live; blue is neutral, and green and white stripes is earth. They are made of multi-strand copper wire, and are invariably separated by a string filling and a layer of braid. Power cables have a thick rubber casing.

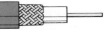

Twin microphone cable is balanced: it allows you to carry two sound signals for stereo recording, and also gives the best sound transmission over long distances. This is a three-conductor cable; it has two connectors surrounded by braiding, which is earthed to provide a screen against unwanted signals. The whole complex is surrounded by an outer casing of tough plastic.

Single-stranded (unbalanced) microphone cable is used for most audio connections. It is used for connections over short distances: to different parts of the video system, for example. The cable would be subject to considerable interference from outside signals if it were not screened from them by the layer of copper braiding which surrounds it.

Ultra high frequency (UHF) cable carries radio frequency (RF) signals which are of a higher frequency than mike signals. It is occasionally used to carry video signals. The central copper conductor carries the signal. The inner core is screened by woven metallic braiding, which also makes it more rigid and incapable of being twisted. With an outer plastic casing, it is a tough cable.

Connecting up
1 Disconnect the TV set from the AC electricity supply.
2 Unplug the TV antenna cable from its socket in the back of the set.
3 Plug the antenna cable into the socket in the back of the VCR marked 'Antenna'/'Aerial'/'RF In'.

4 A short lead is provided with the VCR. Plug one end into the socket in the back of the VCR marked 'Antenna'/'Aerial'/'RF Out'; the other into the socket in the back of the TV marked 'Antenna' or 'Aerial'.
5 Connect the VCR and the TV set to the power supply.

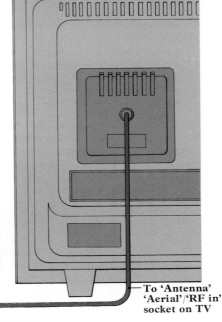

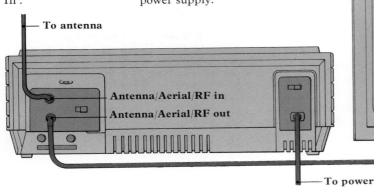

— To antenna

Antenna/Aerial/RF in
Antenna/Aerial/RF out

To 'Antenna' 'Aerial'/'RF in' socket on TV

— To power

Plugs and sockets simplified

It is almost impossible to feed a cable into the wrong input. Cables which have to carry audio signals are entirely different from those carrying the RF signal from the television antenna. Moreover, by fitting them with different connectors it is possible to eliminate incorrect connections.

Nevertheless, there are pointless variations between the types of connector used in different countries and between one model of VCR or audio system and another. Hitherto, manufacturers have followed their own inclinations regarding cable connections between their products. As a result, as soon as you tried to build up a system of different units from different makers, you needed to have special leads made to link the components. Now there is a degree of uniformity.

Broadly speaking, the connectors, as well as the cables to which they attach, split into three classes: those used for RF signals, for video signals, and for audio signals.

There are, in addition, other more specialized cables and plugs, for example, those needed to supply power from the mains, or a battery pack, or to connect a camera (which involves passing video, audio and other signals down a single cable). These, however, often use specially designed connectors, and cables with ten or more different cores to take all the signals, and have to be made up individually.

Treat your connectors carefully, especially when inserting them and pulling them out. When connecting up multi-pin connectors, check that the pins are in line – there is often a slot or pip inside to guide you; when disconnecting, remember that there may be a release mechanism and do not try and force the connectors. Rough treatment could bend or break a pin.

Keep at hand a spare set of the more important cables and connectors in your system. There are adaptors for some of the connector combinations, enabling a cable intended for one connection to stand in, temporarily, for another.

However daunting it may seem, it is worth while learning about connections. Should you eventually extend your video system to incorporate an audio system, games and a camera, the wiring together of the whole system can add up to a maze of cabling and a whole battery of connectors. It will be useful to know how to simplify it.

Connector care check list

1 Keep connectors and connections clean, using specially formulated fluid solvent cleaners.
2 Do not force connectors into sockets. If they do not fit together easily, check to see if you have aligned them correctly. Forcing a connector may bend a pin.
3 Do not jerk connectors out of sockets. If you cannot draw them gently but firmly toward you, there is probably a ring to twist or unscrew, or a release mechanism to operate.
4 Do not bang connectors by swinging cable ends together, or leave them lying on the floor, where they may be trodden on or kicked, or chewed by animals.
5 Be careful with the pins on connectors. If they break the equipment will not work.
6 Do not pull connectors out of sockets by the cables; it causes faulty connections.
7 Do not bend cables. If you do this frequently, the casing will weaken. Coil them in 12 to 15-in (30 to 40-cm) loops.
8 Colour-code your cables for easy identification.

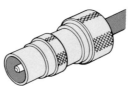 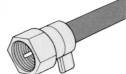

TV Coax Plugs, or Belling & Lee Plugs, *above*, are standard in the UK, Europe, Africa and the Middle East. These push-in connectors transmit RF signals to the VCR and TV set via a coaxial cable.

In America, RF cables are either twin-core 300-ohm cables, ending in two spade-type terminals which are screwed on to the TV set, or coaxial 75-ohm cables fitted with an F-connector, *above*.

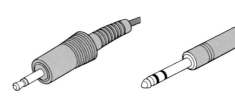

Most domestic video equipment uses unbalanced audio, for which plugs and jacks based on telephone switchboard types are used. The 3.5 mm miniature jack (or mini plug) *above left*, is the most common;

there is also a standard (6.3 mm) size. This connector is usually used in audio cassette tape recorders. The $\frac{1}{4}$-in (6 mm) phone plug *above right*, is used for mike connections by some manufacturers.

One way of keeping the complicated interconnections between different parts of a system as simple and flexible as possible is to wire them through a patch panel, *below*. This may be a panel designed to fit into a rack or a box, and it will have rows of numbered sockets along the front, which can be connected in any combination, using simple jack connectors. By wiring all your video/audio system components into the back, so that each has a set of numbered terminals, you reduce the jumble of connectors, linking them to a neat set of identical cables in one particular spot.

The multiplicity of plug-and-socket combinations may seem daunting, but they are useful because they make it impossible to connect the system up wrongly. Yet, when a connector is damaged, a cable missing, or you need to link into the system components with alien connectors, adaptors are what you need. Familiarize yourself with their names from suppliers' catalogues, or take the parts you are trying to connect along to a store and ask advice.

Adaptors should be temporary. If one seems to be constantly used, have the connector you obviously need made up.

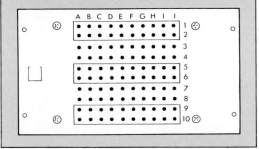

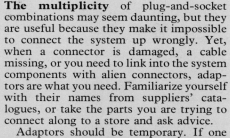

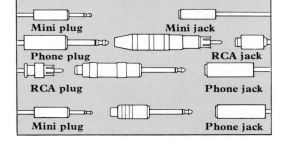

Mini plug   Mini jack

Phone plug   RCA jack

RCA plug   Phone jack

Mini plug   Phone jack

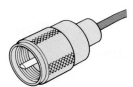

Older models of TV and video equipment usually have UHF connectors, to transmit video signals. They have a central pin and an outer, screw-threaded ring to fasten the plug securely to the socket.

The compact BNC plug, *above*, is gradually replacing the old UHF and F connectors. This is a bayonet-type connector which fastens on a special BNC socket with pins to hold it in place.

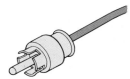

The RCA (phono or cinch) connector is an audio plug for use with unbalanced lines. It loosens easily, and is not really suitable for video use, but it is cheap and, unlike UHF and BNC plugs, is easy to solder.

The multi-pin DIN plugs and sockets are standard throughout Europe as connectors for unbalanced audio lines. They combine input and output connections.

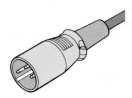

Most good mikes, as well as 1-in (2.5-cm) VTRs and other semi-professional equipment which uses twin-core balanced line cables, will rely on the Cannon (or XLR) three-pin connector, which

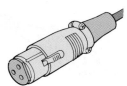

comes in male *above left*, and female, *above right*, forms. An adaptor is available, with a female Cannon plug on one end and a phone plug on the other, to connect an unbalanced recorder to a balanced mike.

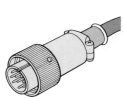

Home video cameras have 10- or 12-pin connectors and professional camera connectors have up to 50 pins. They are usually secured by an O-ring, which must be unscrewed to pull the connector out.

This 8-pin plug transmits both audio and video signals between a VCR and a TV monitor. The 8 pins are unevenly spaced, so check that they are aligned when inserting into the socket.

Tuning in

The VCR has to be supplied with the information which it is to record. If this is a standard broadcast signal from television transmitters it will come via the antenna, which would otherwise be connected to the television. The antenna picks up a mixture of local broadcast signals, but all have different frequencies. By tuning the television to one frequency, it can be made to receive only the signal which has that frequency.

The same is true for VCRs. All non-portable home VCRs have built-in tuners, and portapacks have a tuner/timer as an optional extra. A VCR can be tuned, on its own tuner, to a different station from the one selected on the television's tuner, so that you can watch one channel on the television while recording another on your VCR.

If your television reception is poor, try retuning the set. The tuning knobs and frequency indicators will be underneath a small panel. The fine tuning procedure varies, so if it is unclear, and you have no instruction book, call a service engineer.

Tuning in sounds complicated, but it is quite straightforward. First, choose a spare channel on the television. If this is a new set it may have a button, marked 'AV' or 'VCR', for this purpose. This channel has to be tuned to the channel on your VCR which is pre-set by the manufacturer. This is done by setting the VCR to a special test signal, or by playing a pre-recorded tape. As soon as altering the channel adjustment on the television gives the test pattern or playback picture on the screen, this channel is tuned to the VCR's output channel, which will allow the set to show what the VCR is receiving.

Many tuners on both televisions and VCRs have a button marked 'AFT' (automatic fine tuning), and some have an extra button for making fine adjustments to the tuning. It is important to switch the AFT off while tuning, and to switch it on again when the set is tuned. Once the set is tuned, the AFT will keep the tuning locked into place.

If you get herring-bone interference on your screen the frequency is too close to a broadcast channel. You can alter the VCR's RF channel by a screw control. The manual should tell you how to do this.

The final step is to set the VCR to its normal operating mode and tune in each channel to a different station. Some VCRs have an auto-tuning facility which does this.

Tuning in check list

1 Switch on the TV set and VCR. Select either the 'VCR' or 'AV' channel, or a spare normal channel on the TV.
2 Check with your manual that all the necessary controls are on the right setting for tuning, or you may carry out the procedure with no result.
3 Switch on the VCR's test signal. Most VCRs generate their own test picture, but some have a test signal on a cassette. If you cannot obtain a test signal, substitute any pre-recorded tape, preferably in black and white.
4 Turn the tuning dial on the TV until the test picture is as clear as possible. Then switch the test signal back to its normal setting. If you get herring-bone interference, or if the VCR picks up a TV channel, retune the VCR's RF channel.
5 Tune your VCR channels to the TV as described in the manual. If your VCR has a setting labelled 'AFT' or 'AFC', remember to switch this to 'Off' while tuning and to 'On' again when tuning is completed.
6 Compare the picture you are getting on your VCR channels with the picture you get on the TV on its 'TV' setting. They should not be noticeably inferior. If the picture is poor, first fine-tune the VCR channels again and then, if necessary, the TV. It is worth taking some time and trouble over this, since poor tuning is often the cause of bad video reception.
7 If your picture is persistently poor, consult a service engineer.

Since portable recorders must be as light and compact as possible, they lack the tuning and timing functions of normal VCRs. To enable them to record broadcast television off air, they have separate tuner/timer units. This Panasonic NV-3000 is designed to be used with the NV-V300 tuner/timer, which enables it to be tuned to broadcast RF signals, turning it into the equivalent of a home deck. The most modern tuner/timers have almost as many facilities as other advanced VCRs. To work on the electricity supply, this system needs an AC-DC adaptor/battery charger; some have adaptors built in.

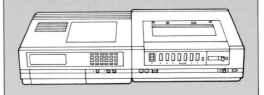

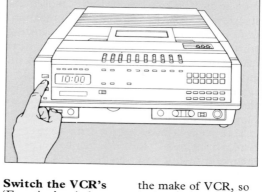

The first stage of tuning in your VCR is to switch on the TV and VCR and select a spare channel on the TV. On new TVs there is a special channel marked 'AV' or 'VCR' for this purpose.

Switch the VCR's 'Function' switch to 'On'. This stage, which bypasses the timer, will vary with the make of VCR, so look through the instructions in your manual again if you are in any doubt.

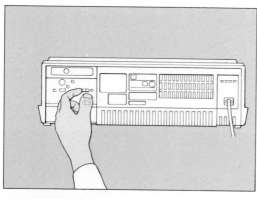

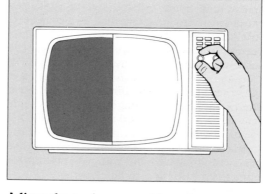

To produce a test signal to which to tune, either put the VCR's test signal switch to 'Test', or play a pre-recorded test tape, such as the one supplied with Grundig's VCRs, or any recorded tape.

Adjust the tuning knob for your TV channel until a clear tuning signal, usually a pattern of black and white stripes, appears on the screen. Then switch the VCR back to its normal (colour) setting.

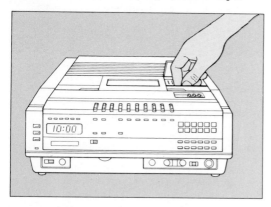

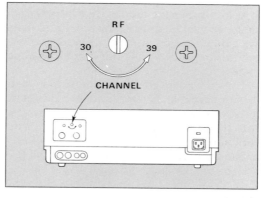

You can now tune each channel on your VCR to a TV station. Compare the picture on the VCR channel with your normal TV picture. If it is inferior, try retuning.

If you get herring-bone interference, or another station on the screen, you can often retune the VCR's RF reception by means of a screw on the back of the VCR.

23

The video cassette

Video cassettes work in basically the same way as audio cassettes, in that a tape made from plastic film and coated with a magnetically sensitive material is passed over a recording head. The signal fed into the head causes a changing magnetic field around the tape. Particles in the tape coating align themselves with the field and so reflect what the magnetic field at the recording head was like when that portion of the tape ran over it.

If the tape is passed at the same speed over a playback head, this is able to read the magnetic information on the tape. The information can be erased by passing the tape over an erase head, which uses a strong magnetic field to realign the particles of magnetic material in the same direction, wiping out the recorded pattern. The video tracks are about a thousandth of an inch (0.025 mm) apart.

Early professional video recorders recorded video tracks across a 2-inch (5-centimetre) wide tape. Since then, tapes have grown narrower and narrower, down to CVC format quarter-inch (6-millimetre) tape. This has been made possible by helical scan, the process of recording tracks at an angle across the tape, done by a pair of recording heads on a high-speed rotating drum. If the heads were fixed, as on an audio recorder, the tape would have to move impossibly fast for enough information to be crammed on it.

The tape follows a complicated path over a series of guides and rollers. Early video tape machines were reel-to-reel models, and threading the tape from the input reel through the machine, around the drum and on to the output reel, was a tricky business. It was only the invention of the pre-packaged cassettes which made loading and removing the tape from the recorder a simple process, but this depended on building the threading system into the recorder.

Sony introduced the cassette in their three-quarter-inch (19-millimetre) U-matic format, where the tape is taken from the cassette and fed into the machine in a path which roughly resembles the letter U. Their half-inch (5-centimetre) Betamax format follows a similar path through the machine. The VHS threading mechanism winds the tape around a more complex path, resembling a letter M; so the tape has to be wound clear of the record/playback path for fast wind or rewind.

The tape follows a complicated path through rollers and capstans for accurate positioning on the video heads. This is done by hand with reel-to-reel machines. Cassette recorders do it automatically.

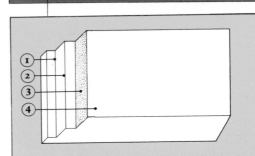

Video tape starts off as a clear polyester base, **2**, which must be thin, flexible, strong and non-elastic. An anti-static carbon backing **1**, prevents static eletricity from building up on the tape as it runs through the recorder. The metal oxide particles, **3**, which store the recorded magnetic fields, are bound to the other side of the base. Finally, to offer the smoothest possible surface to the video heads, the metal oxide is polished, **4**.

The drum in which the video heads are mounted, *above*, is tilted with respect to the tape, so that the video tracks are recorded and played back diagonally across the width of the tape. The drum normally holds two heads. On each rotation of the drum, one head records the even lines and the other the odd lines of the picture, so that a single rotation records one frame. A tracking control on VHS and Betamax VCR, allows the video drum angle to be changed to track the tape more accurately. Video 2000 drums move automatically for better tracking, especially in slow motion and fast picture search.

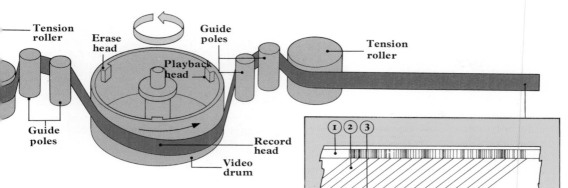

Tension roller

Erase head

Guide poles

Playback head

Tension roller

Guide poles

Record head

Video drum

When a tape cassette is loaded into a VCR, guide poles pull a loop of tape out and wrap it round the video drum. This is called lacing. Tension rollers take up any slack.

At the end of the tape path, just before the tape re-enters the cassette, it is squeezed between a pinch roller and a capstan. The pinch roller is driven by a motor to pull the tape past the video heads. A Betamax cassette is laced up as soon as it is loaded, but a VHS cassette is only laced up when a playback control is operated. Different tape formats lace the tape in different ways.

During playback, the drum spins at 25 r.p.m. (UK) or 30 r.p.m. (USA), producing 25 (UK) or 30 (USA) complete TV pictures per second.

The sound-track, **1**, is recorded along one edge of the tape. Video information is recorded diagonally across the tape, **2**, the full width in VHS and Betamax, or half the width in Video 2000. Pulses recorded on the control track, **3**, ensure that the tape is recorded and played back at the same speed. They are the magnetic tape equivalent of cine film sprocket holes. The quadruplex tape used on reel-to-reel video recorders has a cue track along one side which can be used to store pulses for electronic editing.

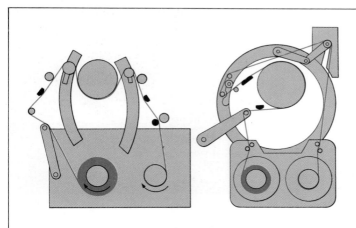

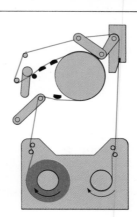

When a VHS tape is inserted in a recorder, the spool locks are released and two guide poles pull a length of tape out of the cassette. Because the tortuous tape path would place severe strain on the tape during fast wind, it is only laced up during normal-speed playback. M-load (or M-wrap) takes its name from the shape of the tape when laced up, *above*.

In the semi-professional U-matic format developed by Sony, the tape is laced up as soon as the cassette is inserted in the recorder. Capstans on a circular guide track catch the tape and pull it round the video drum. Tension arms take up any slack in the $\frac{3}{4}$-in (19-mm) tape. U-matic format has become the standard for the first cable TV stations in the UK.

Betamax, developed by Sony, is a smaller version of U-matic, using narrower $\frac{1}{2}$-in (12.5-mm) tape. Lacing operates in the same way as U-matic, although a smaller mechanism is used. The tape remains in contact with the video heads for all playback and winding functions until the 'Eject' button is pressed. Despite this, there is no excess head wear.

Formats

Video tape is no more than 20 microns thick (a micron is a thousandth of a millimetre). It has to stand up to winding on and off high-speed rotating drums and threading and unthreading hundreds of times during its lifetime, without breaking or distorting by so much as a thousandth of an inch.

The polyester plastic tape which carries the specialized coatings is prone to shrinkage if it gets too hot. Although the tape is stable over normal temperature variations, some shrinkage and stretching can happen with a brand-new tape, so try winding it fully forward and backward before using it.

Video tape records information magnetically on the ferrous oxide layer; so stray magnetic fields can erase recordings. In fact, a tape eraser (called a bulk eraser) works by using a strong magnetic field to realign the magnetic particles on the tape so that they all face the same way.

Keep cassettes clear of any other magnetic fields, such as those produced by magnets in audio speaker cones, in toys or even in magnetic document clips.

The worst effects are produced by collapsing magnetic fields. Switching off a vacuum cleaner close to a television can cause the colour guns to become misaligned, which may result in coloured patches being produced on the screen.

In time, the magnetic particles of the tape coating will be dislodged, causing white streaks on the picture. This is called dropout, and it is usually more common in the first few minutes of a tape. One way of postponing this problem is to begin new recordings at different times over the first five minutes of tape to reduce wear at any given point.

Tape development is now focusing on two areas: cramming the necessary information on to narrower tape, such as the quarter-inch (6 millimetre) Compact Video Cassette (CVC) tape, or the twin-track Video 2000 cassette (the only video cassette on which you can record both sides); and making the tape thinner so that longer tapes can be fitted into cassettes. The latest VHS cassette provides four hours of playing time, but the tape is so thin that some of the older VCRs with heavy threading mechanisms can stretch it. Sony's Betastack gives 13 hours of unattended recording by cycling automatically through four ordinary Betamax cassettes, stacked one on top of another.

Video cassettes have a safety tab to prevent accidental erasure of recordings. When a cassette is loaded into a VCR, a probe detects the presence of the tab. If it has been removed, the tape cannot be erased. If it is necessary to record on the tape at some future date, the tab hole can be covered by a piece of adhesive tape. VHS, Betamax and U-matic cassettes each have one tab. Video 2000 cassettes have two.

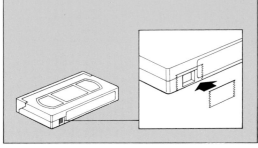

Top half of shell · Spool retaining spring · Protective flap · Tape spool · Tape · Spool lo[ck] · Toothed wheel · Spool l[ock] · Dust g[uard] · Lower half of she[ll] · Tape support · Tape guide · Spool lock

A video cassette might look like an audio cassette, but inside it is very different. The tape spools are mounted on toothed wheels, which are released only when the tape is inside the recorder, to prevent it from slackening. The two halves of the plastic shell are held together by screws (five for domestic VHS cassettes and six, in a stronger arrangement, for industrial machines).

Loading a cassette

Before a cassette can be inserted into a top-loading VCR, the cassette drawer must be opened by pressing the 'Eject' control. Hold the cassette with the protective flap farthest away from you and with the loose spools facing downward. Push the cassette into the open cassette drawer. The cassette drawer must then be closed by pushing it down until it locks into place. The recorder is now ready for playback or recording.

It is not necessary to prepare a front-loading model before inserting a cassette. The cassette is held as before and pushed into the loading slot. When it is about half way in, the motorized mechanism takes over, pulling the cassette away from you and down into the machine.

When loaded, a cassette can be seen through a window in the top loader's cassette drawer. This is not so with an all-enclosed front loader, and in some machines it is possible to insert a second cassette on top of the first. VHS, Betamax and U-matic cassettes can be inserted only if they are the right way up. Video 2000 cassettes can be inserted either way up, but the protective flap must always be farthest away from you.

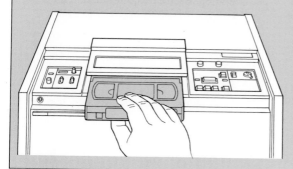

Philips's Video Compact Cassette

Sony $\frac{3}{4}$ in (19 mm) U-matic cassette

Sony Betamax cassette

JVC VHS cassette

There are five widths of video tape in use today. In high-quality professional video, including broadcast, 2-in (50-mm) open-reel tape is the norm. In one 2-in system, Quadruplex (Quad) the video heads write almost at right-angles to the edge of the tape.

One-inch (25-mm) tape is now taking over. There are three formats: A-format was pioneered by Ampex in the sixties, B-format is used by Bosch, IVC, RCA and Philips, while the newer C-format is used by Ampex, Sony, RCA and Marconi.

Sony's U-matic, *top*, is the only $\frac{3}{4}$-in (19-mm) system, and was the first video cassette format. The High-band version gives broadcast-quality recordings. It uses the same cassettes, but will only play back on ordinary U-matics in black and white.

There are two $\frac{1}{2}$-in (12.5-mm) systems, Sony's Betamax, *above*, the smaller of the two, and JVC's VHS, *above right*.

The Video 2000 format uses the Video Compact Cassette, *above left*, by Philips, which has a tape width of $\frac{1}{2}$-in (12.5-mm) but is a $\frac{1}{4}$-in (6-mm) format as it only writes over half the tape width.

The Funai Microvideo system uses a $\frac{1}{4}$-in (6-mm) format tape the size of an audio cassette.

Recording off air

To save needless plugging and unplugging of antenna leads, manufacturers have ensured that as long as there is power running to the VCR, the video signal received by the antenna will pass through to your television set.

It is better to leave the VCR power on all the time as this saves the trouble of resetting the digital clock. There is no electrical hazard associated with such a practice. The machine is over-abundantly supplied with internal fuses and it uses about as much power as an electric clock.

On VHS and Betamax machines, you can use the tuner in the VCR for normal viewing. This means that if you leave the television set tuned to the VCR channel, you can change the channel by pressing the 'Channel Selector' buttons on the VCR. The advantage of doing this is that you can utilize a remote control (most VCR manufacturers offer an optional one if they do not supply one with the machine) to change TV channels – and the VCR usually has more channels available than a television set.

Prepare to make your recording well in advance of the time the broadcast begins. Make sure the VCR is switched to the tuner and that the television is set to the VCR channel. Manufacturers label their switches differently but the principles remain the same; consult your user's manual.

Insert a tape. Check that it is rewound and set the memory counter to zero. Make a short test recording and adjust if necessary.

You can usually hear the tape turning, and on most top-loading machines you can see it rotating. If it does not move, check that you have not accidentally pressed the 'Pause' button. If no picture appears the safety tab at the back may have been removed.

Rewind the tape, watching the memory counter, or using the VCR's memory facility, if the tape is already partly used. Be ready to record when the show begins. Remember to watch for the finishing time of the recording or the VCR will continue to record until the tape ends. Only by using the timer can you program the recording to stop on time.

While recording is in progress you can watch the show, or, because you are not recording from the television receiver but directly from the antenna (or aerial), you can switch the input select mode to 'TV'; the television receiver to another channel, and watch a different show.

Knobs and switches

You can tell a middle-aged VCR by its piano key controls. Pressing a key moves a series of metal levers and links to operate the appropriate solenoids (magnetized wire coils) and relays. Built-in safety checks to ensure that two keys cannot be depressed together exacerbate the slowness of the operation. Each change of function requires the stop mode to be selected in between.

The application of microchip technology has changed all that. The mechanical keys have been replaced by touch-sensitive controls. Only a featherlight touch is needed for these to send a minute electrical current to the microprocessor to instruct it as to which function is required. The microprocessor then operates the necessary switches and solenoids, ensuring that the correct sequence is followed, so you can now switch between functions without having to select the stop mode, knowing that the VCR's brain will sort things out. The removal of mechanical switching has also speeded up the operation of the various functions, drastically reducing the delay between, say, rewind and play.

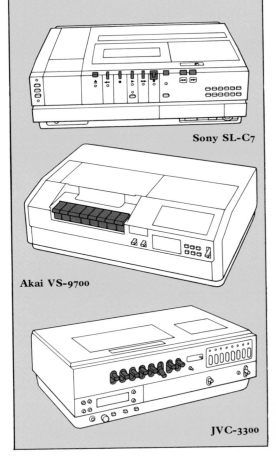

Sony SL-C7

Akai VS-9700

JVC-3300

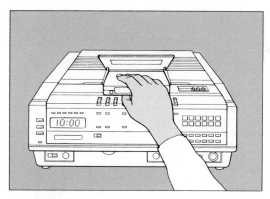

Make sure the VCR is switched on at the wall socket and the VCR 'Power' switch, and that it is not in the timer mode, or the cassette compartment may not open. Insert a tape and press 'Rewind'.

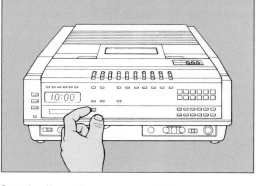

Set the 'Input' or 'Record Selector' or the 'TV/VTR' switch to TV: VCRs with a 'Tuner/Timer' switch should be set to 'Tuner'. On some machines the input selection is made automatically.

Select the channel you wish to record on the channel selector. The channel number will light up. Check that the correct picture is appearing on the screen, and make any adjustments.

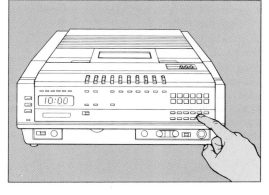

Turn on the TV set and select the 'Video/VCR/VTR or 'RF out' channel on the TV receiver.

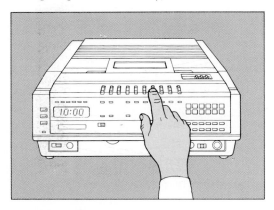

Press the 'Record' button or, on some VCRs, the 'Record' and 'Play' buttons.

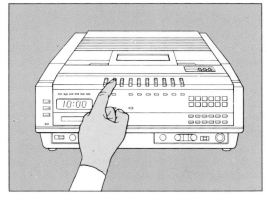

Press 'Stop' and/or 'Rewind' when the recording is complete. Some VCRs automatically rewind when the cassette comes to an end. Remove the cassette.

Time-shifting

In 1972 Philips launched the N1500, the first home video recorder to incorporate a tuner-timer, making the video recorder saleable on the domestic market. Until then, users had to rely on crude mechanical timers; finding the right starting point was something of a hit and miss affair.

These early timers were accurate only to the nearest minute. Modern VCRs have electronic timers accurate to the second.

The timer's job is to switch the VCR on to record at a predetermined time. The simplest timer will record only one such 'event', but most have a repeat facility to record at the same time daily or weekly. Sony's Betastack mechanism allows a number of tapes to be stacked up, giving 14 hours recording time.

Most budget models have a seven-day timer, with a single event capability plus a daily or weekly repeat. Luxury models usually offer eight events over 14 days, but any number of permutations – up to 99 days on the Grundig 2 × 4 Super – are available.

If you use your VCR mainly to record feature films a single event timer is all you will need. It is also easy to set up. The more event capabilities and the longer the timing period, the more complicated is the timer.

It is essential that the digital clock displays the correct time. It may use a 24- or a 12-hour display; so make sure it is not showing 6.00 am instead of 6 pm or 9 instead of 21.00 hours.

A single event timer is programmed with the start time, stop time, day of the week, and repeat facility. A timer that can be programmed over several days will show the days either by name or number (0 = today; 1 = tomorrow, and so on).

Remember to select the correct channel on the VCR before setting the timer, because the tuner will not operate, once the VCR is set to the timer mode.

Multi-event timers need considerably more information, so they are more difficult to program. Each model differs in the method of programming the timer, but the principles remain the same. To save confusion, make a list beforehand with all the information required for each event: 1 Event no.; 2 Channel no.; 3 day.; 4 start time; 5 duration or stop time. If you treat complex programming as a simple question and answer sequence following a logical progression, you will not miss out an essential step.

The timer setting procedure soon becomes second nature, but it is nevertheless easy to leave out an important step, so preventing the machine from making the recording. To stop this happening, before leaving the recorder to make an unattended recording, ask yourself these questions:
1 Is the AC supply switched on?
2 Is the recorder loaded with a cassette?
3 Is the cassette rewound to the correct starting point?
4 Is there a safety tab in place on the cassette? If not, has the hole been blocked by a piece of adhesive tape?
5 Is the digital clock showing the correct time and day?
6 Have the correct recording start time and length, or stop time, been programmed?
7 Is the VCR switched to timer mode?
8 Is there enough recording time left on the cassette for the total length of the show.
9 Should you have pressed the 'Record' button? Check your manual.

For accurate time setting, advance the clock to 1 minute after the correct time. Release the clock button on a radio time signal.

If the clock display flashes, there has been a power-cut and it must be reset.

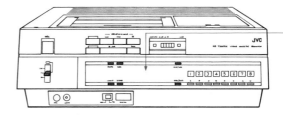

Japanese VCRs, such as the JVC HR7300EK *above*, feature a function switch in a prominent position on the front panel. This is normally set to the 'On' or 'Operate' position for recording and playback. In the 'Off' or 'Standby' position, power is cut off from the recorder section. For unattended operation, once the recording times have been keyed in using the timer setting-buttons, the function switch must be set to the 'Timer' position. The recorder will then appear to switch off. It remains apparently dormant until the start time, when recording begins automatically.

Recording continues until the stop time, when the power is once again cut off.

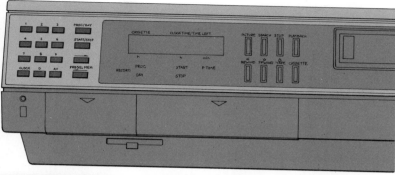

Grundig's 2 × 4 Super offers one of the most advanced timers available to domestic video users. Its tiny computer memory can hold all the information necessary to record up to five events on different channels, up to 99 days later. The method of entering information into this European machine is very different from that of Japanese VCRs.

The computer must first be told that you want to key in some details. Once the correct button has been pressed to start the sequence, the next nine steps necessary to enter all the information to make a future recording must be completed within 15 seconds. If you take longer, the memory is wiped clean. The whole procedure must then be started from the beginning again.

Auto timer recording

1 Press the top 'Presel. Mem' button to start the timer-setting sequence.

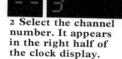

2 Select the channel number. It appears in the right half of the clock display.

3 Press the 'Progr/Day' button to confirm the entry of the channel number.

4 Key the start time using the numerical keypad. Remember, this timer uses a 24-hour clock.

5 Pressing the 'Start/Stop' button confirms entry of the start time into the timer memory.

6 Press the top 'Presel.Mem' button again to switch the timer from time to day setting.

7 The 'H' on the display is German for today (*heute*). Press 1 for tomorrow, 2 for the day after and so on.

8 Press the 'Progr/Day' button to enter the day of the recording into the timer memory.

9 Finally, enter the stop time on the clock, and press the 'Start/Stop' button to enter it into the timer memory.

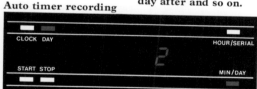

1 JVC's timer setting is typical of Japanese recorders. Hold the 'Day' button down and press the 'Min/Day' button until the recording day appears. Zero means today.

2 If the 'Day' and 'Hour/Serial' buttons are pressed at the same time, a 'd' appears on the clock display, and recordings are made daily at the same time. Most recorders have this function.

3 Next set the start time by holding down the 'Start' button, while pressing the 'Hour/Serial' and then the 'Min/Day' buttons. The hours and then the minutes will cycle round. Release the buttons when the correct time appears on the display.

4 Set the stop time by holding down the 'Stop' button and pressing the 'Hour/Serial' and then the 'Min/Day' buttons until the desired stop time appears. Select the timer position on the function switch, and press the 'Record' button.

Use your memory

The simplest VCR memory facility takes the form of a switch labelled 'Counter Memory'. When this is switched on, the tape automatically stops in fast forward or rewind when the counter reading is zero. It is very useful for finding the beginning of a recording, provided you remember to set the counter to zero when you start recording.

More sophisticated recorders incorporate a system called 'Automatic Program Location' (APL). At the beginning of every recording an inaudible pulse is recorded on the tape. In fast forward and rewind the machine can be made to look for these pulses on the tape and to stop when it finds one.

A further development allows the memory to be used for playback. You can set a start and finish point, so that the machine will play a sequence, rewind and play it again as many times as required – to display advertisements in a store, for example.

The 'Go To' system on Video 2000 recorders makes it possible to program-in a tape location to which the machine will automatically go. To locate a recording which is 1 hour 10 minutes into a tape, punch in the coordinates on the numerical keypad and the machine will do the rest.

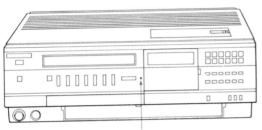

The 'Tape Remaining Indicator' on a machine such as the JVC HR-7700EK gives a rough guide to the length of tape left on a cassette. It takes the form of a series of illuminated bars. The bars are turned off one by one, from left to right, every 10 minutes until, during the last 5 minutes, the last bar flashes. It is certainly a useful extra: a glance at the display shows whether or not there is enough time left on a cassette to make the desired recording, but it is by no means essential. Several top-of-the-range models feature a tape remaining indicator, that on the Grundig 2 × 4 Super is the most sophisticated, with a full clock display.

Most Sharp VCRs, *above,* feature an APL device. It scans the tape in forward or reverse playback, looking for inaudible marker tones, which are recorded on the tape every time the 'Record' or 'Pause' button is pressed, or when recording with a camera begins.

All recorders have a counter, *above,* with three or four digits. The 'Reset' switch sets the counter reading to zero. When the 'Memory' switch is on, the tape automatically stops when the counter reading reaches zero in both fast forward and rewind.

When a cassette is loaded into the Grundig 2 × 4 Super, *right,* the display shows the length of the tape in hours, and the playing time already elapsed. In this case an 8-hour cassette (4 hours each side) is in the machine and 58 minutes have been used; 182 minutes remain free. Unfortunately, this very useful feature is unique to this VCR.

Pressing the 'Time left' button displays the running time remaining on that side of the tape.

The display shows 'Full' when there is not enough tape left for the programmed instructions.

If the display reads 'Cass', it is necessary to insert, change over, or release a cassette from the holder.

Picture search

Probably the most useful of the so-called trick frame facilities, fast picture search, allows the viewer to speed through the tape forward and (usually) backward at between five and ten times normal playback speed, while retaining a picture on the screen. The image can sometimes be almost unintelligible, particularly on the more advanced machines which give more than 20 times normal speed search. Used with discretion, this is a very valuable asset to any VCR, and it is pleasing to see the facility appearing on new models, even at the budget end of manufacturers' ranges.

Video 2000 picture search gives much better picture quality than either VHS or Betamax, because of different head-mounting methods. Indeed, Video 2000 picture search quality on both Philips and Grundig recorders is as good as normal speed playback quality. VHS and Betamax picture search is characterized by bars of white dots (noise bars) stretching across the screen.

Different manufacturers have different names for picture search: visual search, shuttle search or cue and review. Some machines display only a black and white picture in picture search.

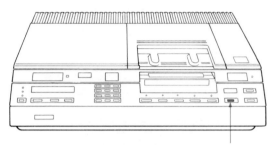

Reverse   Visual search   Forward

Tape movements are controlled by a series of buttons on the front panel. These feed control signals to a microprocessor. However quickly or randomly the buttons are pressed, the microprocessor is programmed to make sure neither heads nor tape are harmed.

The useful 'Go To' function has so far been limited to Video 2000 recorders, *above*. On Philips machines, you press the 'Go To' button and enter a counter number on the keypad. The tape is then automatically wound on or back to the required counter reading and stopped.

Visual search, also called picture search, cue and review and shuttle search, is the most useful of all the trick frame facilities. It provides a quick and easy way of skipping through unwanted sections of recordings, commercials perhaps, to find the beginning of a film. The tape is played faster than normal speed and a picture is shown on the television screen, but there is no sound.

Picture search 25 × faster

The Toshiba 8600 (Europe) 8500 (USA) has a two-speed picture search. Touching the 'Cue or Review' button plays the tape (without sound) at 7 times normal speed. Pressing it down selects 25 times normal speed but it is hard to follow the action at this speed.

Toshiba's APL system is called 'Quick Select'. When activated, it automatically stops the tape at breaks between TV shows in fast forward or rewind. This is very useful for finding the beginning of a show.

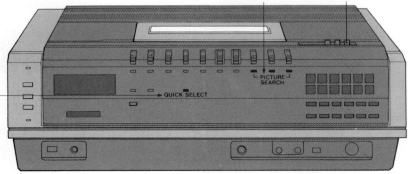

Fast and slow

All but the most basic domestic VCRs now offer a range of playback speeds. These vary from slow motion, which may be a simple half-speed, on-off switch or a continuously variable effect controlled from the remote handset, to high-speed playback, with sound that is just intelligible.

Most common, and perhaps most useful, is picture search. As the name suggests, this offers a picture at, usually, five to ten times normal speed as a means of searching through tape to find a particular sequence. Sound is muted. Some VCRs will search only in the forward direction. Others will search only in black and white, but as search is not used for general viewing, this is not a serious drawback. The fastest search speeds are very difficult to watch.

The pause control usually doubles as a still picture control: the tape is stopped, but remains threaded round the video drum which continues to spin, and the video circuitry remains live. The information on one small section of tape is therefore continually scanned. As this would soon lead to excessive wear of that one piece of tape, a safety mechanism is usually tripped after several minutes to limit the length of pause possible.

1   2   3   4

Picture search, 2, *above,* can be used to find a particular place on a tape, either skipping forward, **1,** through unwanted material or backward, **3,** using fast wind, if you overshoot the desired point. It can be used to wind past commercials.

Pressing the 'Pause' control of a VCR stops the tape and produces a still picture on the screen, **4,** *above right.* Still picture quality varies enormously. It is generally accepted that Video 2000 is the best.

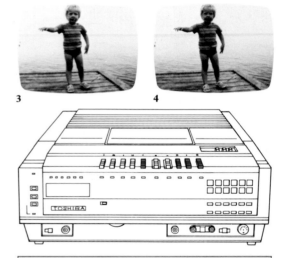

Running the tape at a slower than normal speed causes irritating noise bars across the picture. Some models give a better performance than others, and some very sophisticated models incorporate extra video heads to reduce this problem to a minimum.

The JVC HR-7700 has an unusual slow motion speed control. When slow motion is selected, the playback speed can be varied continually using two press buttons, one to raise the speed, the other to reduce it from normal through slow to freeze frame.

The Sony C7 features triple-speed playback in both forward and reverse directions. It is operated by first selecting playback at normal speed and then pressing the 'X3' button. In this mode of playback, there is no sound. Any noise bars (white dots and streaks) which appear on the screen can be removed by adjusting the tracking control, which should be returned to its usual central position for normal speed playback. The search speed of three times normal is slow, but perfectly adequate.

Sound

Sound has never been a strong point of domestic television sets and the reduction of home video recorders in size and quality from professional U-matic down to the domestic half-inch (12.5 millimetre) format has compounded the problem. There is not enough room on half-inch (12.5 millimetre) tape to store all the information needed for high-fidelity sound.

As home video expands, more and more users are becoming dissatisfied with the quality of the sound on their television and, in response, manufacturers are searching for ways to improve VCR sound quality by adding noise-reduction facilities. The most famous and well-proven noise-reduction system is Dolby, designed to solve problems in audio recording.

Other systems, such as Dynamic Noise Suppression, or Beta Noise Reduction, are attempts to circumvent the Dolby patents.

Many home video users plug their video recorders into their existing audio systems to try and improve the sound. Some hi-fi systems incorporate filters to cut out hiss at high frequencies, or booming at the bottom end, but most merely amplify any weaknesses already present on the recording.

An audio dub facility, *below*, is almost universal on home decks. Simply pressing the 'Audio dub' button at the same time as the 'Play' button erases the existing sound-track. A new sound-track can then be recorded using a mike or other external sound source. Several different shots can be held together by over-dubbing with a new sound-track.

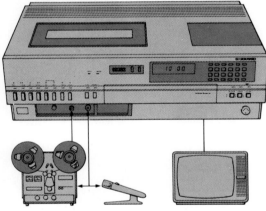

The sound quality of a recording is improved on VCRs incorporating the Dolby system. This effectively reduces tape's hiss.

Betamax VCRs use a system similar to Dolby to reduce the hiss on their sound-tracks. It is known as Beta Noise Reduction, or BNR.

A headphone input socket is useful, not only for monitoring the sound quality of a recording but also to maintain control over simple mixing effects.

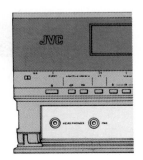

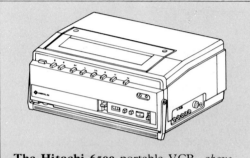

The Hitachi 6500 portable VCR, *above*, features a facility called sound on sound, to record a sound-track without erasing the existing sound-track. This basic mixing is useful for adding music to an otherwise dull tape, or for recording a commentary.

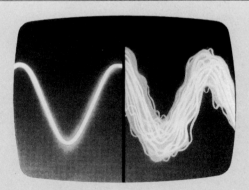

Improved sound quality on Video 2000 VCRs such as Philips VR2022 is achieved by the Dynamic Noise Suppression facility. For any noise-reduction system to work at its best, it must be used in both record and playback modes. It works by boosting high-frequency signals during recording and cutting them (and the hiss) during playback.

Editing

When a VCR plays back a recording, it locks on to a control track which was laid down on the tape as the recording was being made. Any interruptions in this control track will cause picture break-up until the VCR locks on to the new control track.

On the newer models of VCR, particularly on portable versions, a simple form of editing called back-space editing overlaps the new with the old recording, allowing sequences to be assembled one after the other, with clean cuts or edits between them.

More sophisticated models can memorize the control track and align the new recording with the old even if the VCR has been switched off for a while between shots. To insert a picture into a recorded sequence calls for a machine that will cut it in cleanly, and cut it out again to restore the original picture, equally cleanly.

By using a tape with a control track, it is possible to assemble a sequence and cut in further shots without disturbing the original control track. The development of this facility in home portapacks makes them more versatile: you can now shoot a sequence and then cut in further shots without having to use a professional edit suite.

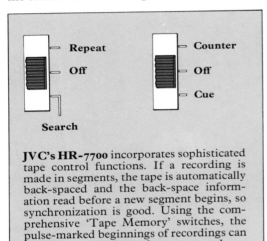

JVC's HR-7700 incorporates sophisticated tape control functions. If a recording is made in segments, the tape is automatically back-spaced and the back-space information read before a new segment begins, so synchronization is good. Using the comprehensive 'Tape Memory' switches, the pulse-marked beginnings of recordings can be found, or sections of tape repeated.

In auto-rewind, when the tape reaches the end it will stop and rewind for the recording to be viewed, *below*. If the tape memory is used with auto-rewind, and the counter set to zero before recording begins, the tape can be made to rewind to the point where the counter reads zero. This is useful for finding the beginning of a recording which is not at the beginning of the tape.

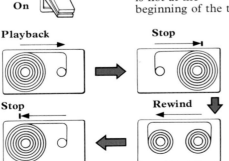

Segment 1

Segment 5

Segment 18

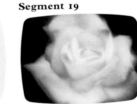

Segment 19

Segment 28

Segment 35

Segment 42

The Sony Auto Search Control can memorize up to 63 segments of a recording. The tape is marked with start and stop pulses on each segment. These may be later located by using the handset, *right*. Any eight of the segments, *above*, can

Segment 60

be programmed to play in any desired order. The cycle can also be interrupted at any point to play a different segment, then return to the cycle. The unit can be used to add a professional touch to presentations or exhibition displays.

Remote control

Most VCRs are supplied with some sort of remote control. The simplest is a pause switch connected to the VCR by a length of cable. Although it is undoubtedly useful for stopping the tape temporarily, it has two major disadvantages. First, the viewer must sit within the cable's reach of the VCR. Second, a trailing cable is a hazard. Some basic or mid-range domestic VCRs use a more sophisticated cable handset with control switches for most of the VCR functions.

Infra-red remote control overcomes many of the problems of cable control. There is no connection between the VCR and handset; commands are transmitted using an infra-red data link, which is an invisible beam. Unlike cable remotes, infra-red units need a power source: a set of batteries. Because the standby current of these units is so small, typically only several millionths of an amp, they can be left on all the time. In fact they cannot be turned off. They should be removed if the remote is going to be inoperative for a long time. When a button on an infra-red remote is pressed, an indicator lights to show that a signal is being transmitted. If the indicator does not light, replace the batteries.

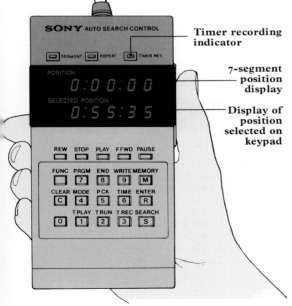

The simplest remote control is a pause switch mounted in a small case on the end of a cable. It can be used to edit commercial breaks out of off-air recordings of feature films. This basic remote control is giving way to more sophisticated infra-red links.

The Sony C7 is controlled by a remote control commander: a handset with press switches for all the main tape transport functions. Information is transmitted to the VCR using an invisible and harmless infra-red beam. Although the beam is directional, the handset can be used up to 30° either side of dead ahead, and up to 30 ft (10 m) away from the VCR. In practice, the beam will reflect off smooth objects such as mirrors and window panes.

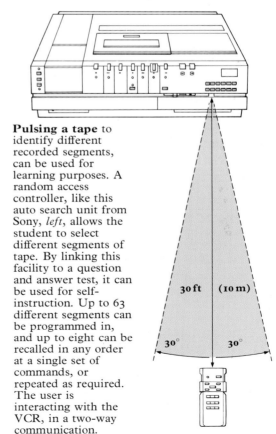

SONY AUTO SEARCH CONTROL

SEGMENT · REPEAT · TIMER REC

POSITION

0:00:00

SELECTED POSITION

0:55:35

REW STOP PLAY FFWD PAUSE

FUNC PRGM END WRITE MEMORY
7 8 9 M

CLEAR MODE PCK TIME ENTER
C 4 5 6 R

TPLAY TRUN TREC SEARCH
0 1 2 3 S

Timer recording indicator

7-segment position display

Display of position selected on keypad

Pulsing a tape to identify different recorded segments, can be used for learning purposes. A random access controller, like this auto search unit from Sony, *left*, allows the student to select different segments of tape. By linking this facility to a question and answer test, it can be used for self-instruction. Up to 63 different segments can be programmed in, and up to eight can be recalled in any order at a single set of commands, or repeated as required. The user is interacting with the VCR, in a two-way communication.

30 ft (10 m)

30° 30°

Faults and how to fix them

The VCR you have bought or rented is likely to be the most complex and delicate piece of engineering in your possession. Indeed, because VCRs are so specialized, any servicing must be left to professionals.

You do not have to be an expert to get the best from it, for the design of a modern VCR is increasingly foolproof, but it is also increasingly complex, and there is a real chance that the time will come when you press a switch and nothing, or the wrong thing, will happen.

Before you call your dealer or reach for a screwdriver, remember that in a survey carried out over thousands of reported video faults, it was established that fully ninety per cent were not faults at all. The errors were in the way the owners had set the controls.

The first rule for trouble-free video is: read your manual. Run through all the processes you are going to use with any regularity and familiarize yourself with them. That way, you will not be baffled if something unexpected happens and, above all, you will not be billed for expensive, unnecessary service calls.

Check list

Some of the most annoying and frustrating faults are the simplest. If your VCR will not work, go through this deceptively simple check list and see if there is anything that you have overlooked.

If the VCR shows no sign of life:
Is it plugged in?
Is the plug properly connected?
Is the wall socket switched on?
Is the VCR switched on?
Has the plug/socket/VCR fuse blown?

If the VCR will not record:
Is the record tab still on the cassette?
Have you released the pause control?
Has the tape come to its end?
Is the dew warning light still on?
Are all the connections plugged in?
If your VCR has a TV/VCR select switch, is it correctly switched to VCR?

If the VCR will not play back:
Is the television switched on?
Has the tape come to its end?
Is the television tuned to the VCR's output channel?
Is the cassette properly loaded?
Is the TV/VCR select switch set to 'TV'?

If the tape will not fast wind:
Has the tape reached its end?
Is the VCR properly connected and switched on?
Has the tape memory stopped the tape?
Is the tape loaded properly?

If the tape will not eject:
Is the VCR in its timer/record mode, waiting to do a pre-set recording?

Connecting up and tuning in

The first and most complicated process you perform on your video is connecting it up, tuning it to your antenna and tuning the television to the VCR. Although manuals are now easy to follow, connecting and tuning need care and concentration. If you miss a step, you may find you have to retune either straight away or, if the tuning drifts out of alignment, in the future. Here are some common tuning problems with their symptoms and solutions.

There are broadcast pictures on the television but no replay picture from the VCR.
The television needs to be tuned to the VCR. If tuning to a pre-recorded tape, check that you are receiving the tape, by operating the pause briefly.

Video tapes play back perfectly but the VCR will not record off air.
The VCR's receiver needs to be tuned to the antenna. Check the VCR tuning sequence (different from the television tuning sequence) in the manual. Although some VCRs have auto-tuning, the picture can sometimes be improved by hand-tuning.

The VCR is connected but the television gives no picture.
The connection between the television, VCR and antenna is wrong. The antenna must be plugged into the VCR, and the lead provided used to connect the VCR and the television. Double-check the correct inputs in the manual.

The television gave a good picture when first tuned in to the VCR, but the picture has since deteriorated.
You have either forgotten to switch off the Automatic Fine Tuning (AFT) when you tuned in the television, or you have

forgotten to re-engage it when you finished the tuning.

Picture faults

Once a picture has been established, you may find that it is not perfect. Here are some common picture faults, their causes and solutions.

Short, fine, white horizontal lines keep darting across the screen.

This is tape dropout, which means that flecks of oxide have fallen off the tape's recording layer. This can happen if the tape is worn, or of poor quality, or if it has been left in 'Pause' too often. This is particularly likely to happen to the first few minutes of a video tape, since these are played most often. Worn tape cannot be repaired, but the ends can be spliced. If dropouts appear on good-quality tapes frequently, and for no apparent reason, call an engineer to look at the VCR.

The picture has become progressively more grainy and the colour and audio poorer. This can happen quickly or gradually.

The video heads need cleaning. For the best results, call an engineer. New heads sometimes get dirty unusually fast. This is because they need to be worn in, and they will settle after a few plays. You can run a blank tape a few times to save wear on recorded tapes.

The recording or timer controls were set carefully, but the VCR did not record.

If nothing was recorded, the VCR was probably not switched to its timer mode. The switch may have been accidentally knocked to 'Off.' If audio and video noise was recorded, the channel selector switch may be switched to a channel not in use. Check these controls when setting up a recording.

Thick white lines appear on the screen on playback, and the VCR makes a noise.

The tape has been creased or crumpled. Do not continue to use the tape, for it may damage the heads. If this happens suddenly and without reason to a known tape, consult an engineer. The VCR may be faulty.

The playback picture is poor, perhaps with marked noise bars. It may break up altogether.

The video heads are mistracking to some degree. If the tracking control does not help and the fault persists, call an engineer. The video heads may be misaligned as the result of a knock to the VCR.

If the tape is borrowed, the VCR it was recorded on was mistracking.

On playback, the top of the picture bends to the right.

This is 'hooking'. It occurs when the television cannot synchronize immediately to the VCR's output. Most televisions can be suitably adjusted by an engineer.

There is herring-bone interference on the screen.

The VCR may be too close to the television, or the VCR's RF output too close to a broadcast channel. Some RF outputs can be retuned by the owner, if the manual gives instructions. Otherwise, call an engineer.

The VCR gives only a monochrome picture.

This may be a sign that the VCR or television needs retuning. Otherwise, the VCR may have a 'Monochrome/Colour' switch which should be set to 'Colour' (or 'Auto') for colour and 'Mono' or 'B/W' for black and white.

White sparks appear on the screen during playback.

There is static electricity on the head drum. An engineer can demagnetize it.

Small, almost static black lines appear on the screen when a pre-recorded tape is played.

This is a recording fault on the tape. Ask your dealer to exchange it.

Regular white streaks deface the video replay picture every few seconds.

This may be radar interference. The VCR's receiver unfortunately amplifies radar signals. You can get a radar filter fitted to the antenna, but it is cheaper and usually more effective to retune the VCR to a new reception channel away from the radar band.

Faults and how to fix them

You are, by now, an expert in the art of using and enjoying your VCR. Your antenna, television set and recorder are all adjusted for the best picture reception. You know your way round the controls and are familiar with the manual. If your VCR fails to record you know how to check thoroughly that you have operated the controls correctly; that your television and VCR are tuned to best advantage; and that all the connections are in the right place before you make an expensive appointment with your service engineer.

This expertise has not been too hard to acquire and you feel at home with your VCR. Now is the time to acquaint yourself with some of the less routine surprises which it might spring on you. The potential problem areas can be divided into cables, tape and breakdowns of the VCR; if you use a portapack, batteries can cause some problems.

Listed below are some symptoms you may encounter, and what to do about them.

Cables

Cables are most likely to become worn or damaged at the point where the cable joins the connector; sometimes the internal cable cores can be broken if they are folded sharply or trodden on. This can be hard to detect from outside. About eight per cent of all video problems are caused by faulty cables.

It is worth learning to do a simple continuity check, using a multimeter or continuity tester. If you know how to splice and solder, repair the cable yourself; if not, it is easier to buy a replacement.

If you are using a screw-together power plug, it is common for one of the wires inside the plug to become disconnected. It is a simple job to open the plug and reconnect it. When doing so, ensure that the metal strands at the end of the wire are twisted neatly together and screwed down tightly, and that the cable is firmly clamped in the plug's cable collar.

Make sure the live wire is as short as possible, so that it will be the first to pull loose if the cable is strained, removing the threat of electric shock should the earth or neutral wire be disconnected.

If you have a sealed AC plug, you may have to replace the cable and plug. However, sealed plugs do not often fail.

Cable problems
The VCR works well near to the television but poorly at a distance.
The extension cable may not be the full-specification UHF coaxial cable which is absolutely necessary for transmitting signals to and from a television receiver. If in doubt, ask your dealer's advice.

You want to use a hi-fi lead for audio dubbing from one VCR to another. The connectors fit perfectly, but you can get no sound from the monitor.
Some audio and video leads look alike, but the connectors are wired differently inside. Ask your dealer for the correct audio lead, or have one made up.

Tapes
Video cassettes are fairly robust if kept inside their cases when not in use. Video tape is very delicate, and small amounts of dust, grease, damp or heat can damage it.

The tape appears to play for a shorter time than is stated on the label.
This is a very common complaint. It is more than likely that the tape memory on the VCR is switched on, and that the tape is not winding back to its beginning.

The picture from one tape is getting progressively worse.
The tape may be wearing out. If a tape is well treated there will be wear eventually, owing to the abrasive effect of the video heads. Tapes used to show signs of wear after about fifty plays, but a good-quality tape with a properly adjusted VCR should last for hundreds of plays in good condition.

If your video heads get dirty quickly, this could be a sign that you are using a cheap brand of tape which sheds its oxide easily, clogging the tape heads.

Once worn, a tape cannot be revitalized. It can, however, be copied: the result will be poor but it will last longer.

A tape has snarled up inside the VCR.
The tape may be caught round the head drum. Call an engineer.

The tape is broken or creased.
You can salvage a broken or partly creased tape by cutting out the creased section and, using a video tape splicing kit, joining the end to one end of the leader tape. Never splice any part of the tape that will contact the video heads.

The cassette is jammed in the compartment.
Cassette housings can become invisibly warped if left near a heat source. Call an engineer.

A cassette housing is broken.
Since cassette housings are screwed together, they can be dismantled and, therefore, it is possible to swap housings with those on a less valuable tape. This requires great manual dexterity: if you handle the tape, you will damage it beyond repair. If the tape is valuable, or you are in doubt about the procedure or its results at any stage, consult your dealer.

If possible, both cassettes should be fully rewound before opening. To open them use a Phillips pattern (cross-headed) screwdriver to undo the screws which hold the housings together. Lay each cassette down with the screw-holes underneath and press the tiny release catch by the hinge of the protector panel which covers the front of the cassette. Hold this panel open and carefully lift off the top half of the cassette.

Gently unthread the tape and lift the loaded spool into its new housing without touching the recording tape. Clean rubber or surgical gloves can be worn as a precaution. If the tape is not rewound, both spools will have to be transferred.

Rethread the tape, replace the top of the new housing, turn it over and replace the screws.

Batteries
Battery problems usually concern recharging. Rechargeable batteries are expensive, so it pays to care for them properly.

The battery pack has suddenly stopped working. They are lead acid batteries.
If lead acid batteries are allowed to go completely flat, they will cease to work.

Tired batteries can cause the tape threading mechanism on the portapack to malfunction, trapping the tape.

The battery pack will only work for twenty minutes. They are nickel cadmium batteries.
It is harmful to nickel cadmium (NiCad) batteries to recharge them when they are only partly used. If done repeatedly, this will inhibit the batteries' ability to accept a charge. Use them until the battery warning light comes on and then recharge them. If stored, discharge and recharge them every six months.

VCR malfunctions
Apart from minor tracking faults and dirty video heads, real problems with the VCR are rare. On older VCRs, damage could result from hasty and incorrect use of the switches. Modern logic-controlled switches are less susceptible, but it is wise to treat electronics with some gentleness. Operate all switches with a brief pause between each operation, and do not be tempted to test the system to its limits.

There are traces of either the audio or video from a former recording on a new one.
The VCR is not erasing properly and requires professional attention.

The cassette keeps ejecting from the VCR.
You may be pressing buttons too fast or in the wrong order, causing the VCR's logic to malfunction.

If you have an infra-red remote control, flashes of sunlight or heat sources can cause it to function unexpectedly. Ultrasonic remote controls can sometimes be set off by whistling or sibilant sounds.

There is a persistent buzz from the VCR.
This can be the first sign that it is drifting out of tune, and needs retuning.

Some people are troubled by traces of audio noise from the VCR. If you are sensitive about sound quality, you need a VCR with a noise-reduction system.

Rewind varies in speed and sometimes stops.
The VCR's drive mechanism may be malfunctioning, or the cassette may be faulty. Consult an engineer.

Understanding the recorder

From the moment you load a blank cassette into the machine the VCR is ready to record signals off air, or from a camera, and to carry out a whole series of other actions in response to the touch of a button.

The VCR's logic circuits are behind the translation of commands into actions. Supposing you select 'Record', the circuitry triggered by the switch sets in motion a mechanical threading system which opens up the guard flap on the cassette, and draws a loop of tape out to a set of moving rollers. These draw it into the machine along a highly complicated path which takes the tape past the fixed audio heads (which record and play back the sound-track); the erase head (which wipes out any existing recording on the tape passing the heads when 'Record' is selected) and the control track head, which writes a regular series of pulses on the tape to calibrate it for accurate timing control. It also winds the tape round the heart of the machine, the helical scan head drum, which records and plays back the video information.

Because of the amount of video information which has to be recorded on the tape, these heads are not fixed, but the drum on which they are mounted spins very fast past the moving tape. The tape transport mechanism swings the tape around the drum at an angle, so that the spinning heads write a series of very narrow tracks at a shallow angle to the length of the tape. This is the helical scan system which all video cassette recorders use. The audio head records the sound-track along one edge of the tape, and the control track is recorded on the opposite edge.

When the recording is finished you touch the 'Stop' button and the machine responds, not only by stopping the tape, but by reversing the laborious tape-threading mechanism, so that the loop inside the machine at the time you stopped the recording is threaded back into the cassette, and the guard flap is ready to unload the cassette.

If all you want to do is wind the tape back to the beginning to replay the recording, this is a more simple process. All the machine has to do is to wind the spools so that the tape is fed back in the reverse direction. This it does by connecting the drive motor to the tape spools rather than to the pinch wheel which pulls the tape loop past the heads for record-

ing and playback. This means that the tape has to be held clear of the heads to allow a fast winding speed: on Betamax machines the tape is retained within the VCR for fast wind and rewind; on VHS machines it is wound back into the cassette first, and on Video 2000 machines the tape can be wound quickly inside and outside the tape path within the VCR.

On selecting 'Play', the tape is threaded back around the rotating head drum and past the other fixed heads. The other functions affect mainly the speed with which the tape follows this path.

Most other features on your VCR will be refinements of these basic systems, or a sophisticated timer-control mechanism, which increase their versatility.

Another option is the automatic program search facility. This is a circuit which records an invisible and inaudible 'blip' on the tape at the beginning or the end of each recording. A control then lets you tell the recorder to fast-wind through a tape, and stop only when it recognizes one of these signals. This will put you at the end of a particular recording, and the beginning of the next, quite automatically.

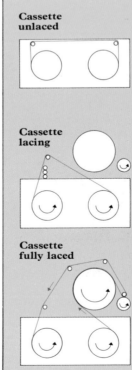

Cassette unlaced

Cassette lacing

Cassette fully laced

When the 'Play' button is operated, a series of pins rises up and draws the tape against the head drum, *left*.

The tape is moved along by the pinch wheel, a rubber wheel which pushes it against a turning capstan.

In 'Fast search' the capstan moves the tape over the video heads faster than in normal playback, and 'Slow motion' slows the tape down. Extra electronics are needed to get a stable picture.

In 'Pause' the pinch wheel releases its contact with the capstan, so that, although the capstan turns, the tape does not move along.

On most VCRs with twin recording heads, 'noise' bars cross the top of the screen when pause or freeze-frame is selected. The Toshiba V-8600 (Europe), V-8500 (USA) eliminates these by doubling the number of recording and playback heads. Instead of tracing two recorded tracks, they trace only one track accurately. As a result, Toshiba offers 'Super Still' and 'Super Slow Motion' facilities on this machine, and also provides fast picture search at up to 40 times normal speeds.

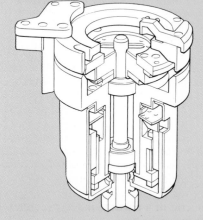

The neat, unruffled exterior of a modern VCR covers a mass of electronic and mechanical machinery which carries out a wide range of delicate tasks with precision and reliability.

The main mechanical part is the head drum which can be seen, ringed by the tape-lacing arm, in the centre of a Sony SL-C7, *below.*

The majority of components, however, are electronic and are mounted on printed circuit boards (PCBs). One PCB may carry several hundred components.

A large VCR factory can turn out over 20,000 machines a day, each one with over 3,000 separate parts. All are tested for a period. VCRs are very reliable; however, the delicacy of some adjustments make them vulnerable to rough treatment. Some parts are set to tolerances 50 times finer than a hair.

The minute slits in the video heads which record the video signal, are so small that particles of dust can clog them, so VCR factories are kept as free of dust as possible. In large factories, much of the work, including PCB assembly, is done by machines.

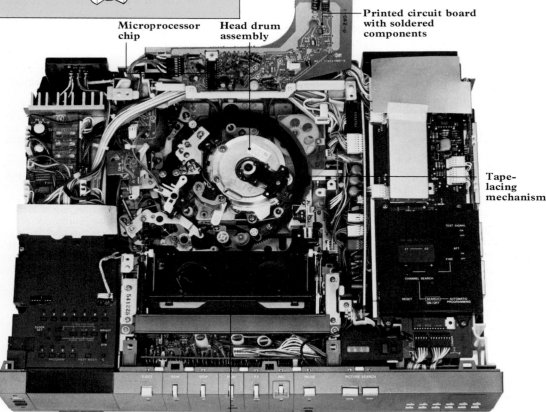

Microprocessor chip

Head drum assembly

Printed circuit board with soldered components

Tape-lacing mechanism

Cassette compartment

Caring for the recorder

What keeps a VCR working well? It needs the right environment to work in: not too cold, nor too hot, humid, dusty or prone to vibrations or magnetic fields. It needs what many engineers call mechanical sympathy on the part of its owner: do not hit it, drop it, shake it, stand heavy objects on it, or spill things into it. Use the controls gently and do not confuse it by trying to give it too many contradictory commands at once because you are unsure about what to do next.

The only repair attention it will need is general cleaning and demagnetizing every so often. It is difficult to be specific about how often chores like these need to be carried out. Most experts say that preventive maintenance (doing the job before the need becomes obvious) is to be avoided.

It is better to watch out for picture distortion or signs of partial erasure on some of your tapes, which are indications that the recording heads are retaining some of their magnetism, before calling a service engineer to demagnetize (or de-gauss) them.

Much more common is the need to clean the heads of particles of magnetic oxide which flake off the tapes in regular use. It is difficult to give an accurate figure of how often this is needed. Manufacturers' and testers' estimates vary from 'up to every 1,000 hours of use' to 'as few as every 400 hours or so' depending on the cleanliness of the atmosphere in which the machine is kept, and the quality of the tapes being used. Poor-quality tapes may shed more oxide particles than the latest, best-quality tapes do.

Once again the answer is to watch for the symptoms. Progressively noisier pictures (that is, grainy and speckled with snow) on all your tapes during playback will indicate that the heads are becoming clogged and that it is time to clean them.

Opinions differ sharply too on whether you should do the job yourself, or call in a service engineer. The problem is that the heads are extremely delicate, and the slightest slip in cleaning them could easily cause damage which would cost far more to repair than the price of having the heads cleaned professionally in the first place. Add to that the fact that most manufacturers' guarantees are rendered invalid by opening up the machine to perform an operation like this, and it hardly seems worth while trying to undertake the work oneself.

Care and maintenance check list

1 Make sure your VCR is horizontal before you operate it.
2 Never stand a VCR on the floor, or on a carpet.
3 Keep your VCR well ventilated at all times. Never cover the ventilation grilles.
4 Do not expose your VCR to direct sunlight or heat; keep it in a cool, dry place.
5 If you have disconnected the machine for some time, do not use it immediately after reconnecting it. Give it time to warm up before playing a tape.
6 Do not expose your VCR to moisture from spilled liquids, sudden changes of temperature, or the damp air near a window.
7 After playing a cassette, remove it from a VHS or Betamax machine, and never transport the machine with a cassette in place.
8 If a fault occurs, do not try to repair it, and do not continue to use the machine. Call a service engineer.
9 Keep the VCR's original packing in which to transport it.
10 Do not use solvent cleaners on a plastic VCR case. Use a little isopropyl alcohol (white spirit) to remove stubborn or oily marks.
11 Wipe the VCR over regularly with a damp cloth, using clean water, or an anti-static cleaning fluid obtained from a video dealer. Dust or vacuum carefully around and behind the VCR to prevent dust and fluff accumulating. Keep the cassette compartment closed when cleaning.
12 Do not use a tape-head cleaner unless you suspect that your video heads are clogged, and then use it sparingly. If in doubt, call a service engineer.
13 Run your VCR in record mode for an hour every couple of weeks, even if you do not wish to record. If you use it only for playback, the heads will gradually become magnetized, causing a loss of picture quality which is a symptom of permanent damage to the recordings. The strong RF signal used for recording reverses this process. If you suspect your tape heads need demagnetizing, call your service engineer.
14 Take care not to drop or knock your VCR. This could cause the video heads to fall out of alignment, a condition which can only be repaired in a video laboratory.
15 Run trailing leads round the edge of the room, or cover them with a mat or rubber electrical cord protector, so that people cannot trip over them or damage them by treading on them.

Although you should never attempt to open your VCR, you should keep a basic tool kit for servicing other parts of your system. As well as standard and cross-headed screwdrivers, you will find that you need Allen keys or hexagon keys or ball-tip drivers, *below*, for hexagon socket screws on tripods, light-stands and video furniture.

For the very small screws on some photographic equipment, jeweller's screw-drivers, **2**, are the right size. When assembling cables or repairing connections, clean wire ends with emery cloth, **1**, and use a soldering iron, **4**, which gives a controlled heat and can take alternative bits, **5**. For stiff tripod joints, use household oil, **3**.

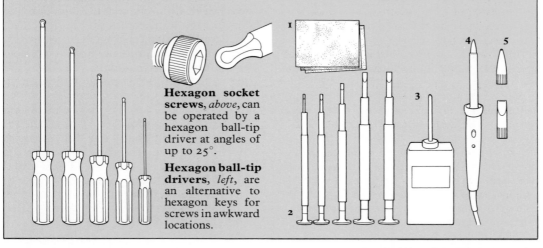

Hexagon socket screws, *above*, can be operated by a hexagon ball-tip driver at angles of up to 25°.

Hexagon ball-tip drivers, *left*, are an alternative to hexagon keys for screws in awkward locations.

Dust is a bitter enemy of the VCR, so much so that it has to be assembled in a constantly filtered, dust-free factory environment, *bottom*.

Dust clogs the video heads, so when your VCR is switched off, put a dust cover over it, *below*. Be careful not to switch it on with the dust cover in place. This can cause overheating.

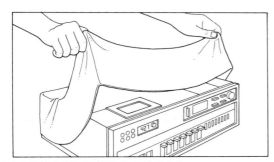

A head-cleaning cassette is a welcome alternative to the use of swabs and sprays to clean clogged tape heads. It obviates any need to open up the machine, and is un-likely to cause damage. All you do is load the cassette in the normal way, and play it for a short time: between 10 and 30 seconds, depending on the manufacturer's instructions. The tape cleans the heads and tape guides by direct abrasive action, so take care not to overdo the treatment.

One type of cassette eliminates the extra wear caused by using abrasives. It has one spool of felt, which has to be dampened with cleaning solvent before use, and one spool of a drying material. The problem is applying the right amount of solvent to the cleaning strips. Dry, non-abrasive, cleaning cassettes use direct contact with a soft material.

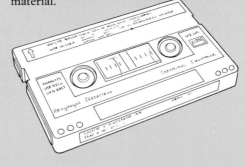

Building a video library

Many of the recordings you make will have a short life. These will be the shows you record because you will be out when they are screened, or because two movies you want to see coincide on different channels.

Yet there will always be some tapes you want to preserve, to play again and again, or to consult at intervals. Some of these you will probably buy. The choice of videograms (pre-recorded video cassettes) has for some time been broadening from the original base of full-length movies. They have penetrated into fields as varied as cookery, cricket and rock music.

However, the price of pre-recorded cassettes makes buying one an investment, worth while only when this repeatability factor comes into play. Classic movies which are only occasionally given an airing on the networks, such as *Casablanca* or some early Hitchcock masterpiece, might be well worth the cost, if you can take them out for a private showing whenever the spirit moves you to renew the acquaintance of such old and valued friends.

Tapes may also merit a place in your library. There are whole series of specialized tapes on diving, dinghy-sailing, rally-driving, fishing, tennis, rugby, football, badminton, soccer, squash and skiing, and the list is growing year by year. Here, the extra facilities on your VCR, such as freeze frame or slow motion, can be of the greatest help, enabling you to study the movement involved in a tennis service or a golf drive really closely, in a way that would not otherwise be possible.

The desire to see over again some of the greatest and most dramatic moments in a truly classic contest may motivate you to expand your library of sports tapes. Here, too, there is a steadily growing choice: provided agreements can be hammered out with the professional bodies involved, sports fans can look forward to being able to watch whole cricket series from the past, closely fought football finals, or Davis Cup tennis.

If you try listing your ten favourite movies, you will probably discover that you remember most clearly their great moments. Few people think of Steve McQueen in *Bullitt* without instantly picturing the amazing car-chase sequence, and perhaps the chess game. Similarly, the final sequence on the vertical cliff-faces of Mount Rushmore is what most people remember about *North by North-West*. Moments like these can form the basis for a specialized collection which will withstand repeated viewing.

How do you build up such a collection? One way is to set aside one cassette to begin a special collection. Every time a movie or a show with a contribution to make appears in the schedules, you watch it through until the moment you want comes up on the screen, and record just that fragment. Unfortunately this has a two-fold problem: first, you cannot pre-set the machine unless you know the exact timing of the segment you want to record; and second, the excerpts will be recorded in the order that the fragments are broadcast on television.

The easiest way round this difficulty is to tape the movie, and the show containing the fragment, in their entirety. Then, wind through the tape to find the parts you want to preserve, and copy them on another tape which you keep purely for these edited highlights. To do this, you will have to borrow another VCR for a few hours from a like-minded friend, for whom you may later be able to return the favour.

The list of edited library tapes you can build is endless: great moments from football games; appearances of your most popular rock band or whole series of comedy shows which may never be repeated.

One word of warning: it is all too easy to lose track of an important recording; just when you remember it, you find that something much less important has been recorded over it. For this reason alone, a proper labelling and indexing system is essential. If you label and index each cassette as soon as you have recorded a show, you will never have to face a dozen unlabelled tapes, having no idea which is the only surviving blank one on which to record a show which is starting in ten seconds.

Finally, as an alternative or in addition to building up your own library, consider joining one. Video libraries are springing up all over the country, with different terms for membership and borrowing cassettes. Joining a good library with a wide selection of tapes of movies and a few special-interest subjects, is a splendid way of widening your choice of tapes in the areas into which your own collection cannot venture: tapes that will be of interest for a single showing at a time.

Copying a video tape

It is quite simple to copy a video tape, but unfortunately a copy is always slightly less perfect than the original. There are ways of minimizing this drop in quality.

In order to copy a video tape, you have to link two VCRs. Do not, however, do this by plugging a VCR/TV coaxial cable into the RF input socket in the second VCR. If you do that you will be playing back the copying signal, converting it to an RF signal in the first VCR, passing this across to the second VCR and there converting it back into video and audio signals.

Instead, buy a pair of video and audio leads, with the correct connectors, to link up the 'Video out' and 'Audio in' of the first VCR to the 'Video in' and 'Audio in' of the second. You will then be able to play back the recorded tape on the first VCR and simply switch the second machine to the record mode for the duration of the piece you want to copy.

By this method you can even copy a cassette on another of a different format, but make sure the copy is made on a cassette which will fit your machine.

Tape care check list

1 Buy a cassette only if it is in a sealed library storage case.
2 Do not touch the tape; it is protected by a flap on the front of the cassette.
3 Never leave cassettes lying on the floor; they may collect dust or be damaged.
4 Do not subject cassettes to strong physical shocks.
5 Always wind cassettes on to the end or back to the beginning before storing them.
6 Store cassettes vertically.
7 Keep cassettes dry: do not have your library near a window. If you take cassettes out of the house, carry them in a waterproof bag or case; do not put them down on damp grass.
8 Keep cassettes cool. Never leave them where sunlight streaming through a window could damage them, such as on the seat of a car, and do not have your library near a fire or radiator.
9 Keep magnetic fields away from tapes.
10 Remove the recording tabs at the back of the cassette from any tape containing recorded material that you wish to keep.

Step-by-step guide to cataloguing

Step 1: Give each tape a number when you buy it, not when you want to use it. All tapes come with stick-on labels and numbers, so stick them on before you need a blank tape in a hurry. Label the first 01. It looks more professional and is easy to identify at a glance. Remember to number both tape and box, and never allow the two to become separated. Make sure you write all labels legibly.

Step 2: Buy yourself a notebook or a set of cards on which you can write the details. Allocate a page for each numbered tape. Only write the details on the labels provided with the cassette when you know it is something you will want to keep. If you have continually to relabel a tape you use over and over again, it will soon become unreadable. If this happens, relabel with self-adhesive labels.

Step 3: On each card, write all the details you need to identify the tape. You will need to note down what excerpts show, and the footage numbers at which they start and finish. Not only does this help you to find sequences quickly, but if you also enter each time a tape, or part of a tape, has been shown, you can work out how much life a recording has had when it begins to lose playback quality.

Step 4: If you remember to reset the counter to zero every time you load a new tape, and to rewind each tape to the beginning after use, you can record footages accurately.

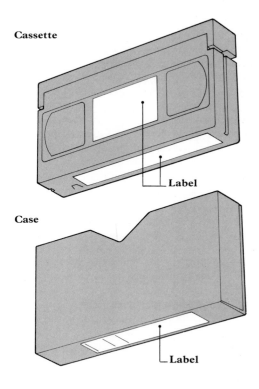

Cassette

Label

Case

Label

Video and the law

Most people who own or rent a VCR are aware that they are, in some way, affected by the law of copyright. There is, however, enormous confusion in the public mind about the extent and implications of that law and the legality of video recording.

The whole principle underlying the complex law of copyright is that creative people should be allowed to control the exploitation of their work, to enable them to secure a proper reward for their creative efforts.

There are two popular misconceptions about the effect of copyright law on video: first that a private individual can record any television programme without obtaining anyone's consent, provided that the recording is intended for home use only; and second, that permission is required for the recording of all television broadcasts. On a strict interpretation of the law, neither is entirely correct, but the second of these two propositions is, in fact, the one nearer to the truth.

A television broadcast usually consists of a number of elements, each of which gives rise to rights belonging to various people as creators of those elements. If you record a television programme, you may breach the copyright of one or more of those elements and, for that reason, break the law. While the copyright of a programme (owned by the broadcasting authority) is not infringed by a video recording made for private, domestic use, the rights of the author of the book on which the programme was based, for example, the composer of the featured music, or the record company who manufactured featured records, would be infringed.

As well as copyright, the 'performing rights' of people such as actors, singers, musicians and dancers are involved. Under the Performers Protection Acts 1958 to 1972 it is a criminal offence knowingly to make a record or film, other than for private and domestic use, from the performance of a musical work, without the prior written consent of the performers. This does not cover live sports and public ceremonies, but there is some doubt as to whether it covers activities such as figure skating and ballroom dancing and the performances of variety artists such as jugglers, magicians and acrobats.

From a strict legal point of view, the main reason why it is illegal to record the vast majority of television programmes off air is that they constitute what the Copyright Act 1956 calls 'cinematograph films', simply because they are pre-recorded on video tape before transmission. The copyright owner of a cinematograph film is the film maker, and so is usually (unless they are broadcasting a commercial feature film) the broadcasting authority. The copyright owner is entitled to control the making of copies of the cinematograph film, and there is no provision in law for copies to be made for private use.

Television programmes, when broadcast live, do not constitute cinematograph film, but often they contain some copyright element, such as the music featured in ice skating events, which would require consent for recording. Even live broadcasts of sporting events contain copyright elements such as theme music or the performance of a brass band at half time. Or they may contain cinematograph film in the form of action replays or other pre-recorded items. The copying of any such film (a cup final is a good example) would, without consent, amount to a breach of copyright.

Even if approached, the BBC and Independent Television companies are usually unable to give consent for copying in respect of all the elements that comprise the majority of their general programmes. The reason is that the BBC, for example, usually obtain, from the owners of the rights in each element, only sufficient rights to enable them to produce the programme and broadcast it. They do not generally acquire the right to authorize others to make recordings of the programmes that incorporate other copyright elements.

There are, however, some exceptions to the rigorous copyright laws which enable educational establishments to make use of certain copyright works. These do not allow schools to record television and radio broadcasts, nor to copy commercial films, but arrangements have been made so that educational establishments can legally record BBC educational programmes. (The exception is Open University programmes which can be recorded only by registered Open University students; otherwise a special licence must be obtained from the Open University.) Even so, a number of conditions must be complied with, and further details can be obtained from the BBC Copyright

Department. ITV will issue a licence to schools to record educational programmes for use in schools. But the limited exceptions for recording educational programmes do not extend to documentaries such as 'Horizon', however educational their content, and do not apply to the VCR owner.

Despite this strict legal interpretation, in practice neither the BBC nor the Independent Television companies complain of recordings made off air for private and domestic purposes. Largely, this is a recognition of their inability to prevent people making recordings in their own homes. Also, the broadcasting organizations seem to recognize that 'time shift' recording harms their commercial interests little, if at all, as long as such recordings are 'wiped' and the tapes re-used for further recordings. This said, they cannot specifically authorize any such private recording.

While turning a blind eye to purely domestic off-air recording, as long as the recordings are not copied, or used for commercial gain, the broadcasting organizations and film distributors recognize the absurdity of the present law, which renders illegal the vast majority of home taping off air, and finance a pressure group to campaign for a change in the law. They would like home taping to be legalized in return for the imposition of a levy on the sale price of blank tapes and VCRs. The money collected would be distributed among the owners of the rights comprised in the programmes. This levy is not intended to legalize the subsequent sale of tapes, even for domestic purposes, nor the copying of pre-recorded commercial tapes from one VCR to another.

Although a commision was set up to examine copyright law, and recommended in 1977 that a levy should be made on recording equipment only, as it is in the German Federal Republic, the British government has decided not to take any immediate steps and has invited further representations from the public and interested parties. In the meantime, the VCR owner will, it seems clear, be taking no risk in taping programmes off air for his own private and domestic use.

Any VCR owners, who produce multiple copies of their recordings and attempt to sell them, could end up at the wrong end of a legal action brought by the film distributors. Large-scale copying of film amounts to fraud, and the court may permit a person's premises to be searched if it is believed that he or she is copying pirate tapes, or storing them. Any counterfeit material is liable to be siezed and used as evidence.

Having made an off-air video tape, is it permissible to show that tape to an audience at home or elsewhere? The answer is that it all depends whether the showing amounts to a 'performance in public'; which depends, in turn, on the nature rather than the size of the audience. If the showing is essentially domestic it is not 'in public'. Otherwise it is.

The fact that some video films are legally made and distributed does not mean that their content is censored, and such films are available to children of all ages. Thus it is important for parents to be careful about vetting films intended for adult audiences only before permitting their children to watch them.

Many video owners make use of goods and services offered in classified advertisements. Most advertisers require full payment in advance, and the would-be purchaser could be left without an effective remedy if an advertiser subsequently went bankrupt without having supplied the ordered goods. Some magazines, however, and certainly those published by IPC, operate a Mail Order Protection Scheme under which the magazine undertakes to consider the customer for full or part reimbursement in the event that the advertiser went bankrupt without supplying the goods, subject to certain conditions being complied with. Otherwise, there is little the customer can do except make a formal claim against the liquidator with little prospect of getting the money back.

If you own a video camera you are, in general, free to film whatever you like, particularly if the film is intended for domestic viewing, and also to sell your movies. You should, however, remember the Performers Protection Acts if you intend filming concerts or the like, other than for home use. Although there is no right of privacy in the UK, some people may object to being filmed, so it is prudent to stop filming if you come up against this problem.

For further information on the legalities of video recording, contact the Video Copyright Protection Society Limited, London NW10, or the BBC Copyright Department.

The video buyer's guide

Acquire a video recorder now, the time is right. Years of competition have brought the prices down, and development has reached the stage beyond which only details have still to be perfected. Eventual obsolescence is unlikely: the VCR's growing role as the heart of the home computer guarantees its survival.

The projected arrival of the video disk, and its likely rivalry with video tape, has caused confusion in buyers' minds. However, you cannot record on a video disk; its potential lies in markets other than those where tape presides. Eventually, each will take its place as an interactive piece in the home computer jigsaw.

Choosing a VCR from among the dozens on the market involves, first, selecting a format. There are three widely available home video formats. VHS (Video Home System), a Japanese system developed by JVC, has so far proved the best seller in the European market. Betamax, another Japanese system developed by Sony, has been more popular in the USA. Video 2000, the late contender from Europe, has yet to make a strong impact in the USA. Complicated though it may seem, multi-format video is likely to persist unless buyers and manufacturers decide to opt for one system. Current trends suggest the opposite.

The choice of format will inevitably be dictated by personal requirements, such as where you live, for example. Each VCR format will play only cassettes designed especially for it: you cannot play a VHS cassette on a Betamax or Video 2000 VCR. If you want to exchange tapes with friends, choose a VCR in the same format as theirs.

If your VCR is to be used mainly for playing pre-recorded tapes, in the UK you will find most material available on VHS; in the USA, on Betamax. However, manufacturers of all three formats are improving market penetration into areas where they are weak, so the balance may be redressed.

In the following pages the differences between the leading formats are discussed in detail. Broadly speaking, however, there is currently the widest choice of machines in the VHS format, while Video 2000 offers the longest-playing cassettes and the most sophisticated timing facilities. Betamax cassettes are the most compact; Sony's portable VCR is smaller and lighter than its VHS competitors. All three have proven quality and

reliability, and there is little difference in price between them. Each format offers low-priced basic machines, and more expensive models featuring advanced facilities.

Weighing up the relative value of sophisticated features takes time. You need to visit stores and showrooms, to see demonstrations and compare models, to read brochures and magazines and talk to friends with VCRs.

Your choice should be based on how you want to use your VCR. If you are often away, you will need a model with a sophisticated timer which takes long-playing cassettes. A machine with remote control is a must if a member of your family is bedridden – or if you just hate getting up to change the television station. Should you want to collect excerpts, or to store off-air broadcasts for educational purposes, you will need a machine with an auto tape-search facility.

Slow motion, combined with frame-by-frame advance and freeze frame, is essential if you want to analyze a recorded sequence – a golf or tennis stroke, for example. If you are training seriously for a sport, consider the possibility of hiring a video camera to analyze your own stroke and compare it with that of a professional. To do that most successfully, you will need a VCR with good roll-back editing facilities.

Consider buying a portable system, if you want to make home movies. With the addition of a tuner/timer it will double as a home deck. The best have all the advanced facilities.

If you want to exchange tapes with friends overseas, you will need a triple-standard VCR. Different countries use different television systems, and so whatever the format, VCRs are designed to record from and play back through the television system of the country in which they are sold. If you want to play a tape of a baseball game recorded in the USA on a French television set, you will need a triple-standard VCR and the television must also be a triple-standard model, which is expensive.

Finally, the enthusiast with professional ambitions might want to invest in an industrial-standard VCR (U-matic, Betamax or VHS). These are more expensive than the domestic formats, but give a higher quality of sound and picture and can be used with sophisticated editing controllers to produce professional-standard video movies.

Before you buy, shop around. Prices fluctuate widely. If you are undecided rent a machine for a period. This way, you pay for the VCR in about three years and lose any resale value; but in return for a commitment of about one year the rental company bears all servicing and repair costs. Portapacks and cameras can be hired for short periods.

You will often find second-hand VCRs for sale. Some will be obsolete formats for which you cannot buy pre-recorded tapes, but blank tapes may still be on sale. Check that servicing is still possible. Even if it is only one year old, discarded in favour of an updated model, run a tape through it to check that it works properly. Later, when you come to update your own machine, think about keeping the old one. It could be useful for editing tapes.

The following pages guide you through the range of video recorders and their accessories currently on the market, and the video disk players you may soon be able to buy. Then, since innovations reported in today's video magazines will be on sale sooner than you think, the last pages take a look at video R & D, to give you a glimpse of what the future may bring.

The Betamax system

The Betamax system was developed by the Japanese electronics giant, Sony, in response to the now-obsolete 'VCR' format developed by Philips. Philips was the first company to enter the domestic video market, but the VCR cassettes were too expensive to attract enough buyers to become well established.

Until that time, Sony had concentrated on its industrial U-matic format. Open-reel VTRs were still the norm for professional video, and cassettes were an innovation. U-matic, with its automatic tape-threading system, called U-loading, became the basic blueprint for Betamax. However, where U-matic uses three-quarter inch (19 millimetre) tape, Betamax uses the half-inch (12.5 millimetre) tape used now by all home decks. This gives a compact cassette only 6 × 4 × 0.9 inches (155 × 95 × 25 millimetres).

Starting from an already-viable format, Sony were able to release Betamax in 1975, a year before its main rival, VHS. Consequently, in the areas where video was marketed vigorously and was quickly adopted – the USA and Japan – it long remained the favourite. In many other parts of the world the VHS system has made more impression. The main result of this is that pre-recorded tapes will be easier to obtain in the locally-favoured format, although, because they are now simultaneously released in both formats, your supplier should be able to order tapes to the format you require.

Betamax has a reputation for technical excellence. The Betamax head drum, with a diameter of 2.9 inches (74.5 millimetres) spins at a speed of 19.2 feet (5.83 metres) a second, enabling the heads to write over a larger area of tape than in VHS. More information can be stored on the tape, and under optimum conditions this should give a better video picture and better audio.

Betamax cassettes are slightly smaller than VHS and Video 2000. This means that portapacks can be smaller and lighter, but also that the longest Betamax tapes give a shorter playing time than the longest VHS, since they are physically smaller. They tend to be cheaper. On the other hand, Betamax is still the only format with an optional tape-stacking mechanism which allows 14 hours of continuous playing.

The U-shaped tape path is thought to place minimum strain on the tape, particularly during on-screen picture search.

Unique to Betamax is Sony's Betastack tape-loading attachment. This is the video equivalent of a disk auto changer; up to four cassettes can be loaded into the cartridge, giving a playing or recording time of 14 hours at normal tape speed. As each tape finishes, it is ejected and a new tape inserted by the autochanger.

An attachment like this is at its most useful with a VCR like the C7, *below*, which has a multi-event timer, so that a long series of features can be recorded. This may account for the fact that video auto changers have not yet become common.

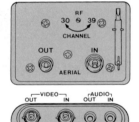

The voltage selector on the back panel of the Sony C7, *above*, gives a choice between 220 and 240V and 110 and 127V. Some voltage selectors give a choice between three or four single-voltage settings.

Methods of tuning a VCR's RF-decoder to the TV vary. In this case, a test pattern is generated by the VCR, and a screw is turned until the pattern shows clearly on another channel.

New from Sony in the USA, the SL-2500, *right*, is the first VCR to be designed to stack with hi-fi components. Modular stacking with other equipment is a natural progression for video, and this is its first realization.

The 2500 has the advanced features of larger VCRs: high-speed tape search (called Betascan), with random access to nine points on the tape, and a direct camera input with roll-back editing.

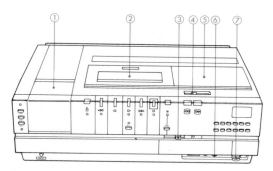 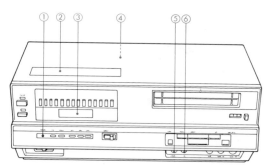

Sony SL-C7, *above*, has been Europe's top-line VCR since 1980. The top-loading cassette compartment, **2**, tuner panel, **5**, and timer panel, **1**, distinguish it from newer front-loaders.

Some older VCRs only have a 3-digit tape counter because they pre-date longer tapes. The C7's tape counter, **4**, has four digits, typical of modern VCRs.

A special tracking control, **3**, can be adjusted to give a good still frame and slow-motion picture.

The C7 was one of the first VCRs to provide a direct camera input, **7**. An input select, **6**, switches between the camera, the TV receiver, and a line 'Video in' input on the rear panel.

The American SL-5000, *above*, is the most advanced of the series which includes the 5400 and 5800.

The 14-switch channel-select panel, **3**, is typical of American VCRs, and will become more widespread as TV stations proliferate. The tuner controls, **2**, include a selector switch for VHF and UHF.

The tape speed select switch, found on many American VCRs, is at the rear of the SL-5000, **4**.

A cable remote control input, **5**, and separate camera pause, **6**, audio and video inputs make this VCR a mixture of advanced and basic features. The clock-set switch, **1**, is operated by a fine-pointed tool.

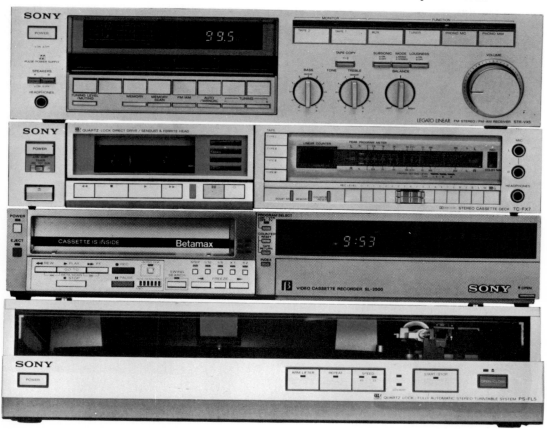

On the market/Betamax recorders

The prospective buyer will notice immediately that there are far fewer Betamax models than VHS to choose from. This is not a disadvantage; VCRs today vary so little from one brand to another that some people may even consider it an advantage.

VCRs fall into three categories: 'budget', 'de luxe' and portable. The lower-priced, or budget, models have few facilities, to minimize costs. The most obvious limiting factor will be the timer, which will allow you only one or two pre-programmed recording events, or one event at the same time on several consecutive days. Many people find that a one-event timer is quite sufficient.

In the second category are the models with more advanced features and a higher price tag. Some manufacturers have several machines on their current catalogue, each slightly more complex and expensive than the one before, so study the most advanced model and then work down through the price range until you find one that suits you.

A portable is built for lightness. Betamax portables are potentially slightly smaller and lighter than VHS, since the cassettes are smaller. However, the choice of Betamax portables is much smaller than for VHS.

Prices tend to reflect facilities rather than picture quality: the best way to study this is to try a model in your own home. This may be hard to arrange if you are not renting; so check whether the store you are dealing with will give you another model if you are not happy. Check that the focus is crisp and the colour true, and that the sound quality is satisfactory for your needs.

All Betamax machines are manufactured under license to Sony. There are fewer manufacturers offering Betamax than VHS: the Sony, Sanyo and Toshiba companies are the primary manufacturers, while others market Betamax machines under their own labels. The choice of facilities and the standards of maintenance and service are much the same for Betamax and VHS.

One point that may decide you between VHS and Betamax is Betamax's faster write speed, which gives it better sound reproduction. However, if audio is an interest, be sure to look for a machine with a noise-reduction system. Sony has its own system, Beta Noise Reduction, but this is apparently less effective than the Dolby system, which VHS has been the first to adopt.

The superb design and engineering for which Betamax is known make it an attractive format. As an example, Toshiba's new model has four video heads instead of two, a facility uncommon at present, but likely to become widespread in the future.

Sanyo VTC-5600 (Europe)

One of the new generation of Betamax, the Sanyo VTC-5600, *above*, has some advanced features at a medium price.

The soft-touch logic controls are a popular modern feature, and are complemented by a record-lock switch to prevent a chance touch from starting the record controls and erasing a tape. On-screen picture search is in forward mode only.

Sony's SL-2000, *below*, is the smallest and lightest ½-in (12.5-mm) portable in the world. Combined with the TT-2000 tuner/timer, it gives many facilities associated with home decks.

The timer can memorize four events over two weeks, and there is a full set of fast and slow frame features.

Important and unusual is the SL-2000's ability to review just-recorded material, in forward or reverse, without disrupting the camera's recording mode. Normally this would happen if the portapack were taken off the 'Pause' or 'Record' setting, causing a burst of video noise on the picture.

Sony SL-2000

Sanyo VTC-9300 (Europe)

Sanyo VTC-9300,
above, is old-
fashioned, but an
inexpensive and
popular machine. It is
identified as first-
generation by its
piano-key style
controls. The switches
are mechanical, and
'Stop' must be
selected between
other modes, or the
controls may suffer
damage or strain.

Typically on old
VCRs, there is no on-
screen picture search.
The VTC-9300 has
held its ground as a
budget VCR because
it offers similar
quality to more
expensive machines.

Sony SLT-7ME
(Europe)

Sony SLT-7ME, a
European triple-
standard version of
the C7, is aimed
specially at customers
in the Middle East,
where PAL and
SECAM are

transmitted, and
NTSC recordings are
on sale. Like most
PAL-based multi-
standard VCRs, it will
play, but not record,
in NTSC. Oddly, it
will not record off air
in the UK.
It is simpler than
the C7, having
monochrome freeze
frame instead of
colour, and a corded
remote, instead of
infra-red.

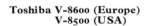

Toshiba V-8600 (Europe)
V-8500 (USA)

Toshiba's new
model is one of the
few VCRs to have
four video heads. The
extra pair are specially
included to overcome
tape distortion during
freeze frame and to
give a noise-free
picture.
Tracking controls
also allow the fast
picture search
functions to be noise
free.
This VCR also uses
the 'Beta Noise
Reduction' system but

this apparently is not
as effective as the
Dolby system, and
the audio is not
exceptional.
A cable remote
control is standard,
with infra-red
optional.

A budget version of
the Sony C7, the
European C5, *above*,
gives the same basic
quality at a budget
price. The timer
allows only one event
to be pre-set over
seven days, and the

Sony SL-C5 (Europe)

freeze frame and
picture search in
forward and reverse
are in monochrome.
Unusually for a
budget model, the C5
has a direct camera
socket, and an optional
cable remote control.

The Video Home System

VHS (Video Home System) was announced by the Japan Victor Company (JVC) in 1976, a few months after the launch of Betamax. By 1978, home and portable machines were widely available, and VHS has become the market leader over most of the world.

For VHS, JVC developed a new tape-loading system known as M-loading. This uses a complex tape path, and the system has been criticized since it was believed to cause tapes to stretch during fast-winding. Therefore, early VHS machines fast-wound with the tape unlaced from the tape heads, so that no picture could be seen. Further developments have alleviated the likelihood of tape damage and given good on-screen picture search.

The VHS head drum is 2.6 inches (62 millimetres) in diameter and revolves at 7.3 inches (2.34 millimetres) a second, giving a slower write speed than Betamax and, therefore, in theory, a slightly inferior picture. In practice, however, if anything has seemed to suffer, it has been the audio quality. Sophisticated electronics have improved this to the point where only serious music lovers will be disappointed, but video sound is generally poor because so little space is allocated to it on the tape.

The VHS cassette is bigger than the Betamax at 7.3 × 4.1 × 9.0 inches (187 × 104 × 25 millimetres). It is much the same size and shape as a Video 2000 cassette. VHS tape has a longer playing time than Betamax, four hours for the longest tapes, and six hours if a long-play machine is used, but since long tapes suffer more from breakage and poor reproduction quality, this is not necessarily an advantage. Video 2000 tapes give a longer playing time as they can be recorded on both sides.

Factors affecting picture quality are so many, and so often external to the VCR (the television receiver and antenna used, for instance) that a sensible comparison can no longer be made between VHS, Betamax and Video 2000 on picture quality alone. Furthermore, fierce competition has ensured that the range of facilities any one format now has to offer does not differ much from that of another. The choice must ultimately depend upon the qualities of one particular model, and local factors (such as availability of video tapes and service), rather than a preference for one format.

JVC's flagship, the HR-7700, is one of the newest, most advanced and most expensive VCRs in any format. It is the ultimate in VHS and, in Europe, has become the successor to the Betamax SL-C7 as the state-of-the-art popular-format VCR. It is expensive, but a luxury machine.

The HR-7700 follows the trend of other, newer VCRs in having a separate RF (radio frequency) output for standard TVs and a video input and output for non-RF monitors and cameras. This, and the good backspace editing facility, make it an ideal VCR to use for simple editing.

The HR-7700, *below,* has a catalogue of advanced features. For audio fans especially, the Dolby noise-reduction system will be attractive. Look for the Dolby logo, **1,** on the front panel.

The 'x2 with sound' facility, **2,** is not just a fast picture search: busy users should be able to watch recordings in half the usual time and still follow the sound-track.

Like nearly all new-generation VCRs, the HR-7700 has a front-loading cassette compartment, **3**.

Slow motion, **4,** frame-by-frame advance, **5,** and still frame, **6,** once considered gimmicks, are now found on nearly all VCRs. The HR-7700 gives colour freeze frame and slow motion pictures which, when the tracking is well adjusted, are virtually noise free.

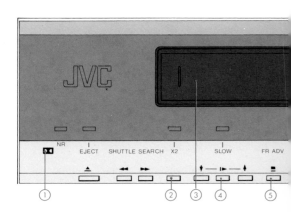

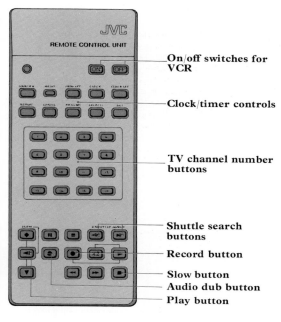

On/off switches for VCR

Clock/timer controls

TV channel number buttons

Shuttle search buttons

Record button

Slow button
Audio dub button
Play button

A full-function remote-control unit is standard with the HR-7700. This controller, *left*, is unusually comprehensive. It uses an infra-red signal, which is more flexible than a cable control, and less liable to interference than an ultrasonic signal.

Remote controllers vary in the distance and angle at which they can be used. Test the unit in the shop and try to find its limitations. You should expect to have infra-red on advanced models in any domestic format.

This unit has a complete set of clock/ timer controls, channel selection buttons, variable-speed functions and audio dub. A light emitting diode (LED) lights up to show when the remote control is operating. One feature of an infra-red control is that is has no 'On/off' switch of its own, needing power only when in use.

The choice of a remote control is a matter of convenience. While a corded remote can be used anywhere within the cord's reach, an ultrasonic or infra-red remote must be aimed at the window on the VCR.

'Audio dub', 7, is another facility appearing on more and more VCRs.

Concealed neatly by an aluminium hatch below the front panel, are headset and mike sockets; a tape memory switch; tracking controls for slow/still frame and x2/play modes; clock/timer controls; auto-sweep tuning; auto tape search (with which the VCR will home in on a key signal recorded along with a broadcast), and a direct camera input.

The soft-touch switches, 9, are logic-controlled, so that any sequence of commands is stored in the VCR's microprocessor before it responds to them. This reduces the risk of damaging the VCR by pressing switches too fast, or in the wrong order.

The display-mode indicator, 10, reads 'Clock', 'Prog' or 'Count', telling the user whether it is in a clock mode, timer-setting mode or tape-counter mode.

The clock display, 11, has fluorescent numerals which give a 24-hour display. The remote control indicator light, 12, comes on when the remote control infra-red is in use.

A line of ten fluorescent segments, 13, can either light up to monitor the auto-tuner's progress as it sweeps the TV broadcast channels, or progressively light up from left to right to show what portion of the tape remains to play.

The TV channel indicator displays the number of the channel which is being pre-set or which is being held in the channel lock, 14.

The sub-power buttons, 15, send power to different parts of the VCR: the power supply is on if the recorder is being used and off otherwise, and the timer power stays on while the timer is set to record. Some power is used at all times to keep the clock running.

On the market/VHS recorders

A majority of manufacturers has opted to manufacture VHS machines under licence to JVC. Primary manufacturers are JVC, Panasonic, Hitachi, Mitsubishi, Akai, Magnavox and Sharp; certain other manufacturers package VCRs manufactured by JVC and Panasonic. As well as the VCRs on the current catalogues, there are often slightly older machines in stock, for which parts and service should present no problem but which may have been reduced in price to clear them. It is perfectly normal for companies to delete a particular model from their catalogue and to stop producing it, but to go on providing parts and supporting services for years afterwards.

VHS is the best-selling format over much of the world, including the UK, the USA and the Middle East. Pre-recorded tapes and to a lesser extent blank cassettes, may be marginally easier to obtain for VHS in these areas, but you can order tapes of other formats.

A good way of inspecting machines is to buy a cassette of the right format and take it to your video dealer. Ask the assistant to record something off air for you, and compare the results with the pre-recorded versions. This may also be a good chance to see in detail how the tuner/timer controls work. You could rent a recorded tape and use it for comparing VCRs in the same way. It is a good idea to try the same model in different shops, if possible.

Another advantage of VHS is that there is a considerably wider range of cameras and portapacks in that format. Cameras are not restricted to one format or another, but it tends to be true that a camera of a particular brand works best with a VCR of the same kind. This is not invariable, though, so test any equipment you buy thoroughly.

Although prices are now fairly consistent from one brand and one format to another, it is worth looking at both VCRs and cassettes in your area to see if one format gives a distinct price advantage. If you are going to build a complete tape library, you will want to choose the format with the cheapest tapes. VHS tends to be a little more expensive per hour (the only meaningful comparison) than Betamax, and Video 2000 is cheaper.

A hard-hitting marketing campaign by JVC back in the seventies accounts for VHS's current domination of the European market. Sony was much too slow.

VHS offers by far the widest choice of individual VCRs of any format. Although all VHS machines are made under license to JVC, other manufacturers have been innovative in their modifications to the system. For instance, Hitachi's VT-6500 portapack is one of few VCRs to offer 'Sound on sound', whereby an extra sound-track can be recorded over the original one without erasing it – music over commentary, for instance.

Although all VCRs are alike in many ways, it is worth while looking closely at several to see what features they offer.

Akai VS-5 (Europe)

Akai VS-5, is a European top-loader. It has a steeply angled front panel making the controls easy to see from all angles: a neglected point with top-loading VCRs.

The VS-5's timer can handle nine events over 14 days. A full-function infrared remote control is standard, and it has a safety lock to disarm the device while recording is in progress, or a tape is being played, to prevent accidental disruption.

If a malfunction should occur during recording, an 'error' buzzer sounds.

This VCR has a channel-tuner with one button to locate stations, and one for tuning.

JVC HR-7200

JVC HR-7200, is a good-value middle-market VCR.

The timer will memorize only one event, up to seven days ahead. However, there is a full-function remote control, and nine times normal speed in forward and reverse, automatic rewind, and tape memory, which return the tape to predetermined points.

Akai VPS-7350 (USA)

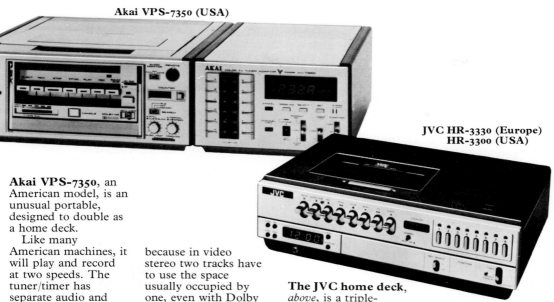

JVC HR-3330 (Europe)
HR-3300 (USA)

Akai VPS-7350, an American model, is an unusual portable, designed to double as a home deck.

Like many American machines, it will play and record at two speeds. The tuner/timer has separate audio and video outputs so that it can be used with older and industrial VCRs, which have no tuners.

There are two audio tracks, allowing stereo recording, but because in video stereo two tracks have to use the space usually occupied by one, even with Dolby noise reduction the audio quality is not particularly good.

The VPS-7350 can be locked, perhaps to prevent children from using it when parents are out.

The JVC home deck, *above*, is a triple-standard VCR based on an older, popular JVC machine.

Its facilities are basic, with no picture search, and a cable remote control with a pause function only.

As is usual for triple-standard VCRs and for some single-standard models, it is possible to select between 110, 127, 220 or 240V and 50 or 60 Hz AC supply.

Panasonic NV-7200 (Europe)

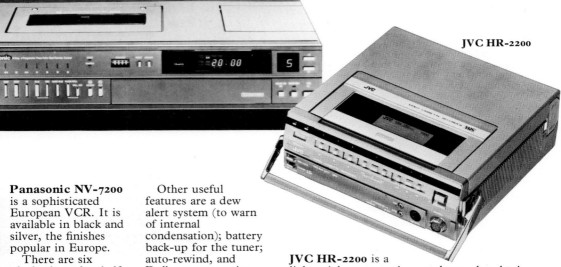

JVC HR-2200

Panasonic NV-7200 is a sophisticated European VCR. It is available in black and silver, the finishes popular in Europe.

There are six playback modes: half- and double-speed, normal, freeze frame, frame-by-frame advance, and nine times normal speed. All are operable from the infra-red remote controller.

Other useful features are a dew alert system (to warn of internal condensation); battery back-up for the tuner; auto-rewind, and Dolby-system noise reduction, giving better than usual audio quality.

Panasonic prides itself on building its VCRs on die-cast, lightweight aluminium chasses.

JVC HR-2200 is a lightweight portapack weighing just over 11 lb (5 kg). Older machines weigh around 19 lb (8.6 kg). It uses rechargeable nickel cadmium ('NiCad') batteries, which are quicker to recharge than lead acid.

The HR-2200 can be powered from its battery pack, an AC supply or a 12V car battery. A built-in RF unit allows connection with a TV.

Video 2000

Video 2000 is Europe's answer to the Japanese takeover of the home video market. Ironically, Philips, co-inventor with Grundig of Video 2000, were the first to market home video with their aptly-named VCR (Video Cassette Recorder) format, but they later lost ground to VHS and Betamax.

In the competitive world of video, as soon as a new model appears, it is safe to assume that a rival has a more advanced model in the pipeline. Outstripped by Betamax and VHS, Philips and Grundig had to produce something to challenge the market.

Video 2000, like VHS and Betamax, uses half-inch (12.5-millimetre) tape. The cassette, at 7.5 × 3.9 × 0.9 inches (183 × 109 × 25 millimetres) is very like a VHS in shape, but it is unique in having two tracks, like an audio cassette, so that the tape can be turned over to give twice as much playing time. (The compact audio cassette, developed by Philips and now the world standard, was the model for Video 2000 cassettes.)

Another major advance is Dynamic Track Following. This process uses a flexible video head which is able to detect the exact path of each video track and follow it precisely, a facility until now only available on professional recorders.

DTF means that the video tracks can be narrower, allowing a more economical use of tape and permitting the two-track format. It also gives very stable freeze frame and slow motion pictures. To achieve this picture stability, the other two formats have produced models with two extra video heads, but they do not give such a good result as the mobile heads. For this reason, there is no tracking control on a Video 2000 machine.

A problem facing Video 2000 is one of market resistance. The video-buying public has become familar with VHS and Betamax. Moreover, the ambiguous name chosen for the Video 2000-format cassettes, Video Compact Cassette (VCC), was intended to draw attention to the link between the Philips system and the successful compact audio cassette. However, the lack of direct reference to Video 2000 on the cassette has given rise to the rumour that Video 2000 cassettes are nowhere to be bought, whereas VCC is widely stocked.

It seems likely that Video 2000 will survive and prosper, and enthusiasts, looking for above-average quality, should consider it.

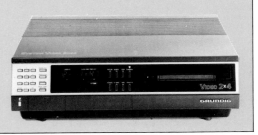

Video 2000's most advanced model, Grundig's 2 × 4 Super, arrived in time to save the format's reputation after poor performances by some of the earlier Video 2000 models. The unique Dynamic Track Following (DTF) system gives outstanding picture quality with still frame, slow motion, frame-by-frame advance, and on-screen forward and reverse and picture search functions, where the picture should be completely noise free: a great asset for anyone using slow motion for analyzing their tennis style, for instance.

The Video 2000 system is different from VHS and Betamax in the style of some of its controls, as well as some of its central technology.

The timer keyboard, **1**, of Grundig's 2 × 4 Super will be familiar to anyone who uses a pocket calculator. It is simple to key in the start and stop times for pre-set recording without running through a sequence of hours and days. However, the VCR's own microprocessor will clear all commands that are not completed or continued in 15 seconds.

The Preselect Memory switches, **2**, are used to alert the microprocessor that you wish to key in a command, or to make the VCR display any instruction in its memory on the clock panel, **6**.

Tuning controls are concealed behind a panel under the keyboard, **3**. There are three channel-search buttons; in the UK only the one marked 'IV/V' is normally needed.

The two fine-tuning switches, **4**, are the equivalent of the AFT switches on some VCRs and radios.

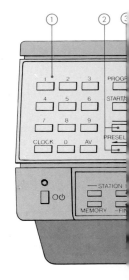

Dynamic Track Following (DTF) is unique in home video to Video 2000. DTF's secret is that the video head can alter its position to follow the video track it is reading. The tiny video head, *below*, is mounted on two bonded strips of piezo-electric ceramic. When an electric current is passed between the strips they bend slightly, moving the head up or down.

The diagram, *below right*, shows how the Video 2000 tape is recorded in two segments like an audio tape. The slanted video track covers less than half the width of the tape, the remaining space being occupied by two audio tracks for each video track, and two cue tracks in the centre of the tape, which could be used later in the format's development for carrying extra control signals. Each half of the tape is a mirror image of the other.

Because the heads follow each track so precisely, there is no need for the guard tracks used on VHS and Betamax to prevent the video heads picking up interference from adjacent tracks.

The video head stays in line by picking up minute traces of signal from the wrong tracks, analyzing and avoiding their source.

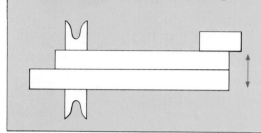
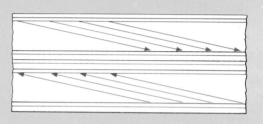

Although there is no tracking control, a crispener lever, **5**, gives the user a choice of sharp- or soft-focus picture. The microprocessor clears its memory after a 15-second delay if left standing, but there is also a manual clear control, **7**, in case the user wants to clear an error as soon as it happens.

The 'Go To' function, 8, is unique to Video 2000. If the user keys in a number of minutes from the start of a tape, the VCR will fast wind to that point. The 2 × 4 Super also has automatic picture search (APS), **10**, which finds the start and end of recordings by homing in on an audio tone.

If the 'Time Left' button, 9, is used, the clock display will show how much time is left for use on the cassette in the machine. It will automatically subtract any recording time stored in the VCR's tuner memory. With this VCR it is practical to base a tape-indexing system entirely on timing.

One confusing point about the 2 × 4 Super is the English wording on some of the switches. 'Stop', **11**, means 'pause', 'Tape', **12**, means 'stop' and 'Cassette', **13**, means 'eject'. The 2 × 4 Super will also display 'Full' if you try to pre-set more recording time than is left on the tape being used.

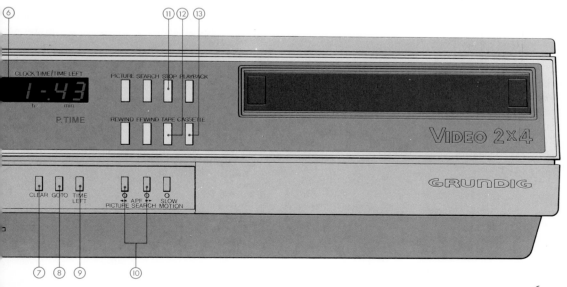

On the market/Video 2000 recorders

The late arrival of Video 2000 on the home video front explains why few models are yet available. The system was developed by Philips and Grundig, in cooperation; Philips machines are packaged by ITT, Pye, and Bang & Olufsen (the last being the only manufacturers to repackage the VCRs in their own style); Pye and ITT have simply relabelled the Philips machines.

Grundig, on the other hand, has designed its own version, aimed at the deluxe end of the market, and this is generally held to be the most advanced domestic VCR on the market today.

The late arrival of Video 2000 has given it advantages and disadvantages, but whereas the disadvantages are commercial (the reluctance of video retailers to commit themselves to stocking a third set of pre-recorded tapes) the advantages are technical.

Philips has been able to learn from the shortcomings of its two rivals. The design of the VCC (Video Compact Cassette) allows it to wind quickly in the housing, as do VHS tapes or, alternatively, in contact with the heads, as with Betamax. The capacity for a second audio channel was built into the VCC from the start, giving stereo or second track audio dub, whereas VHS and Betamax, with their fixed video heads, are limited in the extent to which they can compress the video track and, thus, in the extra space they can allow for audio recording. They can provide the same facilities, but are unlikely to match the quality.

Some models marred Video 2000's reputation because the incredibly sensitive DTF (Dynamic Track Following) system, which keeps the video heads in perfect contact with the tape, did not work properly. Since then, the shadow of these early troubles has been lifted by Grundig to reveal a picture of unsurpassed quality. Freeze frame, slow motion and picture search are especially noise free compared with other formats.

Will Video 2000 be the system of the future? Until it gets a larger slice of the world market it will be hard to tell. However, its popularity in Europe indicates that the enthusiast need not fear its sudden disappearance, and pre-recorded tapes are now readily available. Many enthusiasts today say that Philips's earlier formats, the VCR and VCR-LP are still giving top-quality pictures after many years.

Philips VR-2022 (Europe)

For Philips, the inventors of Video 2000, the VR-2022, *above*, represented an advance. After serious problems with their earlier VCR, the VR-2020, they needed a strong contender. So eager were they to erase the mistakes, that an improved version of the VR-2020, the VR-2021, appeared in the interim.

The VR-2022 has all the trick frame facilities that were omitted from the older models, and these achieve the high quality of which Video 2000 is capable. The 'Search' and 'Store' functions still have to be operated by a point such as a pencil, a seemingly crude method which, however, prevents accidental operation.

Philips VR-2020 (Europe)

The Philips VR-2020, *above*, was the first Video 2000 VCR on the market, arriving in 1981. Although there were problems with this model in its early days, caused partly by the Dynamic Track Following (DTF) system which is Video 2000's great strength, it was seen even then to be a promising format. The troubles with the early VR-2020s may have been precipitated by Philips's desire to put Video 2000 on the market before Betamax and VHS gained an unbreakable hold.

The VR-2020, like Grundig's 2 × 4, is basically a mass-market VCR (if not actually budget) and lacks the still frame facility.

Technicolor Microvideo

At present there are three popular formats in home video, but a trend for specialization may be started by a fourth entirely portable format on sale in Europe and the USA.

The Technicolor 212, *below left*, weighs a mere 7 lb (3.2 kg) and its tuner, the Model 5112, only 4.2 lb (1.9 kg), making them the lightest in the world. As the parachutist, *below right*, shows, this sets a new level of portability.

The Technicolor 212 uses tape only $\frac{1}{4}$-in (6-mm) wide, and cassettes which can play for a maximum of one hour. Video enthusiasts will probably shoot on $\frac{1}{4}$-in (6-mm) tape and then dub and edit the footage across to $\frac{1}{2}$-in (12.5-mm) tape. This portable format will complement a home system.

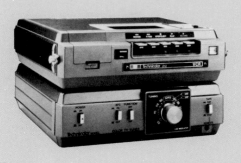

ITT VR-483 (Europe)

The ITT VR-483, *above*, is the Philips VR-2020, sold under ITT's label. Of the models they market, the VR-580 is the VR-2022, and the VR-482 and -483 are the earlier, less sophisticated and cheaper models, slightly restyled.

Another well-known electronics firm, Bang & Olufsen, best known for their futuristic hi-fi designs, are also joining the market with a repackaged Philips VCR. This one, however, looks very different from the Philips model.

The Pye 20VR20, *below*, is the Philips VR-2020 by another name. It is common for makers of electrical goods to market some models bought from other manufacturers, often with little or no alteration besides the change of colour and label. Pye also sell the VR-2022 under the name 20VR22, and a 20VR23.

Unlike Philips, Grundig is so far the sole marketer of its own VCRs.

Pye 20VR20 (Europe)

The U-matic system

When it was introduced in the early seventies the U-matic format revolutionized video recording. Before U-Matic, all video recorders were reel-to-reel, winding from one open spool to another. They had to be threaded, at least partly, by hand, through a tricky tape path (although the tape used was rather tougher than the cassette tape now used). Cassette-loading is much less troublesome, and despite its comparatively narrow gauge of three-quarter inch (19 millimetre) as opposed to 2 inch (50.8 millimetre) for professional reel-to-reel tape, U-matic can give a quality acceptable for editing and broadcast.

As well as a wider tape, the tape speed, at 3.7 inches (95 millimetres) a second, and the writing speed of 26.3 feet (8.54 metres) a second, are much faster than for domestic systems. The cassettes, 8.6 × 5.4 × 1.1 inches (219 × 138 × 31 millimetres) and the machines, 25.4 × 18.2 × 10.4 inches (646 × 425 × 226 millimetres) are about twice the size of the biggest domestic versions. To carry the portapack for any length of time requires a backpack and a certain dedication.

U-matics are industrial machines. In professional terms they are small, mobile, cheap, convenient and easy to use. The range and flexibility of their recording facilities for both video and audio is well beyond that of domestic models, although the gap is narrowing as far as facilities are concerned. However, the sheer extra space for electronics inside a U-matic chassis will ensure that the differential in quality is maintained.

A whole new era in video may well be opened up by the arrival of industrial-quality VHS and Betamax machines, hybrids between the domestic formats and the U-matics. Approaching the quality of U-matic, these VCRs will play ordinary Betamax and VHS cassettes, offering new opportunities for interchange between the amateur and domestic, and the professional and educational user. For broadcast and near-broadcast quality, however, the wider-gauge tape will probably continue to be a necessity.

The main users of U-matics are colleges, industry and video recording studios who need cheap recorders giving professional-quality recordings. For the serious home video enthusiast they are the most ubiquitous of all VCRs, opening the way to full broadcast-quality recording.

JVC's CR-6060ET is a player/recorder VCR which comes in two versions, the standard machine, handling PAL and SECAM signals as a matter of course, and the triple-standard version, also able to replay on NTSC.

U-matics, unlike domestic VCRs, are issued as part of a series designed to work together. Instead of issuing a new model, the manufacturer will bring out a whole new series.

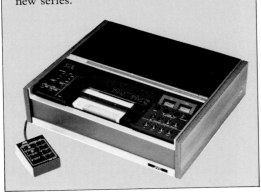

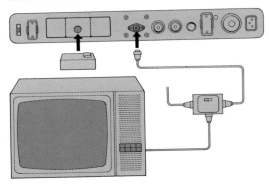

To play a tape on an ordinary TV receiver, the video signal from the VCR must be converted into an RF signal which the TV can receive.

An RF converter, plugged into the back of the CR-6060, must be designed for the same TV system (PAL, SECAM or NTSC) as the TV being used, and tuned to a channel used by the TV receiver.

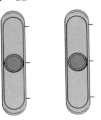

The simple selector, *far left,* switches two audio channels between separate and combined use.

The 'Auto' lever, *left,* will replay a tape continuously if set to 'Repeat'; on 'Search', it will stop when the counter reads '000'.

The 'ET' in the serial number of the CR-6060 stands for 'Europe/Triple-standard'. The same basic VCR is sold in the USA in its NTSC version. The PAL VCR can record and replay in PAL and SECAM automatically, but a switch, **1**, on the front panel, *bottom right*, must be operated for replay in NTSC; recording is not possible in NTSC.

The U-matic control panel, *right*, is a little more complex than that of a home VCR. There are two audio tracks, and one or the other can be brought into use with the audio select lever, **2**. U-matics have audio level controls, **8**, and meters for each channel, and the 'Audio Dub Ch. 1' switch, **7**, allows sound to be added on one audio channel of a recording.

A feature not often found on domestic formats, although likely in future, is continuous rewind and replay, operated on the CR-6060 by the 'Auto' control, **3**.

The 'Colour Lock' control, **4**, enables the operator to adjust aberrant colour effects on colour or monochrome pictures.

The 'Skew' control, **6**, allows the user to adjust picture distortions which would need an engineer on a home VCR.

The 'Timer Record' control, **5**, allows the CR-6060 to be used with an external timer, a facility which enables it to be used for time-shifting.

The CR-6060 is a typical record and replay U-matic VCR. Some of the controls on the rear panel, *below*, will be unfamiliar to home video users.

The 'Playback mode' switch, **1**, has settings for normal playback ('Auto'), monochrome ('B/W'), or for dubbing a video recording on to another machine.

The TV receiver/monitor connector, **2**, is for transmitting video signals to a monitor for playback only, a feature not found on domestic formats, which are made to be permanently connected to a TV.

If recording is to be done from a TV, an RF decoder must be plugged into a cavity, **3**, in the back of the U-matic. The 'Video in'/'Video out' sockets, **4**, the professional VCR's normal connection to another machine, are becoming more common on home VCRs: the 'Audio in'/'Audio out' connection, **5**, is already common.

It is not as easy to alter the supply voltage as it is on most domestic VCRs; although the voltage selector, **6**, can be altered by the user, the manufacturers suggest consulting a dealer for advice.

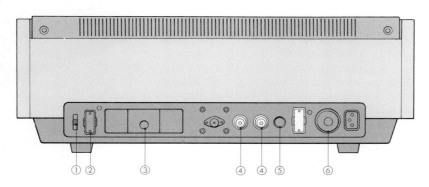

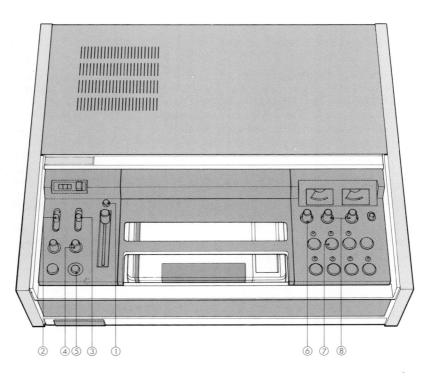

On the market/U-matic recorders

U-matic machines are designed for industrial and professional use; the choice of models is, therefore, arranged very differently from household VCRs. The model you buy will depend more on the application than the price or the facilities. Many of the features common on home VCRs do not exist on U-matics, as they are unimportant in the context in which these machines are used.

The basic U-matic, which is usually used for educational video in schools and colleges, is a playback-only VCR, with no recording mechanism to increase the price and endanger valuable pre-recorded tapes. It can be a triple-standard machine which, with a triple-standard monitor, will play back tapes in PAL, SECAM and NTSC, which is obviously useful for teaching. All U-matics can record and play back two audio channels.

The closest equivalent to domestic VCRs is the player/recorder, which will record from a camera or another machine but not usually from a television, unless the television has its own video/audio output, or a second RF modulator unit plugged in. U-matics normally have auto tape search and pause/freeze frame, but not on-screen picture search.

Dual-sound-track recording is a feature that will come to home VCRs but is now only available in Video 2000 and a few Betamax and VHS machines. You can have a commentary on one track and music on another; You can record in stereo; and the tracks can be played separately or in combination. Dual-sound-tracks are available on industrial VHS and (in the USA) Betamax VCRs.

The portapack is designed to use a small version of the U-matic cassette, with the same spool size and playing for twenty or thirty minutes, and will not take full-size cassettes. Unlike mains machines, portapacks tend to have on-screen picture search and give a very clean edit when shooting.

Many U-matic users want to link their VCRs to a full-function editing suite. This requires the most complex and expensive machines with the full logic needed to control them. These will fast-wind or give slow motion on screen, in order to select an edit point accurate to the nearest frame, and make perfectly noise-free edits. The editing VCR can be linked to a Time Base Corrector so that its signals can be perfectly synchronized with another VCR or camera.

Most U-matics on the market are designed as part of a series of machines from one manufacturer, and even where VCRs from one series are compatible with others, it is safest to stick to machines from one manufacturer for reliable results.

Edit controllers designed to match a particular series are usually compatible only with that system.

Panasonic NV-9200 (Europe)

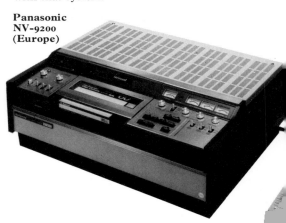

The Panasonic NV9200 is Europe's triple-standard version of a typical U-matic.

The rest of this series includes the basic NV-9210 (which can handle PAL and SECAM, but not NTSC); an editing VCR; an edit control unit; a portapack; and a special 'High-performance' VCR, the NV-9240, which has extra controls to make it a first-class input machine for an editing suite.

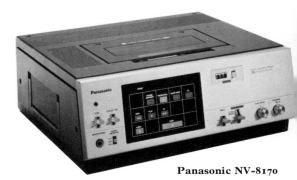

Panasonic NV-8170

The NV-8170, *above*, is a Panasonic VHS machine built to industrial standards. This is the player-only model; there is a record/replay VCR in the series (the NV-8200), and while they are compatible with ordinary domestic VHS models, they can also be used with an edit controller.

In the USA there is already an industrial Betamax series, but this is not fully compatible with home Betamax VCRs: it uses a faster playing and recording speed.

JVC CP-5500

U-matic portapacks such as JVC's CR-4400, *left*, use smaller versions of mains cassettes, which have the same spool dimensions. Portable tapes can be used on home decks, but not vice-versa.

U-matic portapacks are especially rugged. This weighs over 24 lb (11 kg) with built-in rechargeable batteries. It can also run from a car battery.

Automatic assemble edit gives perfectly clean cuts between edits, and the two audio channels have balance controls and an audio peak level limiter.

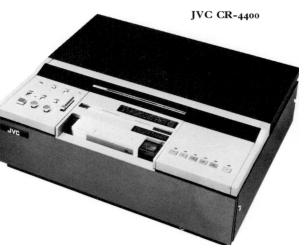

JVC CR-4400

JVC's CP-5500, *right*, is a new-generation player-only VCR with some unusual features.

The CP-5500 and its recorder/player partner, the CP-6600, can be externally sychronized from a Time Base Corrector to give high-quality playback suitable even for broadcasting.

More unusually, these VCRs can take an FM (frequency-modulated) signal directly from the tape and record it on another machine with minimum loss of signal quality.

Usually, the signal has to be converted to video, and back to FM.

Sony's VP-2030, *left*, is a PAL machine; in the USA, the NTSC model is the VP-2000. It is a playback-only VCR. Its sister, the VO-2631 (VO-2611 in the USA), is a player/recorder, which can utilize Sony's Random Access Controller, the RX-353.

This device can record and memorize an audio tone on up to 63 segments of recorded tape. It can return to any of the segments on command, or play back any eight segments in a pre-set order. This facility, especially useful for educational video, is available for most U-matic systems.

Sony VP-2030 (Europe)
VP-2000 (USA)

e **VO-5800**, *right*, VCR belonging to y's new Type 5 es, released in the A in 1982.

Type 5 is the first t-loading U-matic tem, designed to fit -in (48-cm) rack-unt. To make the trols more visible, lower control panel tilts upward.

On-screen picture speeds can be varied continuously from 1/30th normal speed to five times normal by means of a rotary switch, and high-speed picture search is possible when it is linked to an edit controller.

Sony VO-5800 (USA)

Choosing and using accessories

The accessories available to supply the needs of enthusiastic and demanding video users is growing daily. Yet the task of evaluating video accessories is almost impossible, for two reasons. First, the market is in a constant state of change. As improvements are made to VCRs, so some accessories are becoming redundant, while others are being superseded by the demand for more sophisticated, or more fashionable, alternatives. Second, one person's accessory may be another's necessity. Whether it be a device to improve the sound or picture of a recording, or cut out commercials, any video accessory's usefulness is always dictated by its owner.

Although no two video users will agree on the same order of priorities, some items are more or less vital to serious video recording. These include a tool kit for fault-finding and cable repair and, since most of the day-to-day problems involve cables, a set of spare cables. The connections and combinations will depend on the details of your system and the continent in which you live.

Adaptors, which convert one type of connector to another, can be a useful stopgap, especially if you frequently work with other peoples' units. An alternative is to buy a kit which allows you to build a set of interconnections between VCRs, television sets and peripheral hardware, such as games and computer units and video disk players. Some such systems, for example the VAK400 made by Total Video Supply for the American market, provide a set of interconnections to suit most simple needs.

More sophisticated kits, such as the RMS Electronics range, supply signal amplifiers, switchers, splitters and other components. As the ultimate in complexity you could switch all your systems through a box such as VideoMate or Video Commander, although, to date, both of these are still only available in the USA. Whatever your choice, the only rule to remember is to buy with your own system and needs in mind.

From splicing kits to extensive storage systems, dust covers to detailers, cleaning cassettes to crimping tools, the range is vast. If, even so, the precise accessory you want is not available, do not worry. The chances are that it will be on the market soon, or is, in fact, already on sale at a specialist shop – if not in the exact form you want then as an easily modified version of it.

Little black boxes

Many of the accessories most useful to the VCR owner have an unprepossessing box shape. Here is a list of some of the most useful:

1 Commercial cutter: records TV broadcasts but cuts out the advertisements.
2 Stereo simulator: splits the audio signal to give a 'mock' stereo effect.
3 Cable by-pass: useful for cable subscribers. It can record a broadcast on one channel while you are watching a cable-fed broadcast on another.
4 Image enhancer: improves the smoothness of scene changes in tapes edited at home or made jerky by pressing the 'Pause' button during recording to cut out the commercials. It can fade out the signal to black or fade in extra colour as required.
5 Detail enhancer: increases the sharpness of the video signal, so minimizing loss of quality during recording.

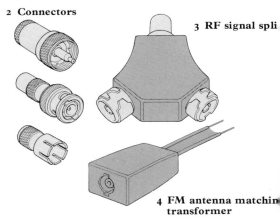

2 Connectors

3 RF signal spli

4 FM antenna matchin transformer

1 Cable ties

A useful selection of video accessories could well include the items illustrated here. Releasable cable ties, **1**, not only help keep your cables neat and undamaged, but are also re-usable. A set of emergency connectors, **2**, will probably be invaluable, especially for the camera owner, to replace snapped-off connections. An RF signal splitter, **3**, can split the signal you receive to serve two TVs or VCRs. An FM antenna-matching transformer, **4**, is the

To splice tape ends, lift the clamps, **1**, then apply recording tape, glossy side up, overlapping over the diagonal slit, **2**, and clamp into position. Holding the tape with a finger, cut across the diagonal slit, **3**, and remove surplus tape. Apply splicing tape, **4**, and carefully cut off any excess.

A crimp tool is often a useful alternative to a soldering iron. First trim the cable, **1**, then insert the central conductor, **2**, which acts to increase the energy supply across the connection. Twist the correct connection on the prepared cable, **3**, and, finally, use the crimp tool to seal the joint, **4**.

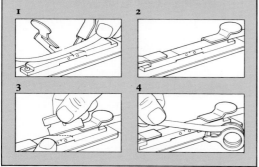

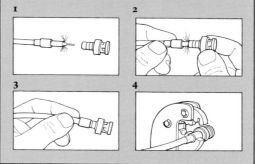

8 Hexagon keys

11 Adaptor kit

9 Dust caps

5 Crimp tool

7 AC test screwdriver

10 Nut spinners

6 Crimps

12 Bulk eraser

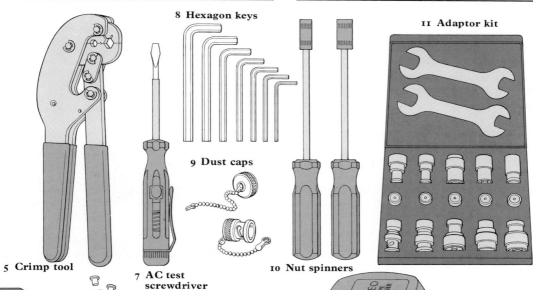

device you need to match the signal from your VHF antenna to an FM tuner. A crimp tool, **5**, with metal crimps, **6**, is the easy way to effect BNC and UHF repairs and reconnections with no fuss or mess. An AC test neon screwdriver, **7**, has a handle which lights up if an AC of 220 to 250V (110 to 125V, US) passes through it, so is handy for testing the integrity of circuits. A set of hexagon keys, **8**, available in metric and imperial sizes, will help you loosen and tighten hexagon sockets effectively. Use dust caps, **9**, over unused sockets and mountings. Nut spinners, **10**, give an improved grip for tackling a variety of electrical connections. An adaptor kit, **11**, comprising a selection of male and female connectors, and spanners, will improve the versatility of your equipment. To make sure that an old video recording does not 'haunt' a new one, use a hand-held bulk eraser, **12**.

Video disks

Video disks look rather like long-playing records. Their surfaces are pitted with microscopic indentations and both visual and audio information is impressed into them. The player is plugged into a television set on whose screen the pictures appear.

The first video disk player, conceived in the twenties by John Logie Baird, had a rotating drum, carrying a precisely arranged set of perforations. This scanned a picture and broke it down into a radio signal. The receiver had a similar drum, synchronized to the camera drum, which reassembled the picture into recognizable images. Baird used the existing technology of the gramophone record industry to produce the 78 r.p.m. video disk. The signals created when the disk was played on a record player were fed into a Baird receiver to give just a dozen stills.

When Baird's television system was killed by the arrival of the EMI electronic system in the late thirties, his video disks died with it. Only in the seventies was the notion revived by the European companies Telefunken and Decca. The resulting TELEDEC machine incorporated an adaptation of an even earlier recording idea – the undulating grooves of Edison's original audio cylinders. The reason for this move was to accommodate more information into narrower grooves on the finished disk. Even so, it had to rotate at 1500 r.p.m. (a speed used by many of today's systems) for acceptable picture quality, and the disk gave only ten minutes' playing time.

As a refinement of the TELEDEC system, Matsushita Electric of Japan produced an ultra-fine pressing that crammed an hour of picture material on a disk scanned by a pressure-sensitive head. This head sensed the undulations and converted them into the video signals fed into the television.

Only with the arrival of the precise, sophisticated technology of the eighties has the Matsushita system evolved into a viable product. First on the scene were RCA with their SelectaVision system. This works by means of a head, which senses billions of undulations in the disk surface and converts the information into a video signal, which varies with differences in the capacitance as the head moves up and down. The JVC Video High Density (VHD) system works in a similar way, but Philips have opted for a novel optical system, LaserVision, in which the disk is 'read' by a laser beam.

The first video disks appeared as long ago as 1928. Constructed from brittle plastic shellac, like the gramophone records of the day, they were played on a gramophone linked to a Baird TV receiver. The disks gave 12 still images of rather poor quality and were sold by Selfridges, the London department store, in the thirties.

In the SelectaVision system developed by RCA, information is etched on a disk as vertical ups and downs in a spiral, V-shaped groove, *below right*. When the disk is played back, a diamond stylus rides in the groove. As the many undulations pass under the stylus, a metal electrode creates the signal readout which is fed into the TV. Unlike an audio system, the stylus does not move in an arc but travels in a straight line across the disk radius, *below left*. This gives a clear, steady picture.

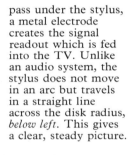

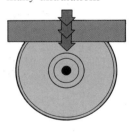

In JVC's VHD system, *right*, information is stored in the disk in 'micropits' of two kinds. Some pits contain audio and video information, the rest tracking data. The scan of the sapphire stylus over the disk (unlike the RCA system it is separated from the disk by a plastic sleeve) is directed by the tracking pits.

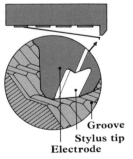

Groove
Stylus tip
Electrode

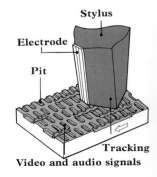

Stylus
Electrode
Pit
Tracking
Video and audio signals

To re-create sound and moving pictures, all video disks have to store a huge amount of information. More than 10,000 pictures are needed for only an hour's visual entertainment. The grooves on the disk have, thus, to be fine, packed tightly together, and etched with great accuracy. All the modern disks are made from plastic. For the RCA and JVC systems, this has to be highly conductive. For the Philips system, it is coated with a reflective material.

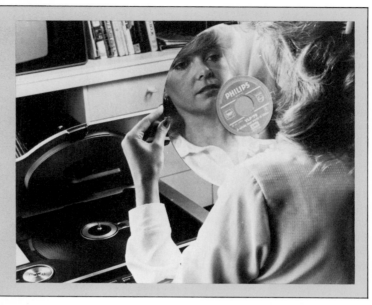

LaserVision, *below*, the brainchild of Philips, uses a completely different technology from the RCA and JVC systems. The great advance is that information, etched on the reflective material of the disk in a series of pits, is read off with a fine beam created by a helium neon laser. By means of a series of lenses, gratings, prisms and mirrors, the laser beam is directed to the disk underside where it is moved by a scanning lens. When it hits a pit in the silvery surface, the beam is reflected. The reflected beam then passes back to the photo diode which creates the signal output.

In a similar system, which is currently being worked on in France by Thompson CSF, the laser beam is not reflected from the surface of the disk, but actually passes through it. Variations in the quality of the beam, created by the information etched on the disk, are then used to construct the electrical signals needed to create a TV picture.

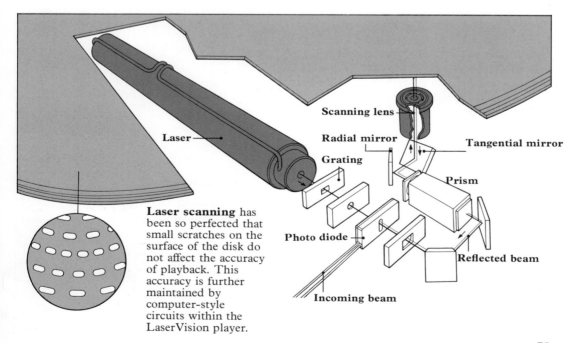

Laser scanning has been so perfected that small scratches on the surface of the disk do not affect the accuracy of playback. This accuracy is further maintained by computer-style circuits within the LaserVision player.

Scanning lens

Laser

Radial mirror

Tangential mirror

Grating

Prism

Photo diode

Reflected beam

Incoming beam

On the market/Video disk players

The video disk could turn out to be the vanguard of a new generation of video, or a complete commercial disaster. For the consumer, deciding whether to opt for a video disk system to plug into your television depends most on what you want video to do for you. Because of the technological requirements of their manufacture, the systems presently available are all players only: they cannot record television broadcasts, neither on nor off air, nor let you record your own material with a video camera.

On the credit side, supporters of the disk system claim that the picture quality is better than that of any tape, and that, in time, prices will be lower. At present it is difficult to evaluate such claims, but there is certainly a possibility that disks protected from physical wear could have a longer life, and be potentially more durable library material, than video tapes.

By the early eighties, the video disk market developed into a three-horse race, with RCA SelectaVision, priced at about $300, having a head start as the only one on sale. Like other systems of its kind, which are being manufactured in prototype by Sanyo, Hitachi, Toshiba, Zenith and Radio Shack, it is susceptible to interference from dust; and even minute scratches on the plastic disk can impair its playback performance.

The LaserVision system by Philips incorporates a machine which looks rather like a conventional record player, but is far from conventional in its laser-operated function. One of the great advantages of this system, available at first only in the USA for around $700, is that the disks are coated with a protective layer of plastic one sixteenth of an inch (1 millimetre) thick. Also, the absence of mechanical friction means that there is no wear on the disk. The Pioneer DiscoVision System, also launched in USA, is laser-operated and programmable.

The JVC Video High Density (VHD) system works, like the RCA system, by contact between stylus and the disk, but as in LaserVision the signal is stored in pits, and the stylus can move freely across the disk's surface in random access. Until all three systems are established and consumers have had sufficient time to use and compare them, there is no knowing which system, if any, will be the most successful.

The oldest form of video disk on the market is the one that has been used since the late sixties for providing action replays on TV sports programmes. The disk is magnetic, and works on the same principle as magnetic video tape. Signals are recorded and stored on the disk in concentric magnetic tracks, each track accommodating 30 seconds of action. The disk can be replayed at any speed, both forward and in reverse, and can freeze frame at the touch of a button.

The range of video disks varies in detail from system to system, but offers an increasingly wide choice, with popular movies at one end of the scale and solely educational disks at the other. The disks, which cost just over a third of the price of pre-recorded video cassettes, play for about an hour on each side, but many of the broadcasts come packaged in multi-disk sets. Of the ranges announced in 1982, that of RCA SelectaVision offered the widest choice of popular entertainment and an increasing amount of educational material, but expansion of the list seems to be limited by the lack of a freeze-frame facility on the disk player. Philips LaserVision, with more sophisticated players, has marketed two sorts of disks – long play disks for straight play through, and active play disks with shorter playing time but with slow motion and freeze-frame potential built in. The JVC VHD system promises disks with the same possibilities as those of the LaserVision system, and a good range has been forecast.

To use the RCA video disk player, you slide the disk into the loading slot, **1**, remove the sleeve, and press the function lever, **7**. Lighted dials, **2** and **3** indicate which side is being played and how long it has been running. 'Rapid access' buttons, **4**, allow you to speed forward or back to a particular time segment, but during this there is no sound or picture. Forward and backward 'Visual search' buttons, **5**, play 16 times normal speed with perfect vision, but muted sound. If it is necessary to stop the disk during play, you press the 'Pause' button, **6**.

The JVC video disk player, incorporating a microprocessor, should give great flexibility. Disks are loaded into a slot, **1**, by pressing the 'Load' button, **11**, and sound selected, **2**, as stereo or bilingual. Lighted displays indicate the chapter, **3**, time, **4**, and the side playing. An array of controls allows such operations as 'Manual search', **5**, and 'Chapter search', **6**, programmed by the machine's chip. For chapter repeats you press the 'Memory' button, **7**. Frame playback in both directions is available, **8** and **9**, and a 'Pause' button, **10**, is a standard fitting on the player.

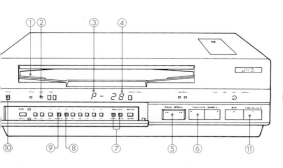

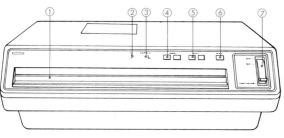

To play a Philips LaserVision video disk, you turn on the power, **1**, lift the lid, **4**, and insert the disk. Closing the lid automatically begins play. The in-play facilities that are offered by this system include still or freeze frame, **2**, which can be moved forward or backward a single frame at a time. Slow motion, **3**, is possible in both directions. For locating particular frames you press the 'Fast forward' button, **5**. Pressing the 'Fast search' button, **7**, plays the whole of one side of the disk, in about 25 seconds with its pictures displayed on the screen. The 'Audio' button, **6**, gives stereo or bilingual sound (in a variety of combinations) on selected disks.

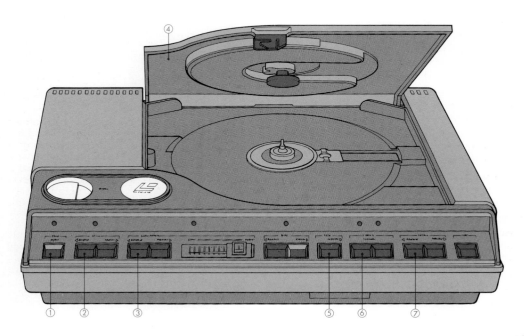

Interactive video systems

When video can be made to respond to the wishes and instructions of the operator, it is said to be interactive. Both video tapes and disks have a role to play in this new application of video, which promises to introduce new methods of learning.

The aim of interactive learning through video is to let the machine take over from the teacher. If it incorporates a programmed tape, a machine on which to play it, a monitor and a device, linked to a print-out, into which the student can punch responses, an interactive video system can check a student's progress and understanding step by step, and discover which areas of study demand the teacher's personal attention.

The next step in sophistication is to link the tape player of the system to a computer such as the Apple II. With the potential of a computer added to the inventory, the level of education can be made more flexible and more technical.

Whenever interactive programs are used with VCR systems, they always meet the same drawback: the access time. This is the time it takes to spin the tape from the end of one section to the start of the next. The solution is to use video disks instead of tapes. Because of the way in which they are constructed and played, video disks allow virtually immediate access to any other part of the disk. All the machine has to do is to move its playback head a few centimetres and the next section of the recording appears on the screen. The player incorporates a microprocessor, so a hand-held infra-red remote control pad can be used to interact with the disk. On advanced machines the sound can be set for stereo, bilingual or a choice of commentaries at two levels of difficulty.

If you already have a television monitor, you could acquire an interactive video disk system for around £1,200 ($600). The limitation of the system, compared with the tape systems so far available, is the lack of facility for teachers and parents to make their own recordings. Instead, they have to rely on material made by the disk companies. Despite this, interactive video disks are already proving useful commercially in the marketing of all types of commodities, from holidays to baby clothes. In the USA, parents can buy a children's disk offering a wide variety of education and entertainment.

Linked to a computer, interactive video disks are proving to have some fascinating applications. The American Heart Foundation, for example, has a disk on mouth-to-mouth resuscitation, in which the computer is linked to a dummy. As the first-aider goes through the course, the program flashes back comments on progress such as 'first breath too hard, third too weak'.

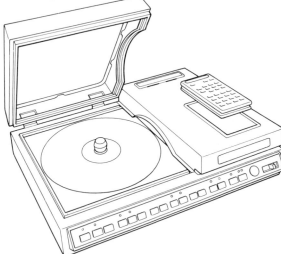

Attached to a TV monitor, the Pioneer DiscoVision player becomes an interactive video system. Sound and picture are both recorded on the video disk, which is played at 1,800 r.p.m. and read by a medium neon laser beam.

One side of a video disk is composed of 54,000 still frames, any one of which, at the touch of a button can be frozen on the TV, for a long period.

For easy reference, each frame on the disk is numbered, but these numbers can be made to disappear during play to prevent them from interfering with the image.

To switch to another part of the disk, you simply code-in the appropriate reference number on the control pad, then press the 'Search' button.

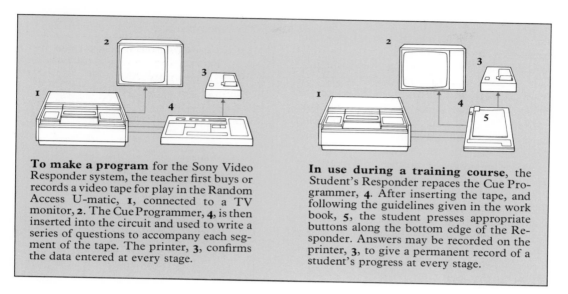

To make a program for the Sony Video Responder system, the teacher first buys or records a video tape for play in the Random Access U-matic, **1**, connected to a TV monitor, **2**. The Cue Programmer, **4**, is then inserted into the circuit and used to write a series of questions to accompany each segment of the tape. The printer, **3**, confirms the data entered at every stage.

In use during a training course, the Student's Responder repaces the Cue Programmer, **4**. After inserting the tape, and following the guidelines given in the work book, **5**, the student presses appropriate buttons along the bottom edge of the Responder. Answers may be recorded on the printer, **3**, to give a permanent record of a student's progress at every stage.

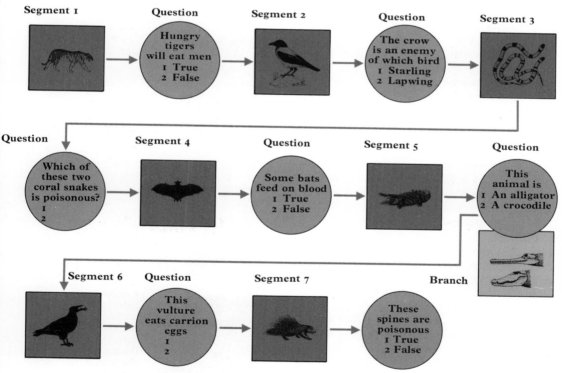

The Sony Video Responder is designed to allow students to progress at their own pace. The tape that is inserted into the U-matic part of the system is programmed in a series of up to seven segments. At the end of each film segment, the student is given a series of questions to answer relating to what has been shown.

In writing the questions to accompany the video tape, the teacher may specify up to three attempts for each question, and make provision for branching into more detailed treatment of any topic. A typical series of questions, and the images on the preceding segment of tape to which they relate, are shown in the program traced out above through seven segments.

The future of video

Video is progressing at such a fast and furious pace that all we can be sure of is that most of today's most outrageous ideas will have become a reality long before the magical date of 2001. Leading the way toward this bright future will be improvements in the versatility, quality and scope of existing systems. On to these will be welded novel technologies which will make video a near-perfect communications system.

As video becomes cheaper and more accessible to all, more and more VCR owners will suddenly become video movie directors. This will be made possible by means of narrower, 8 mm tape and the CCD, or charge coupled device, already being incorporated into the new generation of video cameras. The CCD is a microchip which effectively replaces the camera tube, reducing the camera's weight. Although prototypes do not yet produce recordings of professional quality, this new camera responds to much lower light levels than a conventional video camera and is immune from burning by over-bright light sources.

Today, even the best of video is limited in quality by the coarse screens on which it is displayed. Researchers in Japan are already working toward the 2,000-line television picture which will, for the first time, compete with 35 mm film on grounds of quality. When pictures of such clarity and detail can be scanned by a CCD device and reassembled on large-screen systems, the way should be clear for another step forward, namely increased speed and ease of copying of video recordings. At present, copying involves inevitable loss of sharpness and quality because the copying machine is trying to draw an accurate picture of a fluctuating signal. If, however, the signal is recorded as a set of precise digits, each specifying a particular element of brightness or colour, the recording becomes a rigid set of instructions which incur no loss of quality.

By the end of the century, video will be everywhere: in home, office, school and factory, in supermarket and sports stadium. Video, linked to computers, will spearhead the new industrial revolution. To aid and to entertain, video will change from being a single entity into a whole system, offering the consumer a diverse range of facilities as offshoots from the basic camera, tape and recorder.

The video cassette has a novel future as an integral part of the truly portable video movie camera now being developed by Sony. Replacing the conventional camera tube is the CCD, or charge coupled device, a microchip which splits up the picture into thousands of fragments. These are scanned by logic circuits to create a video signal, which is transferred to 8 mm tape ready for instant playback.

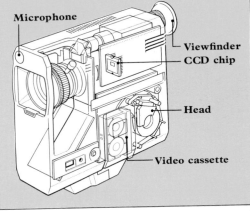

Microphone

Viewfinder
CCD chip

Head

Video cassette

In the Longitudinal Video Recorder (LVR), developed by Toshiba, a high-speed graphite-lubricated tape is divided up into a series of no fewer than 316 separate parallel tracks and so can store a vast amount of information. When played in a specially adapted VCR, the tape shuttles backward and forward so that about 25 seconds of material is played from each track in succession.

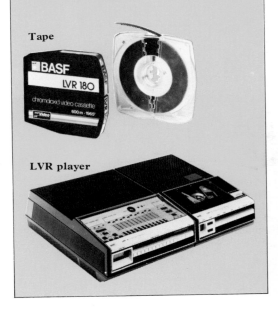

Tape

BASF
LVR 180
chromdioxid video cassette
600 m · 1965'

LVR player

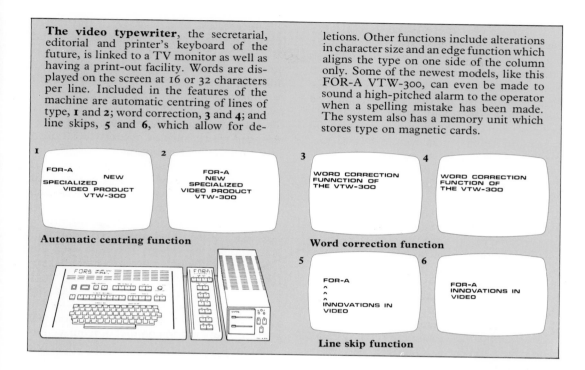

The video typewriter, the secretarial, editorial and printer's keyboard of the future, is linked to a TV monitor as well as having a print-out facility. Words are displayed on the screen at 16 or 32 characters per line. Included in the features of the machine are automatic centring of lines of type, **1** and **2**; word correction, **3** and **4**; and line skips, **5** and **6**, which allow for deletions. Other functions include alterations in character size and an edge function which aligns the type on one side of the column only. Some of the newest models, like this FOR-A VTW-300, can even be made to sound a high-pitched alarm to the operator when a spelling mistake has been made. The system also has a memory unit which stores type on magnetic cards.

Automatic centring function

Word correction function

Line skip function

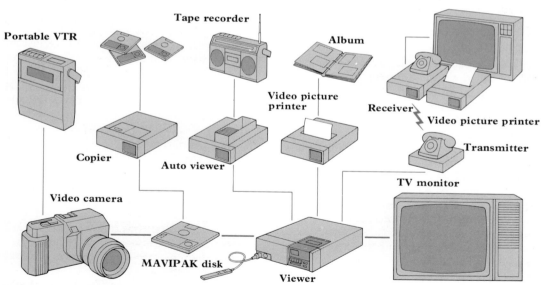

Portable VTR

Tape recorder

Album

Video picture printer

Receiver

Video picture printer

Transmitter

Copier

Auto viewer

TV monitor

Video camera

MAVIPAK disk

Viewer

The Sony MAVICA system plans to offer consumers complete video. The basic elements are a small portable video camera containing a CCD to record signals on a small magnetic disk, the MAVIPAK. With the help of a special playback system, the pictures can be seen at once on a TV monitor.

To these basics can be added a whole set of extras. These include the portable VTR; a copier for duplicating the disks; an autoviewer and tape recorder for separating off the video and audio components of the disk and a video picture printer, which can convert stills into prints.

By means of a transmission facility, the video owner of the future will be able to send signals along the telephone cables to transmit all or part of a video recording anywhere in the world, to be seen by the recipient as a print-out or as a series of images on a TV monitor.

The TV connection

Video grows ever more versatile, but however it is used, there is always a common denominator, namely the television screen on which the visual information is displayed. Without television, video would not have been possible; so a basic understanding of television is vital to any study of video.

Television is arguably the most powerful communications system ever developed, and because it produces its pictures electronically, not chemically like film, it has an immediacy that film could never match. When television first began, broadcasts were always live, with events seen on the television screen a fraction of a microsecond after they had occurred in the studio.

With the advent of colour, and of video recordings, television has changed enormously since those early days, but the basic principles of the transmission of signals and their display on a fluorescent screen remain the same. Advances in television technology, such as sophisticated satellite relay systems, have given live broadcasting a new fillip. Through the medium of television, live events, from battles to baseball, and pageants to pop concerts, can be seen simultaneously in hundreds of milllions of homes all over the world. Never before has it been possible for people all over the world to receive the same message at the same moment. Never before has it been possible for Earth's inhabitants to witness events far out in space, on the moon, or even beyond the planets.

The biggest problem with transmitting television signals is the enormous amount of information that has to be broadcast. A typical television picture transmission is completed in just 64 millionths of a second. In this time, the transmission has to convey signals indicating the thousands of separate differences in light intensity which go to make up every single line on the screen. If the signals were carried in radio space they would occupy more than the entire band taken up by medium-wave radio transmissions. This is why television transmissions have been pushed into the ultra-high frequency (UHF) ranges, and in the USA the very high frequency (VHF) ranges. Here the frequencies needed to transmit from a whole series of television stations can be accommodated without interfering with one another, or with the signals of any other transmission.

The greatest disadvantage of the UHF/VHF transmission systems is that they tend to limit good television reception to areas relatively near the transmitter. Also, high buildings, hills or even low-flying aircraft can interfere with the signals. These are just two of the reasons why it is essential to have the correct antenna for receiving UHF signals, and why it must be properly positioned to obtain the best reception.

The television signals picked up by your antenna are translated into pictures by your television set or receiver. The image that you see is built up from a series of minute dots, which the human eye reassembles into a detailed picture. This image has enormous potential for the viewer. It can be used, for example, to display constantly updated information. This may be transmitted piggy back with regular television broadcasts as the teletext system. Or the screen can be used to provide you with viewdata information fed, at your push-button command, from a computer into the television via the telephone cables. With the addition of a keyboard and mini-computer, your television can be used as an educational aid, a games machine and personal accounts clerk all in one.

The greater the possibilities of television, the more difficult it becomes for the buyer to choose exactly the right television for his needs. So what sort of a set should the VCR owner choose? The answer depends largely on what you want your television to do.

For the VCR owner, or prospective owner, the most important point to look out for is whether the set is a television monitor/receiver. Most ordinary television sets are receivers only, designed to take UHF signals from an antenna. Video signals, however, are low frequency, and when connected to a UHF set, the VCR has to convert the UHF signals to low frequency to record, then convert them back to UHF again to produce an image on the screen.

This two-way switching inevitably results in some loss of quality. The monitor part of the combination takes care of the problem by taking a direct low frequency signal. The monitor cannot act as a receiver: it merely displays what is fed into it; but it is the ideal connection to the VCR because it operates at low frequency.

A television monitor/receiver has a separate channel on the tuning buttons which

selects direct video input. At the back or side of the set there will be separate cabling for attaching to a discrete connection on the VCR. It is possible to convert an existing set into a monitor/receiver.

The diversity in size, shape and complexity of today's televisions reflects both the video and computer revolutions. The versatility of television is being extended way beyond the dreams of its pioneers.

The next novelty will be to have a colour television small enough to put in your pocket, flat enough to hang on the wall like a picture or with the capacity to create a high-definition picture large enough to fill your living room wall. The day of component television, with knowledgeable enthusiasts mixing and matching different parts of television and video systems to produce exactly the results they want will soon dawn.

Along with diversification and development of television will come a vast increase in the amount and variety of television material. Television of the future will cater for minorities as well as the majority. With the development of cable and satellite television, the choice of viewing – and video recording – will become international.

How TV works

Television has become such a commonplace part of our lives that we barely pause to wonder how it works. The form in which this technological revolution first spread across the world was as black and white television, and the basic principle on which all television, even today's complex colour systems, works is the same. Essentially, the picture seen by the camera is broken down into a series of dots of varying brightness which are then scanned in order, and the information passed as a signal to the television receiver. This reassembles the picture on a screen.

Like cine film, television does not consist of moving pictures. Instead it produces a series of still pictures at the rate of 25 to 30 every second (compared with 24 per second for cine film) which deceives the eye into thinking it is seeing smooth, steady motion, since it cannot distinguish the change from one split-second image to the next.

The black and white television picture that appears on your screen starts its life within the television camera in the studio or out on location. The light from the subject being televised falls on the camera lens, and is focused on a target plate whose surface is covered with a mosaic made up of spots of light-sensitive material. Each of these dots corresponds to one of the dots that will make up the finished picture. The light falling on the target plate will vary according to the areas of light and shade in the picture, so that the plate will, in effect, carry a map corresponding to the picture seen by the lens, but made up of electrical charges. The brighter the area, the higher the positive charge carried by the corresponding dot.

The electrical information on the target plate now has to be scanned, first to convert it into a signal for transmission and second to clear the plate ready to receive the next signal. This scanning is performed within the camera tube. A beam of electrons (negatively charged particles) is emitted from a plate (the cathode) and is focused by magnetic coils so that it strikes the target plate in a fine point. Under the direction of the coils, the beam sweeps backward and forward across the target plate in a series of lines, covering the whole surface 50 to 60 times a second. This is double the 'picture scanning rate' because, to prevent flicker, each picture is scanned twice on alternate lines.

The electrons in the scanning beam strike the target plate at a constant rate. As any one dot is hit, the positive charge on the dot is discharged by the negative charges of the electrons hitting it. The greater the charge on any dot, the more electrons are absorbed by it. The electrons which pass on through the target plate fall on a signal plate which lies behind it. Here they are used to generate a signal whose intensity varies directly with the intensity of light in the original picture, and it is this which is transmitted.

When, a fraction of a second after transmission, the signal reaches your receiver, it is used to produce an electron beam which scans the screen. The number of electrons hitting a particular dot on the screen corresponds exactly to the intensity of the original, and the more electrons hit a dot, the brighter it will glow.

The fluorescent screen of the TV tube is coated with dots or particles which glow when struck by the high-speed electrons of the TV signal. The beam of electrons is focused by magnetic coils which cause it to scan to and fro over the screen, making the dots glow in the forward movement only. The brightness of each dot depends on the number of electrons hitting it. When the scan reaches the bottom corner of the screen, it is deflected diagonally back to the top corner.

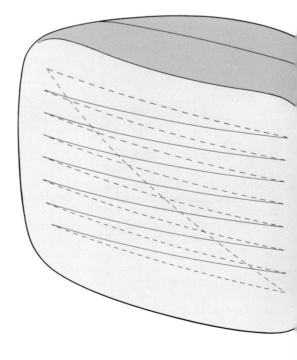

A TV monitor, unlike a TV receiver, does not pick up UHF/VHF signals. It displays a picture fed into it directly from a TV camera or VCR. For the best VCR reproduction, you need a TV monitor and receiver combined, the receiver for picking up UHF/VHF signals, the monitor for high-quality video fed in at low frequency.

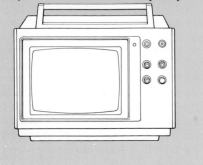

The signal which is transmitted from a TV station, *below,* is first generated as a steady high-frequency wave signal known as a carrier wave, **1** (black). Superimposed on this is the lower-frequency video signal (red). When the video signal is added on in this way, the carrier wave becomes modulated, **2,** so that the height, or amplitude, of the carrier wave (black) is altered to adapt to the video signal it is carrying. When this modulated vision carrier signal is picked up by the TV antenna, it is fed into the TV receiver. Here, the video signal, **3,** is first separated from the carrier wave by the tuner. The video signal is amplified and, after various modifications, fed into the TV picture tube, where it is used to generate a beam of electrons which scans the screen and varies with the intensity of the original signal.

In the TV, visual signals are used to create an electron beam, audio signals to create the sounds emerging from the loudspeaker.

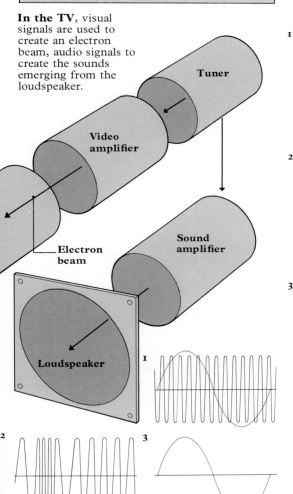

Tuner

Video amplifier

Electron beam

Sound amplifier

Loudspeaker

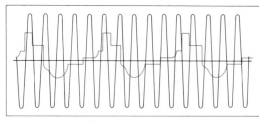

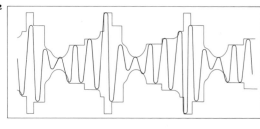

Sound signals, *left,* reach the TV in a similar way to video signals. First, a sound carrier signal is produced, **1,** which is modulated, **2,** by having a sound signal superimposed on it. This sound signal is carried at a frequency just above that of the video signal. In the TV, the tuner removes the sound signal from its sound carrier, **3,** and then amplifies it before feeding it to the loudspeaker.

Colour TV systems

Black and white television was a brilliant achievement, but adding colour was even more spectacular, for colour television involves the transmission of a vast amount of information. Moreover, when transmissions began, the new colour system had to enable people with black and white sets to continue receiving acceptable pictures from colour transmissions, and those with colour receivers to watch in black and white.

Just as the human eye produces a view of the world in two separate components, one a detailed picture in black and white, the other information about colour, so colour television works on a similar principle. One signal, the luminance signal, carries the information needed to build up a detailed black and white picture in exactly the same way as the existing black and white television system, so it can be received by black and white sets in the normal way. The second signal, the chrominance signal, is then added, and directs the television receiver to 'paint' on colours in the correct hues and intensities.

To produce colour television, the colours seen by the television camera are split up into the three primary colours, red, blue and green, by means of an arrangment of colour-separating mirrors or prisms. Each colour is focused into a different camera tube to produce a signal directly related to the areas and intensities of that colour.

Before transmission, the signals are first combined in the proportion of 30 per cent red, 59 per cent green and 11 per cent blue. This produces a completely black, white and grey picture which is transmitted as the luminance signal.

Next, the chrominance signals must be created in the following manner. The luminance signal already carries some of the colour information, since it is made up of the three primary colours in fixed proportions. Transmitter circuits now take the red signal and subtract it from the luminance signal, to produce a signal of green plus blue. Similarly, subtracting the blue signal gives a signal of red plus green. From these two so-called colour difference signals, a set of circuits in the receiver can break the information down to re-create the original red, blue and green signals and produce a picture.

Colour television has considerably complicated the variables between different television systems. The world's first commercial colour system was NTSC (National Television Systems Committee) introduced into the USA in 1954 and later adopted by Canada, Mexico and Japan. The main drawback of the NTSC system is that even slight errors in the phase between the colour difference signals produce errors at the decoding stage so that the set applies too much of one colour; hence the mnemonic for remembering the name: Never The Same Colour Twice. NTSC receivers have a hue control.

The PAL (Phase Alternating Line) system, used in Britain, Australia and most of Europe, produces better colour by means of more complicated receivers. SECAM (Système couleurs à memoire), adopted by France, Hungary, East Germany, Algeria and the USSR is simpler, but does not give such a good picture.

In the NTSC system, *below*, the two colour difference signals, **2** and **3**, created by the subtraction of red and blue from the total signal, **1**, are not transmitted together, but with one a quarter of a cycle behind the other. The signals are then added together to form a single chrominance signal, **4**. When it reaches the receiver, the decoding circuits, **5**, inside the TV break down the chrominance signal and separate it from its carrier wave. The two signals are fed into a matrix, which then combines them with the luminance signal to re-create the three original colour signals. These then create beams in three electron guns.

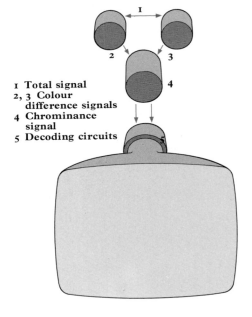

1 Total signal
2, 3 Colour difference signals
4 Chrominance signal
5 Decoding circuits

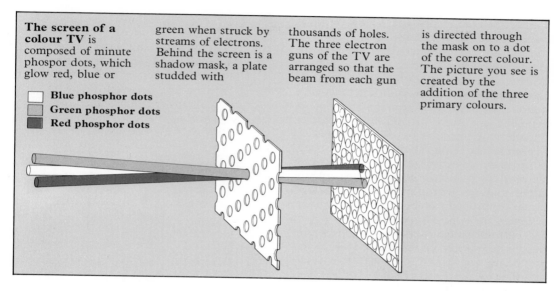

The screen of a colour TV is composed of minute phospor dots, which glow red, blue or green when struck by streams of electrons. Behind the screen is a shadow mask, a plate studded with thousands of holes. The three electron guns of the TV are arranged so that the beam from each gun is directed through the mask on to a dot of the correct colour. The picture you see is created by the addition of the three primary colours.

Blue phosphor dots
Green phosphor dots
Red phosphor dots

The PAL system, *below,* aims to improve the colour picture. The signals are transmitted in the same way, but the receiver delays the information on every line by means of an ultrasonic device, **6,** for the exact time needed to compare it with the signal for the next line. If, for example, a certain line of the picture, as received, contains too strong a red signal, the system ensures the next line will be too low on red by reversing the polarity of alternate lines. The final information passed to the picture tube is the average of the delayed first line and the corrected second one, so cancelling out the error. No hue control is necessary.

The SECAM system, *below,* has a different mode of transmission. The colour difference signals, **2** and **3,** are not arranged a quarter of a cycle apart, but are kept separate by transmitting them on alternate lines of the picture. Delay lines, **4,** inside the receiver then hold up one set of signals so that they can be recombined to build a picture from alternate lines of signals from the original scan within the camera. The SECAM system does not, however, give good pictures on a black and white receiver because it is difficult to separate the signals from their carrier.

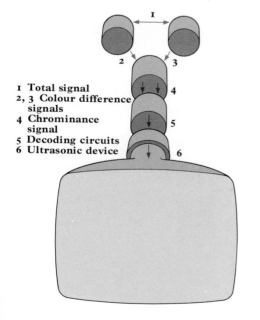

1 **Total signal**
2, 3 **Colour difference signals**
4 **Chrominance signal**
5 **Decoding circuits**
6 **Ultrasonic device**

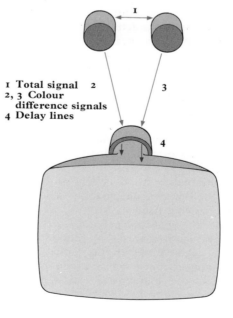

1 **Total signal**
2, 3 **Colour difference signals**
4 **Delay lines**

Antennae

Today's television sets and VCRs can produce pictures of remarkable quality. Nevertheless, however sophisticated your equipment, the biggest limiting factor to picture quality is the strength of the original broadcast signal relayed from your antenna to the input system of your terminal. If that is deficient, nothing you can do to improve or update the electronics of your video system can make the slightest difference. Yet any improvement you can make to the incoming signal will pay instant dividends in terms of better-quality recordings and, as an added bonus, improved television reception.

There are two reasons for a poor signal. Either the broadcast signal is poor, or you are the victim of a geographical accident. If you are a long way from the transmitter, or are overshadowed by hills or tall buildings, then you may have to come to terms with a poor-quality signal. To assess your situation, check with your neighbours; if everyone else seems to enjoy substantially better reception than you do, then there is probably room for improvement.

Whatever the standard of signal you can receive, an antenna adequate for the job is a must. In an area with good signal strength an indoor antenna in the attic, or V-shaped, loop or other antenna mounted on top of the set, may be enough. If these seem inadequate, you may need a roof antenna. These come in many sizes and degrees of elaboration. They may be highly directional (sensitive only to signals coming from one particular direction) which is ideal if your signal suffers from interference from other stations, or from echo causing ghosting. If you are lucky enough to receive reasonably good signals from several transmitters, you may need an antenna with less directional sensitivity to provide the best choice of viewing.

A useful extra to give increased flexibility is an RF signal splitter. This is a plug-in device which can split up the signals into two or more inputs so that either of two television sets can be switched to the VCR, or direct to the RF out for receiving broadcast television, without moving the VCR.

Whatever your needs, the best person to ask for advice is a specialist, who can take accurate test readings of your signal, check the existing antenna, assess the losses that occur down the cabling, and suggest ways to improve a weak or distorted signal.

A UHF amplifier is a useful device for improving the picture on your TV screen. Connected between the antenna lead and the VCR or TV, it can triple signal strength in areas where reception is generally poor.

A distribution amplifier is useful if you have several TVs or VCRs but only one antenna. It obviates the need to change the connection from each VCR as you use it. It can increase the signal strength to each by 75 per cent.

The area over which the receiver, or dipole, of an antenna receives signals can be drawn out as a simple circle, **1**, *below*. The addition of a reflector, **2**, cuts down the amount of signal picked up from the rear; a director, **3**, elongates the shape. Lack of rear pick-up eliminates inter-channel interference when you receive signals from only one transmitter, but you may need a less directional RF out to pick up signals from several transmitters.

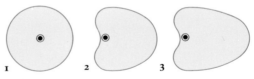

An indoor, set-top antenna, *below*, is most effective if you obtain good signal strength from the transmitter, since a signal weakens as it penetrates a building. Such an antenna can also be an asset if severe power losses are caused by long cable connections to your TV or VCR.

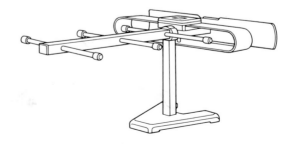

Exorcising ghosts

Poor reception is a problem when the area between the TV transmitter and a house fitted with a UHF antenna is obstructed by tall buildings or hills. In such situations, the most common reception problem is ghosting: the appearance of a shadowy second image to the right of the main image on the screen. What happens is that the antenna first picks up the strong, direct or primary signal from the transmitter, then, a fraction of a second later, picks up one (or sometimes more) weak or secondary signals which arrive by reflection from hill or housetop. Since the strong and weak signals arrive from slightly different directions, the best way to overcome the problem of ghosting is to fit a high-gain antenna, *below right*, on your roof.

If reception from your nearest transmitter is unacceptably poor, a specialist might suggest you tune in to another transmitter.

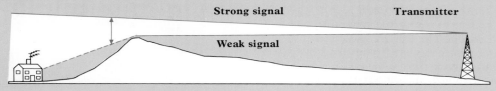

Twin-stacked UHF antennae positioned for best possible picture

Signal bent (diffracted) by hilltop

Strong signal

Transmitter

Weak signal

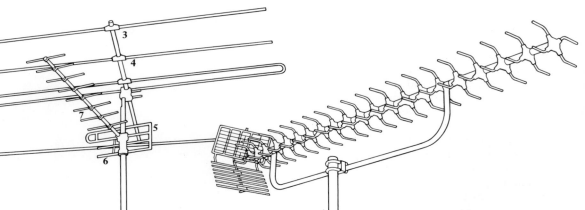

In a combined VHF/UHF antenna, *left*, the VHF part consists of a receiving element or dipole, **1**, on to which signals are directed by means of a reflector, **2**. Two directors, **3** and **4**, are positioned on the transmitter side of the dipole, and help to increase the power of the signal that reaches the dipole. The UHF part of the system has a gate-shaped reflector, **5**, compact dipole, **6**, and many directors, **7**.

A high-gain, group UHF antenna, *right*, is essential to obtain a good TV picture in areas where the signal strength from the transmitter is poor to moderate. Having 21 or more curved directors, the antenna works by picking up signals coming from one particular direction only. By rotating the antenna you may also be able to get rid of ghosts.

85

Viewing data

Silent but lively, videotext is invading our television screens with a dazzling array of computerized information. It was born of an idea conceived only a decade ago by engineers working for the British Broadcasting Corporation, who began sending internal messages along some of the 16 or so unused lines at the top of the television signal. Experiments in transmitting digital information along these lines brought home to the BBC the commercial potential of the discovery and as a result, videotext made its world début on British television in 1976.

Today, videotext comprises two types of service, teletext being the older and simpler. It is a one-way system: it piggy-backs digital data on to the unused portion of the broadcast television signal (it can be superimposed on a broadcast image) and in its unconverted state it resembles a twinkly band of Morse code just above the screen image, visible only when the vertical hold has slipped.

The teletext signal converts directly to a display of words or graphics on your television screen, but in order to receive any videotext system your set must be fitted with a decoder to transform the signal into the display. You can buy adaptors for older sets.

Simply by keying coded numbers on a remote control unit, you can conjure on to the screen news flashes, weather forecasts, sports results, even jokes and puzzles and your horoscope. The information is provided free by the broadcasting company, but only during transmission hours.

Viewdata originated with the British Post Office. It is a two-way system which exchanges information (chiefly by telephone link, but also by two-way cable or satellite) between your television set and data bases filled by commercial organizations such as airlines, financial institutions and retailers.

To receive viewdata you telephone a data bank, identify yourself as a subscriber, and use your remote control unit to call up the pages you want on your television screen. The data, stored in digital form, is converted first to audio signals for transmission by telephone, then back to digital form by the decoder in the television set, before finally being displayed on the screen.

The future of videotext is impossible to predict at so early a stage, but it bestows upon television the potential to become an instrument of information retrieval.

The numbers, letters and graphics that appear on the teletext or viewdata screen are built up as a pattern of dots, *below*. The UK authorities allow 24 lines of 40 characters; the USA broadcasts 20 lines of 32 characters. Both systems have the same visual format, with 96 characters and symbols, **1**, upper and lower case, as well as double size type and 32 control codes for flashing or boxing items, and so on. White, blue, green, red, magenta, cyan, yellow and black are the colours available. The dot matrix is so versatile that it is easily adaptable to display other types of written language such as Arabic, **2**.

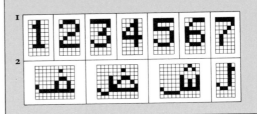

The viewdata system with the most realistic graphics is based on the Canadian Telidon system. This uses an alphageometric technique which gives a more curved display, *above*, than the alphamosaic system developed in the UK; however, it is much more expensive. It has been adopted by the Americans, who argue that the improved graphics will attract advertisers.

Selecting data

A keypad, which usually also acts as the audio-visual remote control and channel switcher for the TV set, is needed to call up teletext or viewdata information. Each teletext system publishes its own book of code numbers, telling you which digits to dial on the keypad for specific information or services, from commodity market prices to subtitles for the deaf.

With a keypad you can freeze a teletext page display for as long as you want it on the screen, or enlarge part of any page to double its size. You can superimpose a page on any TV show you are watching, or have news-flashes and updates, or the latest sports results, flashed up on the screen.

On the viewdata, which is transferred from computer to TV set along the telephone wires, it is possible to use the keyboard to answer back. Punching certain digits on the keypad thus allows you to book theatre tickets, make a hotel reservation and order food for dinner (and pay for all three with your credit card) without getting up from

your armchair. The next step in sophistication is to replace the keypad with a typewriter-style attachment by which the viewdata system can be used as an intelligent mini-computer terminal.

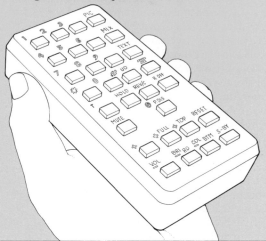

Teletext pages, *above,* are accessed cyclically, like slides in a carousel; the most-used ones are repeated so they may be retrieved in fewer seconds. The viewdata system of supply on request is immediate. the teletext page repertoire is a fraction that of viewdata, but free. With viewdata you pay for the telephone call to the computer, a connection charge and a variable charge per page retrieved. Both systems are constantly updated, but while teletext relies on the broadcaster to act as editor, viewdata is updated by direct input into the computer from many suppliers. Teletext systems in current use include Ceefax, Orbit and Oracle in the UK. Canadian Telidon and French Antiope are teletext systems which can be extended to accommodate viewdata.

Giant screens

The homely, small-screen television is perfectly adequate for most viewing. But when your video tapes begin to seem poor imitations of their wide-screen cinema originals, or when you hanker after re-creating all the atmosphere of a live sporting occasion, if you have the space and the funds, then could be the time to consider acquiring a large-screen television.

A modern large-screen home system consists of three items which may or may not be built into the same unit: a television receiver, an enlarger using one or three lenses for optical magnification, and the viewing screen. The least expensive systems have the screen separate from the projection unit so that the television stands back from the screen rather like a movie projector. This system uses a modified, conventional television set with a huge lens fitted over the screen to project the image on the viewing screen. However, whereas a film projector employs a bright light to boost the illumination on the screen to an acceptable level, the brilliance of a normal television picture cannot be increased, making the vast picture rather dim.

The more elaborate systems use three tubes, each projecting one of the primary colours: blue, red, or green and three lenses which increase the brilliance of the picture and which, with the screen, are contained in one package. A built-in system of mirrors and back projection reduces set size to manageable proportions.

Other techniques of achieving large-screen television include the do-it-yourself conversion of an existing set using a screen, lens and manual supplied by the kit manufacturer. Alternatively, a plastic fresnel lens may be erected in front of the normal television set. The use of most such conversion kits demands considerable technical competence, so they are for experts only.

Apart from home conversions, the most daunting aspect of large-screen television is its cost, which starts at around £800 in the UK and $1,000 in the USA, and rises to as much as £2,500 and $4,000 respectively. But for anyone who relishes the prospect of big-screen viewing at home, for video recordings or ordinary television viewing, then it is certainly worth considering. Projection television systems also have practical possibilities in the leisure industry, in business and in education.

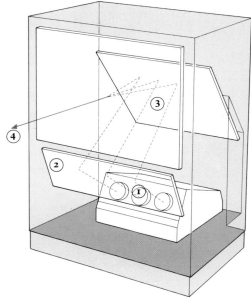

Big-screen TV is made possible by back projection. In this system 3 tubes each project one of the primary TV colours via lenses, **1**, on a mirror, **2**, which reflects them on to a flat screen, **3**. This screen bounces the colours off at such an angle that they are combined, **4**, to form a picture. Sound is also bounced off.

Ample viewing space is essential for watching big-screen TV. Most projection TV systems take up an area of floor space at least 3 ft by 2 ft (1 m by 60 cm) and are designed to be viewed at a distance of 5 to 20 ft (1.5 to 5 m). The primary, and best viewing zone, **1**, is contained within a wide angle, but the best viewing position is well back from the screen. The secondary viewing zone, **2**, provides a less than perfect view of the screen and should be avoided unless the screen is completely flat. To make the most impact, large-screen TV is best viewed in a dimly lit, cinema-like atmosphere with the lights down low.

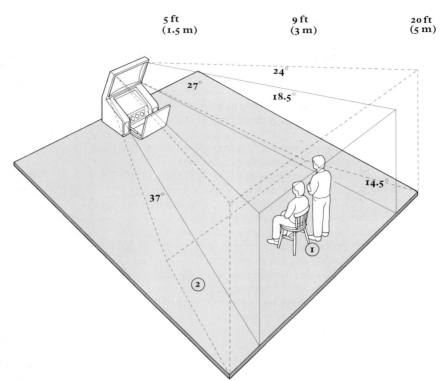

Picture quality on a large screen, with diagonal measurements of 50, 60 or even 80 in (125, 160 or 200 cm), is only as good as the source from which that TV picture originates. Any TV projection system will, by its very nature, magnify any shortcomings in a picture which might well pass muster on a normal TV. This is especially true of snowy, weak or ghosted broadcast TV reception and poorly recorded video cassettes. A good TV signal from your antenna or cable TV system is, thus, the first requirement. Another must for a perfect picture is a screen with a highly reflective beaded glass surface.

Skybirds

For the television of tomorrow, the future will involve both cable and satellite broadcasting. Neither system is novel, but what is new is their potential impact on viewing.

Cable television dates from the earliest days of broadcasting. In these times the coverage of the transmitters was much less than perfect, with several areas, obstructed by tall building or hills, where the signal was either weak or non-existant. The answer was to set up antennae at sites where the signal was acceptable and to pipe it along coaxial cables for distribution to any viewer prepared to pay the subscription fee. The engineering standards employed by these networks were of variable quality, and in many cases the technical system demanded the use of special or modified television receivers.

Modern cable television has developed in many ways, with cable companies sending out specialized broadcasts, often to target audiences. However, the economics of cable television mean that it is viable only in densely populated areas.

Where cable television is too costly, or where isolated communities are cut off from information sources, the answer to improved communications may lie in satellites. Since the launch of Telstar in 1962 satellites have been used to link continents, but satellite broadcasting to the general public is only just becoming an economic reality. With an appropriate dish-shaped antenna and a down-converter to make the signals usable, satellite television beamed from an orbiting 'bird' will soon be available to all consumers for the same cost as a video recorder. In the near future, cable television networks will probably receive and redistribute some of the satellite channels; only serious viewers will need to own a receiving dish.

While the technology of satellite television has been worked out, the politics certainly have not. Hitherto, governments have been able, if they wished, to control the pattern and content of broadcasting, but now transmitters can beam a particular brand of uncensored entertainment, cultural or commercial, into another country.

Cable and satellite television have a linked future and together form an enormously powerful medium for reaching the mass of viewers. While neither is likely to replace conventional broadcasting, they provide a means of catering for special interests.

Cable TV world-wide
Around the world, cable TV has developed in different ways. In the UK the original networks were developed to carry the three broadcast channels and even some of the newer systems have little or no capacity for additional services. In 12 localities, however, feature films are available for a premium subscription

On the continent of Europe, cable TV is more established, with most major cities wired for it. In Belgium, 75% of all homes are wired for cable TV and, apart from the four national programmes, viewers can receive broadcasts from France, Germany, Luxembourg, the Netherlands and the UK.

In the USA, about 45% of homes (a total of more than 20 million) are wired up to cable TV. The majority are in metropolitan areas where 30 or more different channels may be available, providing a wide range of services, including updated displays of news, weather and financial reports. There are cultural, community and ethnic channels, and channels devoted to films, sport and children's entertainment.

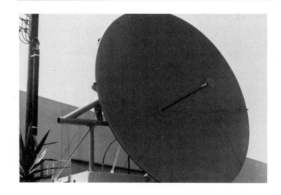

A dish on the roof or in the garden makes satellite TV available at home. Yet even in the USA, where there are over 50 satellite TV channels, and where such dishes are commonplace, the satellites are really intended only to supplement cable TV systems and do not generate their own broadcasts.

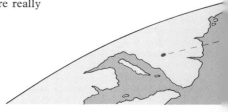

Communications of the future will almost certainly involve the use of optical fibres. Compared with copper coaxial cables now in use, optical fibres carry more data much faster. In this system, electrical signals are converted into a binary code of on-off signals which is then transformed into flashes of light. These are transmitted along transparent glass fibres and, when they reach their destination, are turned back into electrical signals. Some fibres smooth out the overlap between light rays, **1**, but the best, **2**, give higher quality by allowing one ray to pass at a time.

Advances in fibre optics promise wide repercussions for cable TV. In the Japanese town of Higashi-Ikoma, 160 homes are linked by two-way fibre optic cable TV to a central studio and eight other points round the town, including the emergency services. Every home TV set also has a computer terminal equipped with a mike so that residents can call up the various services, see the personnel, and have access to central computer banks. But because the central studio also has a TV window into private homes, the experiment has been considered a violation of privacy.

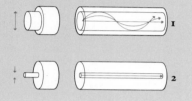

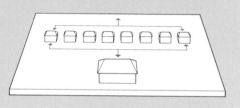

Like a giant bird, a Direct Broadcasting Satellite orbits the earth. In the future, such satellites will beam down signals powerful enough to cover whole countries and allow reception with a dish only a few feet across. The signals will be transmitted at much higher frequencies than our regular UHF transmission of 500 to 800 MHz, so special downconverters will also be needed. With a big dish, say 8 ft (2.4 m) across, it may be possible to pick up signals from satellites sent up by other countries, but the dream of Europeans watching US TV will not be possible until the Americans beam it down on them deliberately.

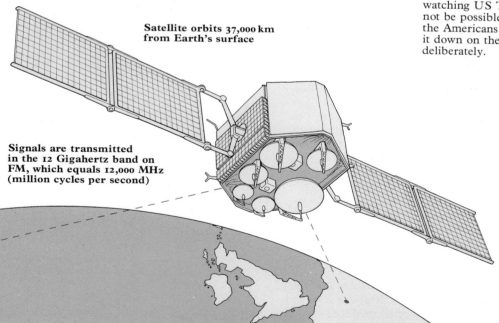

Satellite orbits 37,000 km from Earth's surface

Signals are transmitted in the 12 Gigahertz band on FM, which equals 12,000 MHz (million cycles per second)

TV tomorrow

Television, now inextricably bound to video, has a rosy future. So what does that future hold for us, the viewers? First and foremost, conventional television will quietly improve.

Already American manufacturers are using comb filters to improve picture reproduction, and manufacturers the world over are acheiving new standards of reliability. On the audio side, stereo broadcasting, already a reality in Germany and Japan, will become commonplace.

Soon, we can expect our televisions to be 'user friendly'. By 1988 a television will have, as standard, remote control responding to spoken commands, teledata and cable television facilities, and easy connections for video games, VCR, home computer and reception of satellite broadcasts.

Television will change in shape and size, so that we shall soon become used to large-screen video 'cinemas', and the progressive miniaturization of the screen will be limited only by the abilities of the human eye.

The picture will be given added brightness, either by means of liquid crystal displays, similar to those already used in pocket calculators, or by electroluminescence, created by light-emitting diodes (LEDs) similar to those used today as indicators on a variety of electronic gadgets. Liquid crystal LED displays will also have a role to play in making home computers, linked to televisions, smaller and cheaper. In addition, picture tubes using LEDs, now being developed in Japan and the USA, are proving to be safer because, unlike today's television tubes, they do not run hot and do not use a potentially dangerous combination of glass and a high-pressure vacuum.

High-definition and three-dimensional television are sure to have arrived by the nineties, but are unlikely to be commonplace. The former promises to be most advantageous to the video owner, and could give definition as good as 35 mm film.

With component television, the viewer will have the ultimate in choice. In Japan the Sony Corporation has already introduced the 'Profeel' range for which the consumer selects monitor, receiver and tuner. To this can be added a hi-fi system and VCR.

So (if you can afford it) the future offers a feast of new television. Add to this the promised proliferation of broadcasts, and that future promises to be rich indeed.

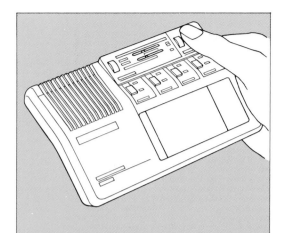

The Microvision pocket TV has a minute flat screen only 3 in (7.5 cm) in diameter, but is able to receive transmissions almost anywhere in the world (France is a notable exception). To do this, the set needs a telescopic antenna, and this, together with the fact that it will not operate in aircraft, trains or automobiles, also limits its usefulness. Despite these drawbacks, miniature TV is likely to be commonplace in the near future, and the day of the wrist-model TV cannot be far off.

Flat-screen TV, hung on the wall like a picture, will have the advantage of taking up less space than today's TV sets. The Japanese are currently working on two possible models. In one, the screen is made up of a matrix of liquid crystal cells; in the other it contains a myriad of minute gas-discharging devices. These sets should also have the added asset of using less electricity in their operation than conventional sets.

In the movie 'Star Wars', Princess Leia asking for help from Ben Kenobi in the Rebellion: it is a 3D holographic image of herself. Such 3D imagery (in realistic colour, not a weird, shimmering blue) is the TV technician's dream. The key to success could well lie with the hologram, a 3D image produced with the help of lasers. To create a hologram, a laser beam is split in two. Half is directed at an object, half at a holographic plate. Where the two beams overlap they set up interference waves which reproduce the shape and depth of the object. Adapting this technology to create truly 3D TV is the exciting prospect for tommorow.

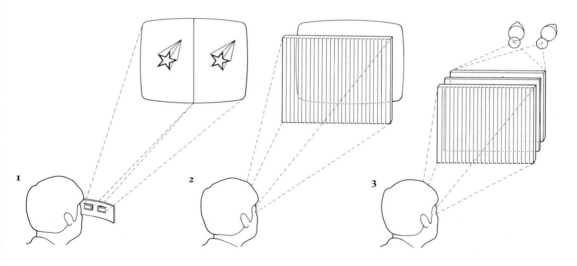

TV in 3D will be on the screen soon. Of the schemes devised to date, one of the simplest, **1**, is to create two identical images, one to be seen by the left eye, the other by the right. The TV is shrouded with a viewing hood containing lenses, to bend the sight-lines outward. Although cheap, this system gives an unacceptably upright image. The direction-selective 3D TV, **2**, has a picture made up of vertical lines with alternate lines designed to be viewed by left and right eyes. In front of the screen is a grooved lens, which translates the visual information and directs it into the appropriate eye. Unfortunately, the picture definition is poor, and even slight sideways movements of the head distort the image. To help solve this problem, **3**, two images from separate tubes are projected on a double-grooved lens. This gives improved definition and restricts viewer movement less.

All about cameras

A video recorder can do more than you realize. In addition to recording broadcast television shows and playing back pre-recorded cassettes, a VCR linked to a video camera is all you need to make your own recordings.

Video cameras are no longer out of the price range of the home-producer. Although a decade ago the only portable colour cameras were professional broadcast models costing thousands apiece, now a compact colour video camera costs little more than a good-quality Super 8 home movie camera. Every year sees further improvements designed to make cameras for home-producers more sophisticated, yet easier to use.

Since portable colour cameras were introduced during the sixties, black and white cameras have dropped in price so dramatically that older ones cost as little as one tenth of the price of a new colour model. These are ideal for beginners to try out. Once you graduate to colour, the monochrome camera will still be useful for adding titles and graphics to your colour movies.

As a result of the revolution in video technology, making your home movies with a video camera is easier than with a Super 8 home movie camera, although it has some disadvantages. One of the most important of these is that the video camera is not yet self-sufficient.

Unlike still and moving film cameras, you cannot load a video camera with film. All it can do is translate the picture framed by its lens into an electrical signal. This has to be passed down a cable to the recorder before it can be recorded on the cassette tape. This means that if your camera is connected to a home deck you can venture no farther than the garden.

For location work, you need a battery-operated portable recorder, which will give you freedom, but at a price several times that of a basic cine film outfit, although film cameras are more versatile. As a compensation, however, the cost of video tape is far less than that of film. Minute for minute, it is roughly one-tenth the price of Super 8 film.

Video has many advantages over film. You can record a shot, then play it back instantly, simply by pressing the 'Rewind' and 'Playback' buttons on the VCR. You will never have to wait, nor pay, for video tape to be processed. If you are not happy with the shot you can wind the tape back and record the next shot over it because tape, unlike film, can be used more than once.

Since your home deck will be connected to a television set, you can try out a shot, watching it on the screen without using the tape at all, to see if it is worth recording. Sound is automatically recorded alongside the picture information on the tape, so you always have a sound-track which is perfectly synchronized with the pictures on the screen. You can play back your movies over the television, without setting up a projector and screen, or darkening the room.

Nevertheless, video cameras are still heavy to operate for more than a few minutes at a time, especially if you are carrying a porta-pack over your shoulder, and film cameras are, by comparison, light. In addition, they can do things video cameras can never do. They can shoot frame by frame, and so create the illusion of movement by showing 24 frames, or separate pictures, every second. The eye's persistence of vision smooths out this succession of separate images into smooth, unbroken movement, a facility which is exploited in cartoons, or in time-lapse effects such as the speeded-up movement of a flower opening.

Luckily you will not have to make a definite choice between video recording and cine filming. Because Super 8 pictures can be copied easily and cheaply on video tape, there are many ways of combining the two media to take advantage of the best of both.

If you have a library of home movies you can transfer them to tape for longer life and ease of playback. You can use a Super 8 camera to shoot film in places where carrying video equipment would be difficult or impossible, and re-record the pictures on tape afterwards.

Finally, because professional editing on video tape can be expensive, limiting most home-producers to recording material in the order in which it is to appear in the finished production, you can shoot complicated sequences on film, edit them by cutting and splicing, and copy the entire sequence into the appropriate place on the tape.

Until you have used a video camera, this sounds complicated, but because tape is so cheap, and because you can see the results of your experiments immediately, you can learn from experience more quickly with a video

SONY

TRINITRON

REMOTE CONTROL KV-1812UB

camera than would be possible with film.

The next few pages show how modern video cameras are removing the guesswork, and making it much easier to produce professional-quality results from the beginning. They progress from the simplest hand-held cameras to the most advanced semi-professional shoulder-mounted models, whose automatic features, adapted from professional broadcasting cameras, do almost all the work for you.

The portable colour video camera has now reached an advanced stage of development, and is unlikely to change a great deal in the near future. The appearance of Microvideo, a new quarter-inch cassette tape format aimed exclusively at the portable market, heralds the birth of a new generation of lightweight portapacks – but these have a very limited playing time.

The innovations of the distant future are, however, just in sight. Sub-miniature tape formats, using microcassettes similar to those you load into dictating machines, will eventually result in a combined deck-and-camera system – a video camera into which you load the tape. Inevitably, too, the micro-chip will invade the video camera.

Basic cameras

Mastering the technique of operating a video camera is easy enough, but the various types and models are so differently designed that whenever you buy a new camera always read through the manual before operating it.

Using the manual, identify the camera's components and put them together carefully. Most of the simpler cameras arrive ready to use, but more sophisticated models may have a separate electronic viewfinder and a microphone, each of which has to be fitted into place and its cables plugged into a special socket. If the lens has to be screwed into its mounting on the camera body take great care not to cross-thread it; the damage may be expensive to rectify. Put the lens cap on to protect the camera tube.

A video camera is designed for use with a portable VCR, but can be used with a home deck, if you connect both to a power adaptor. The various manuals will give clear wiring diagrams. If the camera fails to work the first time you press the stop/start switch, recheck the connections first; then make sure that the camera, the power adaptor *and* the VCR are all switched on. The camera may not produce a picture until two or three of its switches are in the correct position.

Pick the camera up carefully and point it at a well-lit, but not very bright, subject. In a dark room do not point it at a window; the contrast between dark interior and bright surroundings can cause flare if the iris is manually operated, and close down an auto iris so that the interior turns black. If the camera has an optical viewfinder, wait for it to warm up. If it has an electronic viewfinder the picture will appear on its television screen in the eyepiece, but in black and white, not in colour.

Remove the lens cap and zoom in to a subject, holding it in close-up. The picture will probably be out of focus and, if you switch on your television set to see the picture in colour, you may find the colours are unrealistic. Adjust the colour temperature controls, guided by the manual, and then focus the image to give as sharp a picture as possible. It should then remain sharp through the whole zooming range of the lens.

Treat the camera carefully – but at the same time try it out, put it through its paces, experiment with it, find out what it can and cannot do.

Many of the simpler video cameras have been designed along similar lines to Super 8 cine cameras, with pistol-grip handles. However, video cameras are heavier – this Hitachi camera weighs just over 4 lb (nearly 2 kg) – and can be tiring to use and difficult to hold steady. For this reason many pistol-grip cameras are designed to rest on the shoulder, and the angle of the grip is adjustable.

The lens, 6, has three adjustments: aperture or iris (which controls the amount of light reaching the camera tube); focus (which controls the sharpness of the image formed on the camera tube), and the zoom. This allows the focal length of the lens to be varied so that the picture can be framed at any point between a shot of a whole scene and a magnified close-up of its central area. On this camera the iris is fully automatic, the focus, 7, is manually controlled, and the zoom has a power switch, 8, *and* manual control, 9.

Only a few luxury VCRs have an input socket for a video camera. Usually the two have to be connected via a camera adaptor, *below*, recommended by the manufacturer.

All video cameras are designed for use with a particular VCR: this Hitachi with the VT-8500 VCR, *below right*. If you want to use it with another VCR you may need adaptor leads and, depending on the model and

Most cameras have built-in omni-directional mikes. These pick up sound from all round the camera – but that may include the sound of the auto iris and even the operator's breathing. This camera has a uni-directional boom mike, **1**, which picks up the sounds ahead.

You may need a more sensitive extension mike, for which there are special sockets in both camera and VCR. By plugging an empty jack into an external mike socket you can cut the sound.

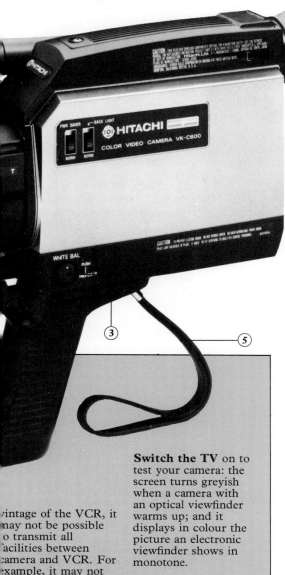

To operate the camera there is usually a stop/start trigger switch near the hand grip, but it may be hard to identify. On this camera it is marked 'Remote control', **4**.

A camera, unlike the human eye, cannot adapt to the colour of light. A white object looks white indoors or out, but through a lens it looks reddish or bluish. The white balance control, **3**, corrects this.

Simpler cameras may have one of four types of viewfinder: an optical viewfinder similar to that on a stills camera; a more sophisticated version which tracks with the zoom, permitting accurate focusing, and gives an idea of the lens's field of view; a TTL (through the lens) device, so called because it gives a picture of the scene framed by the lens; or an electronic viewfinder, **2**. This is a miniature TV monitor mounted in the eyepiece, which displays the picture in black and white.

If the camera has a handle strap, **5**, loop it round your wrist. You will be unconscious of it as you operate the camera, but it will stop it falling if you lose your balance, or if someone bumps into you.

vintage of the VCR, it may not be possible to transmit all facilities between camera and VCR. For example, it may not be possible to stop and start recording from the camera.

Switch the TV on to test your camera: the screen turns greyish when a camera with an optical viewfinder warms up; and it displays in colour the picture an electronic viewfinder shows in monotone.

When you look into the eyepiece of an electronic viewfinder you usually see a number of lines, lights and motifs below or down the side of the screen and sometimes superimposed upon the picture. These are warning lights. In the Hitachi, *above*, 'V' lights up when the camera is recording; 'L' when the object on which the camera is focused is inadequately lit; 'B' when the batteries are running down and 'W' when the white balance is incorrect. For on-the-spot playback just rewind the tape.

Colour correction

An object looks coloured only because it reflects light of a particular colour to the eye. It can do this only if the light falling on it contains the particular colour it reflects. In fact, objects appear in what we see as their true colours only under white light, which is made up of light waves of all colours. Light which is not white, which has one or more constituent colours missing, may distort the colours of the objects upon which it falls. To take an extreme example, an object which looks blue-green under white light would look black under pure red light, since it reflects no red light at all.

This is important in film and video shooting simply because pure white light is surprisingly rare. What our eyes see as white light is usually tinged with blue, yellow or red. In fact, the colour of the light under which the camera is recording tends to vary with the location, the time of day, the weather and the type of lighting being used; and while our eyes automatically compensate for this changing colour balance, so that we always see white objects as white, the camera cannot.

This means that a video camera with its colour responses correctly set up for daylight, which has a distinctly blue cast, will produce pictures with an obviously yellow quality under indoor lighting; and a camera that is adjusted to reproduce the colours in a living room lit by tungsten light (which has a strong yellow tone) in the evening, will 'see' outdoor scenes during the day as much bluer than they seem to the eye.

Film makers solve this problem by using colour correction filters. Whatever the colour of the light falling on the outside of the lens, using the right type of filter ensures that the light reaching the film is always correctly colour-balanced. Similarly, outdoor working presents no problems if a filter which tones down the blue content of the light is fitted to the camera, leaving the light emerging from it perfectly balanced for the film. Many video cameras use filters in exactly the same way for indoor/outdoor adjustment, though they can also produce the same effects electronically. Often a good camera will use both methods: filters for basic colour compensation and electronic correction control for fine adjustment to suit the prevailing light conditions and so will have two sets of colour controls.

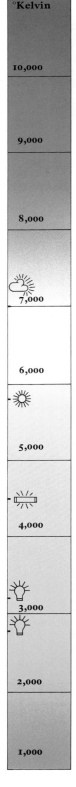

Cloudy sky (7,000°K)

Bright sunshine (5,800°K)

Average daylight (5,000°K)

The different colour balances of different kinds of light can be measured by relating them to the temperatures to which most materials must be heated to produce all the different kinds of light. For example, the reddish light from a candle measures around 1,000° Kelvin, so that is its colour temperature, *left*. Most materials heated to this temperature will produce the same reddish light. Photofloods produce a whiter light at 3,000°K, while flashbulbs, quartz halogen and fluorescent lights range up to around 5,000°K. Sunshine, usually thought of as pure white light, is about 6,000°K, while overcast skies become progressively bluer, at colour temperatures ranging from 7,000°K to 10,000°K. This is not because the sky is hot, but because the scattering of the light produces a bluish cast.

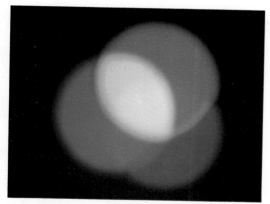

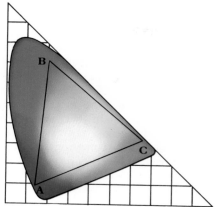

Video uses light of three primary colours: red, blue and green, which mix in the eye to re-create all the other colours you see on the screen. Light beams of these three primaries will mix into a single white beam, *above*, if their intensities are equal. Yet when they are mixed in different intensities, other colours result. The red and green beams, *above*, mix to yellow, the exact shade depending on the proportions of red and green: more red and less green will produce orange; the reverse ratio gives khaki. Moreover, any two colours can be tinted by different proportions of a third colour, and any colour mixture can be paler or darker, widening the colour range.

The chromaticity chart, *above*, shows this colour range. A, B and C mark the primaries. The shades in the inner triangle result from mixtures of these primaries and represent all the colours you see on a TV screen.

The camera's colour temperature adjustment compensates for the type of light being used for the recording. It may consist of a set of colour correction filters moved, often by a 'Daylight Filter' switch, between the lens and the tube, or a switch with up to four colour temperature settings, *far right*. The photographs, *below*, show how the colour of the prevailing light looks natural only when shot under the correct setting.

Instead of using an optical filter to remove excess colour from a scene, turning down the sensitivity of the blue circuits inside the camera has

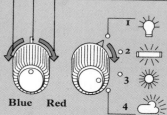

Blue   Red

1 **Iodine lamps (3,200°K)**
2 **Fluorescent lamps (4,500°K)**
3 **Bright outdoors, sunshine (5,800°K)**
4 **Cloudy, rainy (7,000°K)**

the same effect. The Tint, or the White Balance control, *above left*, varies the balance between red and blue. Turning it left makes the picture bluer, and right, redder, *top*.

1 Iodine lamps   **2 Fluorescent lamps**   **3 Bright outdoors**   **4 Cloudy, rainy**

On the market/Basic cameras

Information and test reports on all the new cameras on their way in to the market can be found in all the major video magazines. However, the most important feature of any camera, and one that is not covered directly in the most detailed of specifications, is the quality of the picture the camera produces. This is a combination of sharpness of image, faithfulness of colour reproduction, and ability to capture fast-moving subjects and record at low light levels. The only way to be sure a camera meets all these requirements is to test it.

Take no notice of the photographs, apparently showing what the camera can do, which appear in manufacturers' brochures: they are invariably shot on film, not videotape. The picture a video camera produces is an electronic image and looks quite different. It cannot, however, look as good as the pictures you are used to seeing broadcast on television. These are shot under ideal conditions, using cameras costing thousands.

Begin by comparing the pictures produced by several different video cameras to assess current standards. The manufacturer's showroom or, better still, a video exhibition, may give you the facilities for doing this. Then test two or three systematically.

In a shop, insist on handling the camera yourself. Ideally you should try it with several different tape recorders and through more than one television set, especially if you spot a fault: it may not be in the camera. Point the camera at as many different kinds of subjects as possible. Notice how it copes with well-lit objects, dark areas, high contrasts. Pan the camera quickly across the scene to see whether the picture seems to lag behind the movement of the camera. Many single-tube cameras are faulty on the red colour balance, so notice whether red objects are tinted rust or maroon, and whether faces look too flushed, or pallid.

Most shops are on the dark side, so try to take the camera out into daylight. Record pans, zooms, fades and a variety of still and moving objects on a tape cassette, which you can then take home and compare on your own machine, through your own television, with tapes recorded on other cameras.

Really you need to try the camera out on your own ground, on subjects of your own choosing. You may be able to arrange a short rental or extended trial with the shop.

Hitachi VK-C750

Hitachi produces a large range of single-tube colour cameras. In the earlier models the pictures are sometimes less crisp, particularly in long-shot adjustment, than in those produced by competitive cameras from other manufacturers. The new generation cameras are better in this respect. The VK-C750 is a lightweight model weighing only 4 lb (about 2 kg) and is one of the cheapest colour cameras on the

JVC GX-33

JVC produces a range of colour cameras so wide that it embraces both the cheapest and the most expensive cameras on the market. Their basic model is the GX-33, currently one of the lowest-priced designs in all markets. It has a through-the-lens optical viewfinder and a 3:1 manual zoom. This is an ultra-lightweight camera, weighing only 3 lb (1.4 kg). The

Hitachi GP-41D

Panasonic WV-3000

market. It has an automatic iris, a 2.8:1 zoom lens (the lens allows a 2.8 magnification of the picture in full close-up) with manual control and an optical viewfinder.

The GP-41D has many features the more ambitious enthusiast will want, such as an electronic viewfinder and a 6:1 power zoom lens.

Panasonic was one of the first companies to introduce a reliable colour video camera at a price the amateur could afford. Simple to use, but with a sharp and clear picture, our Panasonic camera performed reliably in locations ranging from the Irish Sea to the Himalayas. The WV-3000 is an up-to-date equivalent, with a 3:1 manual zoom lens and an electronic viewfinder.

JVC GX-88

Panasonic WV-3030 (Europe) WV-3110 (USA)

electronic viewfinder assembly, offered as an optional extra, would add to both weight and price.

The GX-33 comes in PAL and NTSC versions. The GX-88 has a SECAM variant,

electronic viewfinder and a power-operated 6:1 zoom lens. It costs a lot more. It also features the super close-up facility which allows you to focus right in to the outer face of the lens.

The more sophisticated the features offered on a camera the more, as a rule, it will cost. Also, automation accounts for much of the price of the more expensive cameras, such as the

Panasonic WV-3030. It has an electronic viewfinder, a 6:1 zoom lens with macro close-up facility and power zoom control, an automatic iris and automatic low-light-level compensation.

Advanced cameras

Video cameras vary in price and complexity from the basic home-movie type to sophisticated professional models. Drawing a clear line between the two types is difficult because the specifications for the cheaper cameras are improving year by year, and features such as power zoom lenses and semi-automatic colour-balancing, once limited to professional cameras, are beginning to appear on some of the cheaper models.

The biggest single difference between the two is in the way the camera is designed. All semi-professional and professional cameras have electronic viewfinders which, since they need no optical machinery but only a simple cable connection to the camera, can be located at the front of the camera body. This means that the operator can carry the camera on the shoulder while looking into the eyepiece, a much more comfortable arrangement than the pistol grip, and one which enables the camera to be held steady for longer periods.

Essentially, more complex versions of standard fittings make expensive cameras easier to use, more efficient in marginal conditions such as low light levels and more versatile. For instance, the relocated viewfinder on the shoulder-mounted camera can usually be pivoted in all directions, allowing the operator to aim it from the hip, or above the head, and even hold the camera on its side or upside down, and still see into the eyepiece.

Difficult and unusual shots often demand the ability to override automatic systems. As an example, in most situations an automatic iris is a sophisticated device, enabling the camera to react to changing light levels and so relieving you from constant rechecking and readjustment. What happens, though, when you want to zoom out from a close-up of a fairly dark subject to a brighter scene? As the light entering the camera increases, the lens aperture automatically closes down, and this can turn the dark subject into a silhouette. Some cameras have an aperture lock to allow you to guard against this. With the camera set in close-up you lock the iris so that it remains at the same setting as you zoom out. You then reset it to automatic. A back-lighter compensator control is a useful alternative for situations where the subject is standing indoors in front of a window, or is outlined against a bright sky. This sets the lens open, usually by one and a half f-stops, so the exposure should be correct for the subject although the background will then be over-bright.

Most shoulder-mounted cameras, such as the Sony camera illustrated here, have a 'macro' position on the manual zoom control. Selecting it causes the components of the lens system to be rearranged into a different configuration, enabling it to focus on objects as close as the outer face of the lens for really detailed close-ups. However, you cannot zoom at the same time, and providing adequate lighting can be difficult as the camera casts its own shadow over the subject.

A red light, 10, called the VTR Indicator, Tape Run Lamp or Battery Lamp, lights up to indicate to the person being filmed that the tape is running. It also lights up during playback and blinks if the battery is about to run out.

The lens cap, 9, protects the lens from damage and prevents bright light from entering the camera during pauses in recording. On most shoulder-mounted cameras a white plastic lens cap is used, instead of a white subject, to adjust white balance.

The electronic viewfinder, *right,* plugs into a socket just above the external microphone connection, and is fully adjustable. The viewfinder swivels and the eyepiece tilts up and down, giving scope for shots from unusual and difficult angles.

An external boom mike, or a video lamp, can be fitted into this receptacle, **1**. Since the built-in omni-directional mike is useful only to pick up general background sounds, a uni-directional boom mike is often needed. A light fitted to the camera is not so useful. It illuminates only subjects near the camera, and its beam may reflect off a shiny surface into the lens.

Low light conditions may make shooting impossible unless your camera is fitted with a control marked 'Low Light' or 'Sensitivity', **2**. This amplifies the video signal to create a brighter picture. Increased noise makes the picture appear grainier and less sharp, but it does allow the video camera to record an image where this might otherwise be impossible.

The iris control, **3**, has dual functions on this camera: push it in for auto and pull it out for manual control.

To fade the picture out to a blank screen, you usually shut down the lens aperture to the closed position, and you open it up to fade in. To overcome the difficulties of steadying the camera while manually opening and closing the aperture, some of the newer models have a fade control which does the job smoothly and easily. This camera has a pre-set auto-fade switch located on the back panel, **4**.

The camera body is shaped at the bottom to sit comfortably on the shoulder, **5**, but some manufacturers offer an optional, shaped pad that bolts on underneath the camera body and fits snugly around the operator's shoulder.

Every shoulder-mounted camera has a strong hand grip through which the right hand supports the camera, leaving the fingers free to manipulate the power zoom switch above it. The thumb operates the stop/start switch (called 'Tape Run' on this camera) located just behind the grip. The left hand moves the macro lever, the manual zoom and the focusing ring (**6**, **7** and **8**, *above*).

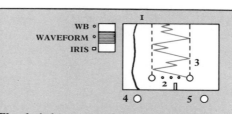

The brightness and sharpness of the picture in the viewfinder can be adjusted by two controls located beneath the eyepiece. With a third switch you select indicators to appear on the screen, *above*. The white balance (WB) indicator causes a white line, **1**, to appear; it moves to the left as the colour balance is adjusted. If the iris indicator is selected the white indicator, **2**, moves left or right as the iris is closed or opened. The waveform indicator causes the waveform, **3**, to peak at the lines only when there is enough light to record an image. Beneath the screen a yellow lamp, **4**, lights up when the light is insufficient and a red lamp, **5**, lights up when the tape is running and during playback.

On the market/Advanced cameras

The more complex shoulder-held cameras have developed directly from the vastly more expensive ENG (Electronic News Gathering) cameras now used by broadcasting professionals. With every new model launched on to the market, features originally introduced to meet television broadcasting requirements are coming into wider use. This makes it easier to predict the changes and improvements that are likely to appear on the next generation of video cameras.

Zoom lenses are now standard fittings on almost all video cameras, but the range of the zoom is being extended. Once a 4:1 zoom lens (allowing a 4:1 magnification of the picture in full close-up) was a popular fitting. Now most zoom lenses in this market are 6:1, with 10:1 and even 14:1 lenses beginning to appear on the costlier cameras.

Most cameras in this part of the market have power-driven zooms, but these work only at a single pre-set rate. The next step is an additional switch to select a slow or a fast zoom or, eventually, a pressure-sensitive zooming control. This allows you to vary the speed of the zoom to suit the shot, or even to vary the speed in a single shot by starting slowly, speeding up and then slowing down to a gentle finish, all using a single control.

Setting up the camera is also being made easier. Many semi-professional cameras have filters which can be slid into place behind the lens to compensate for colour temperature. White balance can be set simply by pressing a button with the camera focused on a test card, or a white object, or with a special white lens cap fitted on to it. Another useful feature is a memory circuit with its own long-life miniature battery. This maintains the control settings on location if the camera has to be switched off in between successive recordings in identical conditions.

Finally, more and more information will be displayed in the viewfinder, where the camera operator can see it most easily. Most cameras have some form of warning light to indicate when the recorder is running. Many have another to warn of light levels below normal operating limits. Other light displays can alert the operator to the fact that battery life is running out, or that the tape in the recorder is nearing its end.

Cameras like these are costly, and produced for the semi-professional operator rather than the home video enthusiast.

Sony HVC-2000 (Europe)
HVC-2200 (USA)

Shoulder-mounted cameras are now being fitted with the newer and more efficient Saticon tube. The immediate benefits are sharper pictures and better performance in marginal conditions. Current low-priced cameras such as Sony's HVC-2000, 2200 in the USA, still have the well-established vidicon tube. However, buyers willing to pay the higher price for the 3000 version will get all the features of the 2000 plus better low-light performance.

Philips V200

The Philips V200, a European model, is the exception to the rule that all low-priced cameras have single-tube systems. For the same price as the more elaborate single-tube models it has three vidicon tubes. In theory, a 3-tube camera should give a sharper colour picture – each tube receives a different primary colour – but 3-tube cameras have recurrent, though readily correctable, registration problems as a result of the tubes becoming misaligned.

Sony DXC-1800

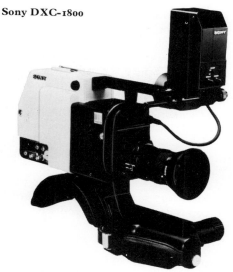

JVC KY-1900

The Sony DXC-1800 costs 3 to 4 times the price of the pistol-grip cameras – but it has most of the features of professional ENG models: a Saticon tube, a 6:1, two-speed, power-operated zoom lens; an automatic iris with a pre-set auto-fade facility; automatic white balance with internal battery circuits to maintain the settings when the camera is switched off, and genlock capability.

Although higher in price than the Sony DXC-1800, JVC's KY-1900 still offers remarkable value. It has three Saticon tubes, a 10:1 power zoom lens (with an optional 14:1), auto iris and automatic white balance adjustment. It also has genlock capability, which allows it to be linked via a special cable into a synchronized, multi-camera system, controlled through a vision mixer or special effects generator.

Hitachi VK-C800

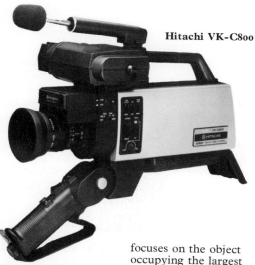

JVC S-100

Hitachi's VK-C800, has an unusual feature: automatic focusing. In theory this takes yet another chore off the camera operator's shoulders, but the manual override may often be needed. The system focuses on the object occupying the largest part of the picture area, but there could be confusion if a zoom-out shot includes objects much closer to the operator; or if you want to shoot your subject past or through a closer object.

JVC's S-100 is expensive – almost twice the price of many of the cameras designed for amateur use – but it has a 10:1 power zoom lens for really spectacular shots, such as zooming slowly in on a football crowd to pick out a small group, or even a single face, in close-up. It has an auto-iris, macro focusing and automatic white balance controls, and a genlock facility, enabling it to be linked into a studio system with other cameras.

Understanding your camera

A video camera works like a television receiver, but in reverse. It breaks down the picture framed by its lens into a coded video signal; the television receiver reassembles it into a complete picture. The heart of this process is the modern camera tube.

Fifty years ago, there was only the cumbersome television camera invented by John Logie Baird, which used a rotating drum and a light-sensitive cell to produce a crude, 30-line picture. Within 20 years cameras had electronic picture tubes called orthicons, which gave better pictures, but which were so large they needed huge lenses to focus the picture. Their average life was only 100 hours, so they often failed during live recordings, and their reaction to red was so poor

that performers had to wear black lipstick.

The vidicon tube appeared in the early fifties. It was a fraction of the size, ten per cent of the price, and had 40 times the life of the orthicon. This is the tube that made possible the first colour television pictures. At first, picture quality was too poor for broadcast cameras, but refinements made it so successful that it is still in widespread use: Sony's Trinicon tube, used on the HVC-3000, illustrated here, is an advanced vidicon.

However, slow to respond to changes in illumination, especially at low light levels, the vidicon is gradually being replaced. The Plumbicon tubes of the sixties use more sensitive photoconductive materials, and

The light that enters the camera is focused by the lens, 1, through the glass faceplate, 2, at the end of the camera tube, and passes through a splitting device, 3. This separates it into its three primary colours: red, blue and green.

The split beam passes through an electrode, 4, and travels to the target plate, 5, which, coated with photoconductive material, gives off electrons (negatively charged particles). These travel backward toward the electrode.

Each electron emitted by the target leaves behind an equal, but positive, charge, so the more intensely illuminated parts of the target emit more electrons than the poorly illuminated parts. At any moment, therefore, the target is

an accurate electrical map of the scene framed by the lens: areas of high positive charge correspond to brightly lit parts; areas with lower charge correspond to darker parts.

The electron gun, 6, converts the electrical charge into an electronic signal. It focuses a fine beam of electrons on the target, and scans across it, progressing from top to bottom.

As electrons from the gun strike the target, many go to neutralize the areas of high positive charge, but more can pass through areas of low positive charge, and hit the electrode. When the target has been scanned, the varying stream of electrons reaching the signal plate reproduces the areas of light and shade in the scene framed by the lens, but in the order in which they were scanned by the beam.

The splitting device in the Trinicon tube is a striped colour filter, 3. Each one of its 240 sets of red, green and blue filter

stripes blocks all colours except its own, which passes through, aligned for the second step in the process.

Each colour stripe aligns the electrons it transmits to strike a specific tooth on the Trinicon tube's comb-shaped

electrode, 4. Each tooth, when struck, transmits to the target an electrical signal corresponding to the colour received.

give a sharper picture and a faster response. They are so compact that four fit into a single camera: one to transmit the luminance (black and white) signal and one for each colour signal, red, blue and green.

In the sixties a single tube fitted into a compact camera made the first portable black and white video camera, and just under a decade later today's small video cameras became available, with all their colour circuits combined in a single tube. In a professional camera this will be a Plumbicon or Leddicon – highly sensitive and very expensive. Semi-professional versions will have a cheaper vidicon, or the Saticon, which is replacing it. This still suffers from lag, but perfection is not for away.

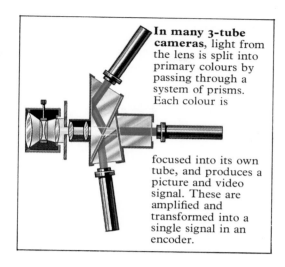

In many 3-tube cameras, light from the lens is split into primary colours by passing through a system of prisms. Each colour is focused into its own tube, and produces a picture and video signal. These are amplified and transformed into a single signal in an encoder.

The changing flow of electrons produces a video signal, which is passed down the cable to the VCR and recorded on the magnetic tape in the video cassette.

The video signal is re-created when the tape is played back through the TV set. The three colour signals are split up and fed into an electron gun in the TV tube, **7**. This fires three electron beams, which pass through a grille, **9**, aligned with coloured phosphor stripes, **10**, which coat the screen. The red phosphors, for example, glow red when struck by electrons from the red gun, the brightness of the colour depending on the intensity of the signal.

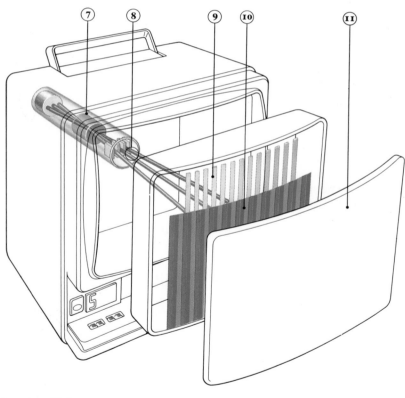

The TV screen, 11, glows brightly in areas where the electron beam striking the phosphors is intense; where the signal level is lower, fewer electrons strike the phosphors, and that part of the screen appears darker. These areas of light and shade correspond to those on the camera target, so the TV screen turns its electrical map into a copy of the scene.

The electron beams, 8, scan the screen at the same synchronized rate as their counterpart in the camera tube, but the number of electrons hitting the screen varies according to the recorded signal. The picture is scanned 25 or 30 times per second, depending on the transmission system.

Caring for your camera

A video camera is much more fragile than a cine camera. Its weakest point is the tube, which is not only the camera's most vulnerable part, but also the most expensive.

Dropping the camera is obviously likely to break or damage the tube. If you use the camera on a tripod, make sure the mounting is secure and all the adjusting screws fully tight after every shot. An unattended camera can flop over on a loose mounting, breaking or damaging the tube or lens.

Apparently trivial bumps, and even prolonged vibration, can disturb the precise physical alignment between the tube and the optical electronic focusing adjustments, resulting in a fuzzy picture. Three-tube cameras are especially prone to misalignment. Leaving the camera in a face-down position can cause flakes from the internal coating of the tube to fall on the screen and form permanent black spots on the picture.

Video cameras deteriorate in heat or cold; so be careful not to leave a camera for long periods in places where the temperature is likely to fall to near freezing, nor to set it down near a radiator or other source of heat. Leaving it on the seat of a parked car could mean exposing it to overheating, if the sun shines on it through a window.

Damp is a great enemy of all electrical equipment, causing short circuits which can result in serious damage. If you have to shoot in the rain, use an umbrella or plastic bag to cover the camera. Special hooded raincoats are available for location work which cover camera and operator, but leave lens and eyes exposed.

Sudden changes in temperature cause condensation, so keep the camera in its case when not in use. It should be as horizontal as possible, and surrounded by packs of silica gel for insulation. These need replacing from time to time, or they can be recharged by warming in a low oven.

Keep the camera away from any strong magnetic fields produced by power transformers, for example, and beware of salt and sand at the seaside. They can play havoc with circuits and lenses.

Video cameras give their best results in bright sunshine, yet this can be a deadly enemy to the tube, particularly its light-sensitive surface. Even bright indoor lights can deliver enough energy to leave a burn inside the tube, if they shine in through the lens, so never rely on the automatic iris to provide complete protection; replacing tubes is costly. It is advisable not to record brilliant sunsets, or scenes with bright lights.

Whenever you finish a shot, close down the iris and replace the lens cap: it is just as easy to burn the camera tube when the camera is not switched on and the auto iris not working. Some cameras have an extra internal shutter between lens and tube. This should be closed when the camera is switched off.

Never tilt the camera upward at the end of a shot. This is a natural tendency with pistol-grip cameras, to relieve the strain on the wrist, and it can easily result in sunlight or artificial light entering the camera tube.

Ninety per cent of apparent camera faults are not faults, but mistakes. Even if you are an experienced camera operator, if a picture fails to appear in the viewfinder, check the connections and make sure the lens cap is not still in place, and that the power is on. Of the remaining ten per cent of problems, fully four-fifths are cable faults, so learn to carry out a simple continuity check, using a multimeter.

The remaining two per cent of problems are caused by electronic faults, and these usually require specialist help. However, tube burns, all too common, are caused by bright light producing a dark spot on the surface of the tube. Depending on the severity of the burn, you may be able to remove it by pointing the camera at a brightly lit white surface and leaving the system in the record mode for an hour or so. If this has no effect, try leaving the camera operating for a day or two, with the lens cap in place.

Some spots on the picture may be caused by specks of dirt on the lens, or even on the target surface of the camera tube. You can clean these surfaces yourself, but always use special lens-cleaning fluid and implements. Apply no pressure; this could remove the lens coating or disturb delicate adjustments. Keeping the lens cap on except when recording will reduce the chances of dirt, scratches and even finger-prints damaging the clean surface.

Remember that tube performance can deteriorate if the camera is out of use for too long. Use it for at least a couple of hours every six months to check that all is well. If it is not, take the camera to a dealer for advice and attention.

Caring for connectors

Cable faults account for almost 8% of all camera problems. These usually occur in the connections which link the ends of the cables to the equipment. Always connect and disconnect cables by holding the connector, not the cable, and never use force. Many camera connectors are designed in such a way that they cannot be disconnected accidentally. The 10-din camera connector, *right*, should be gripped by the O-ring, which releases it from the socket.

Inspect connectors regularly to make sure they are clean and that the pins are not broken. Camera cables have multi-pin connectors, and each pin carries a different camera function, *far right*; so if you drop or tread on a connector, make sure none of the pins is broken or misaligned.

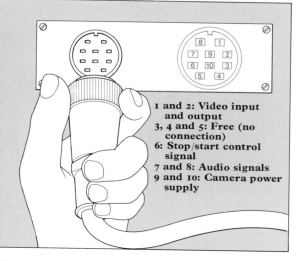

1 and 2: Video input and output
3, 4 and 5: Free (no connection)
6: Stop/start control signal
7 and 8: Audio signals
9 and 10: Camera power supply

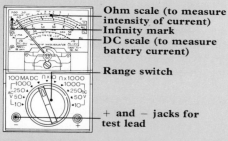

Ohm scale (to measure intensity of current)
Infinity mark
DC scale (to measure battery current)

Range switch

+ and – jacks for test lead

To test a cable, set the multimeter range switch to low resistance scale, and put a test lead probe on each of the cable connector terminals. If the needle deflects, indicating a finite resistance, the cable is intact. If it stays on the infinity mark there is a break in the cable, or one of the pins is not properly soldered to the appropriate wire within the cable.

Keep your camera clean. Blow dust off the lens using a compressed-air product, **1**. Reducing contact minimizes the risk of scratching the surface. Use a large can, and hold it upright, to avoid leaving behind a smudge of vapour. A blow brush, **2**, is convenient to carry around, and both dislodges and clears dust. If the dust is too fine or greasy to blow away, use a cleaning tissue, **3**, or a

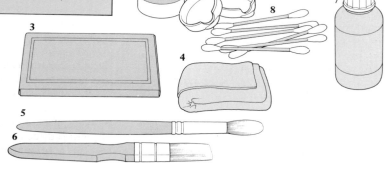

well-washed, soft chamois leather, **4**, with a little lens fluid.

A sable artist's brush, **5**, is a useful dust-brush, and a stiffer brush, **6**, is

needed to remove grit and fluff from the bodywork. Fluid cleaners formulated to dissolve clogging dirt in connections, and provide a protective

coating for metalwork, **7**, should be applied sparingly with a soft cloth. Cotton buds, **8**, are invaluable for removing odd specks of dirt and grease.

The video director

With the simple addition of a camera to your video system you can provide your own input, and make your own recordings on any theme, any subject, any location which interests you. You can create a record on video tape of baby's first words, or an imperishable reminder of a family Christmas, to a travelogue of a specially exciting vacation, or to a commercial for your own business.

You may not have the expensive equipment or the teams of specialists the professional broadcasters use – but the next sections of this handbook show you how to achieve professional results from the simplest and cheapest equipment. The scope is limited only by your imagination and the originality of your ideas.

The first thing to remember about making recordings is that there is a minimum of complicated rules. This is the beauty of video: because the cost of the materials you use in shooting is so low, you can afford to practise and to experiment on a scale which is becoming far too expensive for cine film enthusiasts. Moreover, no one can say that a particular recording has to be made in a particular way, because that way is right and every other way of making the same recording would be wrong. There is only one hard and fast rule to remember: if it works, it is right. If the video tapes you make keep your audience interested, if the pictures are sharp and colourful and well composed, and if they fit together in a sequence that tells the story you want to tell, you have succeeded.

The following pages explain how to use a video camera, and describe the techniques you need to know to create a video production.

Although basic camera techniques are easy to master, putting them together into a good video production is difficult. However, it is usually simple to see what you have done wrong and to ensure that you don't make the same mistake twice, because video's instant replay facility allows you to play back the results within seconds of recording them; a great advantage. By the time a cine film comes back from the processors it is usually too late to reshoot the scene the way you realize it should have been done. One of the difficulties every prospective video director has to overcome is that, if you are eager, you will become your own sternest critic. Yet, because video recording is so creative, be-cause the finished result is so much your own work, there is a powerful satisfaction in seeing your family and friends entertained by something you have conceived, planned and shot according to your own ideas.

Shooting a video production is entirely different from shooting a cine film. Neither is it like shooting professional-quality still pictures. This is because the sequence matters more than the individual shot, which means you can never take a picture in isolation, but only in relation to the shot that preceded it and those you hope will follow it. You cannot cut video tape and splice it together in a different order afterwards as you can cine film or audio tape; therefore you will have to shoot your pictures in the order they are to appear in your finished production.

As a home video director you have to be a researcher, planning what you are going to shoot, and why. You have to be a scriptwriter, working out the sequence of shots with which to build up the finished recording, as well as what you and your subjects are going to say. You have to be the camera operator, handling a piece of equipment that is often heavier and trickier to operate – to begin with at least – than a stills camera. You have to hold the camera steady, not for the fraction of a second the shutter is open to capture the exposure, but to follow the whole action you want to record, smoothly and professionally. You have to be a sound engineer, and a lighting expert, and an editor – because you need to know when and how to finish a shot, and how to start the next one.

This is where our handbook can help: it can give not rules, but practical advice, all of it derived from meeting, and surmounting, the obstacles everyone finds in trying to make recordings. Each two-page illustrated article takes the subject one step further: you need less expertise, fewer ambitious ideas and less experience to make a first tape of a simple subject such as a child opening Christmas presents than you would if you were intending to tape a friend's wedding as a present for him, or trying to capture for posterity the most exciting moments of your local club's tennis tournament. By starting off with the simplest of objectives and the simplest of equipment, it is easy to become expert in handling the camera and recorder, and then to progress to something a little more ambitious – and even more professional.

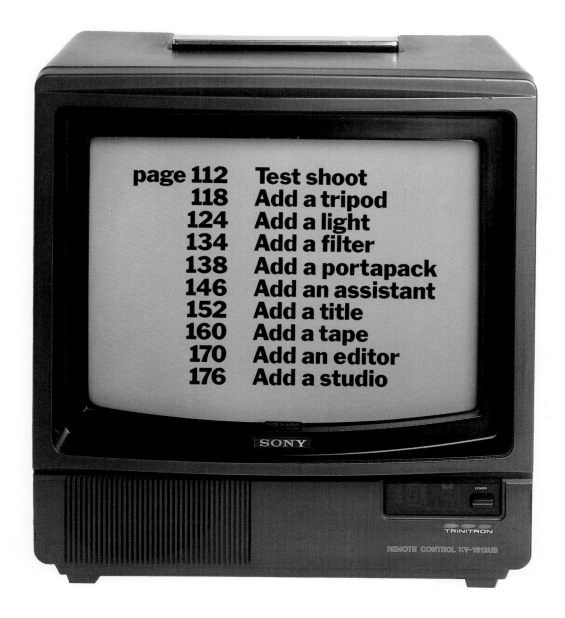

In each of the next sections we guide you through the making of a series of progressively more inventive video tapes. Each one will introduce a different facet of the video-production business – sometimes a different piece of equipment, and sometimes a different technique. However, the emphasis throughout will be on ideas, and on ways of using the new methods and the new assignments to make better productions. By the end of these assignments, while still making use of the cameras, recorders and other equipment now manufactured for the home user, the ideas and methods we feature will be those of the professionals. By the end of this chapter you should feel at home in a professional television studio. Some of the differences, such as the cost and complexity of the equipment, will be obvious; but so, by then, will the similarities. You may be working with video designed for the so-called amateur market, but the results you achieve, and the methods by which you achieve them, will be totally professional.

Handling the camera

Most people have used a camera for taking family snapshots. In some ways, using a video camera follows the same principles. The delight on the face of a child unwrapping a Christmas present; the animation of a party game, the colours and textures of the decorated Christmas tree – subjects like these offer opportunities for captivating still photographs and moving sequences alike.

Yet introducing movement can be a blessing and a challenge. While it allows you to record the whole of an action, rather than forcing you to pick a single moment to tell the story as best it can, good technique imposes its own discipline. When taking still pictures it is normal to tense up at the moment of pressing the shutter release to prevent camera shake; but to do this with a video camera would be fatal. Shooting a single sequence can take a minute or more, you can cope with it only by being as relaxed as possible throughout; by keeping your movements smooth and fluid, and by thinking ahead so that you are not caught unawares in the middle of a difficult shot.

The first step is to get the feel of your camera, learn to handle it, and become accustomed to the weight, the balance, and the position and operation of all the controls. You will get poor results if you grip the camera handle as if it were a loaded revolver, force your eye tightly against the eyepiece of the viewfinder, aim it and then shoot as quickly as possible. The best shots result from following through the action of your subject; so you need to be able to handle the camera without having to stop and remember which button to press.

Once operating the camera becomes second nature, you can concentrate completely on recording the best possible picture sequences. Avoid waving the camera around like a garden hose, trying to capture everything happening around you in a single protracted shot. Try it once, then play it back through the television. You will immediately see how distracting it is to watch a swaying, swerving picture on a stationary screen. Instead, keep the camera as steady as possible for each shot and try to move it only in between shots. At first, use the zoom only to frame each shot properly, so that you are close enough to capture the interest, but not so close that you cannot show all the parts of the picture needed for good composition.

Setting-up check list:
1. Connect camera to power adaptor
2. Connect power adaptor to AC supply; the Video Out and Audio Out plugs to the Video In and Audio In sockets on the VCR (check operating manual)
3. Connect the VCR to the TV set using a coaxial lead
4. Put the lens cap on to the lens to protect the camera tube
5. Set the colour temperature control to Indoors/Tungsten lighting
6. Switch on camera adaptor, VCR and TV
7. Point the camera at a well-lit subject and remove the lens cap
8. Open iris (check operating manual)
9. Check image on TV screen and in camera viewfinder
10. Zoom in on the subject, adjust focus and zoom out to frame a shot
11. Check the colour on the TV screen and adjust Tint/White Balance/Fine Tuning (check operating manual)

The pistol-grip camera is supported by the eyepiece resting against the forehead and the right hand holding the hand grip. Try and keep both eyes open, so that the eye which is not looking into the viewfinder can keep a check on what is happening outside the camera lens's narrow field of view.

Try to hold the camera as steady as possible, but do not lock yourself into a rigid position. You must try to relax as much as you can without shaking the camera. Keep your arms bent and wrists flexible. If your legs and feet are kept slightly apart you will be properly balanced, forming a human tripod. When you need to move to keep your subject in shot, swivel from the hips and bend from the waist. If your knees are slightly bent the movements will be smooth.

When you are ready to play back the recording, replace the lens cap, close the iris, and switch off the camera. Place it carefully either in its box or somewhere where no-one can trip over its connecting lead.

Framing and composing

Every picture you shoot needs careful framing. You must include all of the subject you need, to avoid missing important details, but beware of diminishing the subject by bringing in too much of the surroundings. Do not always put the subject right in the middle of the screen so the picture is split into equal halves and quarters; and do not tilt the horizon, or the horizontals or verticals of a room, unless for deliberate effect. Avoid tangents, or parallax, errors: a shot of grandma in a chair with a vase of flowers on a table behind her can look as if the flowers are growing out of her head; move sideways, bringing the flowers to one side of her. If there are several subjects in a shot: a baby, some toys and the cat sleeping on the rug, find a shooting position that brings them into an interesting group.

Study the framing opportunities (the squared-off shots) the camera operator sees in the family Christmas scene, *below*.

Making a test shot:
1 Load the cassette into the VCR
2 Check tape is at the correct starting point
3 Pick up the camera, hold it correctly and position the viewfinder
4 Set VCR to 'Record' (check operating manual)
5 Press camera operating switch and shoot test subject for 20 sec; press camera operating switch to stop
6 Close the iris, replace the lens cap, switch camera off and put it down carefully where there is no danger of anyone tripping over its connecting lead
7 Press the rewind button on the VCR to wind the tape back to its starting point
8 Press the play button on the VCR and check the replay of the shot on the TV
9 Repeat the process with a variety of different subjects of different colours to see how realistic they look on the TV screen.

Camera angles

Keep your first recording simple; rely on scenes, situations and people you know. Shooting a family occasion may seem a boringly obvious subject, but it has many real advantages. Your family will cooperate while you try to get things right, they will be the most appreciative audience you will ever have, and your video tape will be a record of people and events which might otherwise be forgotten, for nothing can bring the past alive as effectively as moving pictures.

Start as you mean to continue, with a thoroughly professional approach. Remember that those who watch your finished video tapes may not know much about recording techniques and problems, but they are used to a diet of highly professional television every evening. So begin with a proper story line in your mind, if not on paper. What are you going to show in each sequence? How are you going to begin? What will your opening shot be?

Try and establish a length for your recording, and a rhythm. Usually it is best to begin fairly slowly, to attract your audience's attention and involve them in what they are seeing on the screen. You can build up pace through the middle of the recording, slowing down again before the end to prevent a finish which might be too abrupt. Remember that there is more to planning a recording than deciding the basic shape: you need a few seconds' pause every so often.

Your sequences will be made up of individual shots. Try to make each shot as interesting as possible: think of unusual viewpoints, or different camera angles, to enliven an essential shot which might otherwise lack visual interest. Make sure, however, that every shot you use is justified in terms of the story you are trying to tell. Your audience will see only the pictures you choose to show them in the order you record them, so a sudden change of subject, or a jump in time or place, may be distracting or confusing unless your sequence explains it properly. Try to vary the types of shot you use to keep your sequences of pictures as interesting as possible.

Finally, remember that the sounds picked up by the microphone on your camera will be the loudest noises, and these may not relate to the pictures seen through the lens. Always try to ensure that the sounds your audience hears are in character with what they see.

Indoor lighting
Generally speaking, the higher the light level, the better the pictures. Video cameras give their best results out of doors on sunny days; so if your first indoor test shots seem gloomy and flat don't be disappointed – remember how fierce the lighting has to be in a TV studio.

Try shooting your subjects by a window, where they can be illuminated by direct daylight. Adjust the colour temperature for daylight if you do this, and don't point the camera at the window or your subject will appear as a silhouette. Alternatively, you can use what daylight there is and back it up with artificial room lighting – though this can cause colour adjustment problems. Do you set for room light or daylight? Experiment, using your colour TV screen.

Try bringing all your lighting resources to bear on the subject: table lamps, standard lamps and, especially, spotlights or desk lamps with hinged arms – but never point the camera at any light source.

When taking a shot while standing, brace yourself, and the camera, against walls or doorposts, tables or the backs of chairs. This will help keep the camera steady, especially when zooming into close-ups or panning across the scene.

Stand on a chair for an interesting high-angle shot, or sit comfortably on the top step of a step-ladder. Make sure the ladder is really secure before you mount it, and brace the camera firmly on your shoulder, or steady it on your knees.

Starting and ending
Always begin a shooting sequence with a picture that will introduce the subject you are about to record. A good opening shot for this family Christmas tape might be a close-up of the wrapped-up presents at the foot of the Christmas tree, or the star at the top coming into focus. The closing shot should round up all you have been showing in your sequence. For example, the Christmas tree star might go out of focus and then fade gradually to black.

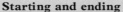

Try kneeling down, with the camera in your lap, to get a low viewpoint. Look up at the action, tilting the viewfinder upwards so that you can see the picture. For a slightly higher viewpoint, shoulder-mount the camera.

You can lie prone to take a close-up, bracing yourself on your elbows. Low-angle shots are especially effective with very small children, or animals.

You need not take every shot from a standing position. A low viewpoint can portray a child's-eye-view of the action; from a high viewpoint you can take in most of the room, or pick out close-ups, clear of people's heads.

Developing technique

Always aim to communicate as directly as possible with your audience. That means building up a sequence of shots in such a way that the viewer is never distracted by the mechanics of the system, nor by mistakes in shooting: wobbles of the camera, for example, or subjects which disappear out of one side of the picture frame, or wander in and out of focus.

The screen on which your recording will be watched is a fraction of the size of the screen you would use for Super 8 home movies. In addition, video produces pictures by electronic means, so the fine detail is not as sharp as in cine film. For these reasons, the best video pictures are usually close-up shots where the action fills a large part of the screen. Yet your recording should be more than a series of tight close-ups. After a while the audience will lose track of where the different close-ups fit into the overall view. Wider shots will remind them of the context. If you shift to a new location, a wide shot will tell your audience where they are now and what they are looking at, so they will then understand a set of close-up shots. You could, however, start on an intriguing close-up, to add mystery or drama.

Vary the subject matter of the picture. Cut from an active shot of someone doing something to a passive shot of someone watching them. Although you will be looking for candid material (that is, people forgetting, even for a moment, that they are on camera), include the occasional deliberately posed shot to add to the variety and the interest. Use such shots sparingly: moving snapshots are a waste of video's possibilities.

Widen your range of shots by including simple camera movements. If someone moves from one side of the room to the other, follow him or her as smoothly as you can. Use your other eye to check what is ahead of the camera, and frame the shot to allow space in front of the subject, so that the camera 'leads' the person through the movement.

Plan each sequence carefully. Stop the tape when each shot is finished, and look around for the unexpected: if you can fit an extra shot into your sequence, shoot it, but remember: however interesting the subject, it must work as part of the whole. Finally, always remember to shoot as though you are telling a story: keep a definite beginning and end in mind.

Panning
Swinging the camera horizontally across a scene, or panning, is useful where you cannot show a complete scene in a single shot – either because the angle you have to cover is too wide, or because you cannot get far enough away with the camera. If, for example, you wanted to show everything happening in a room you would either have to show it in a series of single shots, or pan right across the room in one smooth movement. The movement must be as smooth as possible, starting and finishing slowly and without jerking the camera. Do not over-shoot your finishing point, and never move back in the opposite direction as this is very distracting for the audience. Unless you are deliberately looking for a fast blur effect, pan as slowly as you can. Try a few practice pans and you will find that the one that feels too slow as you record it will be the one that looks right on the screen. In time you will learn how to judge your speed of movement exactly.

1

2

Use camera movements to maintain interest. Instead of cutting from a close-up of one subject – such as the child, *above*, to another, move from one to the other by zooming back and linking them in a wider shot, *below*.

Defining shots

Extreme close-up (ECU)/Big close-up(BCU): eyes, nose and mouth from the middle of the forehead to just above the chin
Close-up (CU): the entire head down to just below neck level, *below*
Medium close-up (MCU)/Chest shot/Bust shot: head down to just above the elbows
Mid-shot/Medium shot (MS): head to waist
Medium long shot (MLS): head to just below knee level
Long shot (LS): subject in full length

3

The zoom lens is so constructed that if a subject is correctly focused in close-up, it will remain in focus as the lens is moved out to the wide-angle position. This is a useful facility: it allows you to begin with a wide-angle shot showing the entire subject, such as a Christmas tree, then zoom in to show a detail – perhaps the star at the top. Alternatively, you can begin with the detail, *above*, and pull out to show it in context.

Subjects such as the Christmas tree, *right*, need a vertical tilt rather than a horizontal pan. This could start at the star on the top of the tree, move slowly down to show the decorations, and end at the parcels at the foot. Hold the start of the shot for a few seconds, tilt the camera slowly and smoothly and, taking care not to overshoot the finishing point, hold the shot there briefly. You could end the sequence by tilting upwards from the foot of the tree.

If an activity you are recording, such as a child unwrapping a toy, goes on for too long, what do you do? Stopping the camera momentarily causes a jump in the action so instead, bridge the gap with a cutaway: focus on another subject, then pick up your shot again.

Camera stability

The most obvious difference between home video recordings and those shown on television is that professional video pictures are steadier. A professional camera operator can hold a camera on one shoulder and still record a far smoother shot than the beginner, but for really smooth sequences the camera is mounted on a tripod. The tripod screws into the base of the camera body – pistol grips usually detach or fold away to allow this. Some have a screw for the tripod in the bottom of the pistol grip but they are less stable since they may move during shooting.

Once the camera is fixed so that it cannot move while the shot is in progress, your work will look a great deal better. However, there are disadvantages to using tripods: a carefully composed shot can be ruined if the subject moves out of frame, yet moving the camera from shot to shot takes time, so you could miss some of the action. Also, in a crowded room someone may trip over one of the tripod's legs and ruin the shot, or damage the camera.

These disadvantages can be minimized by choosing the right tripod for the job. Never economize by using a tripod designed for a still camera: a heavy video camera may be unstable on a lightweight tripod. Moreover, the head is not designed so that you can move the camera smoothly while recording a shot. Buy a tripod which has been designed for video use, with a head which allows you to pan the camera smoothly, to tilt it up and down, and to follow the movements of a subject in close-up. A tripod which suits your camera and allows you to do all these things will enable you to produce really steady zooms, to change focus to shift the viewer's attention from a close-up object to one further away, and even to fix the camera in position and experiment with trick frame effects. For instance, you could stop the camera and restart it when the subject has moved, or gone out of shot altogether. If the camera is absolutely steady on its tripod, the background will remain stationary while you create interest with a moving subject.

The new-found steadiness of your tripod shots will make any hand-held shots you include in a sequence seem even shakier by contrast, so if you need to record hand-held shots, wear a body brace. This is a metal prop that can be fixed to the bottom of a shoulder-mounted camera and rests on the abdomen.

A tripod head, 1, may be a friction type (comprising a fixed lower plate and a rotating upper plate), or a more sophisticated fluid head (so called because the upper plate rotates on a fluid base). A side screw, 2, releases the head for panning; a handle at the back, 3, is twisted to tilt the head up and down.

The height of a tripod may be adjustable from 22 in (56 cm) or less to over 70 in (1.78 m). There may be a pedestal, a centre shaft which is cranked up and down, 4, and the legs may be extensible, 5.

The feet, 6, may be converted from a non-slip rubber dome to a spike.

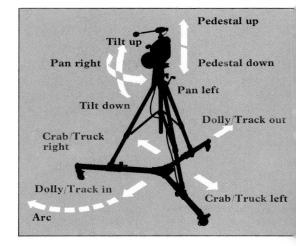

Some tripods can be locked on to a set of wheels, or dollies, 7, which may be collapsible and fitted with brakes, direction locks and guards, 8, to lift stray cables. A tripod head or camera may be fixed to the centre joint, 9, or this can carry a portapack.

Pedestal up
Tilt up
Pan right
Pedestal down
Pan left
Tilt down
Dolly/Track out
Crab/Truck right
Dolly/Track in
Crab/Truck left
Arc

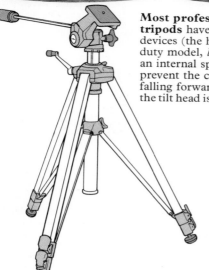

Most professional tripods have safety devices (the heavy-duty model, *left*, has an internal spring) to prevent the camera falling forward when the tilt head is released.

Most good tripods have a spirit level on the platform so that it can be set level on uneven ground. If you then set the head level (some have a second spirit level for this on or near the head) you can keep the horizontals level. Compare the horizon in the hand-held sequence, *above*, with the tripod-mounted version, *top*.

Tripod legs are individually adjustable for shots on uneven ground. Many have legs that splay out, *right*, for low-level shots.

The combination of tripod and dolly has the advantages of both a stable camera platform and flexibility of movement. The tripod head allows the camera to be panned from side to side, tilted up and down and raised or lowered on the pedestal – the central column. The dolly allows the operator to dolly, or track, in and out: that is, to roll the mounted camera toward or away from the subject; or to crab or truck left or right (also known as a travel shot) that is, the camera moves sideways across the shot. The two movements can be used together to make the camera move in an arc.

For steady movement, the surface across which the dolly is moving must be completely smooth.

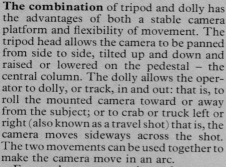

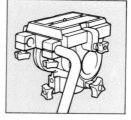

Cheap friction heads with no cushioning between the plates, tend to be jerky. Moving from pan to tilt entails loosening both controls while supporting the camera.

Fluid heads give a smooth action. When panning, the start and stop are barely perceptible. Moreover, you can release the controls to pan and tilt at the same time.

Camera mobility

All tripods designed for use with movie or video cameras have certain features in common. They all have three extensible legs, adjustable so that the camera platform is flat even when the tripod is standing on uneven ground. They have feet ending in rubber pads or screw-out tips to help grip on smooth surfaces. They usually have a pedestal to enable the camera to be raised or lowered. A pan-and-tilt head allows the camera to be swivelled from side to side or tilted up and down; locked in one position or freed in either, or both, planes, and the adjustment is variable to allow variation on the amount of frictional drag on the camera head.

It seems logical that in order to achieve the smoothest camera movement, there should be no friction at all on the camera head. This is not so. If you free the pan adjustment the resulting movement is anything but smooth. With nothing to push against, the slightest tremor in the hand is immediately transferred to the camera and the shot. Moreover, it is difficult to end the pan exactly where you want it to end. If you tighten the friction adjustment so that the camera is difficult to move, this smooths out the movement.

However, frictional drag on the head causes difficulties at the beginning and end of a pan. Sliding friction is less than static friction, so you find yourself increasing pressure on the camera until it suddenly starts to move and the result is a jerky beginning to an otherwise smooth pan. Similarly, toward the end of a pan you use less and less force until the head suddenly sticks: another jerk. A fluid-head tripod solves both problems: it uses either a hydraulic head or a nylon semi-fluid head to produce a smooth transition from beginning to end of a movement.

The camera can be moved bodily in relation to its subject. It can either dolly in or track from a wide shot to a close-up without zooming, or it can dolly out or track away from the subject, or even crab or truck sideways across it. For all these movements the camera needs to be supported on wheels on a smooth surface. If you try to move a dolly across a rough surface, the surface defects will be obvious on the screen. Professionals often ensure smooth movement by laying lengths of miniature railway track for the camera to run on. You can achieve the same effect by having someone push you along in a wheelchair or on a suitable cart.

If your subject has to move through a shot, follow the movement by locking the dolly wheels in the transverse position and trucking parallel.

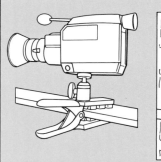

For inaccessible shots, a tripod head fixed to a spring clip, *above left*, or even a webbing belt

tightened between two supports, *above right*, will anchor the camera.

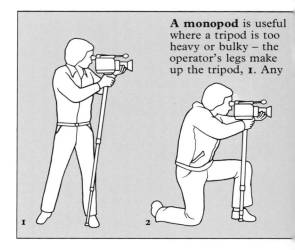

A monopod is useful where a tripod is too heavy or bulky – the operator's legs make up the tripod, **1**. Any

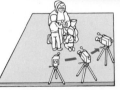

Arcing enables you to alter perspective without changing focus. You use the crabbing movement to describe an arc around the subject.

Most woodwork clamps and lighting clamps will serve to fix a camera to a projection.

A sand or bean bag can be used to weight a tripod for greater stability in wind.

comfortable position may be adopted, but keep the camera steady by bracing the monopod against a knee, **2**, or a foot, **3**. A strap around the neck gives extra support and rigidity if you slip your right arm through it.

Monopods are lighter, more compact and less expensive than tripods. They may extend to 70 in (1.78 m) and fold to as little as 25 in (0.63 cm). Telescope the monopod, if shooting in a vehicle, and brace it against the upholstery.

3

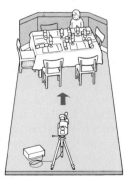

Move from a long shot, *bottom*, to a close-up, *top*, by dollying or tracking: moving the camera toward the subject without zooming, *left*. This gives you more range than the zoom, but you have to change the focus as you move in or out, especially when shooting indoors with a short depth of field.

Linking shots

Once you have mastered the basic camera shots, you may find you need something more concrete than a mental picture of the shape a recording is to take. You need a plan on which shots can be worked out in advance and consulted when shooting – in short, a storyboard.

The problem with planning a video production is that you are working in two media at once: words and pictures. You can write a script which reads well but which is hard to translate into pictures; similarly, the most perfect picture sequence may be difficult to link to any kind of commentary because of sudden changes in the development of the visual sequence.

The storyboard is a device for bringing words and pictures together before shooting begins. In a simple story, such as a record of a family Christmas, a detailed script would be unnecessary. Only a story outline would be needed, as a basis for the order of shots.

To work out such a plan for any video production, ask yourself a set of standard questions. What is the purpose of the recording? (A record of our family celebrating this particular Christmas – this is the *objective*.) At whom is it aimed? (At members of the family, and close friends – this is the *audience*.) What topics will it cover? (The family opening presents; a tour of the house showing different members of the family playing with their presents, preparing a meal; eating; playing games – this is the *theme*.)

The storyboard takes this planning a stage further. The theme of the production is written down one side of each page, and opposite each section of the theme is a series of sketches, one for each shot. These are to remind you how each shot is to be framed, how it will fit into the sequence and what it should show. You may have to guess at certain shots: you may plan a cutaway shot of the cat playing, but it will be possible only if the cat cooperates. The value of the storyboard lies in helping you to decide what kind of shot to look out for.

As you become more ambitious, the storyboard may become more detailed. In a tightly planned production, the timing and length of each shot can be added. The script for a voice-over can be written alongside, so that words and pictures can be matched exactly. The storyboard allows you to try out different approaches before you begin.

1. Establishing shot: LS (to show whole scene. LS cramped in a small room) therefore:

4. MCU (no closer if he is likely to move; stop camera by pressing 'Pause' button);

7. ECU first child (don't linger too long; be ready to change focus, move or stop);

2. PAN to reveal second child (finish panning when in centre of frame);

3. ZOOM in on second child (decide now where you want to finish zoom);

5. TILT up from cutaway shot of tree; (decide direction of next move now);

6. ARC left to bring in first child (stop camera; move tripod in close; crank pedestal up slightly);

8. Crank pedestal up. DOLLY OUT to reveal first child among toys and wrapping paper;

9. TILT up to reveal second child; CRAB right to centre of room; ZOOM out (fade out and stop).

Studio lighting for lifelike pictures

Light is the most important requirement for good video pictures. Your own tapes will be at their sharpest, brightest, most colourful and most lifelike on a sunny day; and on a cloudy day, which seems gloomy by comparison, you will still produce better pictures than you can shoot indoors with domestic lighting. This is because the human eye is much more versatile than a video camera. Our optical system reacts so well to differences in light levels that we hardly notice how much darker it is in a relatively well-lit room than outdoors. A video camera does.

To record an indoor scene successfully, therefore, you need extra lighting. The more lights you can afford the better, but lighting needs care if you are going to achieve the best results with your equipment. The sun is easy to work with because it radiates even light of a constant colour temperature over the whole scene. The different types of artificial lighting radiate light of different colour temperatures, which can play havoc with the colour balance of your picture. Two lights of different colour temperatures will tend to give it a colour cast that can be eliminated only by careful adjustment of the fine-tuning control on the camera. Moreover, every extra light you point at your subject tends to cast deep shadows elsewhere. The only reliable way to produce good indoor pictures is to use several lights of identical colour temperature in a planned scheme.

There is more to lighting than producing bright pictures. Like film, video is a two-dimensional medium and careless, over-bright lighting can make every figure look flat. Good lighting also has to help create the illusion of depth by emphasizing the shape of the subject and the distance between it and the background.

Another problem is that, however carefully you work out your lighting with a subject sitting still, and however closely you stick to the rules, you may find difficulties when your subject moves. That is why every lighting set-up has to be a compromise.

The television screen is the acid test of whether the lighting is doing its job or not. Are the pictures bright enough? Are the colours lifelike? Run through the sequence of actions with your subject, if you are shooting a rehearsed sequence, and experiment with the lights so that you can get the effects you want throughout the scene.

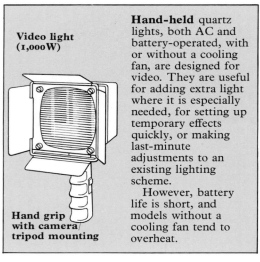

Video light (1,000 W)

Hand grip with camera tripod mounting

Hand-held quartz lights, both AC and battery-operated, with or without a cooling fan, are designed for video. They are useful for adding extra light where it is especially needed, for setting up temporary effects quickly, or making last-minute adjustments to an existing lighting scheme.

However, battery life is short, and models without a cooling fan tend to overheat.

Photofloods radiate a soft, even light which can give your pictures a subtle thirties film quality. If you mix them with other lights, beware of colour temperature problems.

Quartz film lights are ideal for video. They can be adjusted to give a bright spot of light, or a soft pool, so they are useful in most situations. The four

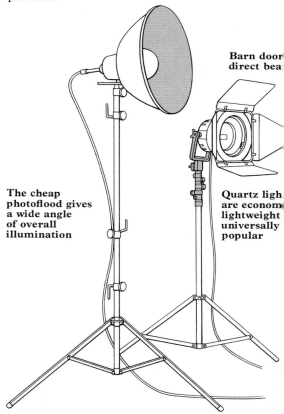

Barn door direct bea[m]

The cheap photoflood gives a wide angle of overall illumination

Quartz ligh[ts] are econom[ic] lightweight universally popular

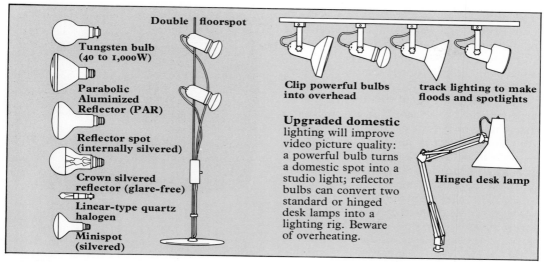

**Tungsten bulb
(40 to 1,000W)**

**Parabolic
Aluminized
Reflector (PAR)**

**Reflector spot
(internally silvered)**

**Crown silvered
reflector (glare-free)**

**Linear-type quartz
halogen**

**Minispot
(silvered)**

Double | floorspot

**Clip powerful bulbs
into overhead**

**track lighting to make
floods and spotlights**

Upgraded domestic
lighting will improve
video picture quality:
a powerful bulb turns
a domestic spot into a
studio light; reflector
bulbs can convert two
standard or hinged
desk lamps into a
lighting rig. Beware
of overheating.

Hinged desk lamp

barn doors, usually
attached, limit the
area of illumination.
A set of three quartz
lights will achieve
most effects, with no
colour temperature
problems.

A fresnel lens can
be mounted in front
of a light to focus the
beam, or to soften the
edges of a spot if it
proves to be too harsh
for the effect you are
trying to create.

**The linear-type
quartz halogen
gives a high-output
wide beam.**

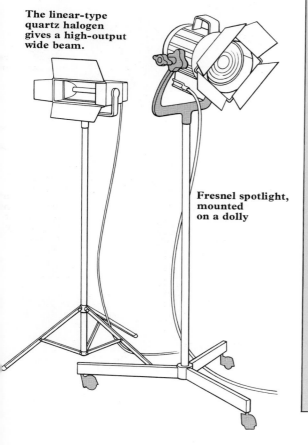

**Fresnel spotlight,
mounted
on a dolly**

Colour temperature check list

Natural light	Colour temperature °K	Artificial light
Heavily overcast sky	10,000	
	9,000	
Haze	8,000	
Lightly overcast sky	7,000	
		'Daylight' fluorescent lights
Sunlight/ blue sky	6,000	
North daylight	5,000	
		'White' fluorescent lights
	4,000	'Cool white' and 'Warm white' fluorescent lights Photographic incandescent bulbs Quartz halogen lamps
	3,000	
		Photofloods Domestic incandescent bulbs
Sunrise/ sunset	2,000	
	1,000	Candle-light

Deploying lighting

The professional way of arranging lights to illuminate a subject brightly while creating an illusion of depth, is called the three-point method. The first light is the key light. It takes over the role of the sun in providing most of the illumination, so it needs to be in front of the subject, and slightly to one side. It should also be set fairly high, though not so high that it makes the eyes vanish into pools of shadow. Usually an angle of 15 to 45 degrees above the subject will be right. This should give sufficient brightness to show up your subject clearly enough.

Sunlight is reflected and diffused in many ways, so the shadows in areas out of its direct range are also quite well lit, but the key light will cast deep shadows on the other side of your subject. As a result, the contrast between over-bright highlights and black shadows may be harsh, and you will want to soften it with a less intense beam from a second light. This is called the fill light. It must be bright enough to eliminate the deepest shadows so that in the picture they look like shadows, not deep black patches.

The job of the third light, the back light, is to make the subject stand out from the background. Again, it needs to be a softer light than the key light.

Your three-point lighting rig need not be expensive. If the room you are using as a studio is fairly well lit you may be able to manage with domestic lighting, or just one professional studio light. A reflector bulb screwed into a hinged-arm desk light makes a serviceable key light; for the fill light you can use overhead lighting – perhaps track lighting fitted with photoflood bulbs. Table lamps, standard lamps and desk lamps can all double as back lights.

If you decide to invest in a studio light you will find quartz film lights the most versatile. They can be adjusted to give a bright spot of light, or a softer pool, and usually have a set of barn doors which can be adjusted to rearrange the area of illumination. A quartz light fitted with a fresnel lens will throw a perfectly even pattern of illumination. Photofloods are good fill lights, but will be incompatible with the colour temperature of quartz or tungsten key and back lights.

Keep the camera switched to the 'Standby' or 'Pause' mode, or put the lens cap on, while moving lights around. A starry reflection from a light could damage your camera.

A key light in front of a subject flattens its shape and form. Placed to one side, it casts hard shadows.

A fill light opposite the key light restores the shape of the subject and softens the shadows.

A back light on the same side as the key light, but above the subject, separates it from the background.

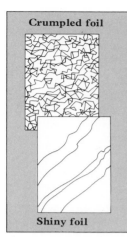

Crumpled foil

Shiny foil

The effect of any video light can be enhanced by using a reflector. You can make one very easily by gluing kitchen foil to a board. One side is made smooth and shiny for direct reflection and the other rough (by crumpling the foil) to give a more diffused reflection. Either side can be used to reflect light back into areas of shadow.

Silk screen

Tracing-paper screen

Eliminate unwanted reflections by tilting mirrors and coating reflective surfaces with matt spray, water mist or black tape, *below.* Lights may be diffused through a silk or paper screen, *left.*

Matt spray

Water spray

Black tape

Daylight streaming in through a window may serve as a boost to domestic lighting, but since the two have different colour temperatures, check the scene carefully on the TV screen before you begin recording, and eliminate any colour problems.

Alternatively, you can boost the daylight by beaming two photofloods through a window, *left.* Here, the light from the photofloods outside is being diffused and softened by a tracing-paper screen fastened over the window. The beam from the photoflood in the room is directed at the ceiling, and so diffused and reflected.

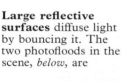

Large reflective surfaces diffuse light by bouncing it. The two photofloods in the scene, *below*, are directed not on the subjects but down to the white napkins and glassware. These reflect the light upward, indirectly illuminating the child and her grandmother, *right.* A third photoflood reflector bulb, hidden by the decorations around the overhead light, directs a beam downward, flooding the table area, which reflects diffuse light all around the room.

The candles' warm glow is mirrored by reflective surfaces all around the room.

Breaking the rules

The conventions of good lighting are broken time and time again on television with perfectly acceptable results. Remember that the rules are there for guidance, and that if you break them, you must have a particular effect in mind.

Putting the back light on the same side of the subject as the key light is the usual way of arranging the secondary lights, but putting it on the opposite side of the subject heightens the dramatic effect. Using two back lights helps to bring extra sparkle to the hair. When you place the fill light, take care not to put it too far to one side of the camera, where it may cast unwanted shadows which can look confusing against shadows from the key light. Instead, try moving it closer to the camera.

The brighter the subject, the less the camera will see the background, particularly if it is dark. To bring out background detail, lighting shone directly on the background will light it up neutrally, but if you want more detail, try shining a light sideways across the background.

Use natural light to aid your indoor shooting, but never use an outside window as a back light unless you want the subject to appear as a dramatic silhouette against the brilliant outside light. While indoor lighting is consistent in quality, intensity and colour temperature, outdoor light tends to vary. Professional film units often insure against this by shooting at night and putting an additional light outside the window to give an illusion of daylight.

In the same way you can create an illusion of night by boosting domestic room lighting with more powerful illumination. If a subject were to sit reading by the light of a small standard lamp, the light level of such a lamp would be too low to produce a good video picture. If you step up the illumination with a hidden light thrown down on to the subject from roughly the same direction it will reinforce the shadows cast by the lamp, and look just as realistic. You can eliminate the harshest shadows with hidden fill and back lighting, leaving the reader seated in a pool of warm light enclosed by a soft darkness.

A carefully planned lighting scheme may lose its entire effect once the subject moves, so think ahead. Light the whole area in which the movement will take place; follow the subject with a hand-held light, or track behind with a light mounted on a dolly.

Lighting practice check list
1 DO NOT use a powerful light bulb in a household light fitting for more than 10 minutes – it will overheat.
2 DO NOT overload power supplies – lights consume a great deal of power.
3 DO NOT shine bright lights directly into your subjects' eyes.
4 DO NOT move lights without switching them off – they may shine into the lens.
5 DO let your lights cool before you move them – they will last longer.
6 DO NOT mount a light on the camera – it might reflect off a shiny surface into the lens.
7 DO NOT put lights behind the camera operator. They cast shadows on the subject.

Lighting sets the atmosphere of a scene and tells the viewers much about your subjects' personalities. A cameo shot, *above*, dramatizes a face. This subject is lit by a single key light which, positioned just to her left, highlights her profile.

A silhouette is a powerful means of eliciting the desired emotion and it can reveal character before the subject walks or speaks. The background light is diffused through a screen to create even illumination behind the silhouette.

Snoots and reflectors

A reflector is a metal shield that fits on a light, and directs the beam; there are many shapes and sizes, **1**. A snoot, **2**, is a metal cone used to narrow a spotlight beam; a parabolic reflector, **3**, throws a near-parallel beam for a spotlight effect. A diffusion reflector, **4**, spreads the beam more widely; a metal cap in the centre reflects and diffuses the beam. A spotlight, **5**, has a reflector and fresnel lens to concentrate the beam on a small area.

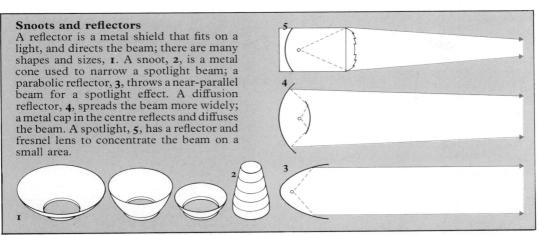

Colour temperature incompatibility may be exploited to create atmosphere, *right*. In this scene the pale daylight is augmented by candles set in trees, in the windows and on the ground.

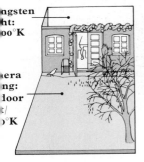

Experiment with the colour controls to exploit the visual potential of such a shot. Setting the white balance to outdoor lighting will emphasize the glow of the candles; turning it towards indoor lighting tones down the orange and makes the daylight look bluer. Check the results on the monitor until you have the balance you want, but be ready to readjust the colour balance when you change frame.

Dramatic scenes can be set up in unusually low lighting conditions, *right*. In this candle-lit scene, the light level seems too low for a video camera, yet to boost it might destroy the atmosphere.

Unconventional but subtle lighting is used to raise the overall light level without spoiling the effect. Two lights set up in an adjoining room are aimed at the white door; using the door as a reflector should increase the light level while diffusing the beams. However, the monitor may still display no more than a white streak on a dark screen and you may have to increase the background illumination subtly by switching on a lamp just out of shot.

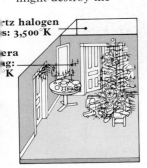

Illuminating movement

Lighting has to be set up to suit the scene you plan to record, and this has a hidden advantage: it obliges you to plan ahead. Imagine, for example, that you want to record a child playing a piano piece. Simply setting up the lights so that you can record the piece as a single shot would give you a record of the player's ability. It would, however, be very boring to watch.

To make it more interesting, you would look for different ways of viewing your subject. An opening shot could bring in piano, player and surroundings, then zoom in to a close-up of the player's hands on the keyboard. Next you could change to an over-the-shoulder shot, showing the music. You might rest on a close-up of the player's face, or the hands from a different angle – perhaps a low shot along the keyboard.

The first of these shots may be close enough to the next for the same lighting arrangement to work for both, but it is more likely that some changes will be needed: a suddenly obtrusive shadow, a key light or back light in the wrong place, which means having to pause while you adjust the lighting.

Since the subject is someone playing a piece of music, this poses problems. Putting the camera into the pause mode means cutting the sound, and missing phrases of the music while you set up the lighting for the next shot. The only way you can avoid breaks in the sound-track is to persuade the player to stop, then start again when you are ready. This demands slick timing from both player and camera operator if the finished result is going to sound as if it were being played through at one sitting.

Yet you must not fall into the trap of trying to get away with two almost identical shots simply to avoid moving the lights. If a shot of the player's hands follows another taken with similar framing, when you cut from one to the other in the finished sequence there will be a jump cut, that is, the picture will seem to jump from the first position to the second, with distracting results. It is far better to wait until you have said all you can with the first shot, then cut to something different, even if it means moving the lights altogether.

Check the lighting before every shot. Make any necessary adjustments with the camera's lens cap in place, before checking on the monitor that all looks right when the lens cap is removed.

Daylight is the best light for video. Use it to bring out subtleties of colour but avoid deep contrasts of light and shadow. Video cameras see more contrast than there is; they react to the light areas, and shadows turn black.

Domestic lighting is less intense than daylight and it is concentrated on a small area. To shoot the scene, *above*, you might need a fill light to lift the overall background level. Add a domestic light, such as an overhead room light.

Shooting a subject against a brightly lit background is a lighting nightmare: the lens aperture closes, reacting to the light, so the subject appears in silhouette.

This can be effective if you plan for it in framing and composition. Alternatively, diffusing the light through a pierced screen, the leaves of a tree or a vase of flowers gives interesting results.

If you want to record a subject in detail, powerful lights are needed to compete with the daylight. If the colour cast looks unnatural, reset the camera for the colour temperature of the lights. The best solution may be to shoot as the outside light fades.

When you light a scene to suit the camera's requirements you commit yourself to changing or moving the lights whenever the subject moves. Here, *above left*, the same two lights will be repositioned so that they stay in the same place relative to the camera and the subject. When the scene changes to a group, *above right*, standard 3-point lighting may not be enough. Add overhead lighting, or reset the studio lights to give a flood and not a spot.

Faces made for lighting

The first thing to remember about make-up for video is that you don't *have* to use any at all. Television make-up artists aim for a much more natural look than in the theatre. There the performers have to look right under much poorer lighting, for an audience which stretches right back to the rear rows of the circle, rather than the other side of the living-room. But make-up is still useful. At the very least it can mask the shine of perspiration created by the heat of intense lighting. At a more ambitious level it can be used to adjust skin tones.

Generally speaking, these considerations are much more important in studio conditions than they are when you are making your own recordings; but make-up can still be used for routine improvements to performers' facial features, and in the much more ambitious area of character make-up clever ideas can change an actor's age or background beyond recognition.

Anyone who appears on television regularly soon learns to apply their own make-up. The first decision is how much make-up needs to be used – skin tones and blemishes can be taken care of with several thin applications of foundation rather than a single thick coating which can produce a mask-like effect. Make-up can be used to tone down over-prominent ears or noses by making them blend more effectively with the colours of the surrounding skin, and faces which become flushed from the heat of the lights can be lightened.

With more skill – and more practice – you can use make-up to correct flaws. Eye sockets which are very deep, causing pools of shadow, can be made to appear less hollow through skilful use of make-up. Eyes which are too prominent or too small, too close together or too wide apart can be 'corrected' by cosmetics, as can wrinkles, or an untidy hair or eyebrow line can be camouflaged. Shiny bald spots, thinning hair and dark five o'clock shadow can all be made much less obtrusive. However, be careful of carrying the improvements too far. Most television directors agree that too much make-up is distracting and far worse than having no make-up at all. The acid test is, once again, your trusty television set. If the changes you make to your face, or those of your performers, look natural and untouched on the screen, you have achieved your purpose.

Begin camera make-up by cleansing the skin with a cream or lotion, then wiping it off with paper tissues. An astringent closes the pores and cuts down perspiration.

For a foundation, use a dry matt cake of compressed powder, applied with a damp sponge, or cream or liquid greasepaint.

Dot the foundation on to nose, forehead, cheeks and chin; then blend it into a thin, even coating over the whole face.

Model the face by shading it in darker foundation colour, and highlighting it in lighter tones. Highlights broaden the features; shading narrows them.

Ideally, eyes are one eye-width apart at the inner corners. Eyes look wider apart if colour is most emphatic at the outer corners. Emphasize far-apart eyes at the inner corners.

Conceal lines and wrinkles by brushing a lighter tone of foundation into them, and a slightly darker shade over them.

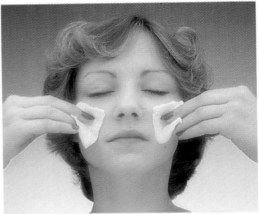

Step 1: cleanse the skin with cold cream or a special cleanser, but wipe it off carefully and close the pores afterwards, or a shine may break out under the lights

Step 4: modelling the eyes is necessary for the camera. A light eye colour makes deep-set eyes look less sunken; dark and bright colours are used for emphasis.

Character make-up

Crêpe hair and greasepaint, bought from a theatrical shop, were the materials used to create this clown. Fix false hair to the skin in tufts with spirit gum.

To give an illusion of age, hair can be greyed with powder or spray tints, or the head balded with a 'bald cap' and false hair added in patches. Shading the facial contours can add years: create wrinkles by rubbing a dark foundation into the facial creases, and shade the hollows of the features, temples and cheeks, under the eyes and at the sides of the nose.

Collodion liquid dries when painted on to the skin, causing it to pucker into 'scars' or, with added imitation blood, 'wounds'. To make *layers* of wrinkles, paint the skin with Sealor and press on to it cotton wool moulded into wrinkles. Seal the 'wrinkles' with Sealor and make up with greasepaint.

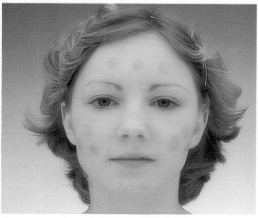

Step 2: apply foundation sparingly in an even layer from hairline to chin, covering surface blemishes. Apply greasepaint with a brush or the fingers.

Step 3: shading the face shapes it. A broad jawline will look narrower if the cheekbones are highlighted and a darker shading used down the sides of the face.

Step 5: contouring the lips gives the face a focal point and balances the impact of the eyes. Avoid bright reds and oranges, they tend to flare on a TV screen.

Step 6: camera-ready make-up should be your normal make-up, but think about the shades you use. A colour looks different under daylight and electric light.

Controlling light

All cameras have to cope with light of differing colour temperatures. Most video cameras can compensate for variations in colour temperature by using their white-balance controls. But there are times when a filter, which changes the characteristics of the light reaching the lens, will give better results. Some video cameras have built-in filters to give simple colour correction – from daylight to indoors, for example – but by adding external filters more ambitious shots are made possible.

Perhaps the simplest filters of all are neutral-density filters. They take out an equal proportion of all wavelengths of light, so that the overall colour balance is unchanged. They are used where the ambient light is too intense, causing the highlights of your picture to flare or the shaded areas to lose their detail. In bright conditions this kind of filter allows you to use a wider aperture (lens opening), to keep your subject in sharp focus against a blurred background.

Colour correction filters do a similar job to the camera's white-balance controls or built-in filters, but there are other useful effects. A magenta filter takes out the excess green apparent when copying old slides on to video tape. A blue filter helps to correct the reddish cast you find when shooting under domestic lighting. Amber filters take out the blue cast of cloudy days and give a warmer tint to skin tones for close-ups and portraits. Ultra-violet (UV) filters take out the scattered ultra-violet haze you find when shooting on the beach or in the mountains. Polarizing filters reduce the amount of reflected light, as opposed to direct daylight, allowing you to shoot through glass without unsightly reflections. Also, when shooting on a sunny day, the sky in the area at right angles to the sun becomes a much richer blue, although the colour temperature of the rest of the picture is unchanged.

Finally, there are special-effects filters which can be screwed on to the lens. These include star filters and cross filters which turn pin-points of light into (as their names imply) stars and crosses. Some screw-on special-effects filters are actually lenses, like the prismatic multi-image lens which surrounds your subject with a number of ghost images in the same picture. Sometimes there is a control for rotating the lens so that the ghost images rotate around a main subject.

Colour correction filters

Filter (apparent colour)	Effect	Application
Neutral density (grey)	Reduces the amount of light reaching the camera lens	Useful where ambient light is too strong or depth of field shallow
Skylight (pink)	Suppresses ultra-violet light	Eliminates bluish shadows cast by a blue sky
Ultra-violet (clear)	Absorbs ultra-violet light	Eliminates blue haze outdoors for clear land- and seascapes
Polarizing (grey)	Absorbs reflected light	Eliminates reflections when shooting through water or windows. Improves clarity and contrast of colour work
Fluorescent (violet)	Eliminates greenish cast	Corrects green cast caused by fluorescent lights. Different filters are available to correct for different fluorescent lights.
Blue (blue)	Absorbs reds, increases colour temperature	Corrects colour balance for shooting under artificial light or in bright conditions if a subject is in shade
Amber (amber)	Absorbs blues, lowers colour temperature	Eliminates any blueness in lighting; useful for portraiture in cloudy weather

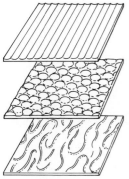

Some filters use the irregularities in the glass to spread light. Soft-focus filters are made from glass in which tiny dimples are impressed in a random pattern. The degree of softening is determined by the size and number of the dimples, while the centre may be clear. A piece of glass held in front of the lens can have the same effect.

Shots are normally framed in the familier television screen shape. If a sheet of card or metal with a central cut-out (a frame) is fixed in front of the lens, the shot is framed inside the cut-out. For instance, a key-hole-shaped frame gives the impression of looking through a key-hole. Popular shapes are star, circle, heart and binocular.

Macro photography

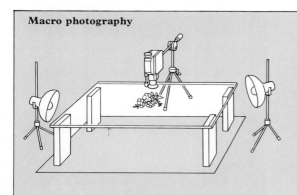

For some shots it may be necessary to get in very close to the subject. Perhaps you want to fill the screen with a watch movement or a single tiny flower. Most lenses cannot focus in so close. However many of the more elaborate colour cameras have a macro facility on the lens, which allows you to move one of the components to reduce its focal length to the point at which small subjects can be brought into focus right up to the lens's outer face.

If your camera does not have this facility, but the lens is threaded to accept standard screw-in filters, you can use a set of the close-up lenses supplied for film cameras. These are slightly more complicated to use than the simple macro position on the lens, but they do have one important advantage: they are fitted on to the front of the camera lens in its normal configuration; so you can still zoom in the normal way, even in super close-up, which is something you cannot possibly do when using a macro lens.

Special effects

By deliberately using the wrong filters, or tampering with the camera's colour balance, it is possible to create special effects. For example, you can set the white balance controls for a bluer light than the one in which you are actually recording. This will give the picture a redder cast which, in moderation, will give your shots a warmer quality, ideal for sequences of people relaxing before a glowing fire. If, on the other hand, you want to record a shot with a colder light, turn the colour balance controls to a lower temperature setting (to an indoor setting, if shooting outdoors or to a tungsten light setting, if shooting under fluorescent lighting). This will give a blue cast to the picture you are recording and can be useful if you want to create 'moonlight' effects under artificial lighting.

Yet, as always when bending the rules, do so only when you have a particular effect in mind. Change the adjustments (or the filters) step by step, and at every stage compare the results by checking the picture on the television screen until you have exactly the quality you want.

Always remember – the more you change things using electronics or optical filters, the more light you need to begin with.

Television studios have complex (and very expensive) special effects generators (SEGs) to produce split-screen pictures, wipes, mixes and other more abstract effects. With a little ingenuity and some extra preparation, it is possible for the home programmer to build in some of these special tricks, using cheaper and simpler methods.

Beautiful colour patterns are created by the feedback caused if you connect the camera to the television, switch on and point the camera at the screen. A glass plate, coated with vaseline around its edges and held in front of the camera lens, produces soft-focus shots with a nostalgic quality. Frosted glass in different patterns and textures creates 'Impressionist' images of subjects.

Many tricks can be done with mirrors: by arranging a large mirror at an angle of 90 degrees between two subjects you can produce a split-screen image of them talking at opposite ends of a telephone wire, for example. Distorting mirrors, or sheets of polished metal, can produce distorted images to simulate madness or drunkenness, or they can be used when shooting dream sequences.

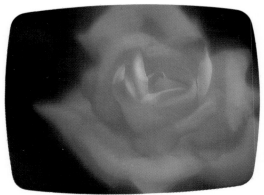

Soft-focus filters are made from glass covered with tiny dimples; the degree of softening depends on their size and number. Soft focus can also be obtained by rubbing vaseline on a plain filter.

Polarizing filters can eliminate unwanted reflections from non-metallic surfaces such as water. Contrast is heightened and blue skies look darker. The filter can be rotated to vary the effect.

A diffraction filter gives its effect by splitting up the colours in the light falling on it. Some simply split the image into its spectral components; others can also multiply the image.

Half colour filters are half coloured and half clear. When mounted in front of the lens they create interesting colour effects. The foreground of a shot may look normal, but the sky may be an eerie red. The division between the coloured and clear halves may be abrupt or graduated. Half colour filters are commonly available in yellow, blue, red, violet, grey, pink and green. They can be used in conjunction with other filters (star burst, for example) for even stranger effects.

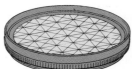

A cross screen is a clear filter with two sets of parallel lines scored on it at right angles to each other. It is useful for enhancing pin-point light sources. If a row of street lights is shot through a cross screen at night, four streaks of light spread out from each light, turning it into a four-pointed star. The same effect can be achieved from point reflections produced by metalwork or glassware under strong lighting. If more sets of lines are scored on the filter, six- or eight-pointed stars appear.

Kaleidoscope effect

Simple wipe effect

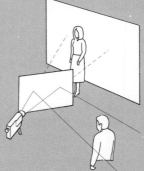

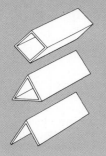

By arranging long rectangular mirrors of equal size into a square or triangular-section tube, and mounting this in front of the camera lens, you can produce multi-faceted semi-abstract shots as kaleidoscopic images of your subject.

A simplified wipe (one picture replacing another by moving in from the side of the screen) can be made using a large mirror. Set up the second shot in front of the camera, and place a mirror at 45° to the camera, *above*. Then place the subject of the first shot so that the camera picks it up from the mirror at the same focus setting as the second shot.

Start recording, then pull the mirror smoothly sideways so the image of the first shot moves off camera to be replaced by the direct second shot.

A video backpack

Making a video movie with a home deck is limiting: the machine is too cumbersome to carry. Moreover, your radius of action is always governed by the length of the power cable and the position of the nearest electrical outlet. A portapack (a portable VCR powered by batteries) is designed to be used on location with a camera.

With a portapack you can make recordings almost anywhere. However, it has a few drawbacks which make video recording a more restricted art than cine filming. Even portapacks are heavy (although new models are progressively lighter) and you have to work within the limitations of your batteries.

Generally speaking, you can operate a camera with a fully charged portapack for between half an hour and an hour at a time, depending on how much power you use in energy-consuming movements, such as zooming, or rewinding the tape. When the batteries are exhausted, they can be replaced with another set, and later recharged with a special unit which can also provide electrical power when a supply is available.

There are relatively few portapacks on the market: most major manufactures offer only one and so there are more VHS and Betamax portapacks, but so far no Video 2000 version. If you have a VHS or Betamax VCR, you need a portapack of the same format for location recording, plus a power adaptor/battery recharger unit. Video 2000 users have to use a portapack of one of the other formats, and copy their recordings on Video 2000 cassettes to play them back on the home deck.

Because they need to be simple and compact, portapacks lack tuning and timing facilities and, therefore, cannot be used for recording broadcast television off air. If you have no VCR, consider buying a portapack and a tuner-timer unit. This will add all the facilities of a home deck to your portable, and recharge batteries used on location.

Generally speaking, it is better to buy the portapack recommended for your camera; if you buy a camera from one manufacturer and a portapack from another, there may be compatibility problems. Picture quality and durability should be just as good with portables as with their home deck equivalents, but a monitor is still necessary for fine adjustments, and a portable monitor would be useful for regular location work.

Location check list
Before setting out on your first location assignment, make a list of all the equipment you are likely to need. When you return, add to it any items you missed and use it as a check list for subsequent trips. Then, on each assignment, follow these rules:–
1 Assemble and pack all the equipment on your check list.
2 Make sure that all batteries (including spares) are fully charged.
3 Check that enough tapes have been packed for the planned recording time and one more in case you overshoot.
4 Connect all the cables securely to their corresponding terminals and ensure that none is under tension or loose.
5 Clean the camera lens and set the controls to give correct picture and colour balance. Check the picture on a portable monitor, if possible.
6 Check the picture in the viewfinder and run a test shot to make sure that audio and video are being recorded properly.
7 After shooting, play back the recording through the camera viewfinder (or the portable monitor) to check all is well.
8 Label the recorded tapes as soon as possible.
9 Clean the camera and portapack before putting them away.

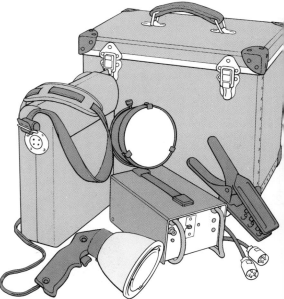

Location lighting is supplied in kits, *above*. A basic kit would comprise two hand-held lamps, with clamps to anchor them and a 12V 100W battery to power them for up to an hour; a battery charger; a daylight conversion filter to eliminate colour temperature compatibility, and a sturdy carrying case.

The transportation of equipment is always a headache for photographers and tape-makers. Everything needed for location shooting can be fitted into a strong, light, waterproof carrying bag or case with plenty of side pockets. The American backpack, *below*, designed for the BVU-110 U-matic portable VCR, provides a useful model.

The carrying straps must be capable of supporting the weight of the fully loaded case. This bag has extensible shoulder straps, **1**, fitted with a comfortable shoulder pad, **2**, to spread the load, and a mike holder, **3**. It also has hand straps, **4**, with reinforced grips.

White panels, 5, held in place by pins or tape, can be used to adjust the camera's white balance controls to suit the lighting conditions.

Loops, 6, can be used to hold a headset, or guide cables.

A flap, 7, protects the portapack and a hood, **8**, shields the camera input socket. The pockets, when filled, cushion the machine from knocks in transit.

The pockets, 9, and **11** are large enough for spare cassettes and batteries, as well as all the equipment ranged *below*. Rolls of tape, **12**, have many uses, from pinning a mike in place, to fashioning a reflector. A camera can be anchored with a clamp, **13**, or a tripod weighted with a string bag, **14**, filled with stones. Filters, **15**, are needed for colour correction and special effects. Pack a stocking, **16** as an extra soft-focus filter, and a roll of kitchen foil, **17**, in case you need a reflector.

The front pocket, 10, is designed to house a 10 ft (3 m) camera extension cable, **18**.

A basic location tool kit, *right*, contains:–
19 Pliers
20 Scissors
21 Stanley knives
22 A measure
23 Screwdrivers
24 Wire strippers
25 Battery lead

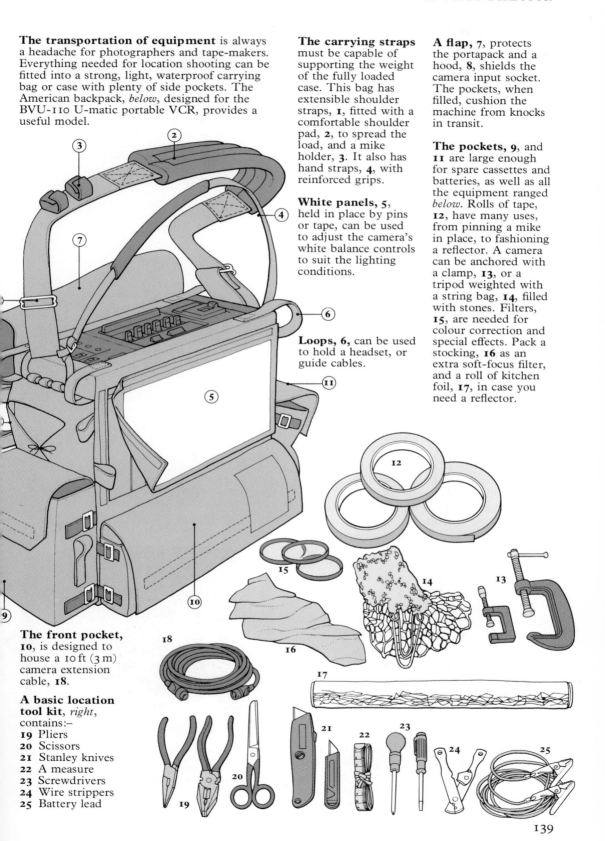

Street scenes

The new freedom a portapack offers brings new problems for you to solve. Although your range and choice may be widened, you lose the tight control over events which you had inside the house. This means you have to learn to recognize good subjects and good shots as they happen. Your planning has to be much more exact, and your reactions much faster, if you are to seize opportunities as they arise.

Take things slowly at first. Move out into the garden and begin by recording any interesting pictures within range. Practise framing and zooming with a greater depth of field (bearing in mind that zooming uses up battery life faster than any other camera movement). Practise being selective: learn to recognize when a shot is not going to work, and be prepared to wait for a better one.

Next, move out into the street. You can try to capture people on tape, zooming in to pick out a face in a group, or following an individual. Eventually, try following a car, keeping it in frame as it approaches and swings past. Keep an eye open for the interesting and the unexpected.

At this stage there is no need to think about building up a logical sequence. You are practising shooting, and worrying about the place each shot might have in a sequence could be inhibiting. In time, you should find you are developing an eye for a good shot.

Look out for useful aids to a more interesting shot; something to shoot a subject through. Try shooting a subject past or through foliage or a fence or, alternatively, focus on the leaves of a tree in front of the subject and then change focus, so that the sharp picture of the leaves dissolves and the subject comes unexpectedly into focus. Done well, this can be a very attractive dissolve between two images.

To make obvious but necessary shots more interesting, try and treat them in a novel way. You can experiment with different camera angles and viewpoints. Shoot from bridges or elevated walkways to give a bird's eye view of a scene; or shoot from subway steps to give a low-angle perspective. Shoot across a busy road at faces on the opposite side, so that passing traffic provides an out-of-focus punctuation to your shot. Learn to look at the apparently unpromising location in terms of the possibilities it presents, and the kinds of shots you can find in it.

Shooting in daylight
Before you venture outside with your camera and portapack, make sure the camera's colour controls are set for the prevailing lighting conditions. You will be operating without a monitor, and so no longer able to make quick visual checks of the colour balance in the picture.

Shooting outdoors means that you can rely on sunlight for most of your lighting requirements, but beware of shooting toward the sun. Even if you are sure that there is no danger of direct sunlight entering the camera lens and damaging the tube, the details of your subjects, particularly people's faces, will be in deep shadow and will tend to look black against the bright surroundings. You can learn to recognize when this is happening, even in a black and white viewfinder, but where the shots are really important, the only insurance is to use a portable, battery-operated monitor.

If you have to follow a subject from a sunny to a shady spot, move the camera slowly. An auto iris will react, but not instantly: there will be a momentary time-lag before it opens enough to compensate. Alternatively, you can fade down, or stop, as the subject walks into the shade. Then, move to a new shooting point, frame up a new shot in the darkened area and begin recording again. This way the changing lighting conditions, and change in shot, can be used to dramatic effect.

Yet another alternative is to lift the patch of shadow, much as you would with a fill light in the studio: a professional might have an assistant aim a hand-held, battery-operated light on the subject from a position at an angle to that of the sun's rays.

Look for out-of-the-ordinary shots. Try shooting a subject reflected in water, or in a shop window, then zoom out to show that it is a reflection. A direct shot may then seem more interesting.

Use groups of people talking to experiment with framing. Shoot across a busy road at faces opposite so that passing traffic provides an out-of-focus punctuation to your shot. Take close-ups of inanimate objects for interesting cutaways.

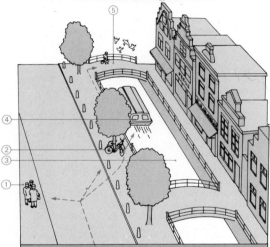

Taking the camera into the street will provide the video novice with a wealth of subjects for essential shooting practice. Use the viewfinder to assess the potential of every view along and across the street. Pick out individuals in a crowd by accurate zooming, **1**, *left*. Look out for shots that summarize the atmosphere of a place, **2**. They often make good opening shots because they establish the location in the mind of the viewer: houses with stepped gables, **3**, say 'Amsterdam' to most people.

Practise following moving objects, and keeping them in frame. Begin with something slow, such as a boat, **4**, or people walking along a road, then progress to faster objects, such as moving bicycles. Learn to take advantage of sudden events, such as a flock of birds taking off from the street, **5**. It demands fast reactions.

Create dramatic interest by opening on a moving subject out of focus: it will appear as a moving blur. Bring some bankside foliage into sharp detail, then gradually bring the boat into focus.

Make the most of every shot by using the zoom to make two shots out of one. Here, you could open with a long shot and then keep still, or follow a pigeon as it flies, and finish by zooming out again.

City walkabout

Having discovered the freedom offered by a portapack, the next step is to make full use of it by putting together a sequence on location. Try not to be too ambitious at this stage; it is much easier to cope with problems in a familiar location than on the top of a mountain, or on the deck of a boat.

Begin by going into town on a Saturday morning. Shoot scenes with plenty of colour and movement: crowds of shoppers or children playing in the park. Concentrate on looking for interesting shots.

There are two main points to remember. First, video equipment is bound to be noticed, so learn to ignore the attention you will inevitably attract. Second, even portable video equipment is heavy, so keep the walking and equipment-carrying to a minimum by planning out the shooting sequence in advance. Make time to tour the location ahead of the day you plan to shoot, and work out a rough sequence of shots. Try sketching out on a piece of paper how the shots will look. Afterwards, your extempore storyboard can be rearranged in a more logical order, to cut out unnecessary moves.

There is no need for a detailed written script, a natural sound-track is often more appropriate than an elaborate commentary. For instance, a shopping trip might open with a shot of people in line at a bus stop. Then you need a shot of a bus approaching. You might want a quick shot of people looking up the road, the bus halting and the people climbing on board. You might then cut to a shot of a bus arriving in town, as a handy way of shifting the location, and follow this with a shot of a store, and so on.

It is important to keep the storyboard simple and flexible, because the shots you record may have to be quite different from those planned. If it is impossible to make a shot planned on the storyboard, keep looking for something similar, or some other shot which will make the same point. Something entirely unexpected might happen – a parade, a ceremony, or an argument in the street. Events like these can be a gold mine to the aspiring video director, but only if they can be fitted into the intended sequence.

Even if your storyboard is no more than a list of shots giving clues to an intended sequence of visual ideas, having a definite plan to work to makes it much easier to take advantage of unexpected opportunities.

Editing in camera

Every time you switch the camera on, the picture takes a few seconds to build up; and every time you stop it, it breaks up again. This means that when you play back your recording, the picture may break up between shots.

If you press the 'Pause' or 'Stop/Start' button on the camera, instead of switching off at the VCR, the recording circuits run back a little before recording begins, and the picture has time to stabilize before new material appears. This is known as backspace editing, and it means that a sequence of several shots can be built up without the picture breaking up between each one; but as soon as you stop recording, the problem of picture break-up recurs.

You can avoid this by fading the picture out. Close down the iris, so that the image darkens. When you are ready to record again, open up the iris, focus and frame, then close the iris down again, start recording and bring the picture up by opening the iris. The picture break-up will happen, but when the screen is dark.

The fade-out-fade-in technique is often used by professionals to show the passing of time between scenes, which is when you are most likely to need to switch the machine off. It can be a problem, however, where one shot is to be linked with the next on a different location. The answer is a device like that on the Hitachi 6500 which, even when switched off, can store in its memory for several days the synchronization of the last shot recorded. The next time any material is recorded, the VCR automatically matches it up to the previous material.

The opening shot in the sequence might be a view along the bicycles in their stand, *above*. Although there is no movement in this shot, natural sounds such as traffic, and the voices of the riders approaching, will create an appropriate atmosphere for the subject.

You should by now be thinking in terms of a series of images combined to put across an idea. Look out for something different: a sequence about a bicycle trip, for instance, might take bicycles, not their riders, as its subject, and follow their progress from bicycle shed or stand to destination.

The subject of the main shot in the sequence, *above*, is undoubtedly a pair of bicycles, yet they are shot through a line of bollards and against a canal back-drop. However, careful framing and selective focusing leave the viewer in no doubt about the subject.

Experiment with different viewpoints before making the shot planned on the storyboard. If the planned shot is not available for some reason, knowing how it is to relate to the others in the sequence will help you think of some alternative, such as a different angle, *above*.

A following shot will make any action sequence more interesting to watch. A camera operator could follow cyclists in a car, and even pass them, *above*, swinging the camera round until they appear to be cycling towards it. You can then shoot them as they dismount.

Making a documentary

During the last few years, the portable video recorder has revolutionized video production. Before that it was necessary to carry heavy mains machines, and miles of extension cable, to try to reach outdoor locations which were still within reasonably easy reach of an electrical power supply. Now, domestic video is making the same move that broadcast television made during the sixties: recording outside the confines of the studio in every kind of location, on every subject.

This means that the immediacy and audience involvement of video can be brought to bear on subjects which would previously have been impossible: from a narrow boat on a canal, to a combine harvester working deep in the countryside. The whole world is there for the recording.

Although your equipment costs and budget will be a small fraction of those of broadcast television, you will encounter the same benefits and the same difficulties as the professional. To begin with, the biggest difference between location work and shooting scenes at home is that both events and subjects are less easily controlled. As a result you can only try to capture on tape parts of the action which seem to you to present an image and give the overall feeling of the subject.

For instance, a horse-racing event, or a canal-boat trip, cannot be shot from start to finish; that would use too much tape and be boring to watch. To make an interesting documentary of such an event, you would have to try, first of all, to isolate the quality the documentary is to put over: the excitement of a horse-race, or the sense of tranquillity of a canal trip, and then plan what kind of highlights are necessary to create that quality.

Keep the planning of a documentary simple and flexible; but better a list of possible shots scrawled on the back of an envelope than no plan at all. Do not plan a sound-track at this stage, but be sure to record enough atmosphere through the camera microphone to give the finished production that extra, lifelike quality. When covering a subject which allows you plenty of time to set things up, try to be slightly more ambitious. On a canal boat, for example, make a point of including all the sounds of the lock machinery being worked, to go with the picture.

The grammar of shooting
The easiest way of working out the relation of each shot to the others in your plan is to think of the whole sequence as a paragraph of text. Each shot is equivalent to a word, and a sequence of shots makes up a sentence. Shots, like words, have to fit together logically, so that the audience can follow the sequence; a shot which is not logical will only confuse the viewer.

Cutaway shots are needed to bridge gaps in the continuity of the main shot. For example, a sequence showing a boat moving into a canal lock, being raised to the next level, and then leaving the lock, would take too long to record. You might try showing brief shots of each phase of the sequence, but when you played back the three shots in order, they would look ridiculous: the boat would seem to jump about on the screen.

Instead, you could separate them with cutaways. After the boat enters the lock, show a close-up of the gates being closed, another of the winding gear being turned and then the boat rising with the water. Then take a shot of the gates opening, one of the steersman opening the throttle, and finally shoot the boat leaving the lock.

Style is as important as continuity. Try to vary the images reaching the viewer by including close-ups in between long shots. Remember to punctuate the end of each sequence visually in some way. You could use a long shot, then cut to another long shot to emphasize a new place and a new time for the next sequence. If a longer pause is required, remember the fade-down-fade-up technique. This can also be used to suggest that a fairly long time has passed between two views of the same subject. It will not matter if there are differences in the details of the two pictures.

It is impossible to shoot an entire race, but you can build up a sequence by shooting the start of one race, *above*, and the middle and end of subsequent races.

Making a documentary about horse-racing presents problems. It is difficult to record a single race from start to finish, unless you have a particularly good viewpoint. It might be more practical, and certainly more effective and entertaining, to try to convey the atmosphere of a horse-racing event, to which the race is only one contributor.

There is a lot of off-course activity: pick out the lead pony on an American course or, in Britain, a bookie, *above*, by careful framing and zooming. Let the mike pick up the reactions and comments of the spectators.

Off-course scenes for cutaways could include shots of grooms leading horses in and out of stables, types and characters around the course, and anxious or triumphant faces in the crowd.

Practise following groups of galloping horses by panning. Make sure you can keep them in sharp focus all the way through the shot, before recording.

A fast pan (called a swish, whip, zip or blur pan) can make a spectacular connecting shot – perhaps between a lagger and the leader during the run up to the finish.

145

Shooting team games

If your family and friends are as intrigued as you are by the demands and the possibilities of video, involving them in the production process will be more rewarding for them than always watching, and reacting to your finished efforts. One person can rarely produce a video recording alone. Although one's inspirations, vision and control may be essential to transfer an idea on to video tape, the help of an inexperienced assistant can make a noticeable improvement.

Planning and shooting even a simple sequence can be surprisingly demanding; it is the thinking and hard concentration that makes video such an absorbing hobby. However, video equipment is still very cumbersome, a fact you appreciate when you have to move around on location. When you add to all the mental effort the physical demands of carrying around and looking after the location kit, the result is usually fatigue.

If you are tired when you are shooting on location, there is naturally an irresistible temptation to stay in one place, rather than to move to a different viewpoint, which might bring you a better, or more dramatic shot. The final results will usually disappoint you, for although no one else may be aware of the shots you missed, you will invariably be your own severest critic. A keen and willing assistant can therefore be a help on the simplest level: by relieving you of some of the physical effort of video production.

An extra person (or more, since there is no reason to limit yourself to just one assistant, if you have more help available) can be particularly useful in helping you to speed up a move between one camera position and the next. This is essential when you are having to react to something which is happening outside your control.

A sporting event, such as a football match, is a good example. Rugby, and the football games played in North America, involve frequent intense battles over a small section of the field at a time. If you are shooting from one position throughout, no matter how dramatic the action, you will miss the opportunities for the thrilling close-ups which make the match visually exciting for the viewer. A tape covering the whole match could be tedious and costly, but your success in catching the highlights depends on your ability to spot trends, and reposition yourself to take advantage of them.

Video camera lenses

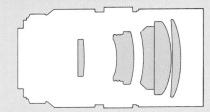

With a telephoto lens on your camera you will be able to cover more of the action. Many video cameras now offer a 6:1 zoom lens, some have 10:1 lenses, and JVC offers a 14:1 zoom lens as an optional extra on its 3-tube KY-1900. You can extend the range of your camera lens by fitting a telephoto adaptor ring in combination with the lens, but unless the optics are precise, you may lose definition in extreme close-ups.

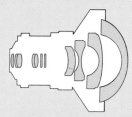

Video cameras are usually made to be used with the lens that comes with them, but if your camera has a standard lens fitting, a film camera lens – perhaps a telephoto lens with an extra zoom, or longer focus, a wide-angle lens or even a fish eye lens, *above* – will fit. Make sure you buy it from an expert salesperson: the geometry of a film camera lens may not adjust to the optics of a video camera without an adaptor.

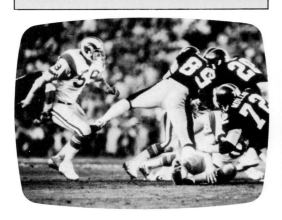

For the viewer's sake, an action shot or foul should be in close-up. At full zoom, steady the camera against something (telephoto lenses magnify shakes) and be ready to zoom out with the ball.

The distorting effect of a wide-angle or a fish eye lens can make an effective opening shot, *right*. Here, a camera, angled from a crouching, kneeling or prone position, emphasizes the players' power and strength. They are not facing the camera, yet the lens transmits the threatening atmosphere.

Do not cross the pitch after you have established your shooting position. A shot from the other side will confuse the viewer over which way the teams are playing.

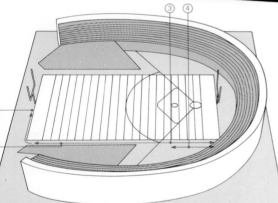

Your freedom of movement will determine the way you cover a sporting event. Set up near the half-way line if you have to stick to one location for the whole match. Position **4**, *left*, gives you a view of the start, and from **3** you have a clear view of the action in the centre of the pitch, **2**.

Your assistant can help you set up, and work the VCR.

If you can move around, try and stay with the team that seems to be gaining advantage. Your assistant's job will be to spot trends as they develop, warn you and help you get from place to place in time. Risk setting up at the goal line, **2**, to wait for a dramatic touch-down, then move round the corner, **1**, to shoot the conversion.

Pan to follow action moving across the field of vision. It needs a steady hand and tripod, but the camera stays in focus longer than when zooming. Move out at intervals to review the game's progress.

Take cutaway shots of spectators, and of players watching the action at the far end of the field. Keep the camera running after the final whistle goes: the crowd's behaviour could make a good end to your tape.

Fast-action shooting

An extra pair of helping hands will not only cut down your response time to developments in the progress of a team sport, it will extend your range of activities. With an assistant you can try shooting sports such as canoeing or slalom skiing, whose locations are invariably harder to reach than a nearby football stadium.

Canoeing, for example, calls for good close-ups at the fiercest rapids, which may mean a long and detailed reconnaissance up and down the course. With an assistant, you can search for unusual viewpoints from which to start and finish the recording, and to provide visual variety. By carrying the equipment up a nearby hill, or on to a bridge overlooking the canoeists' course, you might be able to record a really dramatic bird's eye view. However, have your assistant guard the video kit while you scout; if you both go you double the effort.

Video taping skiing calls for even greater effort, since you have to move through snow. For the most dramatic shots of such fast-action sports you need to know in advance when each competitor is about to appear in camera range. You have to frame the shot and have the camera running, so that in the recording the action bursts upon the viewer. However, in a hilly location you may not be able to see the competitors approaching the spot where you have decided to begin.

An assistant is invaluable in such a situation as this. Work out in advance the spot the competitor will reach at the moment you start the camera, and position your assistant in a place that gives a good view of both you and the oncoming competitor. Then arrange a cue: a wave of the hand will not appear on the sound-track. If there are several competitors, try one or two dry runs with the camera switched off so that you know you can react quickly enough to the cue to begin recording at exactly the right moment. Cueing is essential if the success of a shot depends on timing, especially when you have no editing facilities.

Fast water sports such as sailing or water skiing are difficult to capture dramatically unless you can become part of the action. Look for a place to moor a rented or borrowed boat out of the spectators' line of view, but close to the competitors. Your assistant can help steady you for awkward shots which call for a well-braced camera position.

Shooting on the move
The best location vehicle is a hot-air balloon. It is entirely smooth and gives an open view of the ground. If you use one, keep your scripting flexible: you have no control over the direction in which you fly.

Airliners offer only restricted window space and from the centre of the fuselage you see only an expanse of wing. A high-wing single-engine aircraft gives you a better view. In aircraft or automobile, try mounting the camera on a folded tripod and bracing it against the seat to steady it.

In small boats it is difficult to keep equipment dry, so wrap it in tough polythene bags. On a larger yacht, the sails blot out much of the view, but with an assistant to hold you, there are spectacular shots to be had from the bows.

Trains can offer a good viewpoint for passing shots of town and country. Try using a tripod if the track seems smooth. Never, whether in train, car or aircraft, steady the camera against the window: the vibration will be transmitted directly to the recorded picture. Instead, cradle the camera in your arms and angle the viewfinder so that you can see the picture.

Remember, however, that when shooting from a moving vehicle is part of the story, movement and background noise establish the immediacy of the action. The gentle rise and fall of the sea, for example, reminds the viewer of where the action is taking place.

When shooting from above, do not waste picture space on mountains and sky if there is any action down below. A medium shot, *right*, cuts out the context in which the sport is taking place, but is wide enough to show what is happening. Remember that zoom and telephoto lenses will magnify any unsteadiness in your hold on the camera, and following a moving object smoothly calls for a great deal of practice.

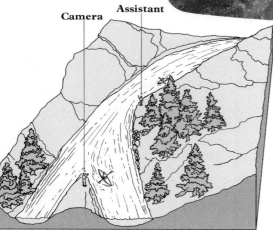

Camera   Assistant

A good vantage point is essential when shooting any sport. Set your camera up in such a position that most of the action takes place at a constant distance. With canoeing this may have to be at the top of a gorge, or on top of a hill, *left*. Station your assistant in a position from which to signal you just before each canoeist is in view.

Always begin with a wide shot so as to establish the scene in the mind of the viewer. Shots from high up make spectactular openers: you could tilt down from the sky and hills to the river below, and zoom out to show the setting from time to time. To close, zoom out, tilt up to the hilltops, and fade out.

Canoeists all look alike in a long or medium shot. When you set up the camera, pre-set it for close-ups and zoom in wherever possible, to show the concentration on the canoeists' faces.

A close-up gives the viewer far less information than a long or a medium shot. Before you zoom in, make sure the preceding shots have made the viewer clear about who or what you are shooting.

The TV interview

By helping in front of the camera, as well as behind it, your assistant can add a new dimension to your recordings. With another person presenting, introducing, commenting, acting as a television reporter, or interviewing other people, you can try out some entirely different ideas. Should your assistant be camera-shy, teach him or her to operate the camera while you do the presenting. Once they see how painless and simple it is they may feel emboldened to try it out.

Good presentation is an art which can be learned: acting schools run training courses designed to teach people to project their personalities under the stare of the camera lens and the glare of the studio lights. For the amateur, it should not be so difficult. Professional television is, to a great extent, a prisoner of its complexity; people tend to be intimidated by the awesome bustle of a large broadcasting studio. Provided you keep the atmosphere informal, and rehearse often, the ease with which most retiring people can learn to feel relaxed and appear professional in front of your camera will surprise you.

Begin by trying it for yourself, so that you understand the problems. Sit in a chair with lights positioned, and the camera set to record you as a straight to-camera presenter (like a newsreader, for example), and deliver a simple statement. You will probably find it easier to make up what you say as you go along, following brief notes, than to commit a speech to memeory. Unless you are a natural actor, the strain of remembering learned lines will show in the expression on your face and in the intonation of your speech. Try and treat the camera as you would an old friend to whom you are telling an interesting story.

Split up the story into parts which are neither too long nor too complex to remember. The camera operator can then maintain visual interest by varying the camera angle, or the framing of the shot, for each part. Timing will be important. You should begin speaking just long enough after the beginning of the shot for the viewer to have taken in the fact that you are on camera and about to say something; but not so long after the beginning of the shot that your viewer is aware of a laboured pause. Practise the timing, until it becomes second nature. You will need a cue from your camera operator so that you know when the recording is about to begin: it should be a signal you can see without seeming to look away from the camera, such as an obvious wave of the hand, or a nod of the head.

Finishing needs good timing, too. When you deliver the final words, continue to look at the camera; do not drop your gaze. Let your assistant know what the final words will be (professionals call it an out-cue) so that the camera can be stopped after a pause of a second or so. Remember your out-cue, so that you don't add something afterwards. You might be cut off in mid-sentence.

Almost everyone is shocked when they first see themselves on screen, just as they are when first hearing their voice on a tape recorder. The reason is partly due to everyone's self-image being far removed from the self they see on the screen. Another cause for alarm is that the personality emerging for the first time through the camera is one reacting self-consciously to a daunting and unfamilar situation, and at first is nothing like the relaxed, everyday self.

Finally, remember that the television screen allows you to study yourself, and anyone else, far more closely than you would be able to in ordinary circumstances. You are likely to be over-conscious of mannerisms or characteristics which seem uncomfortably conspicuous. The viewer, however, will probably not notice them.

In time you will find yourself relaxing in front of the camera. As this happens, you will grow more accustomed to, and more pleased with, the impression you give on the screen. As you learn to think more freely in front of the camera and to cope with more complex cues and routines, you will find a growing pride in your mastery of a difficult craft.

A good presenter should be able to persuade other people to talk to the camera. Your evident ease is the first requirement; it will help other people to respond in kind.

Begin with the easiest possible interview assignment, with someone who knows you well, in informal surroundings, then try asking for an interview with someone you know, but not so well, such as the captain of the local sports club. It may help in both cases to talk through the questions you are going to ask, and the answers you are looking for, before you do the live interview. It will avoid confusion, but do not go over it in too much detail, or the interview may look over-rehearsed.

LS street with crowds. Slow ZOOM in to MCU PRESENTER. Presenter turns to camera.
Presenter: *'Only three days before the elections . . .'*

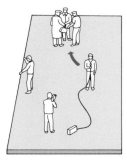

ELS beach. Slow ZOOM in to reveal PRESENTER on shore. PRESENTER turns to camera.
Presenter: *'Here we are on the spot . . .'*

WS looking down valley. Slow PAN to reveal PRESENTER, who turns to camera.
Presenter: *'. . . will we know whether the freeway will be here.'*
PRESENTER turns away. PAN away and fade.

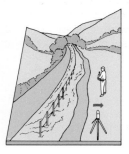

The 'vox pop' interview, where a reporter asks people in the street their opinion on some issue, is more difficult than an interview with a friend or associate. You have to introduce yourself, ask your question as briefly as possible, and hope the people respond. It can be disconcerting if they cross the street when they see you approach with a mike.

You need a long mike cable, and a cue: you must turn to the camera just after the zoom.

Instead of simply cutting to a presenter in time for the first words, try some professional tricks for bringing him into shot. Here, he is too far away to reach with a long mike cable. Signal him to begin speaking with a prearranged gesture when you reach a certain point on the zoom. After shooting, wind back to the cue point, press the 'Audio dub' button on the VCR and record the voice over on playback.

This is one way of ending a documentary and combining a wide shot of scenery which can tend to lack punch when backed only with a voice-over commentary as the final shot. Instead, pan from background to presenter, zoom in during the commentary, then pan away to the scenery before the slow fade out. You will have to cue the presenter to begin speaking, and the presenter will have to establish a cue-out for you to pan away.

Typography for a TV screen

As soon as you start using a VCR, you will find titling useful in keeping track of all the shows and excerpts you record off air. When you start making your own video shows you will realize that not only do titles do an essential job at the beginning and end of each recording, but that titles and graphics can be used together to emphasize or explain points in your recordings, and to make them more interesting to watch.

Titles can be simple or ambitious, but they must suit the medium. Video pictures are not as crisp and detailed as cine film or slides, so titles must be kept simple, and the letters have to be clear and large enough to show up clearly on the screen. The shape of the screen, and its relation to the area seen by the camera, restricts the design of each frame; words should not be positioned too close to the edges of the screen area or they may be distorted, or disappear, when the titles are screened.

These factors limit the amount of information that can appear on a small screen. If you have a lot to say, it is better to spread the information over several frames.

Informal titles are the easiest to make. The words can be written on a blackboard in chalk, or on paper with a paint brush or broad felt-tipped pen. As a rule, it is better to avoid harsh contrasts, such as blue and green on the screen, and to avoid bright colours, especially deep reds, which can cause flares and echoes. Pale buff or light gray paper will look white on the screen without glaring reflections, and pastel colours work better in video.

By using your ingenuity, you can dispense with drawing out titles on card, paper or boards, and at the same time link them more effectively with the theme of the recording. A tape shot at the beach could have the titles drawn in the sand with a stick, for instance. When titles are shot out of doors under natural daylight, reflections and contrast are less important than they would be under indoor lighting.

More formal titles need laying out so that the letters follow the same style and the words appear in the same part of the picture in each shot. The easiest way of ensuring this is to use a set of standard cards marked out to the same measurements, and make up the words from a suitable typeface in one of the ranges of rub-on lettering.

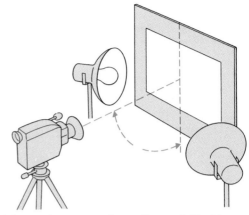

The easiest way of shooting titles is to fix them to a vertical surface, *above*. The camera must be positioned square-on to the surface, or the titles will look distorted. Position a lamp on either side of the camera, angled at about 45° to the card, exactly the same distance away from it, and slightly above the camera.

This animated title was made by cutting up a drawing. The house and snow were pasted on a background card, the lawn on a foreground card. The reindeer, pulling the title, are pasted on a separate card which is pulled between the others by a hidden tab.

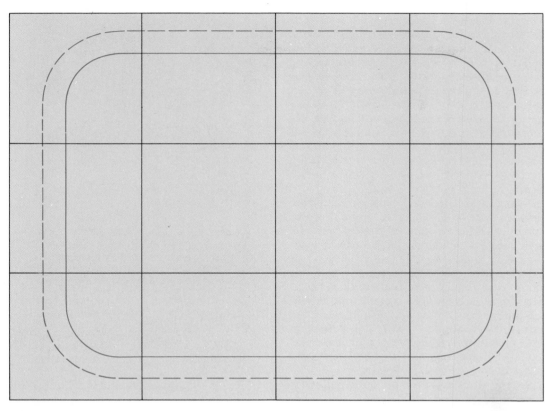

The TV screen is 4 units wide and 3 units deep, and titles have to fit within its shape and size. Titles are best drawn on cards measuring about 9 in (22.5 cm) deep by 12 in (30 cm) wide. The basic grid, *above*, or an enlarged version, may be used as a template for cutting out titling cards. It is best to limit the words or graphics to the safe area, that is, within a border of about 1½ in (3.75 cm) all round. Lettering which extends into this border may vanish during playback.

Titles should be brief, to be effective. Keep the number of words to a minimum, and change the cards quickly.

Lettering should be no smaller than one-tenth of the picture height and should be solid (filled in) *above left*, or a bold outline. Avoid letters with fine lines and serifs (decorative lines extending from the letters of some typefaces): they may disappear altogether on camera.

Avoid using red in titles. The colour contrast in the title, *above left*, will make the letters show up on the screen, but video cameras have problems with the red end of the spectrum and the version, *above right*, will blur into orange.

153

Ways of shooting words

Title cards tell your viewers what you want them to know, but they are essentially a static medium in the middle of a sequence of moving pictures. Perhaps the easiest way of bringing movement into titles is to write the title on a card large enough to allow you to zoom slowly in on it, giving the audience time to read the message before stopping the zoom and cutting to the next shot. However, if several titles are needed, this can be distracting and it might be better to look for straight cuts from one static picture to the next.

Alternatively, the cards can be mounted on a pair of rings on board, rather like a ring-file notebook. A hand, on or off camera, can flip each card out of the way at the end of each successive shot.

Either keep the VCR running so that the whole title sequence is treated as a single shot, (time each card change carefully to suit the time taken for the audience to read the message), or stop the VCR, and restart it after changing the card; this will make the sequence look just like the first method, where each card is shot separately.

Several titles can be built up in different places on the same large sheet of paper. This is particularly useful for setting lettered titles against a background drawing. Start the sequence with the camera aimed at the initial title, give the audience time to read it, and then pan across the picture to the next title, and so on.

The same blend of title and pictures can be achieved by placing the title somewhere in the middle, or to one side, of the scene. You can then cut from the title 'The Christmas Party', written on a card propped up in an armchair, perhaps, to the party happening in the background. In the same way, you can pan across from a shot of people leaving the course at the end of a race meeting, to 'The End', written on any convenient surface in chalk.

If other titles, such as credits (who did what in the production) or acknowledgements (thanks to people who helped) are needed, they can be set up in different places and cut to as a way of building a credits sequence into the last few shots of the recording. All of these techniques attempt to bring a bit of extra interest to a sequence, which might otherwise not hold the audience's attention.

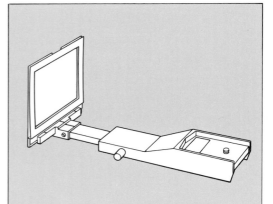

Small title cards can be used close to the camera, but they must be positioned carefully. Sony make a handy camera titler, the HTV 2100, *above*, to hold title cards (which can be as small as a credit card) square-on and at a fixed distance relative to the camera. The macro adjustment on the lens is used to focus on these small cards, and also on colour slides or sections of pictures. You can even use typewriter lettering, provided it is clear, evenly printed and correctly aligned. It is ideal for routine titles.

 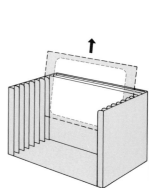

Several titles can be displayed as a moving sequence by mounting them on a long card, *above left*, and tilting the camera down them. A title card box, *above right*, can be used to hold the cards between grooves on either side. When each title has been shown, the card is lifted out of the box to show the next title. Keep each title on camera long enough for the viewers to be able to read it at a reasonable rate.

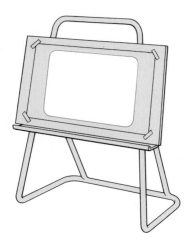

Titles can be drawn out on standard-sized cards and mounted in order on an easel, with the last card to appear on the screen placed at the back. Each card is shown for as long as it takes to read it, and then removed to show the next one. The lines and words should be in roughly the same place on each card, so that the titles do not appear to jump around the screen as the cards are changed.

Clipping the title cards into a ring binder greatly simplifies the card-changing procedure. It is then merely a matter of turning the title pages so that each one appears before the camera in succession. Position the binder so that cards drop in front of the camera in order, or they can be lifted out of sight one by one, to reveal the card underneath. Start and stop the camera from the VCR each time.

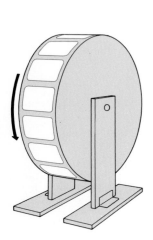

A series of cards that is too long to fit on a concave sheet can be fixed to a drum, *above left*, which is rotated in front of the camera.

Titles can be made to grow, for instance on a wall, *above right*.

Stop the camera, add a letter or a word to the title, then restart the camera. The rate of growth can be matched to the viewers' reading rate.

Titles can be made to appear to change against a constant background. Fix each title or credit to a sheet of clear plastic, and attach the first one as an overlay on a background picture: perhaps a photograph, drawing or map. With the camera clamped to a tripod, shoot the first title, then the others in order, stopping and restarting at the VCR after each one.

Animating graphics

Even a relatively cheap cine camera can be made to shoot frame by frame for cartoon and time-lapse effects. However, with a video camera it is not possible to shoot frames individually, so this kind of animation is not possible.

The shortest sequences that can be shot separately with a video camera vary with the format and the machine, but with a single home deck you can only build up a sequence with a series of shots lasting for two or three seconds at a time. This gives the animation a jerky quality – rather than the smoothly flowing movement possible with film – yet it can be surprisingly successful as an occasional special effect. When the length of time between each of the pauses is just right, the result looks like a fast succession of stills.

All kinds of video animation can be built up on the basis of a simple titling technique. You can draw a graph, or add arrows to a map, by breaking down the material to be added to the background into small components which can be superimposed one by one. Fix the camera securely on a tripod, fix the background card on a wall or easel and draw the first part of the line, or add the first arrow. Run the VCR for a couple of seconds, then press the 'Pause' button; add another centimetre or so to the line, or another arrow to the map, release the 'Pause' button for a second or two, and so on. You may need an assistant to make the additions to the background while you operate the camera.

There are other ways of producing smooth animation with a video camera. A method of producing moving diagrams, used since the earliest days of television, is to construct what are known as pull-outs or reveals. There can be two or more layers of card; the first graphic or title to appear on the screen is written on the top card – the first layer – and the graphic or title which follows it is drawn on the second. The top card is then pulled aside, or a hole is cut in it, and the card behind pulled aside in turn – so that the graphic seems to change, or names appear, in real time, (that is, while the camera is running). A series of titles can be produced in this way as an animation, with the camera running from start to finish.

Pick background music with an appropriate pace and rhythm to accompany your video animation. It is even possible with practice to time the frame changes to music.

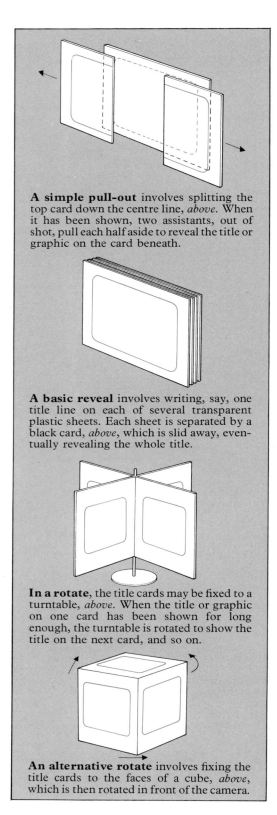

A simple pull-out involves splitting the top card down the centre line, *above*. When it has been shown, two assistants, out of shot, pull each half aside to reveal the title or graphic on the card beneath.

A basic reveal involves writing, say, one title line on each of several transparent plastic sheets. Each sheet is separated by a black card, *above*, which is slid away, eventually revealing the whole title.

In a rotate, the title cards may be fixed to a turntable, *above*. When the title or graphic on one card has been shown for long enough, the turntable is rotated to show the title on the next card, and so on.

An alternative rotate involves fixing the title cards to the faces of a cube, *above*, which is then rotated in front of the camera.

You can transfer slides (and also cine film) to video tape by projecting them on a screen and recording the picture with a video camera. This should be positioned next to the projector and framed on the projected picture. Make sure that the screen provides a bright enough image for the camera without flaring on the highlights. If this happens you may need a less reflective surface, or a telecine adaptor, *below*. The slide is projected through a ground glass screen which brightens the picture and reflects it on a mirror angled at 45° to it. Remember, the mirror will reverse the image.

The click of a stills camera shutter would be an effective alternative to music for the sound-track of the slides, *above*.

Slides and 8 mm frames are 3 units wide and 2 units deep, *top*, wider than the 4:3 aspect ratio of TV screens, *above*. When converting to video, connect the camera to a monitor to ensure that all the important material is framed by the lens.

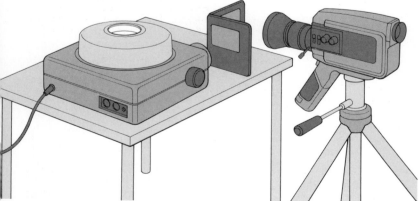

Professional effects

Titles on broadcast television rarely stand alone on a blank white background. They appear superimposed on coloured grounds and mixed in with pictures, but in such a way that the essential information comes over with a minimum of distraction.

To colour a background you have merely to reset the colour balance on the camera, checking the result on the monitor, until you find the hue you want. With similar ingenuity it is possible to advance simple titling techniques to create more exciting effects.

Mount a camera securely on a tripod and focus it on a vertical surface, such as a wall or easel. Eliminate all unnecessary lighting. Now position a slide projector so that the image of a slide is projected on the wall or easel. This requires practice. To avoid distortion, the camera and projector should be side by side, and as far from the screen as is possible without the projected image losing intensity. You may also have to adjust the lighting and colour balance to achieve the most lifelike results with the slide.

Record a few seconds of the slide, then press the 'Pause' button on the VCR. Take a line of the title on a white card and fix it to the wall or easel with pins or tape, positioning it so that it shows up clearly. Make sure the camera does not pick up any tell-tale edges. Release the 'Pause' button and record the shot. The title will seem to superimpose itself on the image.

You can go on to use a succession of title cards with the same slide, or change to a different slide for each card. You can cut from slide to slide with a single projector; but if you have access to two projectors and a dissolve unit, you can mix from picture to picture, printing up a new title once each new picture has been seen. Since the slides do not move, you can stop the camera once the mix from one slide to the next has been recorded, fix the title card, stop the camera again while you remove the card ready for the next dissolve, start it again to record the dissolve, then stop it to put up the next title, and so on.

From there you can progress in whichever direction your imagination takes you. Try shooting some action which is taking place relatively slowly, such as the approach of a slow-moving train, as a series of stills. If you shoot the sequence of one slide dissolving smoothly into the next with your video camera, the result can be sensational.

An SEG can superimpose lettering from a titling camera on a blank screen, or on the image from a colour camera.

The images from the titling and the colour camera may be reversed so that the two motorcyclists change colour.

Cine film can be used, in the same way as slides, as an effective background to titles. Also, where it is easier to record on film: in animation, slow-motion, speeded-up special effects, and so on, you can copy the film sequence, (run at normal speed) on video tape at the right place in the recording.

The transfer of film or slides to tape is called telecine conversion. You can do it by projecting the film on a screen and recording it with a video camera. This is positioned next to the film projector and focused on the screen. Just as when copying slides, a telecine adaptor in folder or box form, *below*, can be used to brighten the projected image and reflect it to the video camera.

Film projector

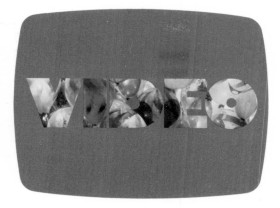

Superimposed titles can be generated by the SEG in monochrome, yellow, magenta, red, cyan, green or blue.

The lettering can become a window, through which the image from the colour camera appears, and may then expand.

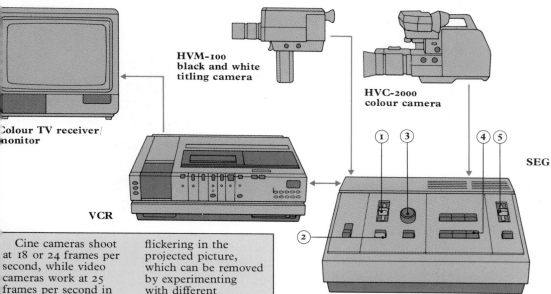

HVM-100 black and white titling camera

HVC-2000 colour camera

Colour TV receiver/ monitor

VCR

SEG

Cine cameras shoot at 18 or 24 frames per second, while video cameras work at 25 frames per second in the UK and 30 frames per second in the USA. This difference can produce lines or flickering in the projected picture, which can be removed by experimenting with different projector speeds. However, 16 mm cameras have a 25-frame setting.

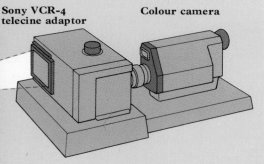

Sony VCR-4 telecine adaptor

Colour camera

Professional effects equipment is now on the market at prices the home enthusiast can afford. A black and white titling camera costs a fraction of the price of a colour camera. It is used to blend titles into a main picture sequence through a special effects generator (SEG), such as the Vel Minimix or the Sony HVS 2000, *above*. This works by switching between two cameras to produce split-screen effects, to wipe one picture off the screen with another, or to combine them in various patterns according to pre-set instructions:

1 Key level (outline) control
2 To reverse superimposed picture
3 Colour adjustment control
4 To remove superimposed picture immediately
5 To remove superimposed picture gradually

Recording sound

Sound is the trump card in the video producer's hand. Whatever the quality and clarity of moving pictures, sound gives them an arresting, life-like immediacy they would never otherwise achieve. Most video cameras have microphones built in, but for a more professional sound, it is better to plug a microphone into the 'Mic in' socket of your VCR, to replace the camera microphone.

Microphones work by converting sound waves in air into electrical signals which vary in exactly the same way. The signal has to be amplified before it can be recorded on magnetic video tape, and when the tape is played back, it has to be amplified again before it can be fed into the loudspeaker of the television.

All the many different microphones useful for video recording can be classified as dynamic or electret condenser in type. The advantage of electret condenser microphones is that, although more expensive, they are smaller and lighter than dynamic ones; they generally give a better, more even response to sounds of different frequencies, and they produce a stronger signal. Their greatest disadvantage, however, is that they run on batteries which must be checked regularly.

According to their design, both dynamic and electret condenser microphones respond differently to the sounds around them. An omnidirectional microphone picks up the sound equally from all around while a unidirectional one picks up sound only from the direction in which it is pointing. Although it picks up some sound from areas at the sides, the unidirectional or cardioid microphone is unable to pick up sound from behind. A unidirectional microphone with a very narrow pick-up range is described as superdirectional. A microphone able to pick up sound from two directions at once, but not from all around, is known as bidirectional.

The type of microphone you choose, its shape and mounting, will depend on the job you want it to perform, but it is worth remembering that a unidirectional microphone can usually be used from farther away than an omnidirectional one.

The more trouble you take to record high-quality sound, the better playback facilities it deserves. Most television sets have small, inefficient loudspeakers, but connecting the 'Audio out' of your VCR to the input of a hi-fi amplifier will give you immeasurably better sound quality.

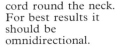

The unobtrusive necktie or lavalier mike is clipped on to clothes or worn on a cord round the neck. For best results it should be omnidirectional.

An omnidirectional mike, *below left*, as its name suggests, has virtually equal sensitivity to sounds coming from all directions, as shown by its typical pick-up or polar pattern, *above left*. This mike is dynamic in type and can be hand-held or mounted on a stand for greater versatility. Useful indoors and out, its sound quality is improved with the help of a built-in wind filter, which reduces breath noise when it is hand-held close to the mouth.

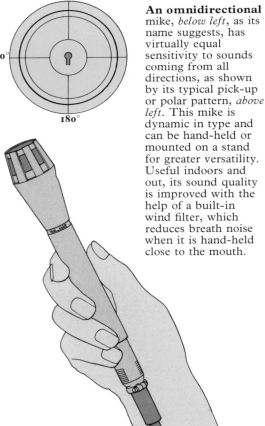

The JVC zoom mike has been designed especially with video recording in mind. The mike is mounted on top of the video camera, and is linked up to the camera lens so that both sound and vision can be varied in concert. This connection means that as the zoom lens of the camera automatically alters in function from wide angle to telephoto, so the pick-up capacity of the mike varies in unison from all round or omnidirectional to unidirectional and finally to superdirectional to give accurate pinpointing of sound.

Mikes used for video recording are classified as either dynamic, *below*, or electret condenser, *bottom*. In the dynamic mike, the diaphragm, **1**, which is placed in a magnetic field, works like an audio speaker in reverse and produces a series of electrical signals as it vibrates in response to the sounds reaching it. In the electret condenser mike, the vibrations of the diaphragm, **1**, are converted into signals by means of a closely attached plate which is charged by a battery, **2**, placed inside the mike's head.

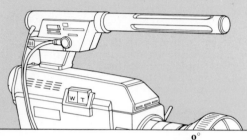

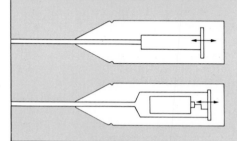

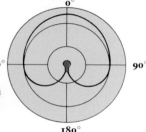

The unidirectional mike, *left*, picks up sound from one direction only, but over a wide area, as its polar pattern, *above*, shows. This heart-shaped trace also gives the mike its alternative name of cardioid.

A mike which is mounted on a boom, *above*, is ideal for picking up sounds in a particular area while, at the same time, keeping out of view of the camera. To make use of this particular mike, it is not essential to have an assistant because the mike extends like a telescope.

Choose a boom mike according to the type of recording you are making. An interview, for example, would be best with a unidirectional mike.

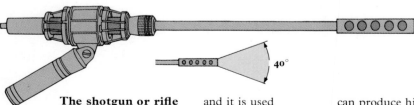

The shotgun or rifle mike is shaped as its name implies, and can be up to 6 ft (1.8 m) long. This is a mike for the specialist, and it is used held over the shoulder. It gives selective pick-up of sound over a narrow angle of only 40° and can produce high-quality recordings of sound from distances of dozens of feet. It is, however, heavy to use and expensive.

Using sound

Built-in video camera microphones are useful for recording general sound atmosphere – the hum of traffic in a busy street or the chatter of a children's party; but when you want to record specific sounds, such as the outburst of delight as your child opens a Christmas present, you need the extra clarity provided by a separate microphone.

Before recording, you must first decide what sort of sound you want to create, then select and set up the correct microphone for the job. If necessary it can be mounted on a stand or boom, but check that it can be easily removed, if required. For recording music, interviews and stage shows, choose an omnidirectional microphone.

Always make sure the microphone is really in the thick of the action, not to one side of it. Use the 'Bass cut-off' switch on the microphone to select the best kind of frequency response for the sound you are recording.

In many situations you will find the miniature, lavalier-type microphone most useful. This is an omnidirectional type used attached to clothes or hung round the neck. It can be cushioned on foam rubber and taped inside a musical instrument, such as a guitar, to give really high-quality sound recordings.

The omnidirectional microphone likely to be of least use to you is the one on your camera, and it is best replaced, if possible, by a directional boom microphone or, even better, the zoom microphone which acts as the audio equivalent of the zoom lens. Any directional microphone fixed to the camera will be much more sensitive than an omnidirectional type to sounds coming from the area toward which it, and the camera, are aimed. As a result, you are much less likely to pick up unwanted background noise.

To pick up only the sound you want, especially sound coming from a single source, use a carefully aimed unidirectional or cardioid microphone. You can also use different parts of the microphone's response pattern to balance two or more sounds blended through a single microphone, for example, a lead singer and backing group. The chief disadvantage of the cardioid microphone is the unwanted echoes it creates.

Most precise of all are the shotgun, or rifle microphone, which can be placed far enough from a speaker to stay out of shot, and the parabolic microphone, which uses a reflector to channel sounds from its target.

Sound-recording check list
1 Do be careful how you position audio cables, particularly when they are used with mikes attached to people's clothes.
2 Do add an extra mike to a setting to give extra atmosphere.
3 Do insulate the base of a desk mike to prevent extraneous noise.
4 Do hide the cord of a lavalier mike. It can be concealed by the folds of a dress, or threaded up a trouser leg.
5 Do place a mike in the correct position for someone who is going to make a speech, and adjust it beforehand.
6 Do remember that if you stop the camera and there are breaks in the sound, you must fade down the sound on camera as quickly as you can, then fade it up again, making sure that you return to the same level. Alternatively, fade down the sound and picture together and change the shot.
7 Do not let subjects handle the mike.
8 Do not leave the mike exposed to view except for interviews or concerts.

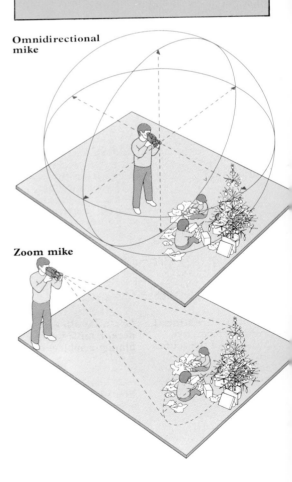

Omnidirectional mike

Zoom mike

The distance between mouth and mike is crucial to the quality of your finished audio recording. When using a fixed, unidirectional mike to record the spoken human voice, the ideal distance is about 1 ft (30 cm). A subject whose lips are too near the mike will produce sounds with explosive 'pops' on the letters 'p', 'b' and 't'. If the subject is too far away, the voice will come over weak and indistinct, and this problem will be made worse by the intrusion of background noise from other parts of the room.

To record an interview in a studio-type setting, use a fixed omnidirectional mike, which produces a sound pick-up area shaped like half an orange. The two people should sit with their knees about 3 ft (1 m) apart. For the best mix of sound and vision and the best variety of visual angles, the scene should be shot over the shoulder and diagonally from the right- or the left-hand corner of the set. Getting a good interview also depends on having a relaxed subject and confident interviewer, who has taken the trouble to do some homework.

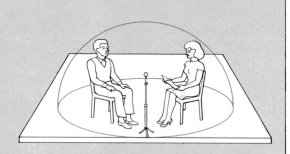

An omnidirectional mike, *opposite top,* picks up all the sounds that go to create an atmosphere, but also extraneous noise, for example from behind. To pick up only the sounds of the children, use a unidirectional zoom mike, *opposite bottom.*

Use a lavalier or necktie mike for filming a subject on the move, *above.* The mike picks up sounds from the subject but not extraneous noise. The only problem is the cable, which may trip the subject up, so it is wise to have a rehearsal.

A unidirectional mike is useful for picking up dinner-table talk, but if you stand it directly on the table it will pick up vibrations. A table-cloth deadens the clattering of plates and cutlery, and a foam pad beneath the stand will help to

insulate the mike.
Position the mike nearest to the main subjects of the recording. Here it is concealed inside a vase of flowers. Brief everyone beforehand not to bang the table or clatter their cutlery while speeches are in progress.

163

Sound on location

Once you have chosen the correct microphone, good sound recording demands, in addition, care, concentration and plenty of advance planning. The problems you come up against will depend on your exact location and whether you are recording indoors or out, but wherever you are you must always be ready to react to those problems.

Shooting indoors gives you most control over extraneous noise (although in a large building you may get unwanted door-slamming and telephone-ringing from some distance away), but the room can give trouble. If there are too many echoes – if all your subjects sound as if they are talking from inside an empty tin – the room is acoustically too 'live'. What you need is more absorbent surfaces, such as carpets, curtains and cushions, to cut down on the amount of sound reflection.

If, however, there are no echoes at all, and everyone sounds as if they are speaking through cotton wool, then your room is acoustically 'dead'. In this case, try to add to the number of reflective surfaces, for example by opening the curtains.

Only practice will tell you when the sound from any room is just right, but wearing headphones while you record will help you, or your assistant, to judge the strength of background noise in relation to the other sounds on the recording.

Outdoor recording does away with worries about acoustics, but you can be plagued by all manner of unwanted noise, from hammer drills to passing aircraft. Apart from choosing your site as carefully as possible, there are few simple remedies for these problems. You can wait for the offending noise to stop; you can move, or come back on another day. If none of these is practicable, put the microphone as near as possible to the subject.

Wind is another potential hazard in outdoor recording, and can produce roars and crackles on the sound-track. To reduce or eliminate this, fit a wind screen to your microphone, or improvise by taping a sheet of polystyrene foam or several layers of folded handkerchief on to it.

Microphone mountings are almost as important as microphones, so give them due care and consideration. Most important of all, remember that the time taken to rehearse at every stage, and to test equipment before you begin, will pay rich dividends.

Mixing sounds

Most domestic video recorders have only a single sound channel. This means that you are automatically restricted in the mixture of sounds you can record at any one time.

If you want to add a commentary or some background music to your tape, you will automatically wipe off the existing sound.

The answer is to build up your soundtrack separately, by copying your video sound-track on an audio recorder. If you then rerecord it as you deliver the commentary, or as you play the background music, you can incorporate several sounds on a single track. If all this sound is on one audio tape it can be put back through the audio channel as a single recording.

The main problem with this technique is getting the sound synchronized with the pictures. As an alternative, you could consider buying a simple audio mixer. This device allows you to mix the inputs from different mikes, together with a prerecorded track from an audio recorder, into a single track, which can then be fed into the VCR. The most sophisticated VCRs, such as the industrial VHS machines and U-matics, have two audio channels for more professional sound-recording.

To shoot sound and vision of a sequence such as a cookery lesson, use an omnidirectional mike attached to a boom held by an assistant, **2**. Use an electret condenser mike to cut down wind noise as the mike is moved, **1**. Rehearse the scene carefully so that the assistant can kneel in comfort while keeping the mike close to the sound source, and so that the camera operator, **3**, can make the correct movements.

Outdoor recording

Making audio recordings outdoors can be problematical. To get a convincing soundtrack to accompany a recording of this canoe race, use the following guidelines:

1 If you are using a camera mike, film from the best, uninterrupted vantage point, in this case standing on a hill. Before shooting, check the sound through headphones to make sure it is loud enough.

2 If you are using a separate mike, plug the lead into the mike input socket in the camera, and take the mike as near as possible to the water. Again, test the sound level before recording.

3 Record water noises and shouts of onlookers separately on an audio recorder and dub this 'wild' track on later (see 6).

4 If you do not have an audio recorder, record 'wild' track by taking your portapack down to the water after shooting and dub the sound on the picture. Remember, however, that sound and vision will not be synchronized.

5 Another alternative might be to attach a lavalier mike to the canoeist, or let the canoe carry an audio recorder, but this is not likely to be practical.

6 To dub commentary on to your soundtrack, shoot the pictures and make a separate recording of sound effects on an audio cassette. When you get home, put the video tape into your VCR and spin it back to the start of the sequence, making a careful note of the footage. Plug a mike into the VCR and press the 'Audio dub' button. As you speak your commentary into the mike, play the audio cassette of sound effects in the background. Any sounds on the original tape will automatically be wiped off and replaced by the mix of commentary and sound effects.

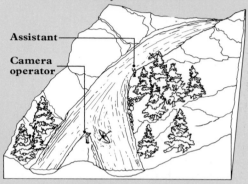

Assistant

Camera operator

For realistic acoustics, aim to cut out all unwanted noise. If the child enters unexpectedly she will be out of shot, but you may record the sound of the door opening, thus making the sound on the finished film confusing. If an unwanted sound, such as the siren of an ambulance should intrude on your recording, repeat the sequence. The whistle of the kettle, however, can be incorporated into the recording.

As the camera operator moves to bring both child and demonstrator in shot, **3**, the mike operator must change places, **2**, without tripping over the wires. She must also ensure, by judging the sound in her headphones, that the audio level stays constant, relative to the background noise. To get the correct acoustics, particularly with noisy crockery, try using plastic plates.

Mixing sounds

The atmosphere of a location, together with any dialogue, will automatically be added to your recordings by the built-in microphone on your camera. Your major preoccupation when shooting will be with the pictures you are capturing on tape. Should some sound occur to complement your sound-track: should a seabird begin to call, for instance, just as you are shooting a yacht setting sail, it would be an unexpected bonus.

Yet sound can add all kinds of qualities to your pictures, and because it is under your control to a far greater extent when the shooting is finished, it offers a wealth of new creative possibilities. You can add atmosphere, blend in a commentary, improve the sound effects and add background music.

To appreciate the power of sound, try recording a completely neutral picture for a minute or so: the front of your house, perhaps, or a close-up of someone looking at the camera with a dead-pan expression. Then add sound. Play happy, up-beat music on your turntable; then try something gloomier with a hint of foreboding. Try a fast, urgent piece, then something nostalgic. In each case you will find the music imposes something of its own quality on the neutral picture.

Sound effects do the same thing. The choice is equally vast: sound effects libraries are stocked with sounds you could hardly imagine. A request for drums will yield drum beats from every corner of the world, drums in religious festivals, in war, celebrating weddings, in jazz combos and rock bands and solo, made by every possible kind of drum.

This overwhelming choice is whittled down to the needs of the amateur in sets of records and audio cassettes. They are released for home use by pre-recorded cassette producers, and by organizations such as the British Broadcasting Corporation. There are records of animal noises, cassettes of transport noises: steam trains; aircraft taking off and landing and even more specialized collections including tracks of people walking and horror sound effects which include screams, creaking doors and moaning wind.

Sound equipment is surprisingly cheap and simple. To record sound on location precisely enough to use afterwards, you need a microphone and an audio recorder. To mix different inputs, such as music, sound effects from a record or tape, a voice-over and a track of the background noise during lo-cation recording, you will need a record or cassette player to play back the library effects, and an audio mixer to bring together the various inputs. These can then be recorded on a single video-tape sound-track.

Alternatively, use two audio recorders and copy the sound between them, adding a new input each time. Provided the drop in quality is not too obvious after all the copying and recopying, you can build up complex soundtracks. These can all be fed into a single sound input which, fed into the video tape's sound channel, becomes the final step in the production.

When you record sound as you shoot, the sound and video channels are automatically recorded in step. If you record sound for mixing and later transference to the video tape's sound channel, you must make sure you have a fixed reference point to help you synchronize sound and pictures.

Film crews do this by including a clapper-board shot in every take they shoot. At the beginning of the shot a crew member holds up to the camera a small blackboard with details of the shot chalked on it. Slamming closed a pair of wooden jaws on top of the board gives a clearly identifiable clap on the sound-track tape. This can afterwards be aligned with the frame where the jaws come together, giving precise synchronization between sound and pictures.

When there is no time to go through this procedure at the beginning of a shot, the clapper-board is included at the end instead. The board is held upside-down to show that it refers to the previous sequence.

If you want to edit your shots afterwards, use a clapper-board, and take it out of the sequence once you have synchronized sound and pictures. As an alternative, ask your assistant to tap the microphone. Provided you can see clearly when the tap is taking place, use it as a synchronization point.

If you are confined to shooting in sequence, and using the roll-back editing facility in the VCR as you are working, you will have to fall back on picking up any synchronization clues in the pictures. In most cases, this will only matter when you are shooting someone talking, either to camera or to an interviewer. Then you have to depend on your subjects opening their mouths clearly enough for you to synchronize on their first words.

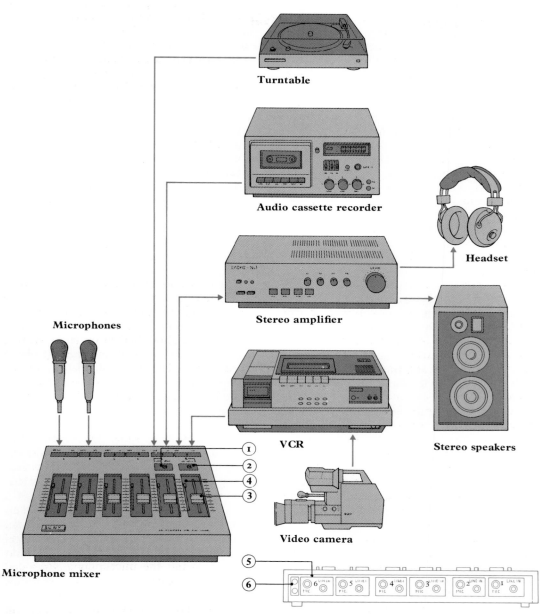

Turntable

Audio cassette recorder

Headset

Microphones

Stereo amplifier

VCR

Stereo speakers

Microphone mixer

Video camera

The Sony MX-7 mixer, *above left*, is designed for home video use. It can mix up to six channels of input and provide two stereo output channels.

The distribution switches, **1** and **2**, control channels 5 and 6, *above right*.

They allow you to feed in sound to be put out through both arms of a stereo system. For mono sound they are set to the centre to ensure equal output from both speakers.

Each slider switch, **3**, is in direct control of the sound level coming through its channel. Beside each slide is a smaller version, **4**. This is used as a reference point, so that if you use the sliding switch to fade or amplify, you have a visual record of the level to which to return.

Each channel has its respective panel, **5**, on the back of the mixer, *above right*, with a microphone and a line-in socket. This takes input from a record player or audio cassette deck. The two sound output channel sockets, **6**, feed the mixed sound into the VCR.

167

Scripting

Some of the best video seems to evolve during production, so having a detailed script at too early a stage may inhibit you from recognizing ideas and opportunities while the action is taking place. On the other hand, working to no more than a sketchy storyboard can leave you floundering. Vague ideas which have not been thought through are difficult to shoot.

The job of a script is to relate the words (which may be a simple summary of what the production is trying to put over to the viewer, or a detailed script of the commentary and/or the presenter's words to camera) to the storyboard. A script for a home movie does not have to be as complex a document as a professional script, but it should give you an over-view of what you are trying to put across.

Your script should give some idea of shooting sequence. In most cases, where the tape is being edited in the VCR using the back-space facility, you will have to shoot the sequences in the order they are to appear in the final production, and a simple storyboard is all you need.

However, in a more professional production there may be all kinds of reasons why you would want to shoot in an entirely different sequence. You may, for example, want to show a particular location in several different scenes and it would obviously be more economical to make one visit and shoot all those sequences together, provided you can edit them into the tape afterwards. A shooting script lays out the whole production in the order in which the sequences are to be shot, giving numbers for each, and cross-references to help at the editing stage.

In every professional production, there will also be a sound script. This is divided up into columns, each one referring to a different sound input. One would be for the sound recorded on location along with the pictures, and this will vary from background effects to the voice of the presenter; another is for library sound effects from records or tape; a third for background music and a fourth for the voice-over commentary. The sound script shows where each particular sound is mixed into the sound-track, where it is faded down behind the commentary, and where different sound effects are put in.

As long as you have a detailed sound script it is surprisingly simple to build up a com- plex sound-track, even without the aid of a mixer. The sound recorded on location forms its basis. This can be transferred to an audio cassette, by connecting the 'Audio Out' socket of the VCR to the audio recorder input. Keep a close eye on the recording level throughout. The presenter's words may be coming through clearly but the background sounds may be too low, depending on your microphone position, and you can correct for this to a certain extent by adjusting the recording level control during the transfer.

Next, add the voice-over commentary. For this you will need another audio recorder and a microphone. Time your commentary first against the recording being played back on your television set and if necessary, cut and adapt it to fit. Play back the sound-track from the first recorder and talk over it, trying to judge that your commentary sound level matches that of the presenter, and that the background sound does not drown you out.

Once you are sure the words and pictures go together smoothly, set the second re- corder to 'Record', set the first recorder (with the audio copy from the video sound-track) to 'Play' and deliver your commentary from the starting point. Pace yourself from the script so that your words mix well with the material already recorded.

You can now take the second cassette, which has a mixture of original sound-track and voice-over, and play that back alongside a record player (with your chosen piece of music or effects track providing the other input) on another tape on the first recorder. This will now pick up both inputs as a mixture. This time, you will have to build up the additional channels bit by bit – if you plan to ensure that music and background effects never occur together you will have to build up only one new channel. If they coincide you will have to build up two additional channels on the one sound-track.

This needs careful work, and takes a long time. You have to be sure that each new piece of sound-track comes in at the right spot in your already recorded track, fades up to the right level so as to mix well with the other sounds, and then fades out at the right point. This is where a good, clearly drawn up sound script is invaluable. It is complicated, but an imaginative sound-track can give your picture sequences an impact, and a professional gloss, they would not otherwise have.

In a professional production there will be several scripts, each with a different job to do. Apart from a shooting script and a sound script, there will be a camera script, presenter pictures with voice-over. Some scripts split the sequences into shots.

script for sequences to camera, and a dubbing script for the voice-over. The program script, *below*, brings them all together.

The sequence number identifies each paragraph in the script in terms of, say,

'FX1' and '2' are sound effects tracks, and there could be half a dozen in a single script. In a battle sequence you

would build up multiple-effects tracks from separate tracks of shouts, screams, shots, trumpet calls and so on.

PROGRAM SCRIPT. Page: 24

Program: THE MOGHUL EMPERORS

SEQUENCE:	TAKE:	PIX:	SOUND:	FX1:	FX2:	MUSIC:
45.		Skyline –WALLS OF RED FORT IN L/S SILHOUETTE.		Cries and shouts.		Indian Music (track 7) fades out
		MCU battlements – camera PANS RIGHT along battlements to towers at gate.			Trumpet calls and gunfire.	
				F/Down	F/Down	
		CU Flag flying from tower.	V/OVER: But the world of the Moghuls, for all its wealth and luxury, was a dangerously unpredictable society.			
		MLS Corner of battlements.				
				F/Out.	F/Out.	
		MS Gateway, camera pulls back to reveal PRESENTER.				
			PRESENTER TO CAMERA: Anyone who seriously meant to make a bid for the supreme power,			

A script evolves with the production. Any shot may need several takes; this column identifies the one used for the editor.

'Pix' are brief descriptions to identify the subject matter for the editor and camera operator, both of whom need on-the-spot information.

The 'Sound' column is divided into 'actuality' sound (recorded on the spot): here, the presenter to camera sequences, and the voice-over sequences which are dubbed on afterwards.

The music is taken separately from the rest of the sound-track and is usually identified by composer, piece and even track.

Instructions to camera operators and details of camera moves are abbreviated:

T/C = title card
COL = colour
RT = running time

2-S = two-shot (a shot including two subjects)
F/G = foreground
M/G = middle ground
B/G = background
L = left
C = centre

R = right
T.I. = track in
T.O. = track out
OB = outside broadcast
Repos = reposition (camera 1 to . . .)
X = exit

How to edit without an edit suite

So far, all the sequences discussed have been put together in the order in which the shots were recorded: in other words, they have been assembled rather than edited. While this may be all right for the majority of home video recordings, once you start thinking in terms of more ambitious productions, the ability to select shots and to combine them in a new sequences quite different from the order in which they were recorded, becomes essential.

The problem with video is that editing is much more complicated than it is with film. After you have shot your cine film and had it processed, you can edit the shots you want in whatever order you like by cutting out the selected shots and splicing them together with plastic cement or transparent tape. You build up a completely new version bit by bit. With video tape, this is not possible.

Video tape narrower than two inches in width must have the picture information recorded on it at an angle, in order to cram it all into the confines of the tape; cutting across the tape would leave some picture information on one side of the cut and the remainder on the other. Apart from that, each section of tape would have to be synchronized so that the picture remained stable across each cut.

So video tape editing cannot be done by cutting and splicing in the same way as audio tape and film editing. Instead, it becomes a copying process. You take a blank tape, and copy your chosen shots from the original tape (or tapes) in any sequence you wish so that you end up with a new video creation.

It sounds simple enough, and in principle it is, but there are technical problems to be solved before a smooth edit can be achieved. These involve the lining up of the synchronization signals in each part of the first tape with each another on the second tape, and there are various expensive and complex machines designed to do this.

However, there is a method of editing you can teach yourself with patience and a pair of home VCRs. This is crash-editing, and it involves a little trial-and-error and a good deal of practice. Even so, you will find that some problems with 'glitches' (picture break-up before a new sequence can establish itself) are inevitable with domestic VCRs, but it is useful practice for editing properly. With care you can turn out quite acceptable results.

Crash-editing check list

1 Choose as your master VCR a machine which gives the best freeze frame picture when in pause mode.
2 Connect the video and audio outputs of a second or 'slave' VCR to the video and audio inputs of the master machine.
3 Connect the master VCR's 'RF Out' terminal to the RF input of the TV.
4 Put your new, blank tape in the master.
5 Put a tape with your recorded material into the slave recorder.
6 Find a point on the recorded tape a few seconds before the point where you wish to start copying.
7 Set the master recorder to 'Record'.
8 As soon as the master is laced up, or within ten seconds, set the master to 'Pause'. Do not leave it too long, or you will have a blank area on the master tape.
9 Set the slave VCR to 'Play' and watch its progress on the monitor.
10 When the sequence you want to copy is beginning, release the 'Pause' on the master. The sequence will be copied on the new master tape.
11 When you reach the end of the extract, press 'Pause' again on the master. Then stop the slave machine. Do not use 'Stop' on the master, or you will get a bad noise burst.
12 Select another sequence from the recorded tape and repeat the process.

Crash-editing is so called because the signals from the two VCRs cannot be synchronized to one another, and the input signal from the slave VCR 'crashes' into the picture-scanning signals for the last sequence recorded on the master VCR, causing a glitch – or burst of video noise – on the picture.

It is impossible to remove this noise entirely when editing with home VCRs, but once you have had some practice with your simple edit suite of master VCR, slave VCR and monitor, you will learn how to time your edit entry and exit points for good results.

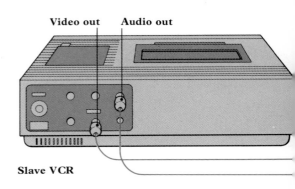

Video out   Audio out

Slave VCR

Use sequences
recorded off air to
enliven a location
shooting which did
not work so well. If,
for instance, in a
concert given by
Camel, you could not

move around to
record from different
angles, you might
vary your sequences
with an off-air
recording from the
local TV news.
  A Camel poster, **4**,

above, would make a
good title card, **4**,
below. You could open
with a news shot of
the band arriving at
the stadium, **2**, then
edit in a number from
your live recording, **1**.

Cut to part of a TV
interview with the
band, **3**, then edit in
the next number from
your live recording,
and so on. End the
tape with the band's
best number.

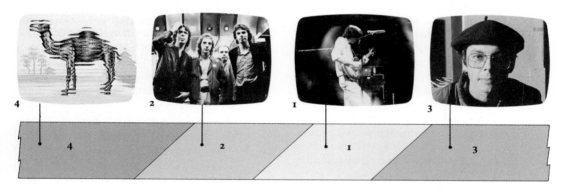

**When you edit
video tape** you pass
an electronic signal
from one VCR to
another, *below*.
  Machines of any
format may be used
together. However,
they must have video
inputs and outputs,

and not just RF
connections. These
are not suitable for
editing. This
eliminates some older
machines, but older
VCRs would not
generally be able to
provide a stable
enough freeze frame.

If you intend to
crash-edit on a Video
2000 VCR you need a
special accessory
(22AV5530) and a
22AV5002 cable to
connect another deck.

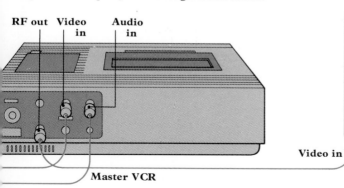

**RF out Video   Audio
          in   in**

Master VCR

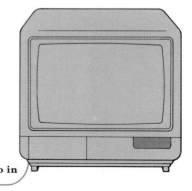

Video in

Professional editing

Although crash editing will allow you to copy sequences on a new tape, it has many drawbacks. However good the VCR and its operator, there will be some noise at edit points which will get worse if copies are made. Moreover, releasing the VCR's 'Pause' button is not accurate enough when you might need to be within a frame or two of a particular point. You sometimes need to be able to time the duration of shots more accurately than you can with a stopwatch or tape counter and you will often want to see whether a particular edit will work visually before committing it to tape.

All this and more can be done on a basic professional two-machine edit suite, linked by an edit controller. Sony's U-matic VCR editing system was one of the first and is still one of the most sturdy and simple to operate. It consists of two edit recorders (although it is not necessary for both machines to have exactly the same facilities), an edit controller and two monitors. One way of reducing the cost of the system is to use as a slave machine a cheaper, simpler player-only VCR, or even a simple player/recorder.

The process, which is simple by professional editing standards, is like this: you load the blank tape into the master VCR and then consult the notes you made as the shots were being recorded, together with their counter numbers, and select a cassette. As U-matic cassettes run for only one hour, there will probably be several sequences, shot in different places at different times, from which to choose. Use the picture-search capability, in U-matics and essential for an editor, to fastwind to the general area of the section you want to use, and then, by playing the tape in varying degrees of slow motion, locate the start of the sequence you want to use to the nearest frame. On newer U-matics, the digital time read-out (a sophisticated tape-counter) displays the position on the tape accurate to a single frame (a fraction of a second), reads the control track pulses on the tape and displays them as a digital time read-out in frames, seconds, minutes and hours.

If the master tape already has material compiled on it, you can find the point from which you want to start your next shot to the nearest frame.

Once you have both VCRs lined up, all you have to do is press the 'Assemble-edit' buttons, and the edit controller will wind both

VCRs into reverse for five seconds. It then stops them, lines them up and starts them both running, correcting the run-up speed until they are exactly synchronized. When the edit point is reached, its memory tells it to start recording from the slave to the master tape, until you press the 'End' button.

If you want to try out an edit without copying it, there is a 'Preview' button. The control unit will go right through the motions without recording, while watching the monitor. The VCR then returns both recorders to their starting point, so that you can run the sequence by pressing the 'Edit' button, or change your ideas before trying another test run.

You can perform another kind of editing, called insert editing, using two machines. If you have a sequence which needs another shot inserted into the middle of it, you start copying the additional sequence using the 'Insert Edit In' control, but when you reach the point where the new shot is to end, you simply press the 'Out' button and the remainder of the original shot is left on the tape.

Two-machine editing
Editing between two machines using an edit controller does allow you to build up a production with a certain flexibility, but you still need to plan very carefully if any special effects are needed.

For example, all the editing system can normally do is cut from one pre-recorded sequence to another as a straight cut. If you want to fade out a particular shot, leaving a dark screen, you have to record it like that when you use the camera. The editor can copy it and insert it into the final scheme, but it cannot do fade-outs, nor dissolves, between two pre-recorded pictures at the editing stage.

Here again, if you want to mix for dissolve from, say, a shot of a rock band to the face of the lead singer, then back to a close-up of fingers on the guitar strings, you will have to record that as a single sequence in the studio, using the studio mixer and a special effects generator. Once it has been recorded on a single tape, you can edit it into the final recording on a two-machine set-up.

All professional editing machines can do insert edits as well as assemble edits – where a new shot is recorded over part of the duration of an existing shot. They can be used to vary visual interest, or to conceal some shooting error.

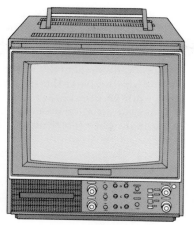

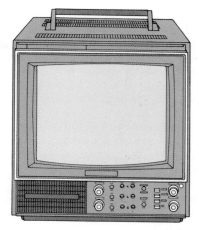

In a professional editing suite each VCR has its own monitor. At least one will be a high-quality colour set such as the Sony PVM-1300E,

above. As the name implies, the monitor's role is to allow the editor to keep track of transmissions from a VCR or from a video camera.

The Sony RM-440 edit control unit, *bottom*, enables the editor to preview edits, program sequences into its memory for automatic

editing, return the tape automatically to pre-set positions and keep a frame-accurate tally of its progress. It has a set of controls for both VCRs.

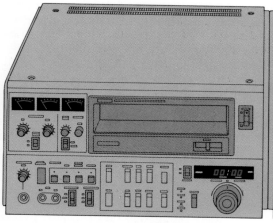

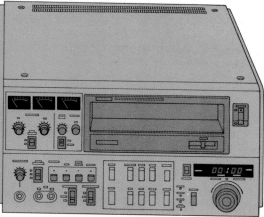

The densely packed control panel distinguishes editing VCRs from less complex models. Representative of the new front-loading generation, Sony's VO-5850, *above*, is so expensive that it is unlikely to be seen outside a professional studio.

The VCR, *above left*, is on 'Playback'. It contains your recorded tape from which you are copying precisely controlled segments,

in the order you decide, on the VCR, *above right*. This is on 'Record'.

The operation is controlled by the edit controller, which decides the precise point at which each segment begins and

ends. It is accurate in time to one frame, that is, 1/50 sec. (PAL) or 1/30 sec. (NTSC).

On the right-hand monitor you identify the end of the last segment to be copied on the master tape.

Then you look on the left-hand monitor for the next segment to be added from the left-hand VCR.

The edit controller will rehearse the edit for you before recording, so you can see what you are looking for. It can determine for you the end point of the edit so that, when you press the 'Edit' button, it will automatically copy the segment on the master tape and stop where instructed.

The special effects generator

What happens if, when editing your tape, you want to mix between images shot with more than one camera, or at different locations on different days? Effects such as these have to be added with a full three-machine edit suite of two input VCRs and a master, with a professional special effects generator.

With a three-machine suite, not only can you compile sequences on your master tape but you can combine the pictures shown on the two input recorder tapes in any way the SEG will allow you; you can mix from one to the other; you can command split-screen effects; do a straight wipe; or even bring the second picture up through a shaped insert in the middle of the first, and transfer the resulting combination to your master.

Equipment as versatile and sophisticated as this is inevitably so expensive that even professionals rarely buy it. They rely on renting it by the day from production or facilities houses, and four-figure prices for a day's editing are not unusual. You can cut costs by first working out your editing sequence in detail on a simple editing suite, and then renting the full professional equipment to translate the sequence you have planned to the finished tape.

There are many places where time can be rented on professional machines, and unless you plan to do a great deal of editing it is hardly worth purchasing one. Should you find you need one eventually, second-hand bargains are constantly available as facilities and production houses update their systems.

However, with a two-machine suite there is an element of trial and error in the editing process: in the pace with which you cut from shot to shot, for instance, or the exact point at which you cut to a new picture. For this reason, an edited production has to evolve stage by stage, in a painstaking and often time-consuming process. Yet the costs incurred are so high that reducing editing time as far as possible is a priority.

One way of resolving this dilemma is to use yet another machine known as a Time Base Corrector (TBC). This is a computer which monitors all parts of a video signal. If a line is out of place the TBC can compensate. It is the only reliable source of accurate synchronization, and accounts for a high percentage of the cost of a full professional edit suite.

There are TBCs which can record, on a separate tape, the exact time and frame number on each input tape of the shots you use at each edit. When you finish assembling that production, the tape number, time and frame of each shot used is preserved as a time code.

This can later be used for building up additional copies of any part of the tape. The information has simply to be fed into the player machine as required, and the rest is done by the control unit, working on the time-coded tape's instructions. A new copy of the whole production can be made in a fraction of the time which would be needed to copy it by other means and, because it is a new original and not a copy of the first edited master, it saves an entire generation of copying; the finished quality is also much higher.

Production and facilities houses have more complex installations which can handle several input machines at once. If the tapes on which shots are recorded can be left permanently in an input machine during the whole editing process, the computer can be used to identify each shot by its time code, and to preview it to your instructions, until you are entirely satisfied that the length and timing are absolutely right.

If you prefer you can build up the whole production as a series of previews, telling the computer which tape the next shot is from, and at what points it begins and ends, so that the production is entirely built up as a set of coded instructions.

A further advantage of time-code editing is that if, for technical reasons, a producer has to shoot a production on expensive 1-inch (2.5-centimetre) or 2-inch (5-centimetre) open-reel video tape, copies can be run off on cheaper U-matic cassettes, which can then be used to produce a time-coded, edited tape. The time-code instructions can then be used to control the much more expensive open-reel editing unit to produce the same sequence, using the open-reel originals, for a fraction of what it would cost to do all the work on those machines.

Unfortunately, home decks are not yet made to be connected to a TBC – that is something only an electronics expert can do. Whether you buy your own equipment or rent someone else's, the most important ingredient of any video production is, and always will be, the originality of your ideas.

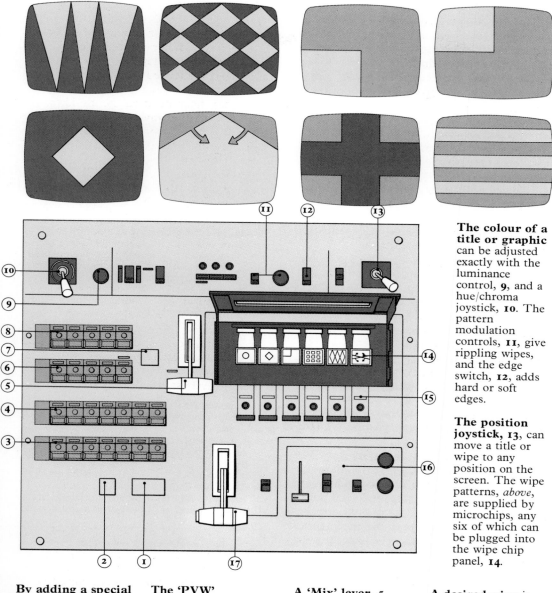

The colour of a title or graphic can be adjusted exactly with the luminance control, **9**, and a hue/chroma joystick, **10**. The pattern modulation controls, **11**, give rippling wipes, and the edge switch, **12**, adds hard or soft edges.

The position joystick, 13, can move a title or wipe to any position on the screen. The wipe patterns, *above*, are supplied by microchips, any six of which can be plugged into the wipe chip panel, **14**.

By adding a special effects generator to your edit suite you can mix between the input pictures from live cameras or recorded sources, or add graphics or decorative wipes for transmission. The 'Take' button, **1**, cuts from the output picture to the input picture which is to follow. 'Soft take', **2**, does this in dissolve.

The 'PVW' switches, 3, select an input picture from a camera or recorder to be displayed on the monitor. The 'PGM' switches, **4**, allow a picture which is being given out by the SEG to be monitored. The operator can run through a sequence of pictures, with effects added, on 'PVW' and then switch to 'PGM' for transmission.

A 'Mix' lever, 5, determines the rate at which the picture from one input mixes to that from another. Two rows of switches, **6** and **8**, can select any two inputs for the SEG to mix between at any one time. The 'AB' button, **7**, will swap one input with another in a wipe sequence, or restore the original order, if operated again.

A desired wipe is added to the input picture by using whichever of the wipe select buttons, **15**, is below the pattern.

On the downstream keyer panel, **16**, are controls which allow graphics to be added from a monochrome camera.

The wipe levers, **17**, position wipes accurately on any part of the screen.

Outside broadcast

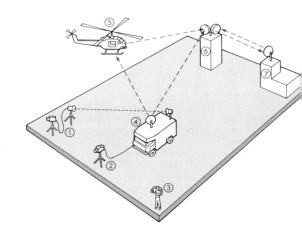

Whether you are doing simple recording or an ambitious production, video is inseparable from television. Watching television with an aware and critical eye is one of the best forms of self-education for the video producer, but amateur enthusiasts tend, consciously or otherwise, to compare their work unfavourably with the output of trained specialists, equipped with expensive cameras and recorders, backed by every kind of advanced electronics, and on a budget infinitely higher than any amateur could ever contemplate.

There is a difference – it shows – in the ultimate quality of the pictures that all this makes possible, but it is heartening to realize how much broadcast television depends on ideas, originality and imagination.

Broadcast television comes closest to home video with location recording. The simplest method is ENG (electronic news gathering), which is one of the newest conquests of video over film. Reporters delivering material from distant trouble-spots used to shoot film, which had to be processed before it could be broadcast. Now, a camera operator and assistant, with a lightweight, high-quality video camera and recorder (costing five to ten times as much as a Betamax or VHS portapack) can record on video tape, which is then rushed, relayed by satellite, or microwaved straight to the studio for broadcast.

The same principles are used for EFP (electronic field production). Shooting an outdoor sequence for a drama production, the camera operator and sound technician are augmented by a crew of four to a dozen people, handling extra portable equipment: lighting, a colour monitor to check the material being shot, and a waveform monitor and vectorscope to give technically precise representations of the recorded signals.

The production techniques are more like those of film, or home video, than studio television. One camera is used, and the feature is built up, shot by shot, to be edited back at the studio. Unlike film, however, shots can be played back on location.

Finally, there is the full outside broadcast coverage of an event such as a sporting occasion. The technique used in shooting, cutting from camera to camera, is more akin to studio production, with the director and video switcher seated at control desks in their self-contained mobile control room.

Video shot on location reaches the TV channels from a number of sources, *above*. A portable camera may have its own small transmitter, **1**, or be linked to a control truck by cable, **2**. A helicopter, **5**, may be equipped with portable cameras to shoot crowded or dangerous situations.

The BCC-20 Digicam camera, *below*, can check and adjust its own circuits to give studio-quality pictures. By changing lens and viewfinder, this camera's versatility can be extended from hand-held portable use to full studio service.

A mobile control truck, **4**, equipped with a microwave relay antenna, can transmit live material direct, or via a relay station, **6**. This passes the signal to the studio, **7**, for broadcasting.

An ENG camera operator, **3**, turns in news to a control van or studio.

The ACM-300 outside broadcast mobile, *right*, was fitted out for the Swiss Army Film Service, who use it both for teaching technique, and to make training tapes for other skills. Modern mobiles are versatile and compact.

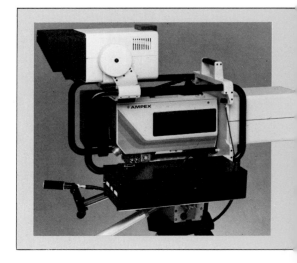

An outside broadcast vehicle, remote truck or mobile control room, *below*, holds enough machinery for full studio operation. There is an on-board petrol engine, **1**, to give an independent power supply, and the production desk, **2**, has full sound and video switching capability.

The colour monitor, **3**, is for colour control, and there are cheaper monochrome camera monitors. The VPR–2B VTRs, **4**, can also replay recorded material in forward and reverse slow motion. A waveform monitor and vectorscope, **5**, give an electronic read-out of the colour and brightness signals. Above the engineer's desk, **6**, is a full set of monitors, camera control units and video distribution amplifiers. Air-conditioning units, **7**, are essential with equipment running in a confined space.

A camera operator can shoot on the move from a hatch, **8**.

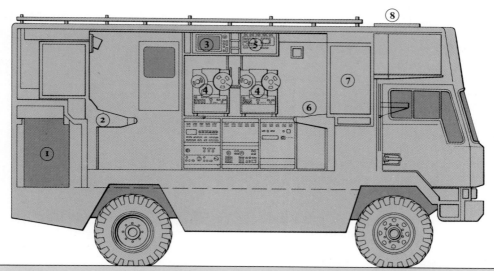

A camera operator working in the field is inured to dealing with the unusual. A helicopter, *right*, is often needed to make possible the shooting of dangerous events, such as large fires or civil riots.

To isolate the camera from the aircraft's jarring, special mounts support the camera in perfect balance, so that its movements are unaffected by the vibrations.

Precision technology cannot always help. One operator, required to record a singer while running down a woodland path, found it impossible to operate a camera while running backwards over fallen branches. The problem was solved only with the help of assistants. The camera operator had to submit to being half-towed, half-carried along the path, with the camera, pointing backwards at the subject, under one arm.

Directing the show

A television studio is a purpose-built environment for television production. Despite an ever-increasing emphasis on location shooting, studio technique is still geared to the assembly of a show in one continuous session, just as it used to be in the early years when most broadcasts were live, and equipment was bulky. The skill and forethought needed to effect an elegant production with a minimum of editing is still a yardstick of professional excellence for a television director.

In drama particularly, a mountain of preparation lies behind the smallest production. The set designer must excercise ingenuity in fitting all the sets into one studio, often making a scale model to test the set's efficiency. Movement of cast and cameras is minimized, and camera positions calculated so that the viewers never see a camera, microphone boom or other giveaway in their picture.

Studio lights are a world in themselves, suspended in their dozens from a gantry high above the action. While the cast rehearses elsewhere, the lighting director coordinates the lights with the required camera angles to achieve the correct light level and, where needed for atmosphere, shadows. During the final camera rehearsal, which simulates transmission as closely as possible, the director can check that the cast and equipment work together for the best effect. During shooting, the final camera script is followed by everyone, although small changes can be made if the director and camera crew agree on them.

The director orchestrates the whole operation from the control desk in the production room, watching the monitors and following a camera script prepared during rehearsals. It is the director's job to cue the vision mixer to switch between cameras, while warning the camera operators in turn what their next shots will be. While camera 1 is on air, camera 2 is picking up shots, which the vision mixer can choose from, and camera 3 may be moving around, setting up a new angle.

In the audio control room, audio engineers mix and adjust the sound from the studio microphones, and add sound effects. A different unrehearsed show, such as a talk show, is a challenge, demanding instant reactions from the whole crew, to pick up the best of what is happening as it happens.

It is the floor manager's job to convey instructions to the cast during shooting by gesturing silently. This sign language is a studio tradition.

On the nose. (We're on time)

Play to that camera

Slow down

Stand by

O.K It's all right

Cut; finish

In a TV studio, *below right*, the sound and vision control rooms, and the production room, overlook the studio floor.

In the video control room, **1**, engineers monitor the colour and contrast levels of the signals from the cameras.

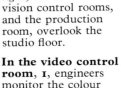

The production control room, **2**, houses the director and assistant director, the vision mixer and the technical director. A bank of television monitors includes a colour transmission monitor, a monochrome monitor for each camera, and others showing outside broadcast, telecine and recorded material.

In the sound control room, **3**, are the audio controller and technicians who mix and switch live and recorded audio sources.

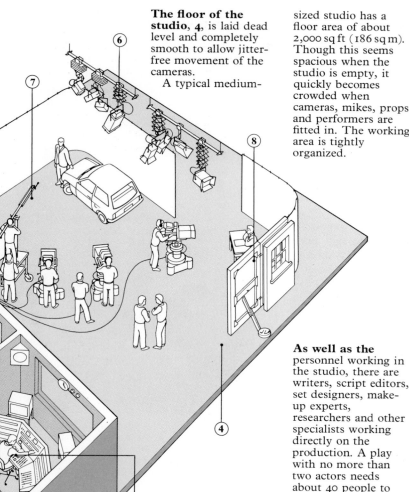

The floor of the studio, **4**, is laid dead level and completely smooth to allow jitter-free movement of the cameras.

A typical medium-sized studio has a floor area of about 2,000 sq ft (186 sq m). Though this seems spacious when the studio is empty, it quickly becomes crowded when cameras, mikes, props and performers are fitted in. The working area is tightly organized.

A studio camera, **5**, is larger and heavier than a portable camera. It weighs about 112 lb (51 kg) and is carefully counterbalanced on a pedestal, whose hydraulics enable smooth movements to be made with finger-pressure. The pedestal is moved around the studio on dolly wheels.

Studio lighting is fixed on a permanent grid, **6**, well above camera level. Some grids are worked by hand, while others are automated. The changing light intensities can be computer controlled.

Mikes, **7**, are operated from the floor, mounted on booms or stands, or attached to the performers, bringing them close to the source of the sound.

Convincing scenery is based on 'flats', **8**, board constructions which can be made into complexes representing the interior of a whole building.

As well as the personnel working in the studio, there are writers, script editors, set designers, make-up experts, researchers and other specialists working directly on the production. A play with no more than two actors needs about 40 people to provide the back-up skills required.

Matting is a technique which can combine on the screen a performer from one source with scenery from another. If one camera is trained on a presenter, a second on another scene and a third on a silhouette called a matte, an SEG can combine the pictures so that the presenter appears within the matte, surrounded by the scene.

Chroma key, *left*, is a more modern and widespread technique similar to matting. The presenter is shot against a pure colour (usually blue, the hue least dominant in human colouring). An SEG can then replace the blue area with a picture from another source, such as this alpine scene.

By means of these techniques a subject can be apparently transported to an entirely different setting – an airport, perhaps, or a tropical island beach.

Electronic wizardry

Drama may bring creative revolution; documentaries may break new barriers in communication, but many people say that the most adventurous television is to be found not in feature television at all, but in commercials. Their subject may be washing powder or after-shave, but their true aim is to pack into thirty or sixty seconds an impact that will remain after the rest of the night's viewing has been forgotten.

This is where money talks. Television audiences are vast; demand for air time is high, and so are costs. Customers are prepared to pay fabulous sums to have their message conveyed as persuasively as possible, and for their money they expect to receive not only flawless technical performance but originality, in a field where, it seems, everything has already been tried.

The shooting of commercials is the province of the production houses, companies which provide the production, editing and special effects equipment which only this rich trade can afford. Their clients may be hiring a two-man EFP team, or commissioning on a budget of millions.

Millions are also invested in machinery for recording and editing film, sound and video: mixers which can mix two camera inputs in dozens of complex patterns – ripples, lozenges, spiral wipes – or chroma key a model safely from a bare studio into a raging inferno. These are analog effects which modify the scanning sequences from the cameras by waveforms representing the desired patterns. Even more costly tricks are performed by computer-controlled frame-store devices. These encode the picture digitally and then stretch and squeeze it into distorted shapes or even rotate it. With the help of computerized edit suites, caption generators and colorizers, the permutations of images available seem limitless.

Perhaps the most precious commodity is the patience and practised judgement of the engineers, directors and editors who produce the commercials. Many essential processes from writing computer graphics programs, arranging props, testing camera angles, and drawing mattes, right down to the simple, but essential jobs such as cooking a fresh dish of baked beans for each new take, can only be done by hand. One professional estimated that he produced twelve seconds of finished work a day: twelve seconds of video perfection.

Using its frame store, a computerized SEG reduces an image to a portion of the screen and swirls it round, leaving a trail of duplicate images behind it.

As it moves round, the image expands. The SEG's next instruction splits the screen and puts the image into one half, with a mirror-image in the other.

In a third stage, the machine opens another picture area. Taking about two seconds to run, this sequence is only a sample from among dozens of effects.

In this modern post-production suite, each piece of equipment has its own control panel, but central control is exercised from the computer keyboard to the left of the main desk.

From this computer, a stereo sound mixer and tape recorder, a vision mixer (video switcher), a digital harmonizer (a device for regulating sound pitch when the tape is running slow or fast), four digital effects devices, a 2-in (5-cm) and three 1-in (2.5-cm) floor-standing studio VTRs, and a dozen or so monitors are coordinated into a system that enables the creation of image sequences so complex and ambitious that to control them by hand might take years, instead of days.

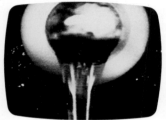

A commercial is built of images from many sources. Here motor oil is shown pouring from a bottle.

Film of a live tiger, shot from a distance to protect the film crew, has already been provided.

A matte is hand-drawn for each frame, to isolate the tiger from the unwanted beach scenery.

With a digital device the editor can enlarge the image of the tiger as if a camera were zooming in.

The whole tiger sequence, from long shot to close-up, is matted on to the background of pouring oil.

In the final stage, the tiger, now standing by a motor engine, is surrounded by an electronic halo.

Making video work for you

Video makes a splendid hobby. Its endless fascination and its limitless challenges to the imagination make the prospect of becoming bored with it seem remote.

Enjoyment is not the only benefit video production can offer. It can be used to help make a living – either indirectly, by contributing to the success of your business or profession, or by becoming your business. Video is already an accepted and increasingly important aid in a variety of fields, from education to salesmanship. Anyone with the skills and equipment to supply polished video recordings to paying customers could easily find their hobby expanding into a profession.

People in commerce and industry are discovering a need for video recordings to sell new products, train workers, communicate with far-flung divisions and branches, reassure shareholders and drum up new customers. So far, the demand for small outfits that can handle video with flair, with imagination and with dedicated professionalism, far exceeds the supply.

Even in the non-commercial world there is immense scope for making many of the tapes, described in the previous section of this handbook, on a profitable basis. People are becoming aware of video's potential for providing an imperishable record of unique family events: weddings; bar mitzvahs, christenings or anniversary celebrations. However, lacking equipment and expertise they need experienced producers to take the whole process off their hands, and to give them the results they want at prices they feel they can afford.

In between these two extremes fall a host of other opportunities ripe for exploitation. Travel agents are beginning to use video to show off hotels or resorts to customers, more vividly than is possible in a brochure. Colleges are using video as a teaching aid wherever repeated demonstrations would be difficult to set up, or expensive. Tapes cover subjects ranging from complex surgical operations for medical students to *haute cuisine* for trainee chefs, and from particle physics to drama. In education and training there are as many possibilities as courses.

At this stage, however, a word of warning. Wide as the market is, it demands a new attitude to video production. From the moment someone commissions you to make a video recording, you are a professional, and you need to bring to your work the attitudes and priorities of a professional.

You cannot afford, for example, to practise at your customer's expense, for video is an expensive item for both individuals and professional organizations to fund. They want competent results, not inspired ideas that failed to work. Stick to methods you know and techniques you have practised.

Eliminate problems as far as you can by pre-planning. Always check your equipment before and after each assignment to make sure everything is working properly. Make check lists. If you can run down a list of numbered points before setting out on location you can be sure you have everything you need. Err on the side of caution. It is easy to forget a vital item when relying on memory; we once drove 200 miles (around 300 kilometres) only to find a tripod was missing because it had been put away in a slightly different place the night before. When you are professional, mistakes like this become expensive.

Begin from the beginning to keep account of the smallest expenditure. Cost each job properly, so that you can be sure you are making a reasonable profit for your skill and effort. It is easy to ignore items such as telephone calls or car mileage which, once you become involved in a busy working schedule, mount up only too quickly. An accountant will advise you about setting operating costs against income tax.

When you start to make money, think about investing some of it in better equipment. A more expensive camera will produce better pictures and may also save you some effort: it may be more simple to operate than a cheaper one. More lights will give a more polished finish to indoor productions. A U-matic machine may be an asset. Even if you know that most of your customers will want cassettes in VHS or Betamax, it will enable you to make higher-quality original copies.

There is no need to buy a lot of equipment to begin with. Rental companies will lend you almost any combination of equipment to suit any assignment, and this gives you an excellent opportunity to try out different formats, recorders, cameras and other equipment. You can also rent the use of an editing suite to liberate yourself from the tyranny of having to edit as you shoot. If the production calls

for it, you can hire elaborate facilities which will allow you to include fully professional special effects – perhaps in a demonstration tape of a rock music band.

Buy new equipment only when you find you need to use it regularly. Putting rental charges on to a bill is a useful reminder of the real cost of attractive extras, and the need to justify the extra expenditure is good practice for salesmanship and self-discipline.

However good your equipment, you will find you need helpers. At first you will need help in carrying equipment on location, and with setting up difficult shots. For this you can call on people on a part-time basis, extending their employment to a more permanent arrangement later, when the volume of work justifies it.

Later, when you have gathered a small team together, make sure it is well looked after. Remember to take enough food on location. Make sure that everyone wears, or takes along, warm clothing: location work is invariably colder than you expect.

In the following pages we explore some of the ways of making video your profession. The field is wide open; there has never been a better time to make video work for you.

Community video

Perhaps the biggest opportunity to make money from video is in recording weddings, birthday parties, christenings, bar-mitzvahs, and other once-in-a-lifetime occasions where a family is quite happy to pay the going rate for an imperishable record of an important event. It is a good place for the enthusiast to start being professional, since the sequence of events is usually preordained.

Do not, however, fall into the yawning trap of thinking that celebratory occasions are easy. There are all kinds of problems and pitfalls for the unwary, and even the experienced can be caught out, because no two locations are ever the same. If you can, try out your ideas on a suitable family occasion before going out to look for commissions.

First, try breaking the event down into a set of sequences. Talk over with your clients the kind of scenes they want to include – for instance, guests arriving, significant highlights of the ceremony and celebrations, activities to be performed by the principal participants, and so on. Then try to enlist their aid in making sure that you can deliver what they want. For example, if you are asked to record guests leaving one location and arriving at another, will you be given enough time to set up the camera at the required place?

Find out in advance whether you will be allowed into the building where the ceremony is to take place. Non-believers are not allowed inside, or are resticted to certain parts of, most places of worship. In others, religious officials may be reluctant to permit lights to be brought inside the building, or to have a camera operator near enough to record the ceremony.

If a camera is not allowed, it may be possible for an audio recorder to be placed where the ceremony is to take place so that at least there can be a clear sound coverage. This can be dubbed on to the video tape later. If you are permitted to record the ceremony, your aim will be to find unusual, interesting and well-composed shots without intruding.

Recording the celebratory meal afterwards poses different problems. Since the whole proceedings usually take far too long to record on one tape, try and capture the highlights, and the most entertaining and amusing impromptu happenings, as they occur. Never relax. Remember you are working and cannot afford to lose concentration.

Planning shots and angles
You need a solid establishing shot on which to fade up and begin the recording. For instance, you might start by framing the building in which the event is to take place and then zoom in for a close-up of an announcement, or banns, or an invitation.

At the celebration, plan to use shots and angles which will suit the atmosphere and mood of the event.

Make the recording of a ceremony more interesting by having close-up shots of individuals interspersed amongst compositions of the whole group. Take into account any existing sources of bright light, such as windows or candles.

If there is to be a change in location, make some link between the two places; for example, fading down on two newly-weds, or parents and child, leaving the church, and up again on the happy couple, or family relaxing at the reception.

During speeches you could fade down the sound and cut to shots of listening faces before coming back to record the final words or toast.

End the film on an appropriate subject which sums up the happy event. Zoom in to close-up, and fade to black.

Pick a suitable angle, either directly in front, *above*, or sideways on, for recording the highlights of a religious ceremony, and slowly zoom in, where appropriate, for close-ups.

Make the most of any planned dramatic moments, *left*, by focusing on the expectant faces of the guests before panning out to the action.

The protagonists: child, parents, bride, bridesmaids, groom, *far left*, should star in the recording, but lack of time may force you to choose between two different events: the groom, or the bride, arriving; the couple leaving the place of worship, or arriving at the reception.

185

Improving your game

Most professional productions involve the making of edited, planned tapes. There are times, however, when you may want to make use of raw video, unedited and unscripted, which can be played back as soon as it has been recorded. If people can see themselves on tape as others see them, they can get a more objective viewpoint of what they are trying to do, and a clearer idea of how they could improve. As well as being useful for actors, public speakers, teachers, interviewers and interviewees, this approach can be of particular value to both professional and amateur sports enthusiasts.

All the equipment you need is a video camera and VCR, and a monitor on which to play back the results. The extra refinements of slow motion, frame-by-frame advance and a still frame hold on the VCR will obviously be advantageous to anyone trying to improve their sporting abilities, since they make possible an analysis of the various bodily movements involved.

Perhaps your local tennis club might be interested in renting your services for the use of its members. Having ascertained the particular action a tennis player wants to study, set up the camera at an appropriate angle so as to capture the whole movement clearly. Once you have recorded a few demonstration shots, wind the tape back and play it over again so that your subject can see where the fault lies.

If the club coach is there, you can shoot before-and-after shots of the subject's service or backhand, for example, at each stage of a fault-correcting talk, so that there is some visual evidence of your client's improvement. As a refinement, you could edit in an excerpt from a recording of a professional's service or backhand alongside that of your subject, for further comparison.

Having recorded a player's service, forehand and backhand, you could then suggest following through part of a match, so that the club coach can highlight more subtle points of tactics or positioning on the court. It may be worth taking a look at one of the prerecorded tennis cassettes for further ideas.

The list of sports activities that can benefit from visual analysis is almost endless. Golfers, karate or judo students, divers, gymnasts and trampolinists can all be given a view of their performance they would otherwise never be able to see.

Viewing themselves on the playback tape, fencing partners get a chance to examine their interacting movements as well as each other's foot and blade work.

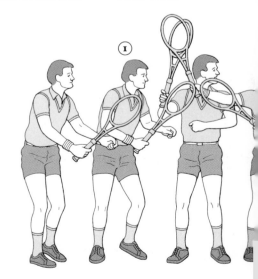

Correct positioning of the arms and hands is vitally important in basketball. Studying movements frame by frame can give a player greater insight into his or her own game as well as into team strategies.

The visual search facility on the VCR enables you to scan the tape you have made at five times its normal speed, either forward or backward, **1**, so that the exact part of the tape you want to see can be swiftly found. Fine slow motion, **2**, shows the action at varying degrees of reduced speed.

In addition, the tape can be made to advance frame by frame, **3**, so that every angle of the action can be analyzed in greater detail. For even closer examination, one single frame, **4**, can be held completely still to be studied.

Using a tripod will help ensure clearly defined pictures, as it keeps the camera steady. Avoid having to zoom out to capture the movement, and do not film against a bright sky or sun: a silhouetted figure will lose some of the important details needed for accurate analysis.

Commercial fantasy

Television advertising is one of the most persuasive weapons a salesperson can have. Although the world of the broadcast television commercial, with its six-figure budgets and trail-blazing ideas, may seem light years away from anything you could do, the difference is one of degree rather than principle.

Television commercials command such huge audiences that the most expensive productions become worth while on a cost-per-client basis. However, many advertisers want to reach a specialized, or local, audience. The owner of a small vacation hotel, for example, may want a tape to show travel agents the attractions of the locale and the accommodation, but will not want to pay television advertising costs. Aim at this market.

Outlets for video advertising are opening up fast. Already, department stores are investing in video playback equipment to advertise new sales lines and promotional events. Manufacturers are beginning to use video cassettes as a form of direct-mail advertising to outlets such as stores. Soon, video cinemas may turn to running advertisements between features, and these are likely to attract local industry and services.

A local hairdresser, or an automobile dealer, would need the simplest of advertisements: perhaps an assembly of slides. These might show the premises; three or four hair styles, or the latest and most expensive automobiles in the showroom; and title cards giving all the relevant information.

This may seem unimaginative, but if it is what your client wants, remember that slides are a useful discipline for thinking about the essentials of a subject. Make sure the slides meet the highest aesthetic and technical standards, and use your imagination in presenting them. Record the advertisement using two projectors and a dissolve unit, so that you can cut and dissolve from one slide to the next. A series of slides of a slowly moving object can be made to appear to move; or, using a battery of projectors, you can work on a complex sequence to make a display of constantly changing segments within a main picture.

If you are asked to shoot a moving sequence, remember that advertisements are always short. Think in terms of each shot taking only a second or two. Look even more carefully for the unusual or unexpected shot to add into the essential information.

Budgeting check list
1 Before you bid for or agree to an assignment, work out your costs as carefully as you can, and include some provision for unexpected expenses.
2 Work out your charges in advance, aiming at a fair return for your time and expertise, and including an element of insurance against depreciation of equipment.
3 If at the beginning it seems necessary to cut profits in order to charge an attractive price, do so, but not too often.
4 Plan out your assignment, and make sure your client agrees to the content, the treatment and the script.
5 If, as you progress, your client wants to make changes, cost them out and quote for the extra work; then let the client decide whether the changes are worth the cost.
6 Remember that the most expensive production may be no better than the cheapest, and that hiring sophisticated equipment adds to the bill, while profiting the hiring company. A cut-price production which pleases your client will give both of you a bigger return.

Try to think of ways of enlivening your production at minimum cost. Advertising agencies and manufacturers' publicity departments often release slides, film and video tapes to anyone promoting their products. The aerial view of an automobile dealer's stock yard, *above*, might be incorporated into an advertisement gratis.

Local celebrities, *left*, are often willing, for a small fee, to appear in an advertisement endorsing a product, especially if it is produced locally. The problem of inappropriate weather on the day when the recording is to be made is an expense you will have to provide for when drawing up your budget.

Home erotica

Video, for many people, means one type of production above all others: that of the so-called adult-only movie. Not only are video magazines packed with advertisements for professional pre-recorded erotica, but the making of erotic home movies by amateurs is now a popular hobby and art form. Some magazines offer prizes for the best and most imaginative recording, which may then be placed on a retailer's list.

Making erotic movies needs more trial-and-error experimentation than perhaps any other video production. It is essential that the person or people being filmed feel relaxed if they are to give a convincing performance, and you will need to give all the help you can from behind the camera, but without acting as an inhibiting influence.

Good results often need more light than seems romantic, however you can always experiment with shooting in low light to start with.

Getting your subjects to over-exaggerate their actions and play for laughs will also help them to throw off inhibition. For example, a girl could try a mimic of a striptease artist's routine. As she warms to the role, the chances are that natural sensuousness will start taking over.

From a technical point of view, you will be using many of the same camera angles as you would for any other kind of video portrait. You want to make the most of your subject; you want to make him or her look as good as possible. Use changes of clothes, locations, or situations to suit several different moods.

Many apparently explicit films, when analyzed, can be found to show nothing that could not be seen on the local beach. So much depends on the context, atmosphere, suggestion and the things the camera does not quite manage to show you. The mere sound of a zip being parted can be extremely evocative, given the right setting.

The erotic home movie is one in which amateurs can almost always turn in better results than the so-called professional movie-makers. Good results depend on originality, a fresh approach, and involvement, and you are more likely to get this when experimenting at your own pace, than turning out a commercial product on an assembly-line production schedule, with models to whom the experience is just an everyday occupation.

Many manufacturers offer a remote control unit as an optional extra which enables you to operate the VCR from a distance. It carries all functions, including tape stop/start, pause, rewind and fast forward, so you can use it to operate a camera positioned to face you. Sony manufacture cameras with detachable viewfinders, and offer a viewfinder extension cable and a remote control unit with a zoom control switch, *below*, so that you can operate the camera at a distance, and still see into the viewfinder.

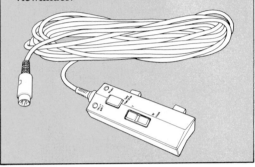

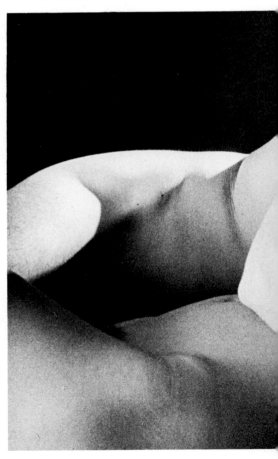

Lighting, background colour and camera position should combine to create the skin tones you are looking for, *above*. Increasing the red response slightly can make your pictures look warm and romantic. A bluer cast projects a more clinical, cold picture. To prevent unsightly close-ups of gooseflesh, heat the room first.

A story line is not essential. You can simply aim for a succession of shots, blending movements and gestures with a suitable sound-track in a way that you find attractive or arousing, *left*. Ask for any changes or improvements that you can think of, and be prepared to throw away, or record over, any unsuccessful first efforts.

191

Portfolio on camera

Anyone who has to put on a performance as part of their professional work – singers, models, dancers, actors – could benefit from using video to sell themselves. A real performance might be immeasurably more persuasive than an audition held under conditions which inhibit concentration.

Professionals will be used to turning in a polished public performance, but they may not be used to working for the camera, so do not try to persuade them to change a well-rehearsed routine without good reason. Let them run through their performance while you work out how to translate it into video as practically as possible. How will you light it? Where should you shoot it: on location where the immediacy of a real performance may make it more convincing; or in a studio where there are none of the restrictions of fitting in with someone else's show? What background does it need? Where do you need close-ups and where would a long shot be better? How can you maintain variety and interest.

There will be room, even in a five-minute video tape, to demonstrate your subject's versatility. A model will need to be recorded in as many different styles as possible; an actor in a variety of roles. You will also want to vary the pace by lingering on some aspect of the performance of which the subject is particularly proud, to give time for the quality of the action to become apparent.

Although professionals are used to interrupting their performance in rehearsals, try and keep recording sessions relaxed. If you have the short shot you wanted, but the subject is deeply involved, let the performance carry on. However, if a take is wrong, say so and ask for a repeat.

You are unlikely to need a script: most performers will want to speak for themselves, but a model demonstrating lounge suits or teenage gear may be enhanced by an appropriate musical background. There may be a case for including relevant personal information as a voice-over and the subject will probably want to be the one to speak.

Always remember that this is one of the most difficult of sales markets to cater for. The professionals who use this kind of portfolio usually work in a buyer's market so the recording should be as polished as possible. On the other hand, avoid overselling your subject; try to let talent speak for itself through the sequences you record.

Video portability

Before video came along, models were restricted to assembling portfolios of still photographs to give advertisers a taste of how they could look in a magazine or on a poster. Almost nothing of the quality of their performances – of how well they could work to demonstrate a product, or how convincing they sound, comes through a photograph. A video tape can be a walking, talking portfolio.

A cassette carefully edited to project a subject just as he or she wants to appear, means that the client is able to turn out a perfect set of performances to order. The cassette may be kept at home to be played back on the client's own machine, or copied and taken to interviews and auditions, even sent to agents or prospective employers, to be played back on their machines and analyzed at leisure. Turning out copies on each of the major formats will not be prohibitively expensive and tapes are not heavy to carry around.

Video is a conveniently portable medium. There are even miniature sales executives' brief-cases equipped with playback machines and tiny monitors so that the whole operation can be self-sufficient from start to finish.

The Nederlands Dans Teater have long been using video as a training aid. Instead of learning roles only in rehearsal, dancers practise alone, using a video recording of a rehearsal.

Recording dancers on stage gives little scope to the camera operator. These shots from 'Miniatures', choreographed by Nils Christe, were taken head-on by a camera at the back of the theatre. They are what the dancers need. If it is to be used as a teaching aid a video recording must be a true, functional record, not an arty rethink of a performance.

Shots like these put over the skills of the subject, rather than of the camera operator.

Presenting your business

A video cassette can be a useful selling tool in many different ways. It can be used to give brief glimpses of holiday resorts for a travel agent to show clients; a real estate agent might consider using video cassettes to interest prospective buyers in certain properties; or an architect, a home builder or an interior designer might want to build up a library of video tapes displaying and analyzing their work.

This kind of production has unusual objectives. It might best be approached as a series of sequences of standard length and format so that each resort, house or room is given fair viewing. Your client will have an idea of the number of homes, say, he or she will want to include on each cassette, so effectively this will decide the length of each entry.

However you, as production expert, should assess the wisdom of your client's views. Too brief a coverage may not do justice to the subject's merits. Moreover, the cost of the recording will depend more on the number of properties your client wants to include than on the time devoted to each.

To cost the job realistically, you must work out how long it will take you to visit each location, set up the equipment and record the material. Include time required for planning shots and packing up, as well as fuel expenses to and from the location. Clearly, it is in your interests to work quickly and efficiently.

Work out before you start shooting all the shots you want and how long each should take. You will be less likely to miss worthwhile pictures, or to end up with too long a recording. Present all the essential details the client's customer will need to see in as objective a way as possible, while making the most of any positive features the property has to offer.

Keep as close as you can to the timings you have estimated for each shot. If you can choose when to shoot the material, make sure the weather is good: holiday resorts and housing look depressing on a drab afternoon. Remember that your client may be the best person to act as presenter or as a voice-over.

Present the edited recording to your client with a list of the subjects and timings of the sequences. If you then charge your client for each property entered, you will find it easy to quote for additional work.

Selling a home

Begin the recording with a bold and simple title card, followed by an establishing shot of the house taken from the road, with perhaps a pan or a zoom up to the entrance.

As the camera pans around the hall, the commentary could establish the numbers and types of downstairs rooms. Extra lighting should be used if needed.

Going from room to room, pick up any attractive features: for example, a long shot down the length of the lounge to emphasise its size; close-ups of bookshelves in an alcove; a shot of central heating radiators or a feature fireplace; the serving arrangement between dining room and kitchen; the shower fittings and bidet in the bathroom.

Try a shoulder-held shot to take you up to the first floor, and include any attractive views through windows, but be sure that the contrast does not make the interior look dark and gloomy. Having filmed the best features of the garden, sum up by explaining in a combination of pictures and words, the proximity of the house to shops, schools, means of transport and other local amenities.

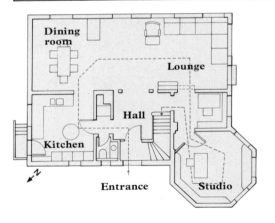

Try to show the viewer how a house fits together as a concept. Record each room in sequence, with the camera shoulder-mounted, so that the viewer sees the dining room through a serving hatch from the kitchen, and the lounge through a doorway.

Set the stairs in context with an establishing shot before recording on an upper floor. In sunny rooms, shoot at an angle to the windows.

A periscope lens can see objects as if through an insect's eye. A detailed architect's model, for example, looks on the screen like a real building, when shot through a periscope lens.

To make one, cut out a piece of smooth-sided corrugated cardboard exactly as in **1**, *below*. Run a finger-nail along the dotted lines in preparation for folding. Cut out a hole large enough to fit over the camera lens; then cut a thin metal sheet into a T shape and wrap the top of the T around the edge of the plano-concave lens (PCV) with masking tape, to form a collar. Mount the lens over the PCV hole with the curved side facing toward the inside of the periscope. The stem of the T can be attached with masking tape above the PCV hole, **2**. With glue, stick a mirror to the inside of each end flap. Close up the periscope body along the folds, and secure with masking tape. To mount the periscope on the camera, bend the aluminium strip into an L shape; then drill a $\frac{1}{4}$-in (6-mm) hole in one end to accommodate a camera retaining screw. Attach the other end to the periscope body with masking tape.

For full-frame magnification you may also need a close-up lens adaptor.

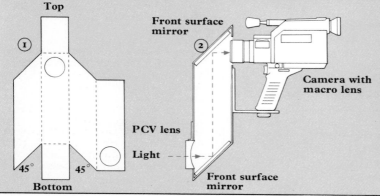

Top

① Front surface mirror

②

PCV lens

Light

Camera with macro lens

45° 45°

Bottom

Front surface mirror

Equipment
Cardboard; aluminium strip, 1 in × 8 in (2.5 cm × 20 cm); thin sheet metal 4 in × 5 in (10 cm × 12.5 cm); masking tape; strong glue; front surface mirror $3\frac{3}{16}$ in × $3\frac{15}{16}$ in (8 × 10 cm) cut in two; PCV lens min 2 in (5 cm) dia.; 56 mm focal length camera retaining screw.

Open your recording by showing the house in its surroundings. Shots of façades are best taken with the light behind you. Try and work out the orientation and plan your visit to coincide with the best light; the sun will bring out details.

If the house has a view, zoom through a window to capture the sweep of the garden, or the landscape. Take various shots to show how the house fits into the neighbourhood.

An interior designer would have you linger on a tablescape, or in an alcove, for subtleties of décor to make their full impact. To avoid extensive post-production editing, shot in 35 mm. It will give you more control over lighting and composition and, when you have worked out an attractive sequence, you can transfer the pictures to video tape.

Alternate stills with shots of plans and preliminary sketches.

Video taping industry

Video can work for commerce in all kinds of ways. It can be used by companies to put across information about their organization, or its product, to potential customers, employees, suppliers and shareholders, and it can be used as a publicity device.

The chief problem in deciding the shape and content of the recording is to convince the customer, who probably has preconceived ideas as to content and presentation, to listen to your suggestions. Planning out the sequence of shots on location, and drawing up a convincing storyboard, may help you to overcome this obstacle.

Whether you are announcing a new product line, or presenting a major extension to the production shops, your main priority at the beginning of the production is to capture the attention of your viewers. The opening shot should be something attractive, or something intriguing. For example, if your subject is the launch of a new automobile, you could begin with a really tight close-up of part of the body emerging from the paint-dipping bath, with the light sparkling on the wet paint. As the camera pulls back in a slow zoom, the body shape is gradually revealed.

Picture possibilities can be found in the most unlikely surroundings. One production made in a television factory produced an almost balletic sequence of sets swaying and gliding past one another on overhead conveyors, which, shot from an unusual angle, had all the grace and formality of a dance.

Another sequence in the same production showed a printed circuit board being conveyed through a bath of molten solder to have all the connections made. Looking along the conveyor, one brilliantly lit area was held in sharp focus, so that the resulting shot showed a dark, unidentifiable shape coming into brilliant illumination on the instant it came into focus. Together, the colours of the components and the bright sheen of the molten solder created a picture with a rare abstract beauty.

Lighting can be a major problem in an industrial location; so survey the premises in advance of the shooting day, to check what you will require in the way of lights and stands. You will have to carry all your equipment, probably along miles of corridors and workshop walkways. Bring a folding cart, or borrow a cart small enough to negotiate through doorways and steps.

Making a training tape

Clarity should be your major preoccupation when making a recording that is to be used for training personnel. Your object is to put over to the viewer clearly and succinctly exactly what he or she needs to know in order to be able to carry out a specific operation.

The information being taught may be complicated and highly technical, and the success of your recording will depend on your assessing such factors as the pace at which you impart the information; how much you can assume the viewer to know already, or whether and where you should pause for a demonstrator to play a sequence over before proceeding to the next stage of the operation.

Ways of tackling problems such as these should be worked out in close collaboration with your client, the client's training officer, or some other person with the specialized knowledge you need. Plan the operation out together, shot by shot, looking out for and solving problems as they arise. This way, the finished product should evolve as an integrated whole. If you can also use your creative abilities to help make the training tape interesting and attractive to watch, you will contribute still more to the success of the project.

Discourage the company directors' likely insistence on the well-worn opening shot of the factory, or office, façade.

Corporate pride could be satisfactorily stated by other visual means – perhaps a portrait of a celebrated founder, *above*.

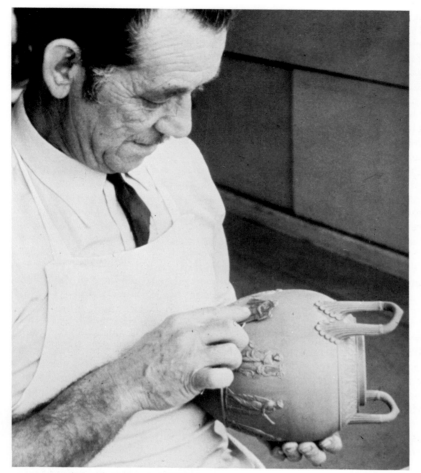

People always make good subjects, especially when engaged in tasks involving skill and concentration. Shoot their faces as cutaways, then shoot their hands, *left*.

If your recording is to be used for training, the picture must be sharp. Work out in advance how close you can position the camera without interfering with the operation you are going to record, and which angles will give you the best view.

Factory and workshop ceilings are usually too high, and the walls may be too distant, to give much reflection, so work out beforehand how much extra lighting you will need to eliminate shadows and boost the light level, and set up well in advance.

Plan any commentary as carefully as the camera angles so that it matches the pictures exactly.

A pottery kiln being loaded could be a spectacular shot, but beware of the danger to the camera. Heat, paint spray, vapour from chemicals and thick dust can damage your camera.

If necessary, film from a distance or from behind a glass screen, searching for long, wide or angled shots to substitute for close-ups. A long shot of a row of objects or people is much more interesting than an unchanging view, especially if you focus from time to time on some specific part of the process.

197

Optional extras

So rich is the wealth of video, and so wide its potential scope, that some of its off-shoots have already become separated from the main trunk of the video business, and have become rooted as growing entities in their own right. These are the 'optional extras' of any video system, and they range from lighting and security systems, through the arcade of video games to the small computer, the child of the silicon chip, which promises to become as common in the home as the television screen on which its store of information can be displayed.

In the world of rock music, video tape linking the action with the sound has become a must for every group or solo performer with an eye on success. Video juke boxes made their début early in the eighties, and video has yet more to contribute to the disco age: those pulsating strobe and pulsed coloured lights, which set the atmosphere in a disco, can now be reproduced to the same quality in the home, not only with a sound-to-light converter but also on a screen.

Connected to a regular television screen, a video synthesizer (an item of video equipment hitherto found only in a professional studio) produces signals which create constantly changing, multi-coloured, abstract patterns in a random sequence having more than 2,000 million possible permutations. By means of a timing button, the pattern on the screen can be made to change as slowly as once every ten minutes, or as fast as twice a second. A synthesizer, looking like a simple audio amplifier, and about the same size, is most effective connected to a large screen.

Apart from the random generation of colour patterns, such devices have much wider possibilities. By connecting a video synthesizer to an external video source, such as a video camera, it can produce identifiable images, but in ever-changing hues. Moreover, by linking it to a hi-fi system or an electric guitar, the colours on the screen can be made to throb in time to the music.

A similar link-up of sound and vision promises to forge another art form. Using a video synthesizer with an audio input produces dazzling but formless patterns. The next logical step forward from this is video art: abstract but at the same time purposeful patterns created on a video screen by the deliberate action of a video artist. This new dimension is given to music by using a computer to program a video disk with a visual pattern, designed to match a specific musical accompaniment. Another possibility for the future could be to program a video synthesizer to make specific visual responses to audio input.

As a kind of hybrid between the fantasy oil projection systems of the sixties and the flashy disco lighting systems of the seventies, the video synthesizer has already succeeded in supplying a vehicle for transporting the public medium into the home. If its price (between £200 and £500; $100 and $500) seems beyond the scope of a personal budget, it may be an attractive item of hardware to hire for a disco party, since it can be linked to a screen to give a wall-to-wall, ceiling-to-carpet display.

Even more than video synthesizers, video games, once the sole province of the amusement arcade, have now begun to find a permanent place in more and more homes. The drug-substitute for kids and adults alike, arcade video games are so compulsive that it was inevitable that they should move indoors to the comfort of the homestead.

Video games are big business, and attract cut-throat competition, with new games (backed by millions of dollars of investment) being pirated by special copying machines virtually overnight. As video games become more and more highly evolved, so their appeal widens and the competition hots up. With tests of logic, numbers and spelling, they are proving their worth medically as aids in the rehabilitation of the disabled.

In an increasingly violent world, amply reflected in the intergalactic wars of video games, guarding the security of persons and possessions is becoming an ever-increasing challenge. Video has provided the answer to security problems everywhere, from the high-street bank to the private house. A better eye witness than any human observer, a video screen connected to a security system can record every last detail of criminal and deed and, simultaneously, note the exact time at which the crime was committed.

Fed information by cameras seen and unseen, the video screen of a security system can not only project a criminal's image but can also be used to check out the innocent by their faces or even their voices. Linked to an alarm, such a security device has already proved its worth in factory and home.

SONY

TRINITRON

REMOTE CONTROL KV-1612UB

Of all the optional extras that can be attached to a video, the use of the video screen as the essential component of any computer system is undoubtedly the one that seems to have the most potential. When connected to even the smallest of home computers, the video screen, fed information from a floppy disk or data bank, can put before your eyes, at the press of a button, a lesson in music theory or a foreign language, the latest situation on the stock market, your bank balance or a list of reference books. Or the computer can be used as a word processor, displaying words on the screen for editing line by line, without the bother of retyping. It can then transfer the edited copy to paper by printing it out.

The possibilities for the computer-video partnership are almost endless. Its only limits are those of inventiveness and imagination. The system is so flexible that it can be tailored to your own personal needs: to supply a recipe idea for tonight's dinner, to help teach your child to do mental arithmetic or to spell, to turn on your television in time for your favourite show, or to list your video recordings. Whatever the future holds, it can only improve the scope of the partnership.

Video security

To set a machine to catch a thief: this is the challenge facing security science as criminals update their techniques to avoid detection. As a visual medium, video can do what other inanimate detectives cannot: a thief recorded on video is not only identified, but actually seen in the act. Security recordings must include a time and date on every frame. It is this which connects the suspect conclusively to the time and place of a crime. Video recordings are now accepted as evidence in courts of law in the USA and the UK.

Security video usually takes the form of CCTV (closed circuit television), where the cameras are connected to the monitors and recorders by cable. Connection by radio is less common. In large stores, overtly displayed cameras and even monitors are a common sight. Elsewhere, a row of monitors, fed by several cameras, will be under surveillance. Many of the visible cameras are dummies; while the live ones keep watch, the dummy cameras act as an effective deterrent. Often staff, as well as the public, are monitored. Cameras with lenses which can film through a hole the size of a pinhole are installed in offices and near checkpoints to combat pilfering; more conspicuous cameras are used at delivery points.

For private homes, one of the most useful devices is the video door telephone. A camera set into the wall by a door is activated by the bellpush; a small screen indoors displays the caller's face. Occupier and visitor can speak through an intercom.

Another form of home video security is a network of concealed pinhole cameras inside the house, which can be turned on from a distance by a radio transmitter (such as a Citizen's Band radio) and the whole house surveyed with a portable monitor. If the network is connected to a telephone, the user can phone a radio signal across the world, and receive pictures across the air, without anyone having to lift the telephone receiver in the house.

Complexes such as oil refineries may use cameras to aid their security staff. If an alarm signal sounds, the guard checks the monitors to make sure the alarm is not false. Video is rarely used to trigger alarms; its movement sensors are indiscriminate, and false alarms result. However, in places where movement is unusual, such as bank vaults, it can be used in this way.

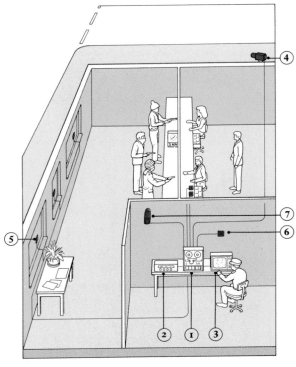

Caught in the act, a team of bank raiders in London are captured on video. A concealed camera was set in operation by a bank employee. Video cameras were not common in banks in the UK in the early eighties, when this raid took place, and the raider was not cautious about keeping his face concealed. The vital time and date appeared on a clock in the background.

This kind of video security must be switched on manually, as the camera cannot tell suspicious movements from everyday ones. A foot switch under the counter, well hidden from view, is sometimes used.

Real-time recording is helpful in this kind of incident, but a recorder left to run by itself would be a time-lapse machine, taking a few frames a second, or minute, allowing it to record for up to 100 hours.

The diagram, *above*, shows how a security system might be arranged. In the room are an open-reel VTR, **1**, a time-encoder, **2**, and a monitor, **3**.

Inside the bank, a small camera, **7**, is concealed. Security cameras are usually monochrome, making them cheaper than colour movie cameras. By the back entrance, a larger camera, **4**, in a weatherproof case, is a visible deterrent.

Alarm sensors, **5**, on doors and windows will set off an alarm, **6**, if there is a break-in while the bank is empty, and can be set to start the recorder.

Screen games

Video games are the new addiction of the eighties. Not only have they revolutionized entertainment, with machines blasting out intergalactic warfare everywhere from the arcade to supermarket, they have also spearheaded the march of computer technology into the home.

In 1972 Pong, a screen table tennis, became the first home video game. Designed for use in conjuction with a television, it consisted of a console containing a collection of integrated circuits to produce the picture, plus rotary hand controls to manipulate the bats on the screen. This, and many similar games that followed, all had the game selection built in, finite and permanent; a system described as 'dedicated' and still used, albeit with refinements, in arcade video games.

For home video games the next step was the semi-programmable game, introduced in 1975 and made possible by the use of individual silicon chips, custom-designed to generate several games. The largest number of games these systems offered was ten.

More far-reaching was the following move to separate the components, making the expensive bulk of the system constant and thus a once-only purchase, and leaving the individual game programs as a series of cartridges (usually called carts), to be slotted in. The constants are a master console, containing the microcomputer for interpreting the carts; the power supply; the television game switch box for attaching to the VHF antenna connection of the television; and the assorted hand controls. The only variables are the chip-containing carts, but the information they contain is permanent, like an audio disk, not re-recordable like a tape. Further refinements have permitted one cart to contain several games with many permutations in the level of difficulty and number of players; most sophisticated are the programmable consoles.

Video games of the future will allow opponents thousands of miles apart to compete, with the aid of a telephone link-up, and have displays that react to the spoken word or the point of a finger. Aside from recreation, or even education, video games promise to prove themselves increasingly valuable medical aids for relieving depression, and helping in the rehabilitation of stroke patients through the relearning of manipulative skills and hand-eye coordination.

Caring for video games
Video game carts are tough enough to withstand rough handling, even by small children, but following these rules will prolong their lives:—

1 Keep game carts clean and dry. Dirt, damp and grease can all impair action.
2 When not in use, keep game carts in their storage cases or in a covered box.
3 Do not let carts become baked by the sun or by the heat from a radiator as this may distort them.
4 When changing games, always switch off the master console to protect both the carts and the console.
5 Do not use force when inserting or removing game carts.
6 For the best game image, turn down the regular TV contrast and manually tune the picture on the display.
7 If games are to be played on more than one TV set in the house, fit each TV with a TV/game switch box to save moving this from set to set.
8 Make sure that players do not tug on the wires connecting the hand controls to the console.

The Intellivision games system has hand controls, *above*, which reflect some of the newest trends in home video games. Each control consists of a key pad with 12 keys numbered 0 to 9, plus keys labelled 'Enter' and 'Clear'. Below is a direction disk; when touched it can sense 16 different directions.

To play a specific game such as 'Space Battle' the player of Intellivision slots a special overlay on top of the keypad. Used in conjunction with a detailed instruction booklet, this overlay gives precise guidance, permitting the player to determine many different aspects of one game.

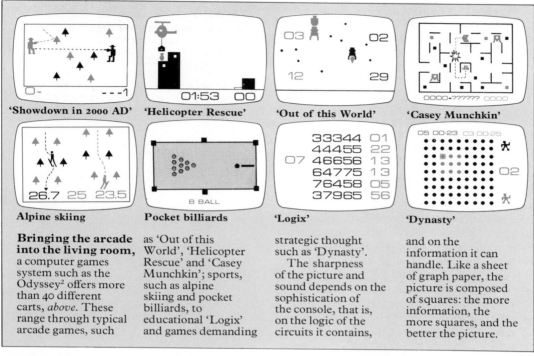

'Showdown in 2000 AD' **'Helicopter Rescue'** **'Out of this World'** **'Casey Munchkin'**

Alpine skiing **Pocket billiards** **'Logix'** **'Dynasty'**

Bringing the arcade into the living room, a computer games system such as the Odyssey² offers more than 40 different carts, *above*. These range through typical arcade games, such

as 'Out of this World', 'Helicopter Rescue' and 'Casey Munchkin'; sports, such as alpine skiing and pocket billiards, to educational 'Logix' and games demanding

strategic thought such as 'Dynasty'.
 The sharpness of the picture and sound depends on the sophistication of the console, that is, on the logic of the circuits it contains,

and on the information it can handle. Like a sheet of graph paper, the picture is composed of squares: the more information, the more squares, and the better the picture.

The heart of a computerized games system is its microcomputer or master console, *right*, plugged into the TV via a games switch box. The keys on the console allow games to be programmed to select different speeds and degrees of difficulty: A 'Basic' (computer language) cart converts the console into a small home computer.

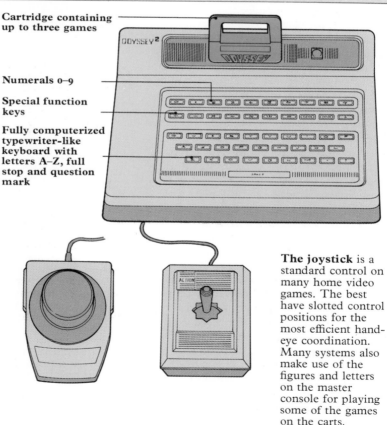

Cartridge containing up to three games

Numerals 0–9

Special function keys

Fully computerized typewriter-like keyboard with letters A–Z, full stop and question mark

The hand control, which rotates freely through 360°, is used with many bat and ball games. The cart, which is controlled by the master console, supplies the ball to the screen, while the player turns the control to alter the position of the bat in an attempt to hit the ball.

The joystick is a standard control on many home video games. The best have slotted control positions for the most efficient hand-eye coordination. Many systems also make use of the figures and letters on the master console for playing some of the games on the carts.

Intelligent video

The computer is the superchild of electronics, the technology fundamental to both computers and video. It is a high-speed calculator with an electronic memory. Very detailed instructions are typed in special languages which bridge the gap between English and the binary machine code in which the computer 'thinks'.

There are already some computers which can receive and reply in spoken English, but the program which enables them to do this must still be written in a symbolic code, where words, letters and numbers stand for specific instructions. These are translated, via binary, into thousands of electrical currents. The signals thus built up allow the computer to calculate, and to operate, through electrical switches, all kinds of machinery.

A computer is no longer just the fortress-like mainframe (a massive machine using far more complex processors and needing a team of expert operators) beloved of science fiction movies. This is the age of the microcomputer, looking like a typewriter and using a single large chip which is called a microprocessor. It is slower than a mainframe, but quite fast enough to be useful in the home or to the small business user.

What could a personal computer do for you and your video? For a start, it could index all your recordings and locate each one instantly; keep a record of unused hours of tape; turn your television on and sound a bleep to tell you a film has started.

In the future there could be a choice of over 100 channels. If a key signal were broadcast, the computer could easily identify wanted material: all kinds of sport or, for instance, if the key signal provided sufficient information, just highlights of the ladies' long jump. It could even edit out commercials.

Computers have already proved effective as teaching aids. They do not suffer from boredom or impatience, and slow pupils get on as well as quick ones, each learning at his or her own speed. Whether used with a library of video tapes or as part of a fully interactive system, which can test the student, rerun the sequence and answer queries, computers, teamed up with video, will give a more personal education. It is well known that children have none of the techno-fear that besets adults.

Basic is the name of one of the most popular languages used to program microcomputers. A program is a set of instructions which are entered via the keyboard into the computer's memory circuits. Once entered, the program can be activated by keying in another instruction, already known to the computer, which will then automatically go through a series of events it has memorized.

This is a program for a simple guessing game you can play with a computer:

```
1ϕ PRINT "HIGH-LOW NUMBER GAME"
2ϕ A = INT (RND( I )*Iϕϕ): B = ϕ
3ϕ INPUT "YOUR GUESS, BETWEEN I–Iϕϕ"; C:
   Iϕϕ LET B = B + I
4ϕ IF C > A, THEN PRINT "TOO HIGH": GO TO
   3ϕ
5ϕ IF C < A, THEN PRINT "TOO LOW": GO TO
   3ϕ
6ϕ IF C = A, THEN PRINT "CORRECT, IN"; B;
   "TRIES": END
```

Iϕ is a number identifying a line of the program. The symbol ϕ distinguishes zero from the letter O. Quotation marks tell the computer that when the program is activated it must print everything within the marks.

In line 2ϕ, A is an unspecified figure which the computer must define. It must be an integer, or whole number (INT), and

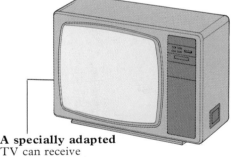

A specially adapted TV can receive teletext or viewdata. Modified further, it can receive computer data through either system, This can be fed directly into a computer memory.

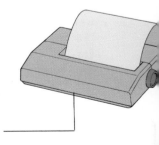

A hard copy printer transfers data from the computer directly on to paper, either by printing like a typewriter, or by burning characters on to heat-sensitive paper with a tiny electric current.

must be chosen at random (RND) between 1 and 100. The computer already knows that it must deal with the command in the inner brackets first, and work outward. When generating the random number, it first takes a fraction of 1 (that is, between 0 and 1). It then multiplies this (* means multiply) by 100 to give a number between 1 and 100, which it rounds to an integer. The colon marks the start of a new instruction in the same line. Another unspecified figure, B, must be equal to zero at this point.

In line 30, the computer is instructed to print out an invitation to guess a number. C must be defined by the player, and so stands for his guess. Any unspecified figure preceded by "if" in this program must be specified from outside the program, that is, by the operator. At this point, the value of B is increased by 1, thus keeping count of the player's guesses.

In lines 40 and 50, the computer is told to return the player to line 30 if the guess is too high or too low.

In line 60, if the guess equals the computer's random number A, the number of guesses made by the player is displayed on the screen at B. The player with the lowest score is the winner.

As satellite and cable TV become widespread, computer data will be sent by the same channels.

Home owners could use a video door phone to speak a code to their computer to gain entrance.

This Apple II, *below*, has a VDU (a monitor designed to be used with computers) and two disk drive units. Flexible (floppy) disks are the usual form of information storage for microcomputers. Illustrated here are some devices which could be linked to a home computer.

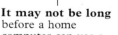

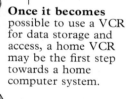

Once it becomes possible to use a VCR for data storage and access, a home VCR may be the first step towards a home computer system.

This little graphics tablet enables the user to draw on the computer monitor by making an electrical contact with the tablet and a stylus.

A computer joystick enables the operator to move a symbol on the screen by hand.
Computers will soon recognize visitors (via a video camera) by their appearance. A time-lapse VTR could then record strangers.

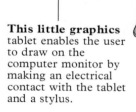

It may not be long before a home computer can use a phone-answering device to identify callers by voice patterns, pass on messages to them, and answer their queries.

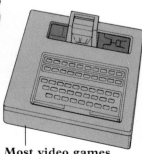

Most video games have an internal microprocessor, but some are so sophisticated that they are almost computers.

Visual display

Whether you start with a VCR and move on to a microcomputer or vice versa, the visual centre of the system will be a television screen. The video signals feeding a computer monitor are the same as those used in broadcast television. Only differences in the way the signals pass from one to the other limit the interaction of VCR, computer and monitor and these differences may vanish before long. Most microcomputers are designed to use a television screen. Some will only display in monochrome, but some can use colour as well. The future may see one large screen, capable of being split into many small screens, handling all the home's video.

A VCR is not fully compatible with a microcomputer. It can be used as an archive memory, but needs a special interface (a device which translates signals from one type of machine to another). However, new interfaces are under development which may allow a home VCR to be used as a data store for a microcomputer.

The advent of viewdata is bringing television and computers closer together. It will soon be routine for microcomputers to order and receive ready-made computer programs by viewdata – perhaps the most direct form of direct mail yet invented.

Some home microcomputers can generate coloured graphics, like those used for teletext, on a colour television or VDU. Coloured captions and pseudo-animations can be created, and even transferred to video with a camera. Some owners may find that their VCRs can record their graphics directly from a television in the normal way.

A professional art computer, by contrast, provides hundreds of colours, can imitate the strokes of a paint brush and could be used to broadcast pictures directly on a television network.

Computer-controlled video can be seen daily on television in the form of multiple or rotating pictures. These need a frame store, a computer which scans a frame of video point by point, gives each point digital coordinates for location, brightness and colour, and immediately displays these on a screen in any order and position. In this way it can move the image around the screen. The speed needed to do so much, so quickly, calls for an expensive multiprocessor computer, so this electronic trickery will remain beyond the microcomputer user.

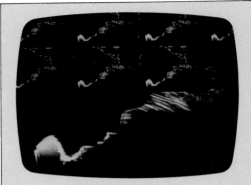

This picture shows an effect devised by using a frame storer. Each point of a single frame is encoded digitally. Enough points are then scanned to reproduce the picture in miniature.

A single frame is here scanned into an area defined by a tambourine. As the tambourine turns, fewer of the horizontal points of the inside frame are scanned, and it also appears to turn.

The rotation of a frame in the same plane as the screen is a newly developed effect. It is also possible to rotate only part of the picture, and increase and decrease the size of the turning area.

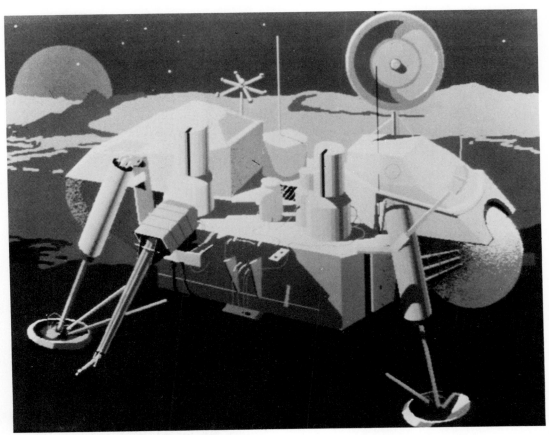

Artists creating computer graphics today are no longer restricted to defining each point on their drawing through a keyboard. Instead, the work area might be an electronically sensitive tablet upon which lines can be drawn with a special stylus, or a light-pen. The signals generated are interpreted by a computer and the picture displayed on a colour monitor.

An area of the tablet will be designated as the paintbox: by touching the right spot, the artist can call up a specific colour on to the screen. Once there, the artist can use it freely until another colour is called up by touching the paintbox on the screen. There may also be a mix mode, so that several colours can be blended, either on a special area of the tablet designated as a palette, or via the drawing surface on the screen.

The range of effects available from the most advanced systems is startling; paint textures and even the handling characteristics of different kinds of paint, pen and crayon, can be imitated.

The picture, *above*, was generated on Flair, a system in current commercial use. It offers a paintbox of 256 colours, and the blending is made more natural by a process called anti-aliasing: each dot on the monitor screen can be varied from its own colour to that of the next, as required. This kind of process is not simple. It is said that computer art enjoys the most advanced electronics outside space science laboratories.

The sequence, *above,* shows how a computer graphic might be drawn in order to rerun the sequence to make a simple animation. This is known as a pseudo-animation. A true animation is a series of still frames, but this is actually a real-time recording of a piece of art-work developing gradually, line by line.

Understanding a specification

All video hardware, be it VCR, camera or power adaptor, has its technical specification. This is usually printed in the owner's manual, and in the manufacturer's brochures.

The specification, or 'spec', is a technical description of a machine's capabilities. Some of the details will be common to all machines working on one set of television standards, American NTSC for instance, and others will outline the capabilities of the particular model being described.

This mass of figures can be daunting, but with a little effort the video buyer can put the data to good use when comparing one machine with another, or when choosing items to make up a complete video system. Here, some sample features taken from hypothetical VCR and camera specifications are explained.

Video recorders and adaptors
Power source: 120v AC ± 10%
The VCR runs on mains (alternating current electricity), at the voltage given, with plus or minus 10% allowance for AC voltage fluctuations. Some VCRs have alternative settings, or wide tolerances, between 220 and 240 volts for instance. Portapacks and cameras use DC (direct current) at 12 volts.
Frequency: 50 Hz (UK); 60 Hz (USA)
Electrical frequency is measured in cycles per second (Hertz or Hz). The VCR must be designed to work on the local supply frequency. Some have a general tolerance between 48 and 62 Hz.
Operating position: Horizontal ± 10%
Home decks need to operate horizontally or very nearly so. 10% is a variation of up to 6 degrees of tilt in either direction.
Relative humidity: 30% to 80%
This gives the percentage of moisture in the air, below condensation levels, in which it is safe to operate the VCR. If condensation is forming in the room, it may also form inside the VCR, causing damage. If the air is dry, as for instance in a closed, centrally heated room, this may cause warping inside the VCR, which can also cause malfunction.
Video recording system: Rotary two-head helical scan, slant azimuth.
This describes the recording system used by all home video systems. Helical scan describes the slanted path the tape takes around the circular head drum; slant azimuth means that the video heads record at an angle greater or smaller than 90 degrees to the tape. Some machines have two extra heads for still frame.
Video signal to noise: More than 42 dBs
Signal to noise (S/N) is the ratio of video signal (picture information) to noise (interference) which the system produces. 'dB' stands for decibel, a measurement of ratio such that with every additional 3 dB the signal strength doubles. A 42-dB S/N ratio is a good reading for a VCR; below 40 would be poor. The higher the figure, the better the picture will be. This ratio is given for the luminance (brightness) part of the video signal, which is more crucial to the sharpness of focus and fineness of contrast than the chrominance (colour) signal.

Resolution: 190 lines centre screen
or: **3 MHz (− 15 dB)**
If a television camera is trained on a test pattern of fine black lines on a white background, the lines will be distinguishable at the centre of the screen. The more lines visible, the higher the resolution and the sharper the picture.

The resolution may be given in MHz (megahertz). At 3 MHz, the VCR is capable of receiving signals over a bandwidth of three million Hz. The higher the bandwidth of the VCR, the more finely distinguished the signals it can receive and, therefore, the higher the resolution. A bandwidth of 3 MHz is normal for a VCR, and is equivalent to about 190 lines.

'− 15 dB' means that the measurement was taken when the VCR was producing a video signal 15 dB below the maximum signal output. A maximum signal of 0.7 V (volts) gives true white on the screen, and 0 volts a true black. A signal 15 dB down on the maximum represents variations between light and dark grey, so that although lines will be visible, they will not be sharply distinguished. Resolution readings are normally given for the luminance signal. Chrominance (colour) signals do not need such a high resolution, as the human eye is less sensitive to the focus of colour.
Video input and output: 1 V p–p, 75 ohms, unbalanced
This is standard for all video signals. When transmitted along a cable, the strength of a video signal is one volt from its highest to its lowest points, from − 0.3 V to + 0.7 V. '− 0.3' describes not an absence of voltage, but a voltage in the reverse direction. Zero volts is the point at which the television screen is perfectly black, and is called the black level. Below 0 volts is the synchronization signal, called the 'sync pulse', which ensures that the electron beam which scans the screen begins its path at the same two points every time it scans. (As a television picture, or frame, is broadcast in two fields, each covering an alternate set of lines on the screen, the sweep pattern has two alternate starting points, one at the top left, one at top centre). This gives a perfectly aligned frame, or a '2:1 fully interlaced picture'. Some very cheap cameras give a random interlaced picture, which is not so good. The video signal is also sometimes described as 'sync negative'.

75 ohms (Ω) is the standard measure of the electrical resistance used in television systems. A cable has little resistance, but its input and output connections must have the appropriate resistance. If this is too low, the signal will rush through, stretching out and losing definition; if too high, the signal will bounce back, sending reflections down the cable and causing ghost images on the screen.

Since the signal is varying, the resistance is different from that for a constant current and is called impedance. 75 ohms impedance is standard for television cable, as the impedance of the cable must match the input and output resistance of the video equipment.
Frequency response: 60 to 10,000 Hz ± 6 dB
Audio, as well as video, signals are measured in

Hz. The higher the frequency, the higher the pitch of the sound transmitted and vice versa. Therefore, the wider the frequency response, the better the sound quality.

'± 6 dB' means that the relative loudness of one part of the sound signal over another can vary by as much as 12 dB.

Distortion: less than 7%

The purity of the waveform from the audio track will be disrupted by electrical noise picked up inside the machine by less than 7%. (Video sound is low fidelity: high fidelity (hi-fi) would allow only around 0.05% distortion.)

Audio input: 100 k ohms, − 10 dB
   or: **− 20 dB (low impedance)**
       (0 dB = 0.775 rms)

For professional and hi-fi audio, a reference level for signal strength is set at 0.775 volts, and taken to be 0 dB. 'Rms' is a method of measuring the voltage of an alternating signal.

Video sound is usually transmitted at a signal strength below that used for hi-fi. This is not a measure of sound quality, but means that if sound is recorded from a hi-fi source the signal may be strong and likely to distort.

Audio sources, such as microphones, are described in terms of their impedance. 100 kilohms (100,000 ohms) is a high impedance; 600 ohms is a common low impedance. A low impedance source may work with a high impedance input; a high impedance source will not work with a low impedance input.

Audio signal to noise: More than 50 dB

This is a good audio S/N ration for a VCR. Less than 44 dB would be poor; hi-fi, however, requires around 70 dB.

External microphone input: − 66 dB, 2 k ohms

'− 66 dB' is, in this instance, the minimum input level the microphone must give for good results. 2 k ohms indicates that the input is low impedance, but, being borderline, will probably tolerate some high impedance microphones.

In audio specifications, a distinction is made between 'mike' (a microphone connection) and 'line' (a cable connection between two machines).

Antenna: 75-ohm external terminal (VHF)
         300-ohm external terminals (UHF)
   or: **75-ohm asymmetrical. Max input voltage 25V (sync level)**

These are standard impedence values needed for VHF and UHF broadcasts. Asymmetrical refers to the unbalanced coaxial cable. The maximum voltage the antenna input can receive is 25 millivolts. For technical reasons, the video signal is broadcast inverted, with the picture information at the lowest power and the sync pulse and black level at the highest power. Hence the highest voltage the antenna can receive is at sync level.

Input sensitivity: 120 μV rms
   or: **TV channels 21 to 68 UHF**

In the UK, broadcast transmissions go out on channels designated numbers 21 to 68. 120 μV is the signal power the antenna must supply to the VCR from the signal it receives. A good antenna can develop more power from a weak signal. The lower this figure, the more likely the VCR is to give an acceptable picture from a weak signal. Check the S/N ratio to see how good a picture is being claimed by the manufacturer.

Modulator output voltage: 3mV rms ± 3 dB

The RF output from the VCR to the television gives a signal of 3 millivolts with a variation over a 6 dB range. If the VCR gives out much more than 5 millivolts the television may be damaged.

Modulator frequency: Channel 30 to 43 (factory set to channel 36)

In order to transmit recorded video from tape to a television receiver, the RF modulator transfers the signal to a channel to which the receiver is tuned. This will be one of the television frequencies in use locally, tuned in at the factory, but may need re-tuning if that frequency is actually being occupied by a local television station.

Cameras

These are some points from the specification which apply solely to cameras:

Pickup system: single-frequency carrier

This merely describes the standard system used with the local colour system. This example is used with NTSC.

Viewfinder: 1.5-in electronic

1.5 in is the normal screen size for television-type viewfinders. If the viewfinder is optical or TTL (through the lens) check to see how accurately it shows the picture you are shooting, especially when zooming.

Colour temperature: indoor/outdoor

This describes the range of settings over which the camera can adjust the picture colour in different lights. Some cameras have four or five settings for colour temperature, but in general 'indoor'/'outdoor' or 'daylight'/'tungsten' are the minimum variations which a good video camera should have.

Synchronization: internal

All home video cameras generate their own sync pulse internally. Professional cameras can be synchronized externally from another piece of video equipment.

Resolution: 270 lines

The resolution figure for a camera is higher than that for a VCR but, in practice, this makes little difference to the picture finally obtained on video tape.

Minimum illumination: 100 lux, F1.4

Lux is a measurement of the amount of light needed; below this amount, the camera will not record a reasonable picture.

F1.4 describes the aperture setting needed for shooting at 100 lux. It is the widest setting; a telephoto setting would give a poorer picture.

Lens: f1.4 × 6 zoom lens; f = 11 to 70 mm

This means that the image is magnified six times between the wide angle and telephoto setting. 'f' designates the focal length of the camera, here in millimetres.

Most home video cameras have fixed lenses. A few have removable lenses, which normally use a mount called a C-mount.

TV standards

The technology by which television signals are broadcast has been developed over a long period. Consequently there are many different methods for transmitting the colour and black and white signals, and for transmitting these signals through the electronics inside the television receiver to its screen.

When video equipment is bought to be used within an area which uses television standards compatible with it, all is well. Problems of compatibility arise when equipment is bought to be taken overseas, or when recorded tapes are sent for replay in another country. In the former instance, the answer is to establish what systems are used in the place of purchase and the eventual destination and, if they are different, to consult a specialist video dealer about buying the most suitable equipment and making any necessary adjustments and modifications. This is often a straightforward process, but requires advice.

In the latter instance, a solution may be harder to find. An ordinary VCR cannot be set up to replay tapes on more than one system. A partial answer is a triple-standard machine, which, however, does not give equally good results with all television systems. Sometimes, an extra gadget can be added to the VCR to allow it to replay on one system tapes recorded on a variant of that system.

The most crucial differences between one set of television systems and another are in the colour standards, as the colour signal is the hardest to encode and decode without loss of picture resolution. There are three basic colour systems: NTSC (National Television Standards Committee), used primarily in the USA and Japan, PAL (Phase Alteration Line) used in the UK, much of Europe and South America, and Australia, and SECAM (Sequential Colour with Memory) used in France, other parts of Europe and Africa, the Middle East and the USSR. There are variations: PAL-M uses a different colour subcarrier, and SECAM is divided into SECAM V (vertical) and SECAM H (horizontal), along with other minor modifications. There are also six monochrome systems: British, Belgian, CCIR (International Radio Consultative Committee), French, OIRT (International Radio and Television Organization) and USA. The differences between these are less crucial than the differences between the colour systems. In addition, there are fourteen separate systems for broadcasting the whole television signal, including sound, and these are designated A to N.

Table 1: World television standards

A specialist can modify video equipment for use with a set of television systems for which it was not designed, once the colour standard, television system and the numbers of the local television channels are known. Table 1, *below*, gives this information for a sample selection of nations where video is becoming popular. Also listed are the electricity supply voltages, on which the equiment must be able to operate, and the frequency in Hertz (cycles per second) of the AC supply. This is, with few exceptions, the same as the number of fields per second broadcast by the local television system, as the number of fields was originally derived from the supply frequency.

Country	System	Channels	Voltage	Hz	B/W
NTSC					
Bahamas	M	A13	110/240/415	60	USA
Canada	M	A2–13, A14–40	120/240	50	USA
Hawaii	M	A2–13	120/240	60	USA
Japan	M	J1–12; 27–62	100/200	50; 60	USA
Mexico	M	A2–23; A14–45	110/220	60	USA
Philippines	M	A2–13	110/220/240	60	USA
(US Forces)	(M)	(A8, 28–74)			
USA	M	A2–13, A14–83	120/230/240	60	USA
PAL					
Algeria	B	E5–11	127/220/380	50	CCIR
Argentina	N	A2–13	220/380	50	USA
Australia	B	Aus 0–11	240/415	50	CCIR
Austria	B;G	E2–12; 21–68	220/380	50	CCIR
Azores	B	E7–9	110/220/380	50	USA
Bahrain	B	E4	220/240	50	CCIR
Belgium	B;H	E2–11; 21–69	220/380	50	Belgian
Denmark	B	E3–10	220/380	50	CCIR
Germany, Fed. Rep.	B;G	E2–11; 21–60	220/380	50	CCIR
Gibraltar	B	E6–11	240/415	50	CCIR
Hong Kong	I	E21–60	200/220/346	50	British
Iceland	B	E3–11	220/380	50	CCIR
Indonesia	B	E4–10	127/220/380	50	CCIR
Ireland, Rep.	I	A–J, 29–43	220/380	50	Belgian
Israel	B;G	E5–11; 25–56	230/400	50	CCIR

Italy	B;G	It A–H; 21–34	127/220/380	50	CCIR
Jordan	B	E3–9	220/380	50	CCIR
Luxembourg	C;G	E7, 27	110/220	50	Belgian
Malaysia	B	E2–10	230/240/415	50	CCIR
Netherlands	B;G	E2–12; 21–60	127/220/380	50	CCIR
New Zealand	B	NZ1–10	230/400/415	50	CCIR
Nigeria	B	E2–12	230/400	50	CCIR
Norway	B;G	E2–12; 44	230	50	CCIR
Pakistan	B	E4–10	230/400	50	CCIR
Portugal	B;G	E2–11; 25–46	220/380	50	CCIR
Singapore	B;G	E5–12; 21–34	230/400	50	CCIR
South Africa	I	14–13, 21–68	220/230/380	50	British
Spain	B;G	E2–11; 21–68	127/220/380	50	CCIR
Sudan	B	E5–7	240/415	50	CCIR
Switzerland	B;G	E2–12; 21–63	220/380	50	CCIR
Syria	B	E4–9	115/220/380	50	CCIR
United Kingdom	I	21–68	240/415	60	British

SECAM

Cyprus	B(H)	E5–11	115/400	50	CCIR
France	L(V)	21–65	127/220/380	50	French
Greece	B;G(H)	E5–12; 21–69	220/380	50	CCIR
Iraq	B(H)	E5–12	110/220/380	50	CCIR
Lebanon	B(V)	E2–11	110–190	50	CCIR
Luxembourg	L(V)	21	380	50	Belgian
Saudi Arabia	B(H)	E5–10	120/208	50 + 60	CCIR
United Arab Republic	B(V)	E3–11	110/220/380	50	CCIR
USSR	D;K(V)	R1–12; 21–69	127/220/380	50	OIRT
Zimbabwe	B	E2–11	230/240	50	CCIR

Table 2: World television systems

In the first column of Table 1, *above*, is listed the designation letter, A to N, of the world's television broadcast systems. In Table 2, *below*, a selection of the most important characteristics of these systems is listed. Systems A, C, E, F and H are now rarely used.

The number of lines describes the number of times the electron beam in a television receiver sweeps across the screen in a single frame, and the number of fields is given for one second in time (a field is half a frame). The colour subcarrier frequency is chosen to separate the colour from the brightness in the television signal. Systems M and N have a lower frequency because their vision signal bandwidth is narrower than normal. The vision and sound separation is very important, since, once correctly set up, it is possible to tune the set to different television channels keeping the sound automatically tuned into the vision.

The vision modulation tells an engineer whether the brightest (white) part of the signal or the darkest (sync pulse) is broadcast at the highest signal power, and sound modulation tells whether the sound is amplitude modulated (by varying the strength of the signal) or frequency modulated (by varying the frequency of the signal). With these basic facts, a television engineer can assess a piece of video equipment for modification to deal with local television conditions.

System	Number of lines	Number of fields	Colour subcarrier	Vision/sound separation	Vision modulation	Sound modulation
A	405	50	none	− 3.5 MHz	Positive	AM
B	625	50	4.43 MHz	+ 5.5 MHz	Negative	FM
C	625	50	4.43 MHz	+ 5.5 MHz	Positive	AM
D	625	50	4.43 MHz	+ 6.5 MHz	Negative	FM
E	819	50	none	+ 11.15 MHz	Positive	AM
F	819	50	none	+ 5.5 MHz	Positive	AM
G	625	50	4.43 MHz	+ 5.5 MHz	Negative	FM
H	625	50	4.43 MHz	+ 5.5 MHz	Negative	FM
I	625	50	4.43 MHz	+ 6 MHz	Negative	FM
K	625	50	4.43 MHz	+ 6.5 MHz	Negative	FM
K1	625	50	4.43 MHz	+ 6.5 MHz	Negative	FM
L	625	50	4.43 MHz	+ 6.5 MHz	Positive	AM
M	525	60	3.38 MHz	+ 4.5 MHz	Negative	FM
N	625	50	3.38 MHz	+ 4.5 MHz	Negative	FM

Names and addresses

Listed below is a selection of addresses in the UK which the video owner might find useful in the case of query or complaint. Each address is followed by a brief note of the range of the company's services, or the goods manufactured. Normally, the owner's first point of enquiry would be his or her own video dealer, but if contacting a manufacturer, ask for the customer liaison department or the product manager. Manufacturers find it easier to be helpful if the customer is as clear as possible about the facts surrounding the enquiry or complaint when writing or calling.

Agfa-Gevaert Ltd., Great West Road, Brentford, Middlesex
(01) 560 2131
Video tapes (VHS, Betamax, LVC, SVC, U-matic).

Akai (UK) Ltd., 12 Silver Jubilee Way, Haslemere Heathrow Estate, Hounslow, Middlesex TW4 6NF
(01) 897 7171
VCRs (VHS), portable systems, cameras, video tapes (VHS), televisions.

Association of Video Dealers, Greystones, Brighton Road, Godalming, Surrey GU7 1PL
Godalming (04868) 23429
Queries and complaints concerning member dealers.

AV Distributors (London) Ltd., 26 Park Road, Baker Street, London NW1 4SH
(01) 935 8161
Agents for Bilora tripods and lighting equipment.

BASF (UK) Ltd., Haddon House, 2–4 Fitzroy Street, London W1P 5AD
(01) 388 4200
Video tapes (VHS, Betamax, VCC, VCR).

R.R. Beard, 10 Trafalgar Avenue, London SE15 6NR
(01) 703 3136/9638
Lighting equipment.

Bell & Howell A-V Ltd., Alperton House, Bridgwater Road, Wembley, Middlesex HA0 1EG
(01) 903 5411
Agents for JVC professional video equipment.

BIB Audio/Video Products Ltd., Kelsey House, Wood Lane End, Hemel Hempstead, Herts HP2 4RQ
Hemel Hempstead (0442) 61291
Video accessories.

British Video Association, 10 Maddox Street, London W1R 9PN
(01) 499 3131
Investigates video piracy and breach of copyright in prerecorded tapes.

Burton Manor, Burton, South Wirral, Cheshire
(051) 336 5172
Short and weekend video courses.

Colortran UK, P.O. Box 5, Burrell Way, Thetford, Norfolk IP24 3RB
Thetford (0842) 2484
Lighting equipment.

Comprehensive Video Supply (UK), 565 Kingston Road, London SW20 8SA
(01) 543 3131
Video accessories from lighting equipment to labels.

The Consumers' Association, 14 Buckingham Street, London WC2N 6DS
(01) 839 1222
Publishes *Which?* magazine; general advice on purchasing and consumers' rights to members.

Council for Educational Technology (CET), 3 Devonshire Street, London W14 2BA
(01) 580 7553
Provides information on media courses and specifications for audiovisual equipment.

Educational Television Association, 86 Micklegate, York YO1 1J2
York (0904) 29701
Professional association to bring together institutions and individuals using television in education and training.

EMI Tapes Ltd., Alma Road, Windsor, Berks SL4 3JA
Windsor (95) 59171
Videotapes (VHS, Betamax)

Grundig International Ltd., Newlands Park, London SE26 5NQ
(01) 659 2468
VCRs (Video 2000), cameras, video tapes (VCC), video disk (LaserVision).

Hitachi Denshi (UK) Ltd., Lodge House, Lodge Road, London NW4 4DQ
(01) 202 4311
Professional video cameras and control systems.

Hitachi Sales (UK) Ltd., Hitachi House, Station Road, Hayes, Middlesex UB3 4DR
(01) 848 8787
VCRs (VHS), portable systems, cameras, video tape (VHS), televisions, accessories.

Introphoto Ltd., Prior's Way, Maidenhead, Berks SL6 2HP
Maidenhead (0628) 7441
Velbon tripods, Hoya photographic filters.

ITT Consumer Products (UK) Ltd., Chester Hall Lane, Basildon, Essex
Basildon (0268) 3040
VCRs (Video 2000, VHS), televisions.

JVC UK Ltd., Eldonwall Trading Estate, Staples Corner, London NW2
(01) 450 2621
VCRs (VHS), portable systems, cameras, video tapes (VHS), televisions, accessories, video disk (VHD).

Kennett Engineering Co. Ltd., The Lodge Works, Drayton Parslow, nr. Milton Keynes, Bucks
Mursley (029672) 605
Tripods.

Maxell (UK) Ltd., 1 Tyburn Lane, Harrow, Middlesex HA1 3AF
(01) 423 0688
Video tapes (VHS, Betamax, U-matic).

Memorex (UK) Ltd., Memorex House, 94–104 Church Street, Staines, Middlesex TW18 4XU
Staines (0784) 51488
Video tapes (VHS, Betamax).

Michael Cox Electronics Ltd., Hanworth Trading Estate, Hampton Road West, Feltham, Middlesex TW13 6DH
(01) 898 6091
Includes mixing and switching equipment suitable for the smaller professional unit.

Mitsubishi Electric (UK) Ltd., Otterspool Way, Watford WD2 8LD
Watford (0923) 40566
VCRs (VHS), televisions.

The National Audio-Visual Aids Centre (NAVAC), Paxton Place, London SE27
(01) 670 4247
Short courses in video production.

National Panasonic Ltd., 308–318 Bath Road, Slough
Slough (0753) 34522
VCRs (VHS), portable systems, cameras, video tape (VHS), televisions, accessories.

Nordmende (UK) Ltd., Units 8–9 Faraday Road, Rabans Lane, Aylesbury, Bucks
Aylesbury (0296) 20501
VCRs (VHS), portable systems, cameras, video tape (VHS), televisions, accessories.

North East London Polytechnic, Short Courses Unit, Longbridge Road, Dagenham, Essex RU8 2AS
(01) 597 7591
Short courses in video production and technique for amateurs and professionals.

Pelling & Cross Ltd., 104 Baker Street, London W1M 2AR
(01) 487 5411
Industrial video hire, including VHS, Betamax; agents for Gitzo, Manfrotto tripods.

Philips Video/Audio, City House, 420–430 London Road, Croydon, Surrey CR9 3QR
(01) 689 2166
Philips Video: VCRs (Video 2000), cameras, video tape (VCC, VCR, LVC), televisions, video games
Philips Audio: video disk (LaserVision).

Polar Video Ltd., 12–18 Brook Mews North, London W2
(01) 724 3736
Video mixer.

Pye Ltd., 137 Ditton Walk, Cambridge, CB5 8QD
Teversham (02205) 2781
VHS (Video 2000), cameras, video tape (VCR, VCC), televisions.

Rank Strand Electric, P.O. Box 70, Great West Road, Brentford, Middlesex
(01) 568 9222
Lighting equipment.

Sanyo Marubeni UK Ltd., Sanyo House, 8 Greycaine Road, Watford, WD2 4UQ
Watford (0923) 46363
VCRs (Betamax), portable systems, video tape (Betamax), televisions.

Sharp Electronics UK Ltd., Sharp House, Thorp Road, Manchester M10 9BE
(061) 205 2333
VCRs (VHS), cameras, televisions.

Sony UK Ltd., Communications Systems Division, Pyrene House, Sunbury-on-Thames, Middlesex
Sunbury-on-Thames (09327) 81211
VCRs and video tape (U-matic; Sony industrial and educational video equipment.

Sony UK Ltd., Consumer Products Division, 134 Regent Street, London W1
(01) 439 3874
VCRs (Betamax, U-matic), portable systems, cameras, video tape (Betamax, U-matic), televisions, telecine, special effects generator.

Survey & General Instrument Co. Ltd., Firecroft Way, Edenbridge, Kent
Edenbridge (0732) 864111
Fujinon, Miller, Quickset tripods.

TDK Tape Distriburors (UK) Ltd., 8th Floor, Pembroke House, Wellesley Road, Croydon CR0 9XW
(01) 680 0023
Video tape (VHS).

Thorn Consumer Electronics Ltd., Great Cambridge Road, Enfield, Middlesex
(01) 363 5353
VCRs (VHS), portable systems, cameras, televisions, video tape (VHS).

3M UK PLC, Recording Materials and Consumer Products Division, P.O. Box 1, Bracknell, Berks
Bracknell (0344) 36726
Video tapes (VHS, Betamax, VCC, U-matic, professional).

Toshiba (UK) Ltd., Toshiba House, Frimely, Camberley, Surrey GU16 5JJ
Camberley (0276) 6222
VCRs (Betamax), video tapes (Betamax), televisions.

Video Electronics Ltd., (VEL), Wigan Road, Atherton, Manchester
Atherton (0942) 882332
Video mixers.

The Video School, 36 Lorne Park Road, Bournemouth, Dorset BH1 1JL
Bournemouth (0202) 28786
Short- and long-term courses in video production.

W. Vinten Ltd., Western Way, Bury St. Edmunds, Suffolk IP33 3TB
Bury St. Eds. (0284) 2121
Tripods.

Glossary of terms

A

Adaptor
A device for converting the format of a plug or socket, for example, from a $\frac{1}{4}$-in (6-mm) jack to a mini-jack.

Amplifier
An electronic device that increases the strength of an electronic signal.

Analog See **Digital**

Aperture
The size of the opening, or iris, in a lens, known as the 'f-stop number'.

Aspect ratio
The horizontal and vertical proportions of a screen. The standard TV format is 4 units of width to 3 units of height.

B

Back projection
The projection of a film or slide on to a translucent screen so that the image can be viewed from the opposite side of the screen to the projector.

Back-space editing
A facility on some VCRs which rolls the tape back slightly each time the camera button is pressed, to give a clean transition from one shot to the next.

Bandwidth
The range of signal frequencies which a piece of equipment can encode or decode.

Boom
An extension arm allowing a microphone to be brought closer to a performer.

C

Camera tube
A glass cathode ray tube using an electron beam to translate the perceived image into electronic signals.

Capacitor
A component used in electronic circuits to store and release voltages.

Cathode
The electrode within a camera or TV tube which emits a beam of electrons to scan or recreate an image.

CCD (Charge coupled device)
A device that replaces the camera tube with a light-sensitive matrix which translates the light falling on each minute portion into an electric charge.

Chrominance signal
The part of the video signal containing the colour signal.

Colour temperature
The colour tonality of a light source, analogous to the colour of a material burning at a specified heat, measured in Kelvins (K).

Commercial cutter
A device for automatically pausing the VCR during commercials.

Control track
A series of signals recorded on the video tape for the VCR to lock onto in playback, to ensure a stable picture.

Crimping tool
A tool for changing a cable end into a connector.

Cycle
In AC (alternating current) a cycle is a complete change from zero voltage to maximum positive voltage, through zero to maximum negative voltage, and back to zero. UK voltage operates on 50 cycles per second; USA voltage operates on 60 cycles per second.

D

Depth of Field
The area (in depth) of a picture which is in focus at any given aperture setting. The smaller the aperture, and the bigger the f-number, the deeper the area in focus.

Dichroic Mirror
A mirror which reflects certain wavelengths of light and allows others to pass through.

Digital
A method of representing a signal by a set of precise numerical values as opposed to a fluctuating current or voltage (analog signal).

Dipole
A VHF antenna.

Director
A reflector plate on a UHF antenna which focuses the signal on the elements.

Dolby System
The trade name of an audio noise-reduction system.

Domestic standard
A standard of technical quality referring to $\frac{1}{2}$-in (12.5-mm) format VCRs designed for the home market. These technical standards are lower than those used in professional equipment.

E

Electrode
A plate at which an electric current is changed into a stream of electrons, or vice versa.

Electron
A negatively charged subatomic particle. (A stream of electrons constitutes an electric current.)

F

Fibre optic
A glass fibre strand capable of transmitting light.

Filter
A transparent material capable of regulating light which passes through it.

Frame
A complete TV picture, composed of 2 fields, which takes 1/25 of a second (PAL) or 1/30 of a second (NTSC) to scan.

Frequency
The number of times a signal vibrates in a second, expressed as Hertz (Hz) or cycles per second.

Fresnel lens
A lens used to focus light into an even concentrated beam.

H

Head
An electromagnetic device that records on, or receives signals from magnetic tape.

Hertz See **Frequency**

Hi-fi
High fidelity audio reproduction as produced by the better quality home audio systems.

Hologram
A 3-dimensional image created by the interaction of two laser light sources.

I

Image enhancer
An electronic device for smoothing out irregularities in the video signal to improve picture definition.

Impedence
A measure of the total electrical resistance (*q.v.*) of a circuit, measured in ohms. Used in describing some electrical equipment, particularly microphones, to ensure connection with compatible equipment.

Infra-red
Electromagnetic waves beyond the red end of the visible spectrum.
Interactive video
Equipment capable of eliciting a response from the user and selecting the information to be displayed according to the user's response.

L
Lacing
The mechanical action of a VCR threading video tape round the record heads.
Lag
An image on the pickup tube of the camera which lingers. This is caused by over-bright subjects.
Laser
A device in which excited atoms produce an intense beam of radiation.
LED (Light emitting diode)
A semiconductor which lights up when a current of electricity is passed through it.
Limiter
An electronic circuit which automatically adjusts audio or video signal levels to a predetermined setting.
Luminance
The brightness of a TV picture.

M
Magnetic field
The area around an object influenced by its magnetism.
Matrix
A rectangular array of qualities or items in rows and columns to make up a single whole.
Microchip
A microprocessor or other electronic component made up of a chip of silica with microelectronic circuitry photographically printed on its surface; a 'silcon chip'.
Microprocessor
A microchip capable of doing complex calculations, used as the 'brain' of a microcomputer or other logic-controlled device, such as a VCR timer; also (loosely) a microcomputer.
Modulate
To alter a signal by adding the waveform (*q.v.*) of another signal to it. To broadcast a TV signal, a plain carrier signal is modulated with video, audio and control signals.

N
Noise
Unwanted audio or video signals which interfere with the normal signal.

P
Parallax
The apparent movement of an object caused by the shifting of the observer's viewpoint.
Photo-conductivity
Electrical conduction caused by the action of light on a surface.
Photodiode
A light-sensitive diode which conducts a current when light falls on it.

R
Real time
A recording or playback which takes the same time as the original action recorded, rather than in slow or fast motion.
Resistance
The extent to which an electrical conductor resists the flow of electricity; measured in ohms.
RF converter
A device to convert audio and video signals into a combined RF signal suitable for reception by a standard TV set.

S
SEG See **Special effects generator**
Signal splitter
A device for dividing an RF signal to feed more than one VCR or TV set.
Silica gel
Quartz crystals with the ability to absorb moisture from the surrounding air.
Special effects generator (SEG)
A device used to mix, switch or process video signals from different sources.
Solenoid
An electro-magnetic device for switching a current on and off.
Standby
The mode in which the VCR has the necessary circuits activated in readiness for instructions.
Switcher
A simplified SEG which selects video signals from two or more sources.

Sync pulse
Synchronization pulse; a signal generated inside a camera or separate generator which ensures that each picture frame is scanned consistently.

T
Telecine converter
A device for transferring filmed material to video tape.
Time-shifting
Recording a broadcast from the TV for later viewing.
Tolerance
The amount by which any technical requirement is permitted to vary without impairing its function.
Transformer
A device for reducing or increasing the voltage of an electric current.
Tuner
A unit incorporated into most domestic VCRs to receive and decode RF signals, from an antenna or other RF sources, into separate audio and video signals.

U
Ultrasonic sound
Sound pitched above the higher limit of human hearing.

V
VCR (video cassette recorder)
A video recorder with tape stored in cassettes.
Vectorscope
An oscilloscope with a round screen, producing information from three colour signals, to allow precise adjustment of professional three-tube cameras.
Video
An electronic signal carrying picture information.
VTR (video tape recorder)
A video recorder with video tape stored on open reels.

W
Waveform
A practical representation of the changing values of a signal.
White light
An equal combination of light of all the colours of the visible spectrum.
Writing speed
The speed at which the video heads revolve, relative to the speed of the tape passing them.

Bibliography

Anderson, C. *The Electric Journalist* Praeger Publishers, New York, 1973.

Baddeley, W.H. *Documentary Film Production* (Fourth edition) Focal Press, London and New York, 1975.

Bensinger, C. *The Home Video Handbook* Video-info Publications, Santa Barbara, California, 1979.

Bensinger, C. *The Video Guide* (Second edition) Video-info Publications, Santa Barbara, California, 1979.

Buckwalter, Len *Video Games* Today Press, Gosset and Dunlap, New York, 1977.

Chorafas, D.N. *Interactive Videotex: The Domesticated Computer* Petrocelli Books, Princeton, N.J. 1981.

Consterdine, G. and Nicholson, R. *The Prestel Business* Northwood Books, London, 1980.

CTL Electronics Inc. *Video Tools* CTL Electronics, New York (Annual).

Davis, D. *The Grammar of Television Production* Barrie and Jenkins, London, 1978.

Fedida, S. and Malik, R. *The Viewdata Revolution* Associated Business Press, London 1979; John Wiley and Sons, New York, 1980.

Foss, H. *How to Make Your Own Video Programmes* Elm Tree Books/Hamish Hamilton, London, 1982.

Foss, H. (Ed.) *Video Production Techniques* Kluwer Publishing, Brentford, Middlesex (Loose-leaf, biannual).

Frost, J.M. (Ed.) *World Radio TV Handbook* Billboard, London, Watson Guptill, New York, 1982 (Annual).

Greenfield, A. and Maltin, L. *The Complete Guide to Home Video* Crown Publishers/Harmony Books, New York, 1981.

Hunt, A. *The Language of Television* Eyre Methuen, London, 1981.

Jones, P. *The Technique of the Television Cameraman* (Third edition) Focal Press, London and New York, 1972.

JVC *Video the Better Way* Victor Company of Japan Ltd, Tokyo, 1980.

Kehoe, V.J.R. *The Technique of Film and Television Make Up for Colour and Black and White* (Second edition) Focal Press, London, 1969; Hastings House, New York, 1969.

Kybett, H. *The Complete Handbook of Video Cassette Recorders* TAB Books, Blue Ridge Summit, PA, 1971.

Kybett, H. *Video Tape Recorders* (Second edition) Howard W. Sams, Indianapolis, IN, 1978.

Murray, M. *The Videotape Book: A Basic Guide to Portable TV Production* Bantam Books/Taplinger Publishing, New York, 1975.

MacRae, D.L., Monty, M.R. and Worling, D.G. *Television Production: An Introduction* Methuen, Ontario, 1979.

Millerson, G. *The Technique of Television Production* (Tenth edition) Focal Press, London and New York, 1979.

Money, S.A. *Teletext and Viewdata* Newnes Technical Books/Butterworth, London, 1981.

National Cable Television Association *Cable Television and Education* NCTA, Washington DC, 1973.

Overman, M. *Understanding Sound and Video Recording* Lutterworth Press, Guildford, Surrey, 1977; TAB Books, Blue Ridge Summit, PA, 1978.

Petzold, P. *The Photoguide to Moviemaking* Focal Press, London and New York, 1975.

Quick, J. and Wolff, H. *Small-Studio Video Tape Production* (Second edition) Addison-Wesley Publishing, Reading, MA, 1976.

Robertson, A. *From Television to Home Computer: the Future of Consumer Electronics* Blandford Press, Poole, Dorset, 1979; Sterling Publishing, New York, 1979.

Robertson, A. (Ed.) *The Home Video Yearbook* Link House Magazines, Croydon, Surrey (New edition annually).

Robertson, A. *International Video Yearbook* Blandford Press, Poole; Sterling Publishing, New York (Annual).

Robinson, J.F. *Videotape Recording: Theory and Practice* (Third edition) Focal Press, London and New York, 1981.

Robinson, R. *The Video Primer; Equipment, Production and Concepts* Quick Fox, New York, London and Tokyo, 1978.

Sexton, B. *First Steps in Television* Fountain Press, Kings Langley, Herts, 1975.

Sigel, E. (Ed.) *Video Discs: The Technology, the Applications and the*

Future Knowledge Industry Publications, New York, 1981.

Sigel, E. *Videotext* Crown Publishers/Harmony Books, New York, 1981.

Sigel, E. (Ed.) *Videotext: Coming Revolution in Home/Office Information Retrieval* Knowledge Industry Publications, New York, 1980.

Shamberg, M. *Guerilla Television* Holt, Rinehart and Winston, New York, 1971.

Sloan Commision on Cable Communication *On the Cable: The Television of Abundance* McGraw-Hill Publishing, New York, 1971.

Smallman, K. *Creative Film-making* Bantam Books/MacMillan, New York, 1972.

Smith, R.L. *The Wired Nation* Harper and Row, New York, 1972.

Utz, P. *Video User's Handbook* Prentice-Hall, Englewood Cliffs, NJ, 1980; Hemel Hempstead, Herts, 1981.

Wilkie, B. *Creating Special Effects for Film-TV* Hastings House, New York, 1977.

Wilkie, B. *The Technique of Special Effects in Television* Focal Press, London and New York, 1971.

Winsburg, R. *Viewdata in Action A Comparative Study of Prestel* McGraw-Hill (UK), Maidenhead, Berks, 1981.

Videography Magazine Editors *The Video Handbook* (Third edition) United Business Publications, New York, 1977.

Zmijewsky, B. *The Consumer's Guide to Video Tape Recording* Stein and Day, New York, 1979.

Periodicals

The Big Reel Drawer B, Summerfield, NC 27358, USA (Monthly; film journal).

Bulletin for Film & Video Information 80 Wooster Street, New York, NY 10012, USA (Monthly).

Cable Information Newsletter Room 852, 475 Riverside Drive, New York, NY 10027, USA (Monthly; cable TV).

Educational and Industrial Television 607 Main Street, Ridgefield, CT 06877 (Monthly)

Filmakers' Newsletter PO Box 46, New York, NY 10012, USA (Monthly).

Hampton's Guide to Pre-Recorded Video PO Box 684, Southampton, New York, NY 11968, USA (Annual; software).

Hampton's Official Video Buyers' Guide PO Box 684, Southampton, New York, NY 11968, USA (Annual; home video).

Home Video 475 Park Avenue South, New York, NY 10016, USA (Bimonthly).

Media and Methods 134 North 13th Street, Philadelphia, PA 19107, USA (Monthly during school year; education).

Movie Maker PO Box 35, Bridge Street, Hemel Hempstead, Herts, UK (Monthly).

Panorama 850 Third Avenue, New York, NY 10022, USA (Monthly; TV).

Popular Video 30 Wellington Street, Covent Garden, London WC2, UK (Monthly).

Television King's Reach Tower, Stamford Street, London SE1 9LS, UK (Monthly).

Television and Home Video Link House, Dingwall Avenue, Croydon, Surrey CR9 2TA, UK (Monthly).

Video 235 Park Avenue South, New York, NY 10003, USA (Monthly).

Video Link House, Dingwall Avenue, Croydon CR9 2TA, UK (Monthly; professional video).

Video A–Z 22 Albany Road, London W13 8PG, UK (Quarterly).

Video Buyer's Review PO Box 684, Southampton, New York, NY 11968, USA (Quarterly).

The Video Exchange Directory 261 Powell Street, Vancouver, British Columbia, Canada V6A 1G3 (Annual).

Hi-Fi for Pleasure 40 Long Acre, London WC2E 9JJ, UK (Monthly; home video).

Videography 475 Park Avenue South, New York, NY 10016, USA (Monthly).

The Videophile 2003 Apalachee Parkway, Tallahassee, FL 32301, USA (Bimonthly; home video hardware).

Video Review 325 East 75th Street, New York, NY 10021, USA (Monthly; software).

Video Review Surrey House, 1 Throwley Way, Sutton, Surrey, SM1 4QQ, UK (Monthly).

Video Today 145 Charing Cross Road, London WC2H 0EE, UK (Monthly).

Video World Galaxy Publications Ltd, Hermit Place, 252 Belsize Road, London NW6 4BT, UK (Monthly).

What Video? 11 St Bride Street, London EC4, UK (Monthly).

Which Video? 145 Charing Cross Road, London WC2H 0EE , UK (Monthly).

Index

The most important entries are indicated in bold type; illustrations are indicated by page numbers in italics.

Acknowledgements

Writers: Bernard Nyman (Video and the law pp 48–49); Ruth Binney (The TV connection pp 80–81; Optional extras pp 178–179); Shelley Turner (Viewing data pp 86–87; Screen games pp 202–203); Andrew Emmerson (Giant screens pp 88–89; Skybirds pp 90–91; TV tomorrow pp 92–93); Helen Armstrong (Video security pp 200–201; Intelligent video pp 204–205; Visual display pp 206–207)
Editors: Ruth Binney; Ian Graham (Assistant Editor, Which Video?); Cynthia Fraser.

The Publishers received invaluable help from the following people and organizations:– Mike Aarons, Stanmore Video Services Ltd (Sonic Sound Audio Group); Akai America Ltd; Akai (UK) Ltd; George Allinson, PTS Electronics Ltd; Ampex Great Britain Ltd; Andy Armstrong, Monode Ltd; Bell and Howell A-V Ltd; John Cammish, Visiting Lecturer, The School of Film and Television, The Royal College of Art; Dr J O Clarke, Head of Resources, North E Wales Institute; English Electric Valve Company Ltd; Fantasy Factory Video Ltd; J O Grant and Taylor (London) Ltd (Agents for Grundig Electronic, West Germany); Grundig International Ltd; Hitachi Denshi (UK) Ltd; Hitachi Sales (UK) Ltd; International Television Association (UK); Introphoto Ltd; Introvideo Ltd; JVC (UK) Ltd; David Klein, Sales Director, Oracle (UK); Maurice Langton, HTV Ltd; Mac MaGowan, MVP Studios (UK); Ken Marsom, DATS Video Ltd; Richard Maybury, *Video Today*; A J Mitchell, Special Effects Director, The Moving Picture Company; National Panasonic (UK) Ltd; Panasonic Co (USA); Eric Parsloe, Managing Director, Epic (Eric Parsloe Industrial Communications) Ltd; Philips Electronics, Video Division; Philips LaserVision; RCA SelectaVision Videodiscs; Cris Rhodes, Comprehensive Video Supply Europe; Sanyo Marubeni (UK) Ltd; School of Communication, Polytechnic of Central London; Sharp Electronics (UK) Ltd; Jim Slater, Senior Engineering Information Officer, Independent Broadcasting Association (UK); Sony Consumer Products Company, Sony Corporation of America; Sony (UK) Ltd, Communication Systems Division; Sony (UK) Ltd, Consumer Products Division; Dave Swan, Head of the Camera Department, Trilion Video Ltd; Technicolor Audio-Visual (USA); Technicolor Viditronics Ltd; Thames Video-Thames TV International Ltd; Thorn EMI Ferguson Ltd; Toshiba (UK) Ltd; Ray West and Frank Wright, PTS Electronics Ltd.

Agfa-Gevaert Ltd; AICO International (UK); Ambico Inc; Ampex Corporation (USA); Apple Computer Inc; The Association of Video Dealers Ltd; Audio Visual (UK); AV Distributors (London) Ltd; Barco Electronic nv (UK); BASF UK Ltd; R R Beard Ltd; BIB Audio/Visual Products Ltd; Braun Electric (UK) Ltd; CEL Electronics (Harlow) Ltd; Cine 60 Inc; Colortran Inc; Colortran UK; Comart Ltd; Computer Aided Design Centre (UK); The Computer Corner (USA); Concord Lighting International Ltd; Creative Film Makers Ltd; Dicoll Electronics Ltd; EDC (Elkom Design Ltd); Educational Television Association (UK); EMI Tape Ltd; ERCO Lighting Ltd; Ercotron AB; Evershed Power-Optics Ltd; EVF Manufacturers Ltd; Leo Fabbri, Sales Director, Video City Productions Ltd; For-A Company Ltd; GEC Computers Ltd; Alan Groves, Chief Engineer, Transcan Video Ltd; Infopress Ltd, PR Consultants to Mitsubishi Electric (UK) Ltd; ISSCO (UK) Ltd; ITT Consumer Products (UK) Ltd; John Garbett (Audio-Visual) Ltd; Keen Computers Ltd; Kennett Engineering Company Ltd; Labgear Ltd; Roland Lewis, Lecturer in Film-making, Polytechnic of Central London; Lightolier (USA); Link Electronics Ltd; Lowel-Light Manufacturing Inc; Lucas (UK) Ltd; Magnavox Consumer Electronics Company (USA); Malham Photographic Equipment Ltd; Marconi Communication Systems Ltd; The Metropolitan Police Crime Prevention Service; Michael Cox Electronics Ltd; Michael Turner and Associates (Public Relations) Ltd; Molinare Ltd; Mothercare Ltd; MPW Ltd; Nicolet Zeta Corporation (USA); Nordmende (UK) Ltd; Online Publications Ltd; Optical & Textile Ltd; Packaged Lighting Systems Inc; PAG Power Ltd; Ripley Pedro, Pedro Computer Services (UK); Pelling and Cross Ltd; Personal Software Inc; Photopia Ltd; Polysales Photographic Ltd; Pye Ltd; Rank Strand (UK); R K Industries (UK); Robert Bosch Ltd; Quantel Ltd; Shinecrest Ltd; Shure Electronics Ltd; Sony Broadcast (UK); Ian Stokes; Survey and General Instrument Company Ltd; Tanenbaum Services (USA); TDK Tape Distributors (UK) Ltd; Techex Ltd; Tele-Jector Ltd; 3M United Kingdom PLC; Times Square Theatrical and Studio Supply Corp (USA); Thomson-CSF Components and Materials Ltd; Thomson-CSF/DTE/France; Total Video Supply (USA); Trilog Inc (USA); Michael Turner and Associates (Public Relations) Ltd; Velbon Tripod Company Ltd (USA); Versatec Electronics Ltd; Vicon Industries (UK) Ltd; Video Electronics Ltd; The Video School (UK); Vidicraft Inc; W Vinten Ltd; Welt/Safe-Lock Inc.

Acknowledgements

Picture credits

b = bottom c = centre l = left r = right t = top
Pages 12–13: Toshiba (UK) Ltd; 16: Schöner
Wohnen/Camera Press; 24: National Panasonic
(UK) Ltd; 27: Peter Smith Studio; 34t: Steve
Back; bl: Image Bank; br: Sony (UK) Ltd,
Consumer Products Division; 36tl: Schöner
Wohnen; tr: Peter Smith Studio; 2nd l:
Schöner Wohnen; 2nd r: Julian Calder; 3rd l:
Peter Smith Studio; 3rd r: Spectrum Colour
Library; bl: Peter Smith Studio; br: Steve
Back; 37: JVC (UK) Ltd; 43: Sony (UK) Ltd;
45: John Sanders; 52: Sony (UK) Ltd,
Consumer Products Division; 53: Courtesy of
Sony Corporation of America; 54t: Sanyo
Marubeni (UK) Ltd; b: Courtesy of Sony
Corporation of America; 55tl: Sanyo Marubeni
(UK) Ltd; Toshiba (UK) Ltd; tr, br: Sony
(UK) Ltd, Consumer Products Division; 56:
JVC (UK) Ltd; 58t: Akai (UK) Ltd; b: JVC
(UK) Ltd; 59tl: Akai America Ltd; bl: National
Panasonic (UK) Ltd; tr, br: JVC (UK) Ltd;
60: Grundig Video (UK) Ltd; 62: Philips
Electronics (Video Division); 63tl, tr:
Technicolor Audio-Visual (USA); c: ITT
Consumer Products (UK) Ltd; b: Pye Ltd; 64:
Bell and Howell A-V Ltd; 66t, b: National
Panasonic (UK) Ltd; 67tl: Bell and Howell A-
V Ltd; bl: Sony (UK) Ltd, Consumer Products
Division; br: Courtesy of Sony Corporation of
America; tr: JVC (UK) Ltd; 70: Barry Fox; 71:
Philips LaserVision Division; 72: Ampex (UK)
Ltd; 74: Peter Smith Studio; 76: BASF
Aktiengesellschaft; 89: Schöner Wohnen; 90:
Science Photo Library; 93tl, tr: Lucas (UK)
Ltd; 95: Peter Smith Studio; 96–97: Hitachi
Sales (UK) Ltd; 98t, c, b: Steve Back; 99tl, tr:
Paul Brierley; c, b: Steve Back; 100t: Hitachi
Sales (UK) Ltd; b: JVC (UK) Ltd; 101tl:
Hitachi Denshi (UK) Ltd; bl, tr: National
Panasonic (UK) Ltd; br: JVC (UK) Ltd;
102–103 Sony (UK) Ltd, Consumer Products
Division; 103: Peter Smith Studios; 104t:
Philips Electronics Video Division; b: JVC
(UK) Ltd; 105tl: JVC (UK) Ltd; bl: Hitachi
Sales (UK) Ltd; tr: Sony (UK) Ltd,
Communications Systems Division; br: Sony
(UK) Ltd, Consumer Products Division; 106:
artwork by permission Sony (UK) Ltd; 111:
Peter Smith Studio; 112–113: Schöner
Wohnen/Camera Press; 114–115: Steve Back;
116–117: Steve Back; 119: Steve Back; 120:
Schöner Wohnen/Camera Press; 121: Steve
Back; 122–123: Steve Back; 126: Peter Smith
Studio; 127: Schöner Wohnen/Camera Press;
128: Peter Smith Studio; 129: Schöner
Wohnen/Camera Press; 132: Spectrum Colour
Library; 133t: Julian Calder; b: Spectrum
Colour Library; 135t: Steve Back; b: Peter
Smith Studio; 136t, c: Spectrum Colour
Library; b: Paul Brierley; 137tl: Steve Back; tr:
Spectrum Colour Library; b: John Garrett;
140: Spectrum Colour Library; 141tl: G.P.
Eisen, *The Daily Telegraph* Colour Library; tr,
bl, br: Spectrum Colour Library; 142–143:
Spectrum Colour Library; 144: Spectrum
Colour Library; 145t, bl, br: Spectrum Colour
Library; 146–147 Leo Mason; 148t: Leo
Mason; b: Jerry Young; 149: Jerry Young;
151t: Spectrum Colour Library; c, b: Mark
Dunton; 152: artwork by Alexander O'Donnell;
156–157: Tony Duffy/All Sport; 158t: Steve
Back; b: Paul Wilkinson; 160: Peter Smith
Studio; 171: Max Hole/Camel; 176: Ampex
Great Britain Ltd; 177tr: Ampex Corporation
(USA); br: The Moving Picture Company;
179: Steve Back; 180: Molinare Ltd; 181:
McCann Ericksen (Nederlands) bv; 183: Peter
Smith Studio; 184–185: Sally & Richard
Greenhill; 186l: *The Daily Telegraph* Colour
Library; r: The Image Bank; 188–189: *The
Daily Telegraph* Colour Library; 190–191:
Octopus Books; 192–193: Nils Christie/Craig
Dodd; 196–197: Josiah Wedgwood and Sons
Ltd; 199: Peter Smith Studio; 201t, b:
Popperfoto; 206t, c: Molinare Ltd; b: Peter
Smith Studio; 207: Logica Ltd.